New Spain's Far Northern Frontier

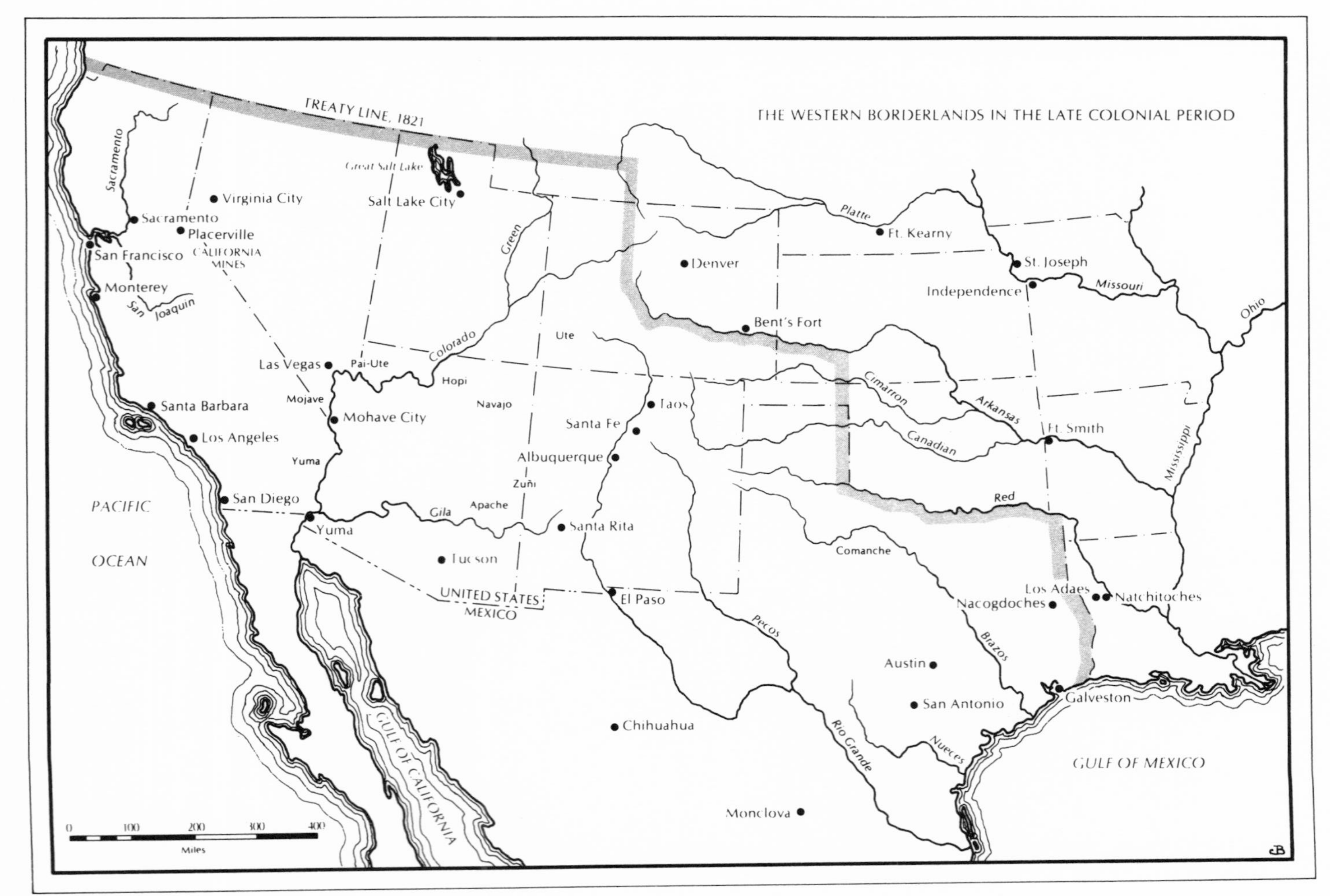
THE WESTERN BORDERLANDS IN THE LATE COLONIAL PERIOD
TREATY LINE, 1821
Great Salt Lake
Salt Lake City
Virginia City
Sacramento
Sacramento
Placerville
CALIFORNIA MINES
San Francisco
Monterey
San Joaquin
Green
Platte
Ft. Kearny
St. Joseph
Independence
Missouri
Ohio
Denver
Bent's Fort
Ute
Colorado
Las Vegas
Pai-Ute
Hopi
Navajo
Mojave
Mohave City
Santa Barbara
Los Angeles
Yuma
Taos
Santa Fe
Albuquerque
Zuñi
Cimarron
Arkansas
Ft. Smith
Canadian
Mississippi
Red
PACIFIC
OCEAN
San Diego
Yuma
Gila
Apache
Santa Rita
Tucson
UNITED STATES
MEXICO
El Paso
Comanche
Los Adaes
Natchitoches
Nacogdoches
Brazos
Pecos
Austin
Galveston
San Antonio
Chihuahua
Rio Grande
Nueces
GULF OF MEXICO
GULF OF CALIFORNIA
Monclova
0
100
200
300
400
Miles
CB

New Spain's Far Northern Frontier

Essays on Spain in the American West, 1540–1821

David J. Weber, Editor

SOUTHERN METHODIST UNIVERSITY PRESS
DALLAS

First Southern Methodist University Press edition, 1988

Library of Congress Cataloging-in-Publication Data

New Spain's far northern frontier.
Reprint. Originally published: University of
New Mexico Press, 1979.
Includes bibliographies and index.
1. Southwest, New—History—To 1848. I. Weber,
David J.
[F799.N48 1988] 1979 88-42631
ISBN 0-87074-280-9 (pbk.)

5 7 9 10 8 6 4

Contents

INTRODUCTION

In 1767, upon inspecting the presidio of San Sabá, situated on the isolated and open plateau country of central Texas, the Marqués de Rubí disparagingly noted that the outpost "affords as much protection to the interests of His Majesty in New Spain as a ship anchored in mid-Atlantic would afford in preventing foreign trade with America."[1] The same characterization might have applied to any of those outposts of Spanish-Mexican culture that jutted north from New Spain into the Indian-controlled lands of what we know today as the Western United States: Alta California, Arizona, New Mexico, and Texas. Spanish officials hoped that those areas might serve as buffers to protect mineral-rich provinces to the south against encroachment by hostile European or indigenous powers. It was not to be. From California to Texas, Spanish-Mexican frontiersmen never achieved sufficient numerical or institutional strength to protect themselves adequately, much less to protect the provinces to the south. Hostile Indians or foreigners could have penetrated the line of presidios, pueblos, and missions that crossed New Spain's far northern frontier as easily as one vessel might skirt another on the high seas.

Although it was tenuous, Spain's hegemony over parts of today's American West was enduring and profound. Her claims to the region began about 1540 with Juan Rodríguez Cabrillo's voyage along the coast of California north to Oregon and the simultaneous explorations of the interior of the continent by Francisco Vázquez de Coronado and Hernando de Soto. From then on, Spain considered a vast swath of today's United States, from Oregon to the Carolinas, to lie within her New World empire. Settled or unsettled, the North American portions of that empire fell within the jurisdiction of the Viceroyalty of New Spain, with its administrative center in Mexico City. The Viceroyalty endured until Mexico won independence from Spain in 1821. Then, for a quarter century, much of what is now the American West constituted the far northern frontier of the Mexican Republic. The Mexican interlude ended when the United States seized the region in the invasion of 1846–1847—an event known to Americans as the "Mexican" War.

During the nearly three centuries that Spain claimed portions of the American West (1540–1821), the scope of her claims expanded and contracted with the fortunes of international wars, diplomatic arrangements, and the vigor of her own colonizing efforts. Louisiana, for example, was first claimed by Spain, but settled by the French, and then ceded to Spain in 1762 as part of the settlement of the Seven Years War. In 1800 Spain covertly returned Louisiana to France, who in turn sold it to the United States in 1803. Thus, Spain's political claims to portions of her North American frontier ebbed and flowed. Meanwhile, Spain's actual settlement of the area grew steadily as a result of the northward advance of missionaries, soldiers, and pioneers. The process of permanent settlement began in the late sixteenth century in New Mexico and ended in California in the late eighteenth century.

Within fifty years of Columbus's discovery of the New World, Spaniards had explored much of the coastline of the United States and had taken a good look at its interior. They did not like what they saw: no strait through North America to the fabled Orient; no wealthy Indians to rival the Aztecs or Incas; and no important mineral discoveries. Why stay when Spain had richer colonies to enjoy? Colonization of today's American West did not immediately follow the exploration of the 1540s. Spain's subjects needed other incentives to abandon the more affluent regions of New Spain and settle the remote and frequently arid areas to the north.

When Spain's pioneers reentered the Southwest toward the end of the sixteenth century, their goals differed from those of the first explorers. The hope always remained that rich minerals would be found, but converting Indians to Christianity and safeguarding the frontier against encroachment by other powers became the most important inducements for Spain to plant the first European settlements in what is now the United States.

Fresh rumors of mineral wealth and Indians to convert brought a wave of explorers north from Mexico to the Rio Grande Valley in the 1580s. Their initial probing led to a government-sponsored party, headed by wealthy Juan de Oñate, which began the permanent European occupation of New Mexico in 1598. Yet, the province had no strategic value at this time and was costly to maintain. In 1608, when the crown learned that precious minerals had not been found, it ordered New Mexico abandoned. Franciscans, however, had already begun to baptize Pueblo Indians. Rather than see them revert to their "pagan" native religion, the crown permitted the Franciscans and the colonists to stay. Missions became New Mexico's sole reason for existence. Santa Fe, founded about 1610, became the third permanent European settlement in the present-day United States, after St. Augustine (1565) and Jamestown (1607).

Connected to the rest of New Spain only by the lengthy, hazardous trail to Chihuahua, the isolated colony grew slowly. The nonaboriginal population of New Mexico probably numbered no more than 2,800 by 1680. That year, in a rare display of unity prompted by the leadership of Domingo Naranjo and Popé, the Pueblos launched a counterattack, forcing the intruders from Mexico to flee southward to El Paso del Norte (present-day Ciudad Juárez).[2] Nevertheless, by 1694 Spanish-Mexicans had regained control of the province. The eighteenth century saw New Mexico grow steadily, despite heavy attacks from Apaches, Comanches, Navajos, and Utes, which drastically reduced the number of Pueblo Indians and kept the *pobladores* confined, in the main, to the Rio Grande Valley between Socorro and Taos, and in the El Paso district. By 1821 New Mexico, which included El Paso, was the most populous province on New Spain's northern frontier, with a population of about 38,500. About a quarter of these were Pueblo Indians, and among those counted by the census takers as "Spanish and other classes" were many Indians who had become Hispanicized.[3]

Arizona, the next area of the present United States to be penetrated by missionaries coming north from Mexico, was part of the province of Sonora and was not a separate administrative entity during the Spanish period. Beginning in 1700, with the work of the energetic Eusebio Francisco Kino, Jesuits extended their mission chain to the north across what would eventually be the international border. Their achievements in southern Arizona, however, remained relatively insignificant. Apache resistance and the area's lack of strategic value hindered further missionary expansion and discouraged mining and ranching. Thus, despite the best efforts of the Jesuits (and Franciscans after 1767), Arizona at the end of the colonial period contained a nominal Spanish-Mexican population, centered in the Santa Cruz Valley. No Hispanic settlements lay north of the presidio of Tucson, founded in 1776, and much of the rugged plateau country north of the Gila River remained unexplored.

Missionaries also led the settlement of Texas and California, but in those two areas defense against foreign powers brought about Spanish occupation. Franciscans had urged since the early 1600s that missions be established in Texas, but not until French colonists, under Robert Cavelier, Sieur de La Salle, built a fort near Matagorda Bay in 1684 did Spain make its first tentative efforts to settle Texas. By 1716, in direct response to heightened French trading activities in Louisiana, permanent missions were established in East Texas near the Neches River. Two years later, in 1718, a mission and presidio were founded at San Antonio as a way station on the trail to East Texas. The chapel of the mission of San Antonio de Valero would become well known as the Alamo.

Besieged by Comanches on horseback, Texas grew slowly, attracting few colonists; its missions failed to expand to the north of San Antonio or to attract a substantial number of Indian converts. By 1785 the Texas missions contained fewer than 500 neophytes and that number declined to 120 in 1809. By 1820 fewer than 2,500 persons of European descent lived in Texas.[4] Only four missions remained active and only three settlements had been founded: San Antonio and La Bahía (later called Goliad), and the faltering town of Nacogdoches in East Texas. From San Antonio west to El Paso, or between San Antonio and Santa Fe, no Spanish outpost stood to challenge Comanches, Apaches, or other tribes for control of the South Plains. No Spanish barrier blocked raiding parties from sweeping across the Rio Grande, through the territory that Spanish officials termed the *despoblado*, into Chihuahua, Durango, Coahuila, and Nuevo León.

As in Texas, Spain also colonized California for defensive reasons, but missions came to dominate the life of the province. Perceived threats to the Pacific Coast from Britain and Russia prompted the sending of the "Sacred Expedition" to Upper California in 1769. Under the leadership of Fray Junípero Serra and Captain Gaspar de Portolá, the expedition established the first mission and presidio in Upper California in 1769. By the time of Serra's death in 1784, Franciscans had completed eight more coastal missions; the northernmost was at San Francisco, where a presidio was also constructed. Working among a dense and diverse population of relatively peaceful aborigines, the Franciscans met greater success than they had in Texas. The California missions numbered twenty-one by 1823. The soldiers and the padres, however, unwittingly introduced new diseases, such as smallpox and influenza, which spread quickly among the natives in the close mission quarters, causing California's Indian population to decline dramatically during the Spanish period.

Despite its salubrious climate, distant California attracted few Spanish-Mexican colonists. Anxious to populate the province, the Spanish government had to offer material rewards to encourage colonization, and it even sent some convicts as colonists. After the Yuma Indian revolt of 1781 closed the only known overland route to California, the area remained dependent upon occasional ships from New Spain for additional colonists, supplies, and news of the outside world. Thus, largely through natural increase rather than colonization, the non-native population of California reached about 3,000 by 1821.[5] A few of these pioneers lived in isolated ranches, but most settled in pueblos scattered along the coast. California had only three self-governing municipalities by 1821: San José, Los Angeles, and Branciforte (today's Santa Cruz). Yet settlements developed near some of the missions, too, such as those at San Luis Obispo and San Juan Capistrano. Settlements governed by military commanders also grew up at each of the four ill-equipped and undermanned presidios that had been built by 1821: San Diego, Santa Barbara, Monterey, and San Francisco.

From the 1540s, then, when Spain's explorers claimed the region for their monarch, until Mexico won independence in 1821, it could be argued that Spain accomplished relatively little in today's American West. She had not populated the region substantially, controlled it with military power, Hispanicized significant numbers of Indians, or brought prosperity and comfort to her own frontiersmen. San Antonio, for example, was described in 1778 as a village of "wretched settlers" whose needs could scarcely be supplied by limited trading possibilities.

> The town consists of fifty-nine houses of stone and mud and seventy-nine of wood, but all poorly built, without any preconceived plan, so that the whole resembles more a poor village than a villa, capital of so pleasing a province. . . . The streets are tortuous and are filled with mud the minute it rains.[6]

Visitors described Santa Fe and Los Angeles in similar terms.

Notwithstanding Spain's apparent failures and the region's poverty and insignificance compared to Peru or central Mexico, New Spain's far northern frontier has fascinated American historians and aficionados of history. That fascination evinced itself a century ago, shortly after the United States occupied the area.[7] Amateur historians, chiefly lawyers, such as Theodore Hittell in California and Ralph Emerson Twitchell in New Mexico, began serious study of their region's Hispanic past based on archival sources. The quintessential amateur of that period, however, was Hubert Howe Bancroft, a San Francisco book dealer and stationer. Overcome by the impulse to collect books as well as sell them, Bancroft amassed an enormous library of rare books, manuscripts, and memoirs. Applying techniques he had learned as a businessman to chronicling the past, Bancroft hired a small staff to help him collect, research, and write. The team eventually produced thirty-nine hefty volumes on the history of the American West, Mexico, and Central America. Bancroft's *Works* (1886 to 1890), which devote considerable attention to the Spanish period in

North America, remain a much-consulted chronicle of events and a valuable guide to sources. Bancroft's library and archive also remain valuable. In 1905 he sold his fabulous collection to the University of California, Berkeley, where it became the nucleus of one of the nation's best collections on New Spain. The Bancroft Library came to be well-used by the man most responsible for cultivating the study of Spanish-Mexican activities in the area of today's United States, Herbert Eugene Bolton.[8]

In 1911 the University of California lured Bolton from Stanford by using the Bancroft Library as bait. Bolton remained at Berkeley until his death at age eight-one in 1953. During his long career he added a new dimension to the way in which American historians perceived their nation's past. Without minimizing the importance of the United States' English heritage, Bolton stressed that a balanced understanding of the nation's colonial past must also include recognition and understanding of its Hispanic origins. Bolton coined a new phrase, the "Spanish Borderlands," to describe the area of Spanish influence in what is now the United States. He defined the Borderlands as a shifting region which at times included Florida, Georgia, Louisiana, and the American West as far north as Washington.[9] The early history of these areas, he argued, belonged to the history of the Spanish empire and not that of the English.

In addition to defining a new field of historical inquiry, Bolton publicized that field through a remarkable amount of research and writing. One of his pieces, "The Mission as Frontier Institution," appears in this anthology. Moreover, Bolton trained his own disciples to continue his work. He directed the graduate training of 103 Ph.D.s, many of whom made their own scholarly contributions to the historiography of the Borderlands and trained still more historians.[10] Meanwhile, scholars who had no connection with Bolton also interested themselves in the new field. One result was the outpouring of so many books and articles on the Borderlands that by 1966 one prominent historian, Charles Gibson, surmised that "it is probable that no other part of Colonial Latin America has stimulated so extensive a program of research."[11]

Such extensive writing on a peripheral and forsaken corner of the Spanish empire is surely out of proportion to the area's historical importance. Indeed, Bolton would have been the first to acknowledge that fact. He once accused some writers of "mistaking the tail for the dog," by suggesting that the nature of the whole of Spanish America could be understood by studying the Borderlands.[12] How can this detailed study of the "tail" be explained?

First, it is well to remember that the "tail" is now in the United States. Like peoples everywhere, Americans have an intense interest in their regional past, in their *patria chica*. Some historians reflect that interest. Unlike their colleagues in other parts of Spain's former colonial empire, however, American historians enjoy a high degree of financial support, research time, and opportunity to publish. There often seems to be a direct correlation between historical scholarship and affluence.[13]

Second, we should remember that failure is relative. Spain's efforts in the Borderlands may be considered inadequate from one perspective, but those who recall her size and population might not question why Spain did so little, but wonder how she achieved so much. With a population of about ten million in the early sixteenth century, and a land mass so small that it would fit inside the present-day state of Texas with room to spare for nearly half of California,[14] Spain managed to explore, conquer, and settle much of the hemisphere, from the Borderlands in the north to Chile and Argentina in the south. Even in the sparsely settled Borderlands, Spanish-Mexicans made a profound and lasting impact on United States culture, be it in such an obvious way as establishing place names or in more subtle areas such as laws regarding community property or water and mineral rights. Moreover, the activities of Spanish-Mexicans in what is now the United States constitute a story of high adventure, drama, and compelling human interest, irrespective of the numbers of people involved or of their ultimate successes or failures.

If, as Allan Nevins put it, an understanding of history "helps men to measure time against eternity; to rise above the heat and dust of ephemeral issues into a serener atmosphere,"[15] then an understanding of the ways in which Spanish-Mexicans pioneered this singular region ought to provide a standard by which modern Americans can gain valuable perspective about themselves and their environment. The diaries, letters, and reports of Spain's explorers, for example, constitute a unique window to the past. Through that window anthropologists, geographers, biologists, zoologists, and others have gained fabulous views of North America's indigenous peoples, plants, and animals at that historical moment just before Europeans altered irrevocably the face of the land with their own flora and fauna and changed forever the indigenous cultures of the continent.[16] Modern Americans have much to learn from a study of Spain's military, religious, and political leaders, who regarded their civilization as superior and who sought to impose it, through propaganda and force, on benighted peoples across the sea. Then, as now, the goals and strategies of civil, religious, and military institutions coincided at times, leading to considerable institutional cooperation. On other occasions, profound schisms occurred among those Hispanic institutions. Then, as now, whites, blacks, browns, and reds mingled, cooperated, and clashed in the New World. Then, as now, people sought to adapt to their environment. Then, as now, ordinary people struggled to support themselves economically, rear and educate their children, and nourish themselves spiritually, artistically, and sexually.

It is enticing for Americans to study these matters at the local level, in an area that is now part of the United States. In that way we gain a sense of immediacy and relevance that would be more difficult to achieve by studying more distant parts of Spain's New World Empire. Perhaps because regional history is so alluring we should recall Bolton's caution not to mistake the tail for the dog. Each corner and cranny of Spain's colonial empire was unique and that uniqueness extends beyond the regional level. Generalizations which apply to California might not pertain to New Mexico, Arizona, or Texas, and vice versa. Beyond that, what is true of southern California might not be true of northern California. When placed in broad perspective, regional and local history ought to help us appreciate the variety and complexity of human response and bring us one step closer to reality. Perhaps that, too, is another reason why the Borderlands has fascinated so many historians.

For a variety of reasons, then, historians have written an extraordinary number of books and articles pertaining to the Spanish Borderlands. Until now, students who sought to examine that literature needed to look far and wide. No single volume existed that contained representative samples of the scholarly literature.[17] In this anthology I have tried to bring together easily readable, interpretive essays which treat some of the major themes with which modern historians of the Borderlands have concerned themselves. Because of limitations of space and in order to achieve greater thematic unity, I have chosen to focus on the western Borderlands, the region from California to Texas. In this region one can see the unfolding of the northern frontier of New Spain into what is now the American West. The Hispanic origins of Louisiana, Mississippi, Florida, Georgia, Alabama, and the Carolinas, on the other hand, belong more properly to the history of the Caribbean than to Mexico, although the whole region fell under the overall administrative supervision of the Viceroy of New Spain.[18]

It seems appropriate to begin this anthology by asking why the topic is important. Donald Worcester (no. 1) provides a clear and concise answer in the opening essay, "The Significance of the Spanish Borderlands to the United States." Worcester's work is followed by two pieces which deal with the theme of exploration. Sweeping across several centuries, George P. Hammond (no. 2) looks at the ways in which "the fabulous" propelled Spaniards into the interior of western North America. Donald C. Cutter (no. 3), on the other hand, describes the explorations of eighteenth-century Spanish scientists. Their scholarly reasons for exploring the Pacific Coast of North America had been downplayed by earlier historians who concentrated instead on the spectacular sixteenth-century motives for Spanish exploration: God, gold, and glory.

In the next four essays historians scrutinize the crucial institutions of Spanish-Mexican settlement on the far northern frontier. Bolton (no. 4) applauds the mission and Odie B. Faulk (no. 5) asks if the presidio was a "Fortress or Farce?" Focusing on Texas, Sandra L. Myres (no. 6) discusses the cattle ranch as a key institution for the settlement of the frontier and Marc Simmons (no. 7) looks at the patterns and evolution of Spanish-Mexican settlements in New Mexico over two centuries.

Reflecting broader trends in American historiography, Borderlands historians have begun to look more closely at the nature of society on the frontier. Using quantitative techniques that are currently in vogue, Alicia V. Tjarks (no. 9) has examined Texas society in the late eighteenth century. Using more traditional historical sources, Manuel P. Servín (no. 8) analyzed California society during the same period. Although their approaches vary, both writers agree that high percentage of the Spanish-Mexican settlers on New Spain's far northern frontier were mixed bloods, or mestizos.

Several essays in this volume, such as those of Simmons and Tjarks, concern themselves with the impact of the frontier on people and institutions. Any consideration of that subject must take into account Frederick Jackson Turner's famed Frontier Thesis. Essays by C. Alan Hutchinson (no. 10) and Silvio Zavala (no. 11) do just that. Like so many writers who have dealt with Turner's ideas, Zavala and Hutchinson come to different conclusions.

As the eighteenth century wore on, Indians and foreigners challenged Spanish-Mexican footholds on New Spain's far northern frontier. Luis Navarro García (no. 12) takes a broad view of Spain's responses to these growing eighteenth-century threats, while Joseph F. Park (no. 13) examines more specifically the successful evolution of Spanish policy toward Indians. Lest we come to view Indians only as adversaries of Spanish-Mexicans, Albert Schroeder (no. 14) reminds us that some Indian groups continued to cope in time-honored fashion with many of the same problems they had faced before the arrival of Europeans. Like Schroeder, George Phillips (no. 15) looks at events from an Indian perspective. In doing so, Phillips arrives at a fresh interpretation of the Indians' role in the destruction of the California missions.

Although the Spanish period in the Southwest ended in 1821, Hispanic culture has lived on. William Wroth's essay (no. 16) outlines the rise and decline of one form of artistic expression among New Mexico Hispanos, the making of santos. The art of the frontier *santeros* began in the late eighteenth century, declined in the nineteenth, and has revived in the twentieth.

The two concluding essays in this anthology treat concerns of many contemporary Americans. John L. Kessell (no. 17) engagingly exposes the distorted vision of the "Pepsi Generation" toward Spaniards and Indians as ravishers and guardians of the environment; David J. Weber (no. 18) explains the roots of Americans' faulty perceptions of Mexicans and Mexican-Americans.

Many fine historians and a substantial number of essays of high quality which treat themes of significance could not be included here for reasons of space or balance. Historians have examined some subjects (such as the mission experience and Spanish-Indian military confrontations) in great detail, making choices difficult for an editor. Other questions have received only cursory examination, forcing an editor to search far and wide. Historians have just begun to explore the social history of New Spain's far northern frontier, for example, and they have largely ignored activities of women. Various writers have touched upon the ecological implications of the arrival of Spanish-Mexicans, but the subject has not yet received systematic exposition. Few historians have compared aspects of the Spanish-Mexican experience in the various frontier provinces.

With the exceptions of Silvio Zavala and Luis Navarro García, a Mexican and a Spaniard, American writers dominate this anthology. That is not by design. Rather, it reflects American dominance of the field. Few Spanish and Mexican historians have interested themselves in the areas of New Spain that the United States seized or purchased. Indeed, for reasons already suggested, American historians not only dominate the history of the Borderlands but threaten to dominate the study of Mexican and Latin American history in general.[19] Among the American historians represented in this collection, only one, Manuel P. Servín, bridges the two cultures. Servín is one of the few Mexican-American historians who has attempted to interpret the early Spanish-Mexican Southwest.[20] Most Mexican-American historians have devoted their research to the late nineteenth and early twentieth centuries when significant numbers of Mexicans became United States citizens.

Notwithstanding this research emphasis on the recent past, Mexican-American historians see a need to understand the years when the Southwest belonged to the Spanish empire and to link those years more closely with Mexican-American history. Many Americans have been blinded to the full dimension of the Mexican-American past by what Carey McWilliams has termed "the absurd dichotomy between things *Spanish* and things *Mexican*."[21] Implicitly, at least, historians have suggested that Spaniards and Indians were the only actors on the Southwestern stage before 1821. It is true that those "Spaniards" who came north from Mexico to explore and settle were subjects of the Spanish crown. Many, however, personified that fusion of Spanish and Indian culture and blood which made them ethnically Mexicans. In the interest of greater accuracy, then, it seems preferable to use the terms Spanish-Mexican or Hispano to identify those pioneers.

If an appreciation of the lengthy and rich Spanish-Mexican heritage of the Southwest is important to Mexican-Americans today, it should be of equal importance to Anglo-Americans. Spanish-Mexican culture continues to flourish in the Southwest beyond the walls of missions and museums. Living bearers of that culture continue to settle and multiply north of the Rio Grande in numbers that suggest the Mexican-American population will continue to grow more rapidly than the Anglo-American population. As José Angel Gutiérrez, founder of La Raza Unida party, predicted:

> Rand McNally may continue to publish maps saying this is Mexico and this is the United States. But in terms of culture and history and heritage and language and tradition . . . the border is going to move a good thousand miles at least—inward into the United States.[22]

The consequences of such a demographic shift will require increased awareness on the part of Anglo-Americans and Mexican-Americans alike.

My role in the making of this anthology has been mainly that of a compiler. This collection is actually the work of those scholars who have contributed to it. I am grateful to them for granting permission to reprint their work. In a broader sense, the anthology belongs also to those historians whose writing is not included here for reasons of space, but upon whom all of us have relied. For examining the manuscript and confirming or denying my selections, I am especially grateful to Iris Wilson Engstrand, of the University of San Diego, Donald C. Cutter of the University of New Mexico, Michael Mathes of the University of San Francisco, Oakah L. Jones of Purdue University, and my students at SMU. For help in assembling illustrations for this volume, I am indebted to Linda Laury, who made the initial selections; to the staff at Fikes Hall of Special Collections, SMU, who graciously made old sketches and lithographs from the DeGolyer Collection available to us; and to Bill Dworaczyk, who did the photography.

If this book were to have a dedication it would be to Marvin D. Bernstein of the State University of New York at Buffalo, who with wit and wisdom first guided me toward the history of Latin America, and to Donald C. Cutter of the University of New Mexico, whose infectious enthusiasm drew me to the study of the West in the years when it still formed part of the Spanish Empire.

David J. Weber
Southern Methodist University

NOTES

1. Robert S. Weddle, *The San Sabá Mission, Spanish Pivot in Texas* (Austin: 1964), p. 170.

2. In a remarkable article, Pohé-Yemo's Representative," *New Mexico Historical Review,* 42: (1967):85–126, Fray Angélico Chávez suggests that Domingo Naranjo, son of a mulatto father and a Tlascaltec mother, impersonated the god Pohé-Yemo.

3. Lansing B. Bloom, "New Mexico Under Mexican Administration, 1821-1846, *Old Santa Fe,* 1: (1913):27–30.

4. Odie B. Faulk, *The Last Years of Spanish Texas, 1778–1821* (The Hague, Netherlands: 1964), pp. 75, 102.

5. Hubert Howe Bancroft, *History of California,* vol. 2 (San Francisco: 1886), pp. 251, 392, 653.

6. Fray Juan Agustín Morfi, *History of Texas, 1673–1779,* trans. and ed. Carlos Eduardo Castañeda (Albuquerque: 1935), 1:92.

7. For an excellent discussion of this question see Burl Noggle, "Anglo Observers of the Southwest Borderlands, 1825–1890: The Rise of a Concept," *Arizona and the West,* 1 (1959): 105–31.

8. For a biography and assessment of Bancroft's work see *Hubert Howe Bancroft: Historian of the West,* by John W. Caughey (Berkeley: 1946).

9. Some writers have included the northern tier of Mexican states, from Baja California to Tamaulipas, in their definition of the Borderlands. Bolton's treatment of the subject, however, in the book in which he popularized the phrase, focused on the area north of the present United States–Mexican border. See *The Spanish Borderlands: A Chronicle of Old Florida and the Southwest* (New Haven: 1921).

10. John Francis Bannon has written a full-dress biography of his mentor, *Herbert Eugene Bolton: The Historian and the Man* (Tucson: 1978). Bannon's briefer portrait of Bolton appears in his introduction to *Bolton and the Spanish Borderlands* (Norman: 1964).

11. *Spain in America* (New York: 1966), p. 189.

12. "Defensive Spanish Expansion and the Significance of the Spanish Borderlands," in Bannon, ed., *Bolton and the Spanish Borderlands,* p. 34.

13. A recent University of Texas Press release, for example, suggested that scholars take delight in current border problems because those problems generate research grants: "For scholars the problems of the United States-Mexican border area are like a shower of sweets from an exploded piñata, releasing many varied and intriguing research possibilities. Quoted in *The Texas Observer,* November 18, 1977.

14. Jaime Vicens Vives, *Historia de España y América social y económica,* 2d. ed. (Barcelona: 1971), 2:360.

15. *Gateway to History,* rev. ed. (New York: 1962), p. 407.

16. For an example of the way in which a geographer has used Spanish sources see Carl Ortwin Sauer, *Sixteenth Century North America: The Land and the People As Seen by the Europeans* (Berkeley: 1971).

17. Only one other anthology in English exists: *The Spanish Borderlands—A First Reader,* edited by Oakah L. Jones, Jr. (Los Angeles: 1974). Although it contains many articles of quality and a fine introduction and commentary by Jones, that anthology includes articles from only one source, *The Journal of the West.* A Spanish-language anthology, edited by David J. Weber, appeared in Mexico in 1976: *El México perdido: Ensayos sobre el antiguo norte de México, 1540–1821,* translated by Ana Elena Lara Zúñiga, Hector Aguilar Camín, and Isabel Lil Sánchez. The present volume represents a considerable expansion and revision of that book.

18. Those interested in reading further on the eastern Borderlands will find excellent guidance in Jack D. L. Holmes, "Interpretations and Trends in the Study of the Spanish Borderlands; The Old Southwest," *Southwestern Historical Quarterly,* 74 (1971): 461–77.

19. For a discussion of this question see "History and the Social Sciences in Latin America," by the late dean of Mexican historians, Daniel Cosío Villegas, in *Social Science in Latin America*, ed. Manuel Diégues Júnior and Bryce Wood (New York: 1967), pp. 121–37. María del Carmen Velázquez is one of the few Mexican historians whose work focuses on the portions of New Spain that now form part of the United States. See, for example, her *Establecimiento y pérdida del septentrión de Nueva España* (Mexico City: 1974), and *El Marqués de Altamira y las Provincias Internas de Nueva España* (Mexico City: 1976). See, too, a provocative article by ethnohistorian Miguel León Portilla, "The Norteño Variety of Mexican Culture: An Ethnohistorical Approach," in *Plural Society in the Southwest*, ed. Edward H. Spicer and Raymond H. Thompson (New York: 1972), pp. 77–114.

20. A major exception to this statement is Carlos E. Castañeda, whose monumental *Our Catholic Heritage in Texas*, 7 vols. (Austin: 1931–1958), focuses on the colonial period. As this anthology went to press, articles by Antonio José Ríos-Bustamante, "New Mexico In the Eighteenth Century: Life, Labor and Trade in la Villa de San Felipe de Albuquerque, 1706–1790," and Janie Louise Aragón, "The People of Santa Fé in the 1790s," appeared in a late issue of *Aztlán*, 7 (1976): 357–90, 391–418.

21. Quoted in *Foreigners in Their Native Land: Historical Roots of the Mexican Americans*, ed. David J. Weber (Albuquerque: 1973), p. 22.

22. Quoted in an Associated Press dispatch, Crystal City. Texas, in the *Fort Lauderdale News and Sun Sentinel*, June 16, 1974.

1

The Significance of the Spanish Borderlands to the United States*

Donald E. Worcester

Editor's Introduction

In this clear and concise summary, Donald Worcester describes Spain's enduring impact on a variety of aspects of life in the modern United States: agriculture, ranching, irrigation, architecture, literature, and law among them. In addressing this subject, Worcester joins a small group of historians, both Spanish and American, who have sought to demonstrate that our cultural debts do not go back to England alone and that the study of Spain in America is of more than antiquarian interest.[1] Worcester has added a new dimension to traditional considerations of this question, however, by extending the usual temporal definition of the Borderlands to include events of the last century and a half. Although the Borderlands are no longer under the control of Spain, Worcester notes that "the

*First published in the *Western Historical Quarterly*, 7 (1976):5–18, this essay is reprinted by permission of the author and the Western History Association. The author expresses thanks to Professors Lawrence Kinnaird and Malcolm D. McLean for reading the manuscript and making valuable suggestions.

Spanish language frontier is moving steadily northward." He exhorts Borderlands historians to extend their vision past 1821 and to include Mexicans, Cubans, Puerto Ricans, and other Spanish-speakers in the "new" Borderlands history.

Professor Worcester speaks with the assurance of a historian who has practiced his craft for nearly forty years. His numerous articles include studies of Navajos, Apaches, and the spread of Spanish horses among the Plains Indians. His books relating to the Borderlands include an editing of *Instructions for Governing the Interior Provinces of New Spain, 1786,* by Bernardo de Gálvez (New York: 1951), and an overview of Apache history, now in press. He has also written books on Latin American and American history, including *The Growth and Culture of Latin America* (New York: 1956), *Brazil* (New York: 1973), and *Bolivar* (New York: 1977), to name but a few. This versatile and prolific writer, presently Lorin A. Boswell Professor of History at Texas Christian University, has been honored by his fellow historians with the presidency of Phi Alpha Theta (1960–62) and the Western History Association (1974–75). He is a member of the Texas Institute of Letters, a former president of Western Writers of America (1973–74), and currently president of Westerners International.

NOTE

1. Among the American writers who have examined this question or aspects of it are: Harry Bernstein, "Spanish Influence in the United States, Economic Aspects," *Hispanic American Historical Review*, 18 (1938): 43–65; William R. Shepherd, "The Spanish Heritage in America," *Modern Language Journal*, 10 (1925): 75–85; Arthur P. Whitaker, "The Spanish Contribution to American Agriculture," *Agriculture History*, 3 (1929): 1–14; and Otis E. Young, "The Spanish Tradition in Gold and Silver Mining," *Arizona and the West*, 7 (1965): 299–314. Among the Spaniards interested in this subject are Dario Fernández Flóres, *The Spanish Heritage in the United States* (Madrid: 1965), and Carlos M. Fernández-Shaw, *Presencia española en los Estados Unidos* (Madrid: 1972).

The Significance of the Spanish Borderlands to the United States

Although it is true, as patriotic and ethnocentric historians on occasion inform us, that the main currents of American history have flowed from east to west, there were other currents flowing northward from Mexico and the Caribbean. These currents converged in the Southeast and the Southwest when European nations competed for footholds in North America and for control of Indian tribes and their trade. Competition among governments is rarely friendly, but on the fringes of empire the equality of poverty is a palliative, and the participants may subordinate imperial interests for the sake of survival or welfare. At this level cultural exchanges occur, consciously or otherwise. Americans have usually treated the westward movement as a human juggernaut that rolled relentlessly over Indian and Mexican as a vast and wonderful land was plundered in the name of progress. We have tended to ignore the Spanish, Mexican, and recently Puerto Rican and Cuban northward movements, even though they have made the Spanish-speaking population of the United States larger than those of some Spanish American republics.

Spanish influence in American national history has been present from the beginning. In the early decades the British monetary system was abandoned in favor of the dollar based on the Spanish peso, the most valuable and available specie. The pieces of eight into which the peso was divided became our two bits, four bits, and six bits. The peso and the United States dollar remained about equal in value for much of the nineteenth century, and Anglo bounty hunters were happy to be paid in pesos for Apache scalps in the 1830s and 1840s.

Still other signs of Spain's presence in many areas of the United States are numerous. Spanish place names cover the land from Florida to California, although in some states local pronunciation of such names effectively conceals their origins. Many modern cities such as San Francisco, Los Angeles, San Diego, Tucson, Santa Fe, El Paso, San Antonio, Pensacola, and Saint Augustine were built on Spanish foundations in the form of presidios, missions, and pueblos. Most of these cities still have large Spanish-speaking populations. The Presidio of San Francisco has served continuously as a military post since its founding in 1776 as a defensive outpost against potential Russian expansion into the Pacific. In 1976 its purpose is surprisingly similar to what it was two centuries ago, for it is the headquarters of the Sixth Army, a gigantic military complex representing this nation's military power on the west coast.

Spain's contributions have been especially significant to farming and ranching, including the livestock the Spaniards brought—horses, burros, cattle, sheep, goats, and swine—as well as plants such as alfalfa and a variety of fruits, including grapes. Although there were Anglo cattlemen on the frontiers of the southern English colonies, and they held roundups of range cattle at the various cowpens, raising contented cattle in forest and savanna was quite different from handling fleet-footed, bad-tempered Longhorns on open prairies. There is, incidentally, a Georgia brand book that goes back well into the eighteenth century; whether or not branding was introduced by Spanish ranchers in Florida has not been determined. The vast cattle industry of the United States owes much to its Spanish origins in Florida and the Southwest. Only in those regions were there laws favorable to cattlemen rather than farmers, a legacy of the Spanish *mesta* or stock raisers' association.

The Anglos who first began "cow hunts" in Texas soon learned from Mexican vaqueros and borrowed their riding gear, methods, and with more courage than elegance, their vocabulary. The southwestern cowboy was in fact a blend of southern frontiersman and vaquero. Few equalled the vaqueros' horsemanship and skill with the lasso, but they learned enough to justify the old saying, "Ropers south, riders north." The cowboy's lingo is largely Spanish in origin, as a few examples will show: lariat from *la reata*, buckaroo from *vaquero*, cinch from *cincha*, chaps from *chaparejos*, hackamore from *jáquima*, hoosegow from *juzgado*, bronco, mustang, and so forth.

There have been a number of studies of the *mesta* and the growth and spread of Spanish cattle ranching.[1] Additional studies might include the transformation of the roundup into the modern rodeo, and the story of that open range equine specialist, the cutting horse. Separating wild and uncooperative steers from herds required unusual horse sense, muscle, coordination, and the ability to move catlike between a herd-bound beast and its bovine associates. Today cutting horse competition is widely popular; like the rodeo it is a modern, highly competitive sport that grew out of Spanish cattle-handling techniques. Anglos also borrowed trail herding practices, road brands, regulations concerning cattle raising, and stockmen's associations inspired by the *mesta*.

The cattle and horses brought by the Spaniards had a revolutionary impact on the nomadic tribes of the Southwest and plains. Livestock raising is an economic activity well suited to occupying vast expanses of land with relatively few men, but in the Southwest the hostile tribes quickly learned the value of horses in hunting and warfare as well as for food, and became the primary predators. The result was that the Apache and Comanche checked the Spaniards' northward advance at the Rio Grande valley and southern Arizona, and came close to causing the total depopulation of Chihuahua and Sonora.

Because of the intensity of Apache raids the Spaniards developed distinctive institutions to cope with them. To punish raiders in Sonora and Chihuahua the Spaniards created *compañías volantes* or flying companies, highly mobile cavalry forces. And in the eighteenth century Spain introduced a unique colonial institution, the Commandancy General of the Interior Provinces, for the sole purpose of protecting the long and exposed frontier against the Apache. The commander general, unlike the viceroy and captain general, had only military responsibilities, so that he could concentrate on the all-pervasive Apache problem. The commandancy general was altered and reorganized several times in vain efforts to make it more effective without providing an adequate military force.

Considering the severe limitations in men and means, the officials of the Provincias Internas did a creditable job in staving off total ruin. Their greatest military successes were the result of persuading Apache to fight Apache. When the United States took control of the region as a result of the Treaty of Guadalupe Hidalgo we promised to prevent the Apache and other tribes from raiding across the border into Mexico. This proved so difficult that in the Gadsden Purchase treaty a few years later we abrogated that agreement. It required half a century of the hardest campaigning, the invention of more effective firearms, and most of the United States army to subdue the Apache. But final victory came as a result of Gen. George Crook's "discovery" that only the Apache could effectively fight the Apache in their mountain retreats. In view of the long and costly warfare between comparatively large and well-equipped United States forces and the Apache, the accomplishments of the small and poorly armed presidio garrisons and flying companies appear remarkable.

During the Apache wars, when pack mule trains proved vital for maintaining troops in the field, most of the packers, equipment, and terminology were borrowed from the mining regions of northern Mexico, as the Spaniards had borrowed the terms and techniques from the Arabs. *Aparejo* was the pack; *jalma* was the Arabic word for packsaddle. The saddle cover, *sobre-el-jalma*, Anglos corrupted into suvrin hammer.[2] As any student of General Crook's career will know, he made mule pack trains a science, with excellent results. Speaking of mules, we should not forget that the mule raising business in the East received a significant impulse because of the two splendid jacks the King of Spain sent to George Washington, or that the famous "Missouri mule" was a by-product of the Santa Fe trade.

Irrigation techniques were another Spanish contribution to those living in the arid lands of the Southwest. Although native Americans had developed irrigation systems centuries before the Spanish arrived, Anglos and their English forebears had never faced such problems. Spanish missionaries were the pioneers of the western irrigation frontier. Spanish laws regarding water usage and rights were also introduced.

Architecture is another important and visible feature of the borderlands, especially in the Southwest where it is a blend of Indian, Spanish, and Anglo styles. The Southwest is the only area in the United States where the architecture of the Indians, with its two-thousand-year tradition, has made a permanent impression.[3] Pueblo style architecture has furnished inspiration for both Spanish and Anglo construction. While adapting the adobe the Indians used in constructing their multistory pueblos, the Spaniards added their own distinctive features such as arches, patios, stucco, tile roofs, and decorative wall tiles. Anglo architects of the Southwest have been indebted to both traditions. And the popular barbecue found in countless patios of American homes across the country came from the Caribbean islands by way of Mexico and the Southwest.

With regard to literature, most of the voluminous writings of the Spanish and Mexican periods are accounts of travel beginning with Cabeza de Vaca's story of the ill-fated Narváez expedition to Florida, followed by the various reports on the Coronado and De Soto expeditions. These and many later narratives have been translated.[4] There was, in addition to the military and religious reports, an epic poem—Villagra's seventeenth-century account of the conquest of New Mexico.[5]

The borderlands have also been the inspiration for scores of Anglo writers and the setting for fiction, history, biography, and folklore. Among names familiar to all are Herbert E. Bolton, J. Frank Dobie, C. L. Sonnichsen, and Frank Waters. A few of the novelists whose books have had settings in the same region are Mary Austin, Willa Cather, Harvey Fergusson, Helen Hunt Jackson, Eugene Manlove Rhodes, and Conrad Richter.[6]

Political practices, at least at the local level, were also influenced by Spanish and Mexican town governments. In many localities Mexican officials continued in office after the Anglo occupation began.[7] There have been and still are officials with Spanish surnames in the borderlands states, including the present governor of Arizona. In several states Spanish surnames predominate in some counties.

Within the realm of folklore, folk tradition, myth, and legend there are indigenous ones and imports from Spain. The Seven Cities legend brought from Spain is germane to the Southwest as well as to other parts of the hemisphere because of the seven Zuñi pueblos and their role in attracting the Coronado expedition. There is also the legendary Amazon Queen Califia, for whom California was aptly named. Myths and legends the Spaniards found in the New World, and which had a vital bearing on the accumulation of geographical knowledge, were the Fountain of Youth and the Gran Quivira. Later ones concern lost mines and buried treasure, such as the famed Lost Dutchman Mine presumably somewhere in the Superstition Mountains of Arizona.

Racial and cultural blending has ever been characteristic of the borderlands for the Spaniards often sent non-Spaniards to frontier outposts. Many of the so-called Spanish colonists were in fact mestizos and mulattos. Spain also sent colonies of "civilized" Indians to the northern frontier to help in defense and to serve as examples to the wild tribes. Settlements of Tlascalans were established at Saltillo and in Texas near modern Eagle Pass and at San Sabá.[8] In the eighteenth century Spain also founded colonies of Canary Islanders at San Antonio and in Louisiana, where their descendants still live.

When Britain seized Florida during the Seven Years War most of the Spanish families withdrew from Saint Augustine and Pensacola, and few of them returned when Spain recovered Florida in 1783. Dr. Andrew Turnbull's Minorcan and Greek colonists abandoned New Smyrna in south Florida and moved to Saint Augustine, where Minorcan family names, traditions, and folklore are still found, yet the myth that the oldest city is Spanish survives. Among the Minorcan descendants who have won recognition are the Benéts and Admiral David Farragut of "Damn the torpedoes" fame.

One of the most significant and least familiar by-products of the borderlands experience is the Spanish legal heritage. Many Anglo jurists and lawmakers found existing institutions and legal concepts more humane and better suited to local conditions than their own common law principles, especially Spanish concepts concerning family relations. Spanish adoption laws, for example, were drastically different from Anglo-Saxon legal tradition, which made no provision for accepting an outsider as a lawful member of the family. Anglo-Saxon law even made it impossible to legitimize children born out of wedlock despite the fact that the parents having committed adultery, eventually atoned for their sins by committing matrimony. Texas law continued the principle of legitimization and in 1850 Texas was the first state to legalize adoption. Spanish law did not, on the other hand, recognize common law marriages.[9]

Texas and Arizona also borrowed the Spanish practice of allowing children of fourteen years or older to witness wills, and in Texas children must consent to adoption and may state a preference for a guardian. Also following Spanish custom, the Texas legislature enacted laws of descent and distribution which deny the right of a parent to disinherit children, for any cause other than violent attack or an attempt to defame the parent by accusing him of offenses punishable by law.[10]

Arizona, Texas, and California described property acquired during a marriage as the common property of husband and wife.[11] The principle known as community property regulates property rights of married couples in a number of western states under laws derived from the Spanish code, and is much more favorable to women than the English common law.[12] In the Spanish tradition the married woman's identity was distinct, and she had the right to enter contracts and to manage her own property, a right her Anglo-Saxon counterpart did not have. Under the common law all property owned by a woman prior to marriage became the property of her husband, as did any wealth the couple accumulated after their marriage, the wife retaining only a dower right, about one-third of the property. Under the laws derived from Spain the wife has a half-interest in all profits the couple earn, and no sale or encumbrance of real estate can be made without her consent.[13] The Spanish doctrine apparently stems from the Visigoths rather than the Romans or Arabs; the Visigoths took their womenfolk with them when they went on raids, and the women shared in both the dangers and the plunder.

Probably the most significant extension of the Spanish doctrine of community property is the joint income tax return, which appeared first in the borderlands states. In 1948, because of its obvious advantages, this benefit was extended to all married couples in the United States for income tax purposes.[14] Some of the flexible Spanish provisions concerning the making of wills and probate administration have also been retained in the borderlands states, and these provisions reduce the cost of probate and give greater freedom from expensive and time-consuming processes through the courts.

Another important legacy from Spain is protection for debtors, which goes back at least to the time of Ferdinand and Isabel, who decreed that oxen and other work animals as well as tools of farmers could not be seized except for debts to king or overlord. A century later this prohibition was extended to include cultivated lands, and ultimately, to artisans' tools of trade.

In 1824 Stephen F. Austin, who himself had left some unhappy creditors in Missouri, sought relief for colonists facing suits over debts incurred before coming to Texas. Learning that Spanish and Mexican laws were more favorable to debtors than those of the United States, he recommended that the Mexican Congress extend similar protection to Texas colonists. In 1829 the legislature of Coahuila and Texas passed laws that went beyond Austin's expectations, for they protected lands, farming equipment, and tools of trade against seizure for debts. The basic protection of these homestead exemption laws was maintained under the constitutions of the Republic and the State of Texas, which also prohibits garnishment of wages for debts.[15] Many other states have adopted similar laws.

Long before the United States passed the Homestead Act, Spain and later Mexico had a policy of allotting large acreages to settlers, giving each sufficient land for farming or ranching, depending on the adequacy of rainfall or water for irrigation. Use and occupancy for a number of years and a minimal tax earned title to the land. Spanish and Mexican land policies were much more liberal than those of the United States. In 1799 Daniel Boone, who had found it difficult to acquire title to frontier land in the United States, moved into Spanish territory, where Charles Dehault Delassus, lieutenant governor of Upper Louisiana, gave him 845 acres on Femme Osage Creek above the town of Saint Charles. He also named Boone syndic or civil magistrate for the Femme Osage district, a post he held until the region was ceded to the United States. In 1825 the *Missouri Advocate* attributed immigration to Texas to the difference between "a republic which gives first class lands gratis and a republic which will not sell inferior land for what it is worth."[16]

The Treaty of Guadalupe Hidalgo and the Gadsden Purchase guaranteed protection of the property rights of Mexican nationals in the territories annexed, but only the part of Texas between the Nueces and the Rio Grande was included in this guarantee. Spanish units of measurement are still used in parts of Texas to determine the limits of landed properties. The vara or Spanish yard could be anything between thirty-two point eight and thirty-five inches until 1919, when the Texas legislature fixed it at thirty-three and one-third inches.[17] Spanish law was obviously advantageous to Texas in the tidelands oil controversy, for the Spanish rule for offshore limits was three leagues rather than three miles—a league being three and a half miles.

In the Southwest where the possession of or right to use water is absolutely vital to agriculture, Spanish irrigation practices, terminology, and legal principles are still generally applied. Because the common law doctrine of riparian rights was unsuitable in areas of limited water resources, the Arizona legislature enacted a statute declaring that the common law doctrine of such rights "shall not obtain or be of any force in this Territory."[18] There was much litigation over rights to water, and the rulings of the Arizona courts were generally based on Spanish and Mexican laws, under which the right of prior appropriation was sustained. Both Arizona and New Mexico consistently followed the Mexican rule denying riparian owners the exclusive rights they would have had under the common law.[19]

The distinction between law and equity was abolished in Texas in 1840 when the legislature adopted the simple Spanish system of pleading cases in court. Under the common law system of pleading, the skillful lawyer was favored over right and justice. Under the Spanish system the plaintiff was required to tell the court his troubles in concise and straight-forward language. This simplified system has, since its adoption in Texas, been almost universally adopted in American and even English courts.[20] Even though some of the early laws based on Spanish legal principles were eventually superseded in the borderlands states, they nevertheless contributed to the body of legal tradition and their influence is still felt.

Spanish and Mexican mining techniques were borrowed by Anglo prospectors, but Spanish mining law did not survive as long as some other legal principles, for the new states were selective in what they retained. In 1783 Charles III promulgated a mining ordinance applicable to all of Spanish North America; under it all minerals belonged to the king, but his subjects could extract them according to specific rules. Charles III's Ordinance of 1783 remained in effect after Mexico's independence and became part of Mexican law. In 1836 the constitution of the Republic of Texas stated that "All laws now in force in Texas not inconsistent with this Constitution shall remain in full force until declared void, repealed, altered, or expired by their own limitations."[21] On entering the Union in 1846 Texas retained the Spanish system.

In California the question of mineral rights on former Spanish or Mexican grants arose with regard to Las Mariposas grant purchased by John C. Frémont. In 1861 the courts decided that the mineral rights had passed to the United States as private property; Frémont had, therefore, acquired title to all minerals on his grant by virtue of the patent issued him confirming his title. The Spanish-Mexican system remained in effect in Texas until the state constitution was amended in 1866.[22]

The borderlands have been well researched for the Spanish period by Dr. Herbert E. Bolton, whose book, *The Spanish Borderlands* (1921), popularized and delineated the field, by his students, and by many second generation Boltonians.[23] Investigations of this period are still being produced and published as if Spanish Borderlands history ended when Spanish officials left the scene. But if Spanish-speaking peoples are accepted as an essential element in our history, the Spanish Borderlands area of the United States has become increasingly important with each decade. The Spanish language frontier is moving steadily northward as the English language frontier moved westward a century and a half ago. The Spanish Borderlands have expanded and are still expanding, yet the horizons of borderlands historians have remained limited to the colonial era. It is time for historians to take a broader view of this phase of American history, for it is in the field of the new Spanish Borderlands that infinite opportunities for historical research are to be found.

The Spanish-speaking population of the United States is the second largest minority group today, an estimated twelve million with an annual increase of upwards of half a million. According to conservative projections this Spanish-speaking population will outnumber the black population in fifteen years. The Spanish-speaking borderland has obviously expanded far beyond the Spanish Borderlands of yesteryear. Today every state in the Union has Spanish-speaking residents. New York City became part of the Spanish-speaking frontier when the United States acquired Puerto Rico; it now has more Puerto Ricans than San Juan.

The education of Mexican Americans and other Spanish-speaking children is an area in which only belated efforts at improvement have been made. Until the 1930s no significant studies of their educational needs were available. During the 1950s Mexican American political and social organizations began to question the effectiveness of educational practices for their children.

The 1960 census provided much information on the 3.4 million people with Spanish surnames living in Arizona, California, Colorado, New Mexico, and Texas. The median years of school completed by Spanish surname citizens ranged from 4.7 in Texas to 8.6 in California, while the "all white" median was between 10.8 in Texas and 12.1 in California. The high dropout rate indicated by these figures is a reflection of the failure of school systems to make school attendance rewarding for Mexican Americans.

In the 1960s a number of organizations comprised of Mexican American educators began to play an important role in the development of techniques for the education of Spanish-speaking children. The studies they produced attracted the attention of state and federal agencies. In 1967 the federal government held a cabinet-level conference in Texas at which time Mexican Americans discussed problems with the secretaries of agriculture, interior, and health, education, and welfare. All agreed that educational problems required immediate remedy. As a result of these various activities Congress passed the Bilingual Education Act (1968) and provided funds for the development of bilingual education programs. However, the creation of an effective program of education for rural and urban Spanish-speaking children remains a challenge.[24]

The problem of providing effective education for children whose mother tongue is Spanish becomes ever more critical partly because of the high percentage of Mexicans among the estimated 6 million illegal immigrants in the Unted States. No accurate count can be made of the number of wetbacks entering the United States from Mexico each year, but in 1974 alone an estimated 1,200,000 arrived, and the number coming each year has been rising. Some return to Mexico, voluntarily or otherwise, but the majority remain.

A recent trend in borderlands studies has been the effort to give the neglected Mexican Americans a sense of identity and cultural homogeneity. Even as late as the 1960s they were referred to as forgotten Americans, but efforts to unionize farm laborers and growing political awareness have attracted attention to Mexican Americans.[25] The result has been an outpouring of books which too frequently have lacked historical perspective by slighting or misconstruing their history before the Treaty of Guadalupe Hidalgo. In attempting to give Mexican Americans a feeling of cultural unity some writers have overlooked the regional and other variations in both Mexican and Mexican American cultures.[26] There is little to be gained by trading old myths for new ones.

Since the Castro take-over in Cuba there has been a large Cuban migration to the United States, especially to south Florida. Cubans have so quickly become a part of the Florida scene that in 1974 the Dade County Commission passed a resolution proclaiming metropolitan Miami to be officially bicultural and bilingual—Cubans already constitute more than half of the area's population. It seems likely that Spanish-speaking majorities will appear in a number of other cities in the future and Dade County's action probably foreshadows similar developments elsewhere.

One hundred or more television and radio stations in the United States broadcast in Spanish most or all of the time, and there are Spanish language newspapers and first-rate newsmen who speak Spanish. Spanish American athletes and entertainers have had great success and popularity in the United States. Organizations such as La Raza Unida have given Spanish-speaking citizens more economic and political influence. One of the indications of growing awareness of the existence of a Spanish-speaking population is the increasing number of stores displaying the sign Aquí Se Habla Español.

Writers thus far have generally focused their attention on Mexican migrant farm workers and their plight. Urban dwellers are today at least numerically much more important. The thousands of Spanish names listed in the telephone directories of our major cities are revealing. A family with a telephone has not only a permanent address but the business and social contacts that make a telephone necessary. Such families are part of our permanent urban population, not migrant workers. For historians who are more interested in socio-economic progress than in social ills there are endless opportunities for investigation. The story of the progress and achievements of Spanish-speaking citizens of the United States in the professions, politics, business, and military service would fill many volumes and reveal their role in advancing a new linguistic, cultural, and ethnic frontier.

Frederick Jackson Turner's thoughtful and provocative essay, "The Significance of the Frontier in American History," delivered at the 1893 meeting of the American Historical Association, has had a profound and enduring influence on American historiography. Yet the frontier of which Turner wrote with such insight ended in 1890, and its disputed influences have largely been dissipated or have receded before urbanization. The old frontier has gone, but the Spanish Borderlands remain, still expanding and more important than ever. It is unnecessary to look at long-past events such as the laying of the foundations of great western cities or the origin of our monetary system to become aware of their significance. The Spanish language and cultural frontier is a present and manifest reality. A historian who views the statistics on the number of Spanish-speaking people already in the United States and the great waves arriving each year may be left with the justified feeling that a new and different form of Spanish conquest has begun.

NOTES

1. For example, Charles W. Arnade, "Cattle Raising in Spanish Florida, 1573-1763," *Agricultural History*, 35 (July 1961), 116–24; Donald Brand, "The Early History of the Range Cattle Industry in Northern Mexico," *Agricultural History*, 35 (July 1961), 132–38; William M. Dusenberry, *The Mexican Mesta: The Administration of Ranching in Colonial Mexico* (Urbana, 1963); Odie B. Faulk, "Ranching in Spanish Texas," *Hispanic American Historical Review*, 45 (May 1965), 257–66; Richard J. Morrissey, "The Northward Expansion of Cattle Ranching in New Spain, 1550–1600," *Agricultural History*, 25 (July 1961), 115–21; Sandra L. Myres, *The Ranch in Spanish Texas, 1691-1800* (El Paso, 1969).

2. John G. Bourke, *On the Border with Crook* (Glorieta, 1971), 150–52.

3. Trent E. Sanford, *The Architecture of the Southwest: Indian, Spanish, American* (New York, 1950).

4. For example, Morris Bishop, *The Odyssey of Cabeza de Vaca* (New York, 1933); Herbert E. Bolton, *Spanish Exploration in the Southwest, 1542–1706* (New York, 1916); Edward G. Bourne, ed., *Narratives of the Career of Hernando de Soto in the Conquest of Florida*, 2 vols. (New York, 1904); Charles W. Hackett, ed., *Historical Documents Relating to New Mexico, Nueva Vizcaya, and Approaches Thereto, to 1773*, 3 vols. (Washington, 1923–37); Frederick W. Hodge and T. H. Lewis, *Spanish Explorers in the Southern United States, 1528–1543* (New York, 1907); Lawrence Kinnaird, ed., *Spain in the Mississippi Valley, 1765–1794*, 3 vols. (Washington, 1949).

5. Gaspar Pérez de Villagrá, *History of New Mexico*, tr. and ed. Gilberto Espinosa (Los Angeles, 1933).

6. For surveys of southwestern literature see Lawrence Clark Powell, *West Southwest: Essays on Writers, Their Books and Their Lands* (Los Angeles, 1957); and Mabel Major and T. M. Pearce, *Southwest Heritage: A Literary History with Bibliography* (Albuquerque, 1972).

7. Among recent studies are Jack D. L. Holmes, *Gayoso: The Life of a Spanish Governor in the Mississippi Valley, 1789–1799* (Baton Rouge, 1965); Marc Simmons, *Spanish Government in New Mexico* (Albuquerque, 1968); Helen H. Tanner, *Zéspedes in East Florida, 1784–1790* (Coral Gables, 1963); John J. TePaske, *The Governorship of Spanish Florida, 1700–1763* (Durham, 1964).

8. Marc Simmons, "Tlascalans in the Spanish Borderlands," *New Mexico Historical Review*, 39 (April 1964), 101–10.

9. James M. Murphy, *The Spanish Legal Heritage in Arizona* (Tucson, 1966), 39, 43.

10. Gerald Ashford, *Spanish Texas, Yesterday and Today* (Austin, 1971), 259. See also Bennett Smith, *Marriage by Bond in Colonial Texas* (Fort Worth, 1972).

11. Murphy, *Spanish Legal Heritage*, 38.

12. Murphy, *Spanish Legal Heritage*, 31, 32.

13. Ashford, *Spanish Texas*, 258, 259.

14. Ashford, *Spanish Texas*, 259.

15. Ashford, *Spanish Texas*, 238, 239.

16. Ashford, *Spanish Texas*, 236, 237. See also C. Richard Arena, "Land Settlement Policies and Practices in Spanish Louisiana," in John Francis McDermott, ed., *The Spanish in the Mississippi Valley, 1762–1804* (Urbana, 1974), 51–60.

17. Ashford, *Spanish Texas*, 251.

18. Murphy, *Spanish Legal Heritage*, 16.

19. Murphy, *Spanish Legal Heritage*, 20. See also Richard E. Greenleaf, "Land and Water in Mexico and New Mexico, 1700–1821," *New Mexico Historical Review*, 47 (April 1972), 85–112; Betty Eakle Dobkins, *The Spanish Element in Texas Water Law* (Austin, 1959).

20. Ashford, *Spanish Texas*, 259.

21. Wallace Hawkins, *El Sal del Rey* (Austin, 1942), 7–12.

22. Hawkins, *El Sal del Rey*, 24–27.

23. Among general and bibliographical studies are the following: Hubert Howe Bancroft, *History of the North Mexican States and Texas*, 2 vols. (San Francisco, 1884) and *History of Arizona and New Mexico, 1530–1888* (San Francisco, 1889); John Francis Bannon, *The Spanish Borderlands Frontier, 1513–1821* (New York, 1970); Herbert E. Bolton, *The Spanish Borderlands: A Chronicle of Old Florida and the Southwest* (New Haven, 1921); Carlos E. Castañeda, *Our Catholic Heritage in Texas*, 7 vols. (Austin, 1936–1950); Charles C. Cumberland, "The United States-Mexican Border: A Selective Guide to the Literature of the Region," supplement to *Rural Sociology*, 25 (June 1960); Odie B. Faulk, *Land of Many Frontiers: A History of the American Southwest* (New York, 1968); Dario Fernández-Flórez, *The Spanish Heritage in the United States* (Madrid, 1965); Jack D. Forbes, *Apache, Navaho, and Spaniard* (Norman, 1960); Eugene Hollon, *The Southwest: Old and New* (New York, 1961); Billy Mac Jones, *Health Seekers in the Southwest, 1817–1900* (Norman, 1967); Howard R. Lamar, *The Far Southwest, 1846-1912: A Territorial History* (New Haven, 1966); D. W. Meinig, *Southwest: Three Peoples in Geographical Change, 1600–1970* (New York, 1971); Lynn Perrigo, *The American Southwest: Its Peoples and Cultures* (New York, 1971); Rupert N. Richardson and Carl Coke Rister, *The Greater Southwest* (Glendale, 1934); Francis Borgia Steck, *A Tentative Guide to Historical Markers on the Spanish Borderlands*, new ed. (New York, 1971); Henry R. Wagner, *The Spanish Southwest, 1542–1794*, 2 vols. (Albuquerque, 1937); Arthur R. Whitaker, *The Spanish-American Frontier, 1783–1795* (Boston, 1927).

24. "Mexican Americans, Education of," *Encyclopedia of Education*, 1971. VI: 343–46.

25. Ralph H. Vigil, "The New Borderlands History: A Critique," *New Mexico Historical Review*, 48 (July 1973), 189. See also Julian Samora, ed., *La Raza, Forgotten Americans* (Notre Dame, 1966); and George I. Sanchez, *Forgotten People, A Study of New Mexicans* (Albuquerque, 1967).

26. Vigil, "New Borderlands History," 190, 191.

An Early Explorer.

2

The Search for the Fabulous in the Settlement of the Southwest*

George P. Hammond

Editor's Introduction

Few subjects hold as much interest and dramatic potential as exploration, and few historians know more about that subject than George Hammond. After earning a doctorate from Berkeley in 1924, under Herbert Eugene Bolton, Hammond went on to become the leading authority on sixteenth-century Spanish terrestrial exploration in northern New Spain. He has edited most of the significant documents on that subject, ranging from the first *entrada* by Francisco Vázquez de Coronado in 1540 to the settlement of New Mexico by Juan de Oñate in 1598. Until his retirement in 1965, Hammond served as director of the Bancroft Library and professor of history at the University of California, Berkeley.

**Utah Historical Quarterly*, 24 (1956): 1–19. Reprinted with permission of the author and the State of Utah, Department of Development Services, Division of State History. Dr. Hammond has graciously made minor corrections and augmentations to the original article. His sources, however, continue to reflect his original scholarship and have not been updated.

He has yet to retire as a historian, however. In 1976, in his eightieth year, Hammond published a book-length biography of British-born trapper and trader Alexander Barclay.[1]

In "The Search for the Fabulous," originally an address delivered to the Utah State Historical Society in 1955, Hammond lucidly outlined the familiar story of the impact of myth, legend, and credulity on Spanish exploration to the north of Mexico. In addition to such famous and fanciful notions as the Seven Cities of Cíbola, which Hammond discusses, Spaniards also learned that among the indigenous peoples of North America was a "tribe who sat in the shade of their own generous-sized ears; and still other people who did not eat their food, but lived on smells."[2]

Because they believed these tales, Spaniards might seem unusually gullible to twentieth-century readers. We must, however, take seriously Dr. Hammond's reminder that the atmosphere of the sixteenth century was "supercharged with dreams." Spain's explorers had not only absorbed popular legends of chivalry, in which fact and fiction melded indistinguishably,[3] but those same explorers knew that in the New World dreams beyond imagining had come true. For the discoverers of fabulous Aztec cities in the Valley of Mexico, it required little stretch of imagination to suppose than an even more fabulous new Mexico might lie somewhere else.

Lest we judge Spaniards too hastily, we should remember, too, that myths and legends remain strong in our own times. It appears that we cannot do without them.[4] The legend of Aztlán, for example, has served the Chicano movement since the mid-1960s as a symbolic name for the southwestern United States. The ancestral home of the Aztecs before their thirteenth-century migration to the Valley of Mexico, Aztlán existed somewhere to the north of Mexico City, according to Aztec oral tradition. Notwithstanding anthropological evidence to the contrary, some Chicanos place Aztlán in the present-day United States. They hope that the name "Aztlán" will not only serve as a symbol of the return of Mexicans to their homeland, but will also give the Chicano movement a broad regional identity that transcends state or local levels.[5] In this regard it is curious and ironic that a seventeenth-century Franciscan, as Hammond suggests, mistakenly supposed that the ancestral home of the Aztecs was at a place called Lake Copala in the area of present-day Utah.

NOTES

1. With Agapito Rey, Hammond has translated and edited such works as the *Narratives of the Coronado Expedition, 1540–42* (Albuquerque: 1940), *The Rediscovery of New Mexico, 1580–1594* (Albuquerque: 1966), and *Don Juan de Oñate, Colonizer of New Mexico, 1595–1628,* 2 vols. (Albuquerque: 1953). His most recent book is *Alexander Barclay, Mountain Man* (Denver: 1976).

2. Herbert Eugene Bolton, "Defensive Spanish Expansion and the Significance of the Borderlands," in *Bolton and the Spanish Borderlands*, ed. John Francis Bannon (Norman: 1964), p. 40.

3. Perhaps the best discussion of this is in Irving Leonard, *Books of the Brave* (Cambridge, Mass.: 1949). For the application of one of these legends see Donald C. Cutter, "Sources of the Name 'California'" *Arizona and the West*, 3 (1961): 233–43.

4. Barrows Dunham provides a delightful if somewhat dated discussion of this question in *Man Against Myth* (Boston: 1949).

5. David J. Weber, *Foreigners in Their Native Land: Historical Roots of the Mexican Americans* (Albuquerque: 1973), p. 4.

The Search for the Fabulous in the Settlement of the Southwest

Any discussion of the Southwest, its exploration and settlement, brings to mind Spain's tremendous record in the New World in the sixteenth century. This century, as you will recall, had been Spain's Golden Age, the period of Cervantes' *Don Quijote*, the time of Ferdinand and Isabella's Conquest of Granada, bringing to a climax Spain's long fight against the Moor; it was the time also of organization of the national state under Ferdinand and Isabella, centralizing power in the Crown; it was a period of great religious fervor, when everyone must be brought to believe in the one true God, according to the Catholic dogma. Spain believed in these things. Thus, with Church and State well organized, the Crown was in a position to exploit fully the discovery of America, which came, as if by divine favor, in the later years of the rule of this unique pair, Ferdinand and Isabella. Columbus' discovery in 1492 opened a new world, not only to Spain, but to all the world. But it was Spain's opportunity to exploit it before any other.

In the first half of the sixteenth century came the original occupation of the West Indies Islands, immediately after the discovery of America by Columbus; then followed the exploration of the northern coast of South America, the Florida area, the Caribbean Sea, and those celebrated voyages into the Gulf of Mexico that led to the expedition of Hernán Cortés and the discovery and conquest of the native civilizations of Mexico and Central America, an adventure story that has ever been one of the celebrated chapters of world history, a tale that makes Robinson Crusoe pale into insignificance by comparison. Cortés' exploits were duplicated in a measure in Central America, where the noted Pedrarias conquered the natives with a cruel and ruthless hand; in Guatemala, where Pedro de Alvarado subjugated a kingdom; in Peru, where Francisco de Pizarro, descendant of a family so poor and lowly that he has been called the Swineherd of Estremadura, broke the power of the Inca Empire and reduced it to allegiance to Spain; in Chile, where Pedro de Valdivia began the conquest of the indomitable Araucanian Indians; or in New Granada (the modern Colombia), where Gonzalo Jiménez de Quesada established the power of the Spanish king in the fabled land of the Chibchas.[2] Here originated the tale of El Dorado, popularized by Adolph Bandelier as *The Gilded Man*, where, in a religious ceremonial, a native chieftain, bedaubed with mud and sprayed with gold dust, dived into a lake to wash off the golden dust and so propitiate the gods.

These events had come to pass by the middle of the sixteenth century. The second half was marked not only by further conquests, but by consolidation of what had been gained. Among the new areas that came into view was the distant New Mexico, of which marvelous tales had been heralded by frontiersmen and explorers for half a century, tales which envisioned lands to exploit and peoples to convert.

First of these storytellers was Alvar Núñez Cabeza de Vaca, a castaway of the Pánfilo de Narváez expedition to Florida. Cabeza de Vaca had been stranded by shipwreck on the Texas Coast in 1528, lived among the Indians of the Gulf Coast till he made his escape and returned to Mexico in 1536 by way of Mexico's west coast, full of romantic stories of what had happened on that fabulous but dangerous frontier; and tales of the land and its people, according to rumors he had picked up along the way, as well as to what he had seen.[3]

We shall never know all of Cabeza de Vaca's stories, for he told some to his barber and other gossips, and still others to the officials of the government, few of which have been recorded. We do know what happened, however, and that was the sending, by the viceroy of Mexico, of Fray Marcos de Niza on a great reconnoitering expedition to the north to verify Cabeza de Vaca's reports and to search for the fabled Seven Cities, thought to exist in the north somewhere.

The legend of the Seven Cities, with all their gold, originated in medieval Europe.[4] With the discovery of America, they skipped from place to place, from the West Indies to Mexico, but always beyond the horizon, until Fray Marcos now sought to find them on this trip. As he plodded along with his guide Estevanico and some Indians in modern Sonora, he sent Estevanico on ahead to reconnoiter and arranged to communicate with him by signs. That is, if Estevanico found good news, he was to send back an Indian bearing a small cross; if more important news, a larger cross; and if he should discover a country richer than Mexico itself, a great cross. Lo and behold, four days later an Indian messenger brought Fray Marcos a cross "as high as a man" and urged the friar to push forward at once. Fray Marcos did so, and is supposed finally to have approached Zuñi, in New Mexico, but to have seen the pueblo only from a distance, for the Zuñians were hostile, had killed Estevanico, and his fleeing companions did not need to urge Fray Marcos to flee for his life. It may be that he had seen Zuñi in a mirage, a common characteristic of the dry, mountain country, as all of us who have lived in it can testify. In any case, Fray Marcos, on his return to Mexico, gilded his narrative profusely with stories of rich cities. The Seven Cities, indeed, now were given the name Cíbola, a new word which he had heard from the Indians. Ever since then it has been applied to Zuñi and the group of pueblos that surrounded it in ancient times.

"The city," wrote Fray Marcos, "is larger than the city of Mexico . . . The doorways to the best houses have many decorations of turquoises, of which there is a great abundance." According to what the friar heard, "Cibola is a big city in which there are many people, streets and plazas, that in some sections of the city there are some very large houses ten stories high . . . They say that the houses are of stone and lime . . . that the portals and fronts of the chief houses are of turquoise."[5]

Let it be noted that the friar's excited listeners apparently failed to grasp the fact that while the friar had seen the town, he had not seen its riches. He had only heard about them from the Indians.

But such was the atmosphere of the sixteenth century, an atmosphere supercharged with dreams—dreams of Indian souls to convert and Indian gold to exploit.

With the return of Fray Marcos to Mexico, the viceroy lost no time in organizing and sending out the Coronado expedition the very next year, 1540. At Cíbola, Spanish hopes were dashed. Coronado himself, distinguished by a gilded helmet, was struck down by an Indian warrior from a terrace, though the soldiers soon captured the town. But it had no turquoise-studded doors, no ten-story houses; there were only adobe buildings, poor in Spanish eyes.

Now Coronado sent out his captains to explore, while he settled down with the headquarters detachment of his army at Tiguex, about twenty miles north of present-day Albuquerque. They explored as far as the Grand Canyon of the Colorado on the west to Kansas in the east. They heard of numerous kingdoms, especially of golden Quivira—reputed to have so much gold that the ordinary dishes were made of "wrought plate," the pitchers and bowls of solid gold, and the chief of the kingdom slept under a tree laden with little golden bells that lulled him to rest during his siesta. What a dream—Golden Quivira! This kingdom was sought for so long and was so well publicized that it became an established point on the maps of European mapmakers. They might locate it anywhere from Kansas to California, but there it was—a definite place on the chart. Elusive? Yes, indeed, but for future explorers a lodestone of magic power.[6]

The Coronado venture was soon forgotten. Such forgetfulness was made easy by the colossal events about to be revealed as the curtain of history opened on another scene. This scene was played on Mexico's northern frontier, on the hills around modern Zacatecas, 150 miles northwest of Mexico City, then the home of hostile Indians, but where Spanish miners and cattlemen had begun to penetrate. In the conflict that ensued between white man and red, an Indian woman, so the story goes, who had been befriended by a Spaniard, revealed the existence of a lode of silver ore. This was the famous Bufa at the top of one of the hills of Zacatecas. Here was treasure—treasure such as the Spaniards had not yet found in Mexico, and miners flocked in. All of northern Mexico came under the pick of the prospector. The Indians were pushed back, or pacified and civilized, settlements followed, with cattle ranches and the usual accompaniments of a frontier society. Northern Mexico became famous for silver production.[7] Even today, promoters diligently invite people to invest money in Mexican mines—there must be more where there was so much at one time!

The steady progression of settlements northward from Mexico City in search of silver and gold led more and more people into the new country, and soon more accurate information became available of what the land and its people were like. There were rumors, too, picked up in Chihuahua and reported to Mexico City, of more distant inland regions, where there were people who lived in houses many stories high, who wore clothes, who, in short, must be rich and numerous and worthy of exploitation and civilizing.[8]

These rumors had reference to the Indians of the present New Mexico and Arizona, people who lived in great houses, in marked contrast to the wild and uncivilized Indians of northern Mexico. Now, at last, there seemed to loom up on the distant horizon another kingdom such as Cortés had found in Mexico, or Pizarro in Peru. Today we recognize that to these men the wish was father to the thought—we know so much more about the Southwest than they did. But the sixteenth century was not practical or scientific, but rather romantic and idealistic. Anything was possible. Had this not been proved by many, many conquerors—Columbus, Cortés, Pizarro, and others?

So when, in 1580, miners and slave hunters had reached modern Chihuahua—laborers were needed to work the mines—and the rumors of these new kingdoms persisted (just as they had in Coronado's day)—plans were set on foot by a friar, Agustín Rodríguez, to investigate. Permission to make the exploration was obtained by the friar, and the soldiers went along for his protection; that is the official story. In fact we know that by the New Laws of 1542 and the new regulations of 1573, the oldtime expeditions such as had been made by Coronado, De Soto, and many others, were no longer legal, and it became necessary to adopt different procedures to gain permission to visit the unexplored frontier.[9] It was for this reason that all the expeditions after this date had a strong tone of religious leadership, although the presence of the soldiers and captains of industry made the search for new silver mountains, or new centers of Indian population, equally certain.

On this basis New Mexico, as this northern region was now being called, was rediscovered. In 1580–81, Friar Agustín Rodríguez, two other friars, and Captain Francisco Sánchez Chamuscado with less than a dozen companions, peacefully invaded New Mexico and visited all the pueblos before returning to report on their remarkable discovery. To them and their generation it was a discovery, for knowledge of what Coronado had done forty years earlier had been so thoroughly buried in government archives, in short, so completely forgotten, that now it was not even suspected he had been in this same land.[10]

The very next year, 1582, another expedition visited New Mexico. It was headed by Antonio de Espejo representing the military and Fray Bernardino Beltrán representing the Church. The immediate reason for the trip was anxiety over the fate of two friars who had chosen to remain among the Pueblo Indians in order to begin the Christianization of the people. Espejo, a merchant by profession, wanted to explore; and this he did, visiting the entire pueblo area from Pecos on the east to the Moquis (Hopis) on the west, and to Taos on the north. The reports of this band as to the wealth of the land and the many people who lived there were so encouraging that the Crown in Spain, by royal decree, authorized the "pacification and settlement" of New Mexico, and instructed the viceroy to find a suitable leader to carry it out.[11]

Now followed a spirited contest for the position of "governor and captain general" of New Mexico. It might well be likened to the nomination of a presidential candidate by a political party in the United States today, as candidates tossed their hats into the ring. The final selection of the successful candidate was made by the viceroy of Mexico, who kept in close touch with the Council of the Indies and the Crown in such matters. But as the official who represented the king directly, he made the choice, and he issued the instructions for the conquest, in conformity with the laws regulating such matters. The conquest of so rich a province demanded the attention of the highest officials, both of Mexico and Spain.

Eight or ten influential men offered to make the expedition; largely at their own cost: Lómas y Colmenares, a big cattle baron; Urdiñola, a governor and military chief; Juan de Oñate, who had taken part in the subjugation of the wild Indians of Nueva Galicia and whose father and grandfather had opened great silver mines around Zacatecas; ambitious soldiers like Hernán Gallegos, who had gone on the first exploration in 1581; and there was the merchant adventurer, Antonio de Espejo—who headed the expedition in 1582. But the man nominated was Juan de Oñate of Zacatecas, whose family moved in the same social and political circles as the viceroy himself. In other words, Oñate was not only a man of wealth and experience, but had good connections, and the viceroy chose him to undertake the great adventure.[12]

Oñate's petition to the viceroy asking to be appointed governor and offering to carry out the exploration largely at his own expense was drawn up in accordance with the laws and ordinances regulating new conquests, particularly the laws of 1573.

These laws had set an entirely new pattern of conquest. Hereafter, any expedition that might be sent into the Indian country should seek only the conversion of the heathen, not discovery of mines or subjugation of the native people.

It shall not be my purpose on this occasion to dwell in detail on the events of the Oñate expedition to New Mexico. This I have done in some published books, but I do wish to make a few general observations to illustrate the significance of the expedition and the importance attached to it by the Spanish government.

In my judgment, it would be a fair comparison to say that the Oñate expedition was considered as important as that of Hernán Cortés which conquered Mexico in 1519. Cortés had set out to conquer new kingdoms, and had stumbled on the great Aztec society in the valley of Mexico. Oñate had reports of kingdoms too, apparently verified by several reconnoitering expeditions. There was this difference: Cortés acted pretty much as a private entrepreneur, in the name of the king, whereas Oñate went with the blessing of the Crown itself, and with the government paying the costs of the six friars who accompanied him, as well as of the cannon, quicksilver, lead, and certain other specialized goods. Oñate promised to enlist not less than two hundred men, fully equipped, to provide food and supplies for the trip, to provide several thousand sheep, goats, cattle, and horses, and many other things, such as footgear, medicine, iron, cloth—all too numerous to mention here. Altogether it represented a tremendous investment, most of the cost shouldered by Oñate and his friends and relatives.

With this force Oñate took command personally on the northern frontier in Chihuahua, where his army was stationed, but he had to wait nearly three years before finally being authorized to proceed. These vexatious and costly delays were due to jealousy of others who sought to displace him, to official vacillation caused by a change of viceroys in Mexico late in 1595, after Oñate had been appointed governor, and to the cumbersome nature of the Spanish administrative system itself. Nevertheless, in 1598 he finally set out for the Promised Land, with a reduced and somewhat bedraggled force (it had been held on the extreme northern frontier of settlement where supplies were difficult to procure), crossed the Rio Grande at modern El Paso, where he took possession of the land in the name of the Crown, and proceeded up the great river, visiting the Indian pueblos on the way. In general, the natives were frightened of the foreign invaders. At modern Socorro, where the Indians fled across the river in fear, Oñate took a supply of corn from the homes of the Indians to feed his own men. The journey had been long, the supplies inadequate, and the men were starving. At Santo Domingo, half-way between Albuquerque and Santa Fe, he met the chiefs of seven pueblos in the kiva of the town, and there, on bended knee, they swore allegiance to the Spanish God and King, after having listened to a sermon on the benefits they would gain as subjects of Spain.

Shortly thereafter the Spanish force set up headquarters at a pueblo which they christened San Juan de los Caballeros, modern San Juan, about thirty miles north of Santa Fe. Later they moved across the river to San Gabriel, where the ruins of the old pueblo may still be seen. This remained the capital until Governor Pedro de Peralta established Santa Fe in 1610.

Now came Oñate's exploration of New Mexico, the land that was supposed to rival Mexico in its riches. Within a few months he had toured the entire pueblo area, visiting the Jumano pueblos at Abó and Gran Quivira in the Estancia Valley east of Albuquerque, those up the Rio Grande as far as Taos, the Jemez group to the west in the Jemez River Valley, and Acoma and Zuñi still farther west. One of his captains, Marcos Farfán, visited the Moqui pueblos and the Verde River region in search of mines and staked out mining claims. Everywhere the picture was much the same—a large Indian population living in houses of adobe, often built to a height of more than one story. But these Indians possessed neither silver nor gold, nor abundant or fertile farms, nor good mining prospects, though the soldiers did stake out quite a number of mining claims and boasted of their richness. Still, Oñate considered New Mexico's prospects great, as shown by a letter of his to the king dated April 7, 1599, wherein he said: "I trust in God that I shall give your majesty a new world, greater than New Spain, to judge from the reports I have received and from what I have seen and explored, and I shall persevere in this effort to the end of my life."[18]

These reports probably referred to Quivira, news of which had been picked up in the exploration of the country. According to the Indian Jusepe, who had visited this land some years earlier and who now was one of Oñate's guides, it was a vast country with a great population and enormous riches. Such testimony was enough to set the imagination afire, and Oñate made plans to visit and claim this fabulous land.

So in the summer of 1601, after he had received a reinforcement of eighty men, Oñate went to Quivira, just as had Coronado sixty years earlier, and reached approximately the same place, beyond the great bend of the Arkansas, where it is joined by the Walnut River, not far north of the Oklahoma border. He found the population very large, but some of the people were hostile, and he was forced to turn back for safety.

The fertility of the land had impressed the Spaniards, however, and though they turned back, they hoped to return and conquer this wonderful country at some future date.[14]

Full of hope and plans, Oñate and his little force returned to their capital at San Gabriel. Not only had they found a land of surpassing fertility and promise, but they had heard of other lands and kingdoms farther on—*más allá*—as the Spanish reads—which could be explored from Quivira. All these hopes were dashed to bits on their return, for at San Gabriel most of the soldier-colonists had mutinied and abandoned the province. Only twenty-five or so, a mere remnant, remained behind. This was a disaster. At one blow Oñate's dreams of further conquest had been shattered.[15] Indeed, his little force was in danger of attack and destruction by the Indians, who might seize the opportunity to wipe out the invaders. The returning malcontents, it was sure, would have other stories to tell than those sent out by Oñate, a fact that he must have contemplated with chagrin. The situation was all the more serious from the fact that up till this summer of 1601, he had maintained a tight censorship, had not permitted any letters to be sent to Mexico by members of the colony, and his own letters had been tinged with a superlatively rosy hue that would now be denounced by the deserting colonists.

Indeed, this is just what happened. The deserters lodged grave charges against the governor, accusing him of misconduct, mismanagement, and even more serious offenses, while Oñate accused them of the crime of desertion. The viceroy, in far-off Mexico, unable to sift fact from fancy in this fire of countercharges, refused to permit further reinforcements to be sent to the infant colony until the situation could be clarified. Oñate, still powerful though at a disadvantage, struck back with all the resources at his command. Through friends and relatives in Mexico he appealed to the viceroy and Audiencia; and through his brother, Don Alonso, and the poet-soldier, Gaspar de Villagrá, whom he sent to Spain to intercede with the king and the Council of the Indies for support.[16] At the same time he made preparations for a final throw of the dice, for one more major exploration, in the hope of finding new riches and of impressing the government with his achievements. This exploration was aimed at finding the Pacific Ocean, or South Sea, as it was then called, and its reputed wealth in pearls, of discovering a seaport close enough to New Mexico to permit easier transport of supplies and reinforcements, and of prospecting for mines or new Indian populations that would restore royal confidence in him and confound his opponents and critics. With but a handful of men, approximately thirty, Oñate hoped to succeed, "to strike it rich," in this final gamble.

This journey he made in the winter of 1604–5, and it took him to the head of the Gulf of California, not to the Pacific Ocean proper. Of the events that took place en route we have an extraordinary diary by Father Francisco de Escobar,[17] extraordinary especially because of its tales of new wonders and Oñate's signature in imperishable rock, chiseled on an overhanging cliff of Inscription Rock, near Zuñi, on the return journey in April, 1605. There it may still be seen, the oldest inscription ever found in the West. The site is now a national monument.

Oñate's dreams of empire in the north foundered on the solid rock of fact, the fact that man would have to struggle in the sweat of his brow to wrest a living from the soil; that the line of communication and supply between the new land and Mexico City was too great; that there were no rich kingdoms to subdue and exploit, but rather innumerable people who required the white man's help to raise their standard of life. For a time the government seriously considered giving up New Mexico, but a few missionaries and a handful of settlers remained, waiting for the government's decision. The king's conscience finally decided the issue, for he was not willing to abandon the recent converts to relapse into heathenism. Then, in 1608, came word from New Mexico that "seven thousand" Indians had been converted and that there were thousands more "ready unto the harvest," whereupon the government decided, somewhat reluctantly, to retain its foothold there as an outpost at the cost of the Crown. As a consequence, a new governor, Pedro de Peralta, was appointed, Oñate was sent home and punished for his alleged misdeeds, Santa Fe was founded as the new capital (to get away from San Gabriel in the Chama Valley, which lay on the route of the Navajo Indians), an escort of fifty soldier-citizens was maintained at the capital for protection, a handful of missionaries was distributed among the chief pueblos, all at royal expense, and the northern frontier, purged of its dreams of finding another Mexico, settled down to a humdrum existence.

New Mexico was, in fact, one of the most isolated of Spain's colonies in North America, a situation that prevailed for two hundred years—or until Lieutenant Zebulon M. Pike and frontiersmen from the new United States visited the province in the early 1800s. Throughout this two-hundred-year period the Spaniards had maintained New Mexico, in spite of the many threats of Indian uprisings and in spite of the successful Pueblo Revolt in 1680, when the Indians rebelled, killed four hundred or more Spaniards, and drove the rest out, a force of perhaps twenty-five hundred—but the Spaniards came back, regained control over the natives, and converted and civilized the populace to the best of their ability.[18] The process was naturally a two-way operation, for the Spaniards married Indian women and maintained something of a mixed society. But it was a Spanish—a European—society, which cultivated its inheritance of sixteenth-century ideas in government, religion, literature, and speech, until its isolation was disturbed by invasion in the nineteenth century.

Though New Mexico was remote and cut off from its sister provinces in Mexico, its occupants continued to dream, and some of its governors played with the magic of finding new and rich kingdoms, long after the early rumors of Quivira had been so completely scuttled. One of these dreams was of a certain Sierra Azul, or Blue Mountain, apparently a mountain of silver.[19] In the time of Governor Diego de Vargas, who reconquered New Mexico after the disastrous Pueblo Revolt of 1680, the viceroy of Mexico wrote him, in 1691, urging the discovery of certain quicksilver deposits, thought to exist in the form of small lakes and pools in the province of Moqui, according to information he had received. Vargas in turn did not fail to emphasize the possibilities of finding riches in the Sierra Azul, using this as a fulcrum to keep the royal officials interested in the reconquest of New Mexico. In fact, one can hardly escape the conclusion that the bait of the Sierra Azul was tailored to fit the desires of the Crown, eager to re-establish Spanish control over the pueblos in New Mexico that had rebelled. The psychology of the times nourished such thinking. The Sierra Azul continued to dance about, like a distant mirage, every time an expedition went out to explore. It did not vanish till a better knowledge of geography dispelled its attractive power in the nineteenth century.

These tales of elusive wonders in the west that have charmed man for many years require some reference to Copala and to Teguayo.[20] The kingdom of Copala, marvelous to relate, was first heard of in the time of Diego de Ibarra, he who became one of the original millionaires on the discovery of mines at Zacatecas about 1545. Like Coronado's Quivira, Copala was just over the horizon. Francisco de Ibarra, nephew of the millionaire, was commissioned to find it, and in 1565 he did make a tremendous exploration of the country north and west of Zacatecas. He probably reached the Casas Grandes area of northern Chihuahua, may even have seen a part of southern Arizona, but found no kingdom of Copala, no rich Indian communities to conquer, only a wild country inhabited by nomadic tribes.[21]

The lure of Copala persisted, however, and with the passage of the years, tended to vault over hitherto unknown regions only to appear again in some new place, conjured up, perhaps, by the vivid imagination of some captain, sitting around a campfire on the Indian frontier and listening to the tales of his local scout and interpreter, who really understood neither what the Spaniard sought, his language, his customs, nor his peculiar fascination for gold and silver. Under the circumstances, the interpreter would naturally try to please his visitor, especially since it usually meant presents of food and some of the wonderful gadgets that the

European brought along—perhaps a knife, a gun, or some other marvelous gift.

An illuminating example of this occurred on Oñate's expedition to the Gulf of California in 1604, of which we have two accounts, one written by Fray Francisco de Escobar, who accompanied the party, and the other written by Fray Gerónimo de Zárate Salmerón, who wrote about 1626. Escobar makes no mention whatever of a lake called Copala, or of having heard of it from the Indians, though he spins some fantastic yarns. Zárate, on the contrary, has a wonderful story, gathered, he says, while he was a missionary among the Jémez Indians, one of whom had actually visited the country. He wrote that while among the Mojave Indians they heard of the lake called Copala, that here was the original home of the Mexicans, that is, the Aztecs, that the Indians spoke the name Copala very plainly, and that the said lake was situated a fourteen-days' journey to the west-northwest.[22]

What a wonderful story! Now we have Copala pictured as the mythical place of origin of the Mexican people, who had of course migrated from somewhere in the north. And we have the story of Lake Copala intertwined with other stories of the unknown. With each advance of the frontier, these kingdoms tended to disappear over the horizon. In this instance Copala did not find a fixed resting place till the Domínguez-Escalante expedition of 1776 into Utah, when it found lodgment in the valley of the Great Salt Lake.

It remains to bring into this family of fabulous kingdoms still another—that of Teguayo, a relatively late entrant into this society of mythical wonders. But since it was to point toward the land of the Utah Indians, or perhaps to lands beyond, it has found a prominent place in the story of Spanish expansion in the Southwest.

To the Spaniard, it should be remembered, distance meant but little. There was no boundary beyond which he could not go—except through the lands occupied by hostile people, and these he would consider proper subjects for conversion to his religion and submission to his government. Hence, Spanish officials and friars alike were alert to the existence of such new people, for they might live on that renowned Strait of Anián, or Northwest Passage, thought to connect the Atlantic with the Pacific. Hence it was incumbent on every official on the frontier to be vigilant and to report new developments.

When, therefore, the kingdom of Teguayo was reported about the middle of the sixteenth century in New Mexico, it became an object of speculation and official concern, especially after Governor Don Diego de Peñalosa, who had gotten into trouble with the Church and had been humiliated by the Inquisition, fled to France and sought to interest that government in establishing a base on the Gulf of Mexico from which

France might conquer the interior of North America, and, in particular, acquire the wonderful kingdoms of Quivira and Teguayo![23]

This threat from an old enemy, France, called for action. The viceroy of Mexico was instructed to investigate and report. Fortunately, he had at hand a well-informed man, Fray Alonso de Posada, who had been a missionary in New Mexico for many years before retirement from the mission field. Posada gave a famous report of the northern country, about 1686.[24] By this time Quivira had become firmly rooted northeast of New Mexico, and he placed the mythical kingdom of Teguayo far to the northwest, beyond the lands of the Utahs. It was, he said, the same place as Copala, according to the Mexican Indians. He had obtained his information while a missionary among the Jémez Indians, one of this tribe having visited Teguayo and having been imprisoned there. Father Posada urged that an exploration be made, but he did not repeat the usual stories of great riches to be found in the new region.

The exploration that Father Posada contemplated was not made for another seventy-five years, when a fortunate combination of circumstances—the right men in the right places—led finally to an exploration of these various mysteries to the north and west. This was the Domínguez-Escalante expedition of 1776, organized to explore the possibility of bringing reinforcements overland from Santa Fe to the new settlements in California. Such a route would supplant the dangerous sea voyage from Mexico to Monterey and the trail up the peninsula of Baja California. But the Domínguez-Escalante party found there was no such new route. They did, however, pioneer a trail to modern Utah through some of the most difficult and picturesque country in the Southwest. Several English translations of their journey's diary have been published, the latest at the time of my remarks being that of Herbert E. Bolton in 1950.[25]

The Domínguez-Escalante expedition, which explored the mysterious Utah—or shall we say the kingdoms of Copala and Teguayo—in the very year that American patriots on the eastern seaboard declared their independence and organized to fight for their liberties—made known for the first time the real nature of this region and set at rest forever those rumors of reputed wealth that had buzzed about on the Spanish frontier since the days of Columbus and his successors.

Stories of the fabulous were an integral feature of the age of discovery of America and the conquest of its native peoples. The stories might be legion, but nature was perverse, especially in the Southwest, and tolerated only rumors of kingdoms, not the substance. In spite of the niggardliness of the soil, however, and the lowly stature of the people who inhabited it, Spain planted her culture, conquered and civilized many of its people, and held the land till another age. When the Mexican War came and she had to give up the vast northern fringe of her territory, stretching from Texas through New Mexico and Utah to California, others were ready to make a reality of Spanish dreams. In the ancient Copala and Teguayo, the Mormon pioneers did so; in California, the discovery of gold drew thousands to that land of the wonderful; in New Mexico and Texas, other pioneers built on a similar scale. Throughout this region the great discoveries in our own day of gold, silver, copper, oil, uranium, and other riches proved that Spanish dreams had, after all, been founded on fact.

NOTES

1. Herbert E. Bolton, *Guide to Materials for the History of the United States in the Principal Archives of Mexico.* Washington, 1913.

2. See for example Germán Arciniegas. *The Knight of El Dorado.* New York, 1942. A delightful story.

3. One of the best known of the recent books on this adventurer is Morris Bishop. *The Odyssey of Cabeza de Vaca.* New York, 1933. More scholarly is Cleve Hallenbeck, *The Journey and Route of the First European to Cross the Continent of North America.* Glendale, Calif., 1939.

4. Portuguese navigators sought these Seven Cities in the unknown Atlantic in the fifteenth century, without success, and also an island called Antilia, supposed to be very rich. E. G. Bourne. *Spain in America.* New York, 1904.

5. There are several translations of the Niza narrative, the most recent by George P. Hammond and Agapito Rey in *Narratives of the Coronado Expedition, 1540–1542.* Albuquerque, 1940. See pp. 66–79.

6. There are two translations of the Coronado documents. The first was George Parker Winship's, "The Coronado Expedition, 1540–1542," in *Fourteenth Annual Report,* Part I, Bureau of Ethnology. Washington, 1896; the other by George P. Hammond and Agapito Rey, cited above.

7. H. H. Bancroft, *History of Mexico* (6 vols., San Francisco, 1883–89), II. chap. 26. For a recent study, see Philip W. Powell, *Soldiers, Indians, and Silver* (Berkeley, 1952), chap. 1.

8. An excellent summary of this movement is found in Herbert E. Bolton. *The Spanish Borderlands.* New Haven, 1921.

9. Both of these codes were published in the Pacheco y Cárdenas, *Colección de Documentos Inéditos . . . de Indias,* XVI. Madrid, 1871. Henry Stevens and Fred W. Lucas translated them in *The New Laws of the Indies.* London, 1893.

10. A member of the party, Hernán Gallegos, kept a diary of the expedition; published by the Historical Society of New Mexico, Santa Fe, 1927, translated by Hammond and Rey.

11. *Expedition into New Mexico Made by Antonio de Espejo.* George P. Hammond and Agapito Rey, tr. Los Angeles (Quivira Society), 1929. See also Herbert E. Bolton, *Spanish Exploration in the Southwest* (New York, 1916), pp. 161–95.

12. George P. Hammond, *Don Juan de Oñate and the Founding of New Mexico.* Santa Fe, 1927. See also George P. Hammond and Agapito Rey. *Oñate, Colonizer of New Mexico.* Albuquerque, 1953; and Charles W. Hackett, *Historical Documents Relating to New Mexico,* I. Washington, 1923.

13. Hammond and Rey, *Oñate, Colonizer of New Mexico*, I, 492.

14. The report of this expedition is translated in *ibid.*, 746–60.

15. The original documents telling of this catastrophe are given in *ibid.*, 672–739. See also Hammond, *Don Juan de Oñate*, 140–53.

16. In Spain, Villagrá wrote the famous *Historia de la Nueva México*, published at Alcalá in 1610, an historical poem glorifying the exploits of the conquerors of New Mexico.

17. Herbert E. Bolton, "Father Escobar's Relation . . . ," in *Catholic Historical Review*, V; also given in Hammond and Rey, *Oñate, Colonizer of New Mexico*, 1012–31.

18. A good account of this period is José Manuel Espinosa's, *Crusaders of the Rio Grande*. Chicago, 1942.

19. See "The Legend of Sierra Azul," *New Mexico Historical Review*, IX (April, 1934), 113–58.

20. See S. Lyman Tyler, "The Myth of the Lake of Copala and Land of Teguayo," *Utah Historical Quarterly*, XX (October, 1952), 313–29.

21. The chief account of Ibarra's expedition was written by an old soldier named Baltasar de Obregón. It was published by George P. Hammond and Agapito Rey as *Obregón's History of Sixteenth Century Explorations in Western America*. Los Angeles, 1928. See also J. Lloyd Mecham, *Francisco de Ibarra and Nueva Vizcaya*. Durham, N.C., 1927.

22. Zárate Salmerón's narrative was published in *Documentos para la Historia de México*, 3rd Series. Mexico, 1856.

23. Consult William E. Dunn, *Spanish and French Rivalry in the Gulf Region of the United States, 1678–1702*. Austin, Texas, 1917.

24. See Cesáreo Fernández Duro, *Don Diego de Peñalosa y su Descubrimiento del Reino de Quivira*. Madrid, 1882.

25. Herbert E. Bolton. *Pageant in the Wilderness*. Salt Lake City, 1950; Herbert S. Auerbach. "Father Escalante's Journal with Related Documents and Maps," *Utah Historical Quarterly*, XI (1943); W. R. Harris, *The Catholic Church in Utah*. Salt Lake City, 1909. [A fresh translation of *The Domínguez-Escalante Journal* by Fray Angélico Chávez, edited by Ted J. Warner, was published by Brigham Young University Press in 1976—ed.]

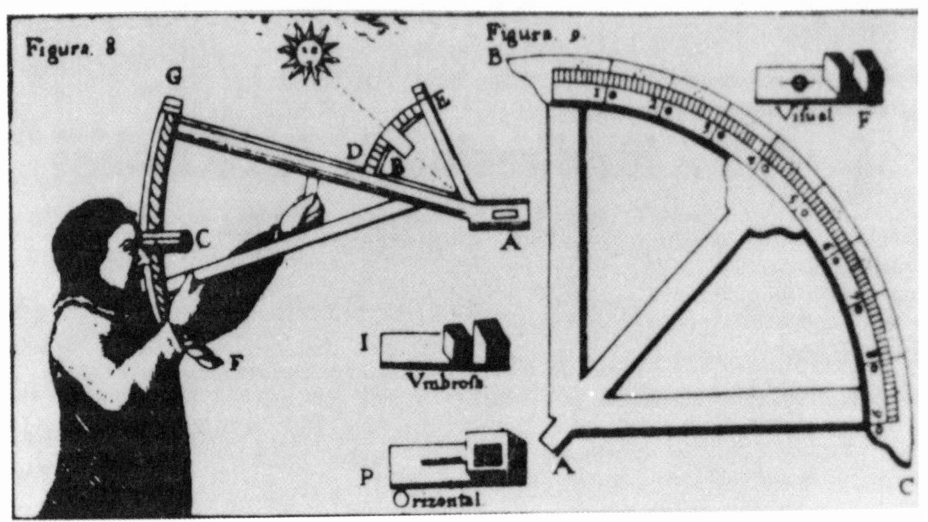

Figura. 8
G
D
E
B
C
A
F
I
Vmbrosa
P
Orizontal
Figura. 9
B
Visual
F
A
C

3

Spanish Scientific Exploration Along the Pacific Coast*

Donald C. Cutter

Editor's Introduction

As the previous article by George Hammond suggests, Spaniards' hopes of locating the "fabulous" in North America remained alive after two centuries of exploration. In the eighteenth century, however, emphasis shifted to more prosaic matters. Due in no small part to the influence of the Enlightenment on Bourbon Spain, the pursuit of empirical knowledge came to rival other motives for exploration and the Spanish Crown under Charles III sponsored a series of scientific expeditions to the New World. As described here by Donald C. Cutter, some of those expeditions probed the Pacific Coast of North America from Baja California to Alaska. Although Spain's wandering scientists hoped to locate a waterway through North America, they devoted their attention to matters such as botany, zoology, cartography, geography, astronomy, and

*This essay appeared originally in *The American West: An Appraisal,* ed. Robert G. Ferris (Santa Fe: 1963), 151-160; 243-45, and is reprinted with permission of the author and the publisher.

ethnology. As a result, they harvested a wealth of scientific data in the form of artifacts, written descriptions, and careful drawings. Many of those data remained in Spanish archives, unseen and unappreciated, until the pioneering research of Donald Cutter brought them to scholarly and popular attention.[1] Indeed, largely through Cutter's efforts a remarkable collection of artifacts and art work, taken along the Pacific Coast in 1791 by Alejandro Malaspina, was brought from Spain to the United States in 1977. Exhibited in museums from Washington to Portland, the collection heightened appreciation for the work of Spain's explorer-scientists.[2]

Donald Cutter's interest in Spanish maritime exploration began at Berkeley where he studied under Herbert Bolton and Lawrence Kinnaird. His teaching career began at San Diego State (1950–51) and the University of Southern California (1951–61); he has been professor of history at The University of New Mexico since 1962. Among his publications are *The Diary of Ensign Gabriel Moraga's Expedition . . . 1808* (Los Angeles: 1957), *Malaspina in California* (San Francisco: 1960), and a re-editing of *The California Coast: A Bilingual Edition of Documents from the Sutro Collection* (Norman: 1969). Much of his time and energy has been devoted to training and encouraging graduate students and they, in turn, have flocked to study in the enthusiastic and supportive environment which he provides. In 1976 he joined the distinguished group of historians who have been honored with the presidency of the Western History Association.

NOTES

1. Cutter's work has been followed by some of his students, most notably Iris Wilson Engstrand. A translation and editing of *Noticias de Nutka: An Account of Nootka Sound in 1792*, by José Mariano Moziño (Seattle: 1970), stands among her contributions to this field. See, too, Juan Carlos Arias Divito, *Las expediciones científicas españolas durante el siglo XVIII* (Madrid: 1968).

2. See Cutter's account of this exhibit in "The Return of Malaspina," in *The American West*, 15(1978): 4–19.

Spanish Scientific Exploration Along the Pacific Coast

Possessing claim to a large share of the earth's surface because of the explorations of Columbus, Balboa, and others, Spain was early interested in the uniqueness evident in the New World. Indeed, the acknowledged father of natural scientific inquiry in the New World is the oft-quoted, highly respected author of *Historia General y Natural de las Indias, Islas y Tierra Firme del Mar Oceano*, Gonzalo Fernández de Oviedo y Valdés, whose multi-volume work was written between 1535 and 1557, though his experience in the Americas dated back to his first visit there in 1514. Oviedo, however, was more of a chronicler than a naturalist.

More in the spirit of true scientific inquiry was the activity of Dr. Francisco Hernández. Virtually a contemporary of Oviedo, he and his young son Juan traveled in New Spain from 1570 to 1576. A true naturalist, he dedicated himself to a study of the botanical, animal, and mineral kingdoms of the extended viceroyalty. So avid was his research that his health failed and he returned to Spain in 1577, though his enlightened monarch, Phillip II, had desired that he continue his labors in the South American viceroyalty of Peru.[1]

Hernández prepared for publication sixteen volumes of materials concerning his findings in New Spain, but like many other Spanish projects of a worthy nature they were left unprinted, in the archives of *El Escorial*, near Madrid, only to gather dust and finally be destroyed by fire in 1671. Fortunately, in the late eighteenth century, the prominent historian Juan Bautista Muñoz discovered copies of the first six volumes. He set the leading Spanish botanist of the period, Casimiro Gómez Ortega, director of the *Real Jardín Botánico* (Royal Botanical Garden) to work on publishing them, especially the botanical material.[2]

At this propitious point, the first Spanish scientific group to be interested in the Pacific Coast was organized. Probably oblivious of the work that Ortega was doing, an Aragonese physician residing in Havana, Dr. Martin Sessé, a graduate of the University of Zaragoza, suggested in a letter to him his willingness to direct a full-scale scientific expedition in New Spain that would complete the work of Dr. Hernández.[3]

As a result, Sessé was soon in the field in Mexico with three other scientists. The expedition, known as the *Botánica Mexicana*, was really interested in all aspects of natural history. It also became interested to some degree in the Pacific Coast from San José del Cabo to Nootka Sound and beyond.

A second important scientific exploring expedition of the late eighteenth century, which explored the Pacific Coast, was the Malaspina group, a naval contingent headed by the Italian-born Spanish naval career officer, Alejandro Malaspina, who was ably seconded by Captain José Bustamante y Guerra.[4] This expedition had the same objectives as those of the ill-fated Captain James Cook of the Royal Navy and of the French Count of La Pérouse, whose disappearance was still a mystery to the world at the time of Malaspina's departure from Cádiz in late July of 1789. By May 1791, the two-vessel Spanish naval task group was on the west coast of Mexico, poised for a trip to California and the Pacific Northwest coast.

The expedition had strong political overtones. A major objective was to seek the fabled, elusive, and strategic Strait of Ferrer Maldonado, a sort of reverse Northwest Passage leading to the Atlantic.[5] If such a strait existed, the Spanish proposed to claim it. Despite the prevailing doubts about the existence of the strait, the Malaspina group was confident of success, for it issued orders to some detached personnel indicating that the vessels would next be at Veracruz, after having made the passage.

A second objective of the expedition was even more politically opportunistic, concerning as it did investigation of the Spanish claim and military posture in the Nootka Sound area of the west coast of Vancouver Island, at 49° 30′ N. latitude. The situation at this focal point of international rivalry had been magnified to undue proportions by the reports of an untrustworthy British captain, and by the acts of a stubborn and opinionated Spanish junior officer.[6] Both courts had become embroiled; war seemed possible.

Additional Spanish naval scientific activity had preceded and would follow the Malaspina group, but the outstanding personnel and organization of this group enhance its importance. However, it should be noted that an earlier Spanish naval expedition had visited Baja California in 1769 for astronomical observations. Led by the Tarragonese officer, Vicente Doz, and accompanied by the French Abbé Chappé and Lieutenant Medina, this expedition sought to obtain an accurate observation of the transit of Venus and to correlate this with other sights in the interest of a more accurate geographical determination of west coast points, long a subject of some controversy. Failure of this earlier expedition resulted from the death of all the prominent members except Vicente Doz.[7] Any significant result was soon more than overshadowed by the multiple methods of longitudinal observations employed by Malaspina's group.

A third naval scientific voyage was an offshoot of the Malaspina exploration. After their visit to the Northwest coast, the Spanish naval scientists of the Malaspina expedition were not yet convinced that they had determined one way or the other the existence of Ferrer Maldonado's strait. Though Malaspina was convinced that he had not missed the strait north of Nootka, he was uncertain about the area around 48 to 50° N., in which existed the strait known as Juan de Fuca, named for a fictitious Greek pilot of a much earlier period. The relatively deep drafts of the *Descubierta* and *Atrevida* had made Malaspina cautious about any attempt at the close inspection of inland waterways. But the Nootka Sound dispute with England demanded a thorough inspection. The area in question was the tangled skein of waterways and canals that stretch inland both north and south of the Strait of Juan de Fuca, the northern outlet of which is Queen Charlotte Strait.

Therefore, when Malaspina reached Acapulco after the Northwest coast phase of his expedition, in cooperation with the viceroy of New Spain, the Conde de Revilla Gigedo, he sent two small, forty-six-ton sailing vessels, the *goletas Sutil* and *Mexicana*, constructed at the Spanish Naval Department of San Blas for the purpose of detailed coastal exploration.[8] They were commanded by four of Malaspina's top officers, Dionisio Alcalá Galiano, Cayetano Valdés, Juan Vernacci, and Secundino Salamanca, and manned by a mixed crew of Malaspina veterans and San Blas personnel. The activities in 1792 of these men, all later to become prominent Spanish senior officers, are related in some detail in *Relación del viage de las goletas Sutil y Mexicana*, probably written by their scribe, artist, mapmaker, pilot, and jack-of-all-trades, José Cardero.[9]

The group followed approximately the same operational procedures as the Malaspina expedition. It cooperated with British Captain George Vancouver and his men, who were on a similar expedition but had other political motives. Artist Cardero drew an unusually interesting series of illustrations during the reconnaissance of the Strait of Juan de Fuca. A set of good maps was prepared, as well as a lengthy description of operations. The expedition named various places for Spanish naval figures, particularly members of the Malaspina group.[10] Though an abbreviated version of the final report of this expedition has been published several times,[11] the original and complete version still awaits publication.[12]

Of special anthropological note is the word list and extensive catechism of the Rumsen and Esselen Indians of Mission Carmel, prepared by the expedition toward the end of its reconnaissance, after it had traced the coast southward from Nootka to Monterey in the fall of the year. An abridged version of the word list was published with the *Relación del viage*.

Another scientific exploration of two sorties was made along the Pacific Coast in 1791 and 1792 by several members associated with the *Botánica Mexicana* expedition. The first of these sorties—made by José Longinos Martínez, a native of Logroño, accompanied part of the way by his associate, Jayme Senseve—was a brief study of the area from the tip of Baja California to as far north as Monterey, and perhaps beyond. The emphasis was on botany and certain physical phenomena.[13]

The second sortie—and the final effort by Spain in exploring the Pacific Northwest—was led by José Mariano Moziño, accompanied by botanical illustrator Atanasio Echeverría and natural scientist José Maldonado, all three of whom were attached to the more politically oriented expedition "Of the Limits to the North of California."[14] Headed by the San Blas commandant and leading Pacific Coast naval figure, Juan Francisco de la Bodega y Quadra, this expedition had been sent to reconcile the differences between England and Spain at Nootka, and to ascertain Spain's ability to maintain its interests in the northern area. The prominent Creole doctor-naturalist Moziño, a well-trained Mexican-born botanist, conducted some notable studies at Nootka, where he was located for nine months, from April 1792 to February 1793. After learning the language of the Nootkans, he compiled a comprehensive linguistic study and dictionary.[15] In conjunction with the dictionary, he prepared an interesting ethnological, geographical, and zoological work entitled *Noticias de Nutka*, which was scheduled to be published in the Universal History of North America.[16]

Except for the two expeditions to Baja California, all of them had a common denominator. To each was assigned one or more sketch artists, whose function was somewhat analogous to the photographer of today. Though occasionally one of them might employ artistic license, for the most part they illustrated with fidelity to detail the items deemed of interest by their superiors. Their wealthy pictorial record speaks well for the thoroughness of the eighteenth-century scientific expeditions. The artists played a key role in the attainment of scientific objectives.

Though some of them specialized in one type of drawing, their range of abilities had to be extensive. Sometimes they paid special attention to fauna and flora, strictly from the botanical and zoological standpoint, but at other times as part of a more general scene. Their sketches of native Indian types and their unique customs have enhanced the ethnological record.

Coastal profiles, some much like modern hydrographic office charts, were drawn as aids to future navigation and as proof of the thoroughness of exploratory endeavor.[17] Numerous sketches were made of the Spanish settlements visited on the Pacific Coast—Nootka and Monterey.

The most comprehensive Spanish exploring expedition of the period was that of Captain Malaspina.[18] Organized in Spain with the strong support of the Minister of Marine, Antonio Valdés, the expedition set sail in 1789, staying abroad until 1794, a total of 62 months. Every effort was exerted to recruit well-qualified personnel and obtain the best equipment. Originals or copies of pertinent documents at various archives were abstracted. Seamen were recruited from the areas of Vizcaya, Asturias, and Santander, where they were presumed to be hardier.[19]

Malaspina, who was permitted to select his officers from among the active list of the navy, picked those having the requisite qualifications and experience. Felipe Bauzá, Chief of Charts and Maps, had been engaged in a general mapping of Spain under Vicente Tofiño; Alcalá Galiano, under the command of Captain Antonio de Córdova Lazo in a 1785 study of the Strait of Magellan, "had busied himself with observations on the soil, climate, aspect and composition of the land, animal and vegetable products, and human races"; Secundino Salamanca was considered to have ability in history; Vernacci in astronomy; Ceballos in cartography; and Hurtado in art. Surgeon Pedro María González assisted in astronomy and natural history, and some of the men doubled as scribes. Perhaps not insignificantly, Cayetano Valdés was the Minister of Marine's nephew.[20]

The two vessels used by the expedition, the *Descubierta* and *Atrevida*, which combined security, comfort, and economy, were constructed in an identical manner. Each was 120 feet in length and displaced 306 tons, having a loaded draft of approximately 14 feet. All personnel were Spanish naval officers and men, except for Chief of Natural History Antonio Pineda, an army colonel; the natural scientists, Botanist Luis Neé and Naturalist Tadeo Haenke; and the original artists. All except Haenke, who was Bohemian, were Spanish subjects.[21]

Before departure, the Spanish archives were combed for materials that would shed light on the objectives of the expedition; and subsequently, at each major stop, officers obtained all available source materials from local archives. In this manner, Malaspina obtained considerable information about the Pacific Northwest coast as a basis for further inquiry. In the Mexican viceregal archives, Lieutenants José Espinosa and Ciriaco Ceballos hopefully sought: 1) maps of Guadalajara and California prepared by Jesuit Father Consag; 2) "memorials of Alarcón, perhaps an ex-Jesuit who left important notices about the geography and civil history of the nations of the Río Colorado"; 3) the printed account of Sebastián Vizcaíno; 4) maps made by Kino of California, Sonora, Pimería, and the Río Colorado; 5) papers or old Mexican volumes of Boturini; and 6) "a dictionary and grammar of each of the languages known on the north coasts of Mexico."[22]

Though not all of these documents were found, other worthwhile ones were, such as the many journals of the San Blas naval officers, who since 1769 had been making regular supply runs and periodic exploratory trips along the Pacific Coast. The Minister of Marine, Antonio Valdés, produced some unexpected aid when he forwarded to Malaspina seven maps that had been sent in by Brigadier of the Navy Josef Bermúdez, commander of the Cavite Arsenal in the Philippine Islands, some of which concerned the coasts of America along what was then considered to be California.[23]

Other documents obtained for use by the expedition included Palóu's biography of Junípero Serra, Miguel Costansó's diary of the Sacred Expedition, some of Anza's journals, diaries of both Bruno de Hezeta and Juan de la Bodega, and many other documents concerned more with the *Provincias Internas* than with the coastal region itself.

Some half dozen or more separate accounts were kept by expedition members, not to mention the guard books of each of the two vessels, maintained only while in port. Special reports on various topics were compiled with regularity by the more competent members.

Three stops were made by the *Descubierta* and *Atrevida* along the Pacific Coast. The first, and northernmost, was a nine-day stop at Mulgrave Sound, Lituya Bay, Alaska, at approximately 59° 30′ N. and 140° W., or 133° 45′ West of Cádiz, the prime meridian for Hispanic explorations. Among the Tlinget Indians, whose friendship was soon temporarily won, Malaspina and his men carried out extensive observations. The nearby glacier, now called Malaspina Glacier, was studied; the height of Mt. St. Elias was calculated;[24] and the bays in the area were explored. An observatory, in the form of a tent, was established for scientific headquarters. In the tent, experiments were conducted with the simple pendulum for gravitational calculations in cooperation with the French, who were attempting to establish an international standard of weights and measures.[25]

Though many "lunar distances" were shot and geographical positions were calculated using marine chronometers, poor weather hampered astronomical and meteorological observations. A lumber summary was compiled,[26] birds were described scientifically,[27] and colored zoological plates were drawn. The artists sketched several curiosities, including sea-otter kidneys, and the local Indians.

The initial friendship with the natives and with their chief, Anaku, was temporarily destroyed by an incident ashore. However, because of the chief's interest in peace and trade, harmony was soon restored. Trade with the Indians was controlled, the Spaniards seeking mainly artifacts, such as native arms, articles of dress, and manufactures. Whenever possible, for security's sake, negotiations were conducted on land rather than on board ship. Severe punishment was prescribed for any men who violated trading regulations. In attempting to learn the native language, the officers were "to pay special attention to those words which have the most direct connection with our needs and with all the objects of good management."[28] A word list that was compiled was shipped back to Spain, along with some artifacts, for purposes of later classification and correlation. Other artifacts were similarly shipped from Nootka and Monterey.[29] Ballast, wood, and water were taken aboard at Mulgrave Sound to replenish the depleted stores on the twin vessels.

Upon departure from Mulgrave Sound, the expedition moved southward, inspecting the shoreline, making geographical observations, drawing profiles of the promontories, and to a great extent proving the lack of existence of any strait leading to Hudson's Bay. Stopping at Nootka Sound on the large offshore land mass now known as Vancouver Island, Malaspina was at a site of diplomatic controversy between England and Spain.

He inspected the physical location of the Spanish settlement and fortifications at Yoquot and Hog Island and sought any other information that might be helpful to the viceroy, Conde de Revilla Gigedo, or to his representatives at Nootka.

To this end, and to strengthen the Spanish hand, Malaspina and his men won the confidence of the vacillating chief of the Nootkans, Maquinna, by treating him with great respect. This important chieftain, who held a potential high card in the Nootka controversy, was a willing informant for anthropological purposes[30] and was a testator to the validity of Spanish claim to the area based on priority of discovery and legality of purchase of land from the natives.[31]

The sketch artists were particularly active at Friendly Cove, Nootka. They made many drawings of local Indians and of their cultural activities. Tomás Suria, artist-engraver on loan to the expedition from the Mexican mint and disciple of the prominent Gerónimo Antonio Gil, composed several classic representations of Nootka chiefs and kept a journal of his activities.[32] The drawings of young José (Pepe) Cardero, formerly cabin boy of Lt. Cayetano Valdés, were becoming increasingly skilled. This skill, combined with bravery and application, would win him an assignment as artist with the *Sutil* and *Mexicana* in the same area the following year and subsequently a commission as a lieutenant in the Naval Supply Corps.[33]

At Nootka a series of good maps were either drawn or collected. The observatory was again established, this time on shore near the headquarters of the military commandant, and the customary series of calculations, annotations, and observations were effected. Felipe Bauzá spent considerable time in drafting appropriate maps, establishing ranges, and taking bearings of all significant landmarks. Naturalist Tadeo Haenke observed the natural phenomena of the area; and a small group, led by José Espinosa, explored in detail the labyrinth of canals that led inland from Friendly Cove in the direction of Tasis Mountain and Maquinna's interior village site.[34] This group in 1791 explored Nootka Sound, circumnavigating Nootka Island, which lay offshore from Vancouver Island.[35] In 1792, Galiano and Valdés, in the *Sutil* and *Mexicana*, circumnavigated Vancouver Island, which at that time was being called "Vancouver and Quadra's" Island, for both the Nootka commissioners. Later this was shortened to Vancouver Island.

After a two-week stay among the Nootkans, Malaspina and party again moved southward, planning to follow the coastline as closely as possible. Unfortunately, foggy weather and an imperfectly known coastline forced them somewhat farther out to sea than anticipated until about 41°, from which point southward to Monterey a fairly close inspection of the coast was possible.

In California, which Spain had settled in 1769, twenty-two years prior to Malaspina's visit, the expedition made primary observations and obtained useful second-hand information. Some of the founding fathers were still available to act as informants, and a number of "firsts" in California history were established. Haenke became the botanical discoverer of the *Sequoia sempervirens;*[36] several species of oak were subsequently discovered and botanically described for the first time by Botanist Luis Neé, from samples brought from California by the paymaster of the expedition;[37] and the first California original pieces of art still extant were drawn by artists José Cardero and Tomás Suria. Four of the pieces of art were California birds in color and three were coastal profiles.[38]

California was primarily of interest to the expedition because of its frontier character. One of the leading Hispanic frontier institutions, the mission, was studied by the visitors. Despite the reputed liberal tendencies of the Italian-born commander, the mission system was not only given a clean bill of health, but it was also eulogized—especially the self-sacrifice of the Franciscans led by the well-known Father Fermín Francisco de Lasuén.[39] Lasuén was particularly helpful to the scientific ends of the expedition, especially in providing guides for field trips and obtaining artifacts.[40]

No less helpful, in his own way, was the commandant of the local presidio of Monterey. In an effort to meet the secondary purpose of Malaspina's visit, that of the three R's of navigation (rest, recreation, and relaxation), Lt. José Darío Arguello provided mounts, daily *novilladas* in the courtyard of the presidio, and liberal quantities of fresh provisions, including milk.[41] So helpful were the Californians that the explorers were able to complete their observations—botanical, mineralogical, and general—within a two-week period, and sail southward to rejoin those members who for several months had been carrying out commissions in Mexico proper.

The *Relación del viage*, expurgated of all mention of the expedition commanded by Malaspina, and with the commander's name deleted, is about all that saw light of any of the Malaspina ventures for almost a full century. According to Baron Alexander von Humboldt, Malaspina was "more famous for his misfortunes than for his discoveries."[42] A plan which allegedly would have supplanted Spanish Chief of State Manuel Godoy as Queen María Luisa's lover and confidant with Malaspina apparently backfired to the suave round-the-world explorer's disadvantage.[43]

Because of the decline of its sea power in the Pacific, its abandonment of the centuries-old claim to exclusive sovereignty there, and increasing commitments in Europe, Spain reaped little or no advantage from the numerous well-equipped and well-staffed scientific expeditions it dispatched to the Pacific Coast. However, the westerner of today can at least appreciate the notable efforts of these eighteenth-century Iberian men of science.

NOTES

1. José Luis Benítez Miura, "El Doctor Francisco Hernández, 1514–1578," *Anuario de Estudios Americanos*, 7 (Sevilla, 1950), pp. 367–405.

2. Published as *De Historia Plantarum Novae Hispaniae* (3 vols., Madrid, 1790).

3. Sessé to Ortega, Havana, Jan. 30, 1785, in Archives of the Real Jardín Botánico, Madrid, 4ta División, legajo 19.

4. The career of Malaspina is summarized in "Antiguidades de los oficiales de guerra de la Armada," Museo Naval, Madrid, tomo 1161 bis. Museo Naval hereafter cited as MN.

5. Lt. José Espinosa y Tello had extracted the narrative of Ferrer Maldonado from the Archivo General de Indias prior to departure of the expedition. See "Correspondencia relativa al viage de Malaspina," hereafter cited as Malaspina Correspondencia, Tomo A, ff. 47–48, MN 583.

6. Half-pay Captain John Meares and Ensign Esteban José Martínez were the principal catalytic agents in the controversy.

7. Documents on the observation of the transit of Venus by Medina and Doz are found in "Papeles Apreciables," II, MN 147.

8. A list of equipment is in "Viaje al Estrecho de Fuca," Tomo II, MN 144. Manifests of the *Sutil* and *Mexicana* upon departure from San Blas are contained in Archivo Histórico Nacional, Madrid, Estado 4290, as are also Malaspina's instructions to the crews (Estado 4288). Archivo Histórico Nacional hereafter cited as AHN.

9. For biographical data on Cardero, see Donald C. Cutter, *Malaspina in California* (San Francisco, 1960), pp. 12–16.

10. To name a few: Galiano Island, Valdés Island, Quadra Island, Maurelle Island, Tejada Island, Tofiño Inlet, Salamanca Canal, Cardero Island, Vernacci Sound, Toba Inlet, and Haro Strait.

11. Published in Spanish in *Relación del viage hecho por las goletas Sutil y Mexicana en el año de 1792*, as well as in an atlas on the voyage published in Madrid in 1802 and again in 1958; and in English in Cecil Jane, ed., *A Spanish Voyage to Vancouver and the Northwest Coast of America* (London, 1930) and in Henry R. Wagner, *Spanish Explorations in the Strait of Juan de Fuca* (Santa Ana, California, 1933).

12. "Vargas Ponce," MN 1060, seemingly in the hand of José Cardero. Manuscript copies

of the shortened version of the "Voyage of the Sutil and Mexicana" are located in AHN, Estado 4290; Archivo General de la Nación, Mexico, Historia 31; MN 143, 144; MN 468. Archivo General de la Nación hereafter cited as AGN.

13. Lesley B. Simpson, trans. and ed., *Journal of José Longinos Martínez* (San Francisco, 1961). For a scholarly treatment of Longinos' activities, see Iris H. Wilson, "Scientific Aspects of Spanish Exploration of New Spain During the Late 18th Century" (Ph.D. Dissertation, University of Southern California, 1962).

14. "Viaje a la Costa N. O. de la America Septentrional por Don Juan Francisco de la Bodega y Quadra. . . ." (1792), Manuscript No. 145, in Archivo del Ministerio de Asuntos Exteriores, Madrid; also in Vol. XXX, Revilla Gigedo Collection, in Bancroft Library.

15. Sessé to Revilla Gigedo, Mexico, May 9, 1793, in AGN, Historia 527.

16. The dictionary is available in many places in manuscript; Alberto M. Carreño edited a version which was published in Mexico in 1913. Though of great interest for its anthropological information, it has never been published in English [see p. 36 *n* 1 . . . ed.]. Manuscript copies can be found in MN 142 and 468; Vol. XXXII, Revilla Gigedo Collection, in the Bancroft Library; in the Beinecke Collection, Yale University Library; in the Sociedad Mexicana de Geografía y Estadística; and in the AGN. The original illustrations have never been discovered. Only recently did some copies come to light. A copy of the entire series became available in the Revilla Gigedo Collection in the Bancroft Library, and a second copy (Manuscript No. 146) was discovered by the author of this paper in the Archivo del Ministerio de Asuntos Exteriores, in Madrid.

These two sets had been executed with considerable care at the Academia de San Carlos by Echeverría's associates: Tomás Suria, José Cardero, Gabriel Gil, Julián Marchena, J. Vicente de la Cerdá, José María Montes de Oca, Francisco Lindo, José María Guerrero, José María Vásquez, M. García, José Casteñeda, Mendoza, Nicolas Moncayo, José Mariano de Aguila, Miguel Albián, and Manuel López; Suria, Cardero, Lindo, and Cerdá all had been associated with the Malaspina enterprise. Some of these drawings doubtless were sketched during an excursion Echeverría made with Naturalist José Maldonado on a side trip out of Nootka under the command of Lt. Jacinto Caamaño in 1792. The journal of this expedition is presented in "Extracto del Diario de Navegaciones, exploraciones y descubrimientos hechos en la America Septentrional por D. Jacinto Caamaño. . . . del año de 1792," Manuscript no. 10, in Archivo del Ministerio de Asuntos Exteriores, Madrid.

17. Chief of Charts and Maps Felipe Bauzá of the Malaspina expedition was particularly proficient at costal profiles. Most of the profiles are on file in the Museo Naval.

18. Almost a century afterwards, some of the results of the Malaspina expedition were published in Pedro de Novo y Colson, ed., *La Vuelta al Mundo por las corbetas DESCUBIERTA y ARTEVIDA al Mando del Capitán de Navio D. Alejandro Malaspina desde 1789 a 1794* (Madrid, 1885). Hereafter cited as *Vuelta al Mundo*.

19. Malaspina Correspondencia, Tomo A, ff. 12–16, MN 583.

20. *Ibid.*, f. 48.

21. Haenke has recently been treated extensively by Joseph Kuhnel, in *Thaddaeus Haenke: Leben und Wirken eines Forschers*.

22. Malaspina Correspondencia, Vol. I, f. 81, MN 278.

23. Valdés to Malaspina, Madrid, July 21, 1789, in *ibid.*

24. Table of apparent altitudes of Mt. St. Elias is in "Curiosidades Sueltas," MN 169.

25. The simple pendulum experiments are described in "Papels Apreciables," III, MN 148.

26. "Relación de maderas de Mulgrave, de Nutka, de Monterey in Pacífico América," Tomo I, MN 126.

27. "Descripciones del Sr. Gonzáles hechas en el viage a los 60° N," in Pineda Notes in Archivo del Museo de Ciencias Naturales, Madrid.

28. "Libro de Guardias, Descubierta," MN 729; "Libro de Guardias, Atrevida," MN 755.

29. Malaspina Correspondencia, Tomo A, ff. 98–99, MN 583.

30. "Noticias que nos dió Maquina," in California y Costa N. O. de America, Tomo I, MN 330.

31. A copy of the purchase of land from the Nootkans, appropriately notarized, is in AHN, Estado 4290.

32. Justino Fernández, *Tomás de Suria y su viage con Malaspina*, 1791 (Mexico, 1939). The original journal is in the Yale University Library.

33. Alcalá Galiano and Valdés to Revilla Gigedo, Mexico, March 3, 1793, in AGN, Marina 82; Joseph Cardero, "Expediente matrimonial," in Archivo General Militar, Segovia.

34. Malaspina to Josef Espinosa, Nutka, Aug. 17, 1791, in "Apuntes, Noticias y correspondencias pertenecientes a la Expedición de Malaspina," MN 427.

35. "Libro de Guardias, Descubierta," MN 729.

36. Willis L. Jepson, *The Silva of California* (Berkeley, California, 1910), p. 138.

37. *Anales de Ciencias* (Madrid, 1801), 3.

38. All the California drawings are published in Cutter, *Malaspina in California*.

39. *Vuelta al Mundo*, p. 447.

40. Felipe Bauzá, "Viaje alrededor del Mundo, 1789–96," MN 749.

41. *Ibid.*; Cutter, *Malaspina in California*, p. 31.

42. Baron A. de Humboldt, *Ensayo Político sobre Nueva España* (Jalapa, 1869), 1, p. 261.

43. The appropriate document is entitled "Relativo a la causa reserbada que se les formo a Don Alejandro Malaspina, P. Manuel Gil, Sra. Marquesa de Matallana," in AHN, Estado 3150.

4

The Mission as a Frontier Institution in the Spanish American Colonies*

Herbert Eugene Bolton

Editor's Introduction

This influential essay has been reprinted several times in English since its first publication in 1917. The essay reveals Bolton's breadth of learning and his ability to synthesize. His thesis is clear: "The value of the missionaries as frontier agents was . . . clearly recognized, and their services were consciously utilized by the government." If this idea seems unremarkable today, it is because Bolton's argument has influenced many writers who have incorporated it into their books, thereby making it commonplace.

This is not to suggest, however, that Bolton, whose importance as a historian is suggested in the introduction to this anthology, is beyond criticism. As with all historians, the passage of time has revealed factual errors in his writing, such as his assertion that Spanish law required missions to be secularized after ten years. More important, historians

**American Historian Review*, 22 (1917): 42–61. Bolton's essay is reprinted here in a slightly abridged form.

have quarreled with Bolton's interpretations and moved on to new areas of inquiry. See, for example, George Phillips's essay in this anthology.

Bolton chose to stress only the positive aspects of the missionary experience, ignoring matters that concern more recent historians. He does not mention that missionaries unwittingly introduced European diseases to Indians, fostered contagion in the mission environment, and contributed to the premature deaths of thousands of Indians. Nor does Bolton concern himself with the unpleasant reality of forced labor and corporal punishment at the missions, or question the right of the missionary to forcibly indoctrinate Indians. Two anthropologists, Daniel Matson and Bernard Fontana, for example, recently termed the missionary an "aggressor," and argued that

> Simply to "spread news of great joy" is one matter; to invade the most scared inner precincts of another man's being, and thereby to defile him, is something else again. It seems to us there can be no greater form of violence that this.[1]

Bolton avoided digressions into these matters in his 1917 essay. He had another point to make, and he made it convincingly and gracefully. Uncharacteristically, Bolton did not document this essay. At the outset he explained: "My conclusions are based on the study of documents, unprinted for the most part, which have been gathered mainly from the archives of Mexico and Spain." Bolton frequently refers to his sources in the text of this article rather than in the customary footnotes.

NOTE

1. Daniel S. Matson and Bernard L. Fontana, translators and editors, *Friar Bringas Reports to the King: Methods of Indoctrination on the Frontier of New Spain, 1796–97* (Tucson: 1977), p. 31. Researchers have uncovered substantial data regarding the precipitous decline of indigenous populations due to diseases brought by missionaries. See, for example, *The Conflict Between the California Indian and White Civilization*, by Sherburne F. Cook, first published serially in the 1940s and reprinted in a single volume in 1976 by the University of California Press.

The Mission as a Frontier Institution in the Spanish-American Colonies

Of the missions in Spanish America, particularly those in California, much has been written. But most of what has been produced consists of chronicles of the deeds of the Fathers, polemic discussions by sectarian partisans, or sentimental effusions with literary, edifying, or financial intent. They deal with the heroic exploits of individuals, with mooted questions of belief and practice, or with the romance that hovers round the mission ruins. All this is very well, and not to be ridiculed, but it is none the less true that little has been said of these missions in their relation to the general Spanish colonial policy, of which they were an integral and a most important part. . . .

Each of the colonizing nations in America had its peculiar frontier institutions and classes. In the French colonies the pioneers of pioneers were the fur-trader and the missionary. Penetrating the innermost wilds of the continent, one in search of the beaver, the other in quest of souls to save, together they extended the French domains, and brought the savage tribes into friendly relations with the French government, and into profitable relations with the French outposts. In the English colonies the fur-trader blazed the way and opened new trails, but it was the backwoods settler who hewed down the forest, and step by step drove back the Indian with whom he did not readily mingle. In the Spanish colonies the men to whom fell the task of extending and holding the frontiers were the *conquistador*, the presidial soldier, and the missionary.

All of these agents were important; but in my study of frontier institutions in general, and in my endeavor in particular to understand the methods and forces by which Spain's frontiers were extended, held, and developed, I have been more and more impressed with the importance of the mission as a pioneering agency. . . .

The functions of the mission, from the political standpoint, will be better understood if it is considered in its historical relations. The central interest around which the mission was built was the Indian. In respect to the native, the Spanish sovereigns, from the outset, had three fundamental purposes. They desired to convert him, to civilize him, and to exploit him. To serve these three purposes, there was devised, out of the experience of the early conquerors, the *encomienda* system. It was soon found that if the savage were to be converted, or disciplined, or exploited, he must be put under control. To provide such control, the land and the people were distributed among Spaniards, who held them in trust, or in *encomienda*. The trustee, or *encomendero*, as he was called, was strictly charged by the sovereign, as a condition of his grant, to provide for the protection, the conversion, and the civilization of the aborigines. In return he was empowered to exploit their labor, sharing the profits with the king. To provide the spiritual instruction and to conduct schools for the natives—for Indian schools were actually prescribed and maintained—the *encomenderos* were required to support the necessary friars, by whom the instruction was given. Thus great monasteries were established in the conquered districts.

But the native had his own notions, especially about being exploited, and he sometimes fled to the woods. It was soon discovered, therefore, that in order properly to convert, instruct, and exploit the Indian, he must be kept in a fixed place of residence. This need was early reported to the sovereigns by *encomenderos* and friars alike, and it soon became a law that Indians must be congregated in pueblos, and made to stay there, by force if necessary. The pueblos were modelled on the Spanish towns, and were designed not alone as a means of control, but as schools in self-control as well.

Thus, during the early years of the conquest, the natives were largely in the hands of the *encomenderos*, mainly secular landholders. The friars, and afterward the Jesuit priests, came in great numbers, to preach and teach, but they lacked the authority of later days. In 1574 there were in the conquered districts of Spanish America nearly nine thousand Indian towns, containing about one and a half million adult males, representing some five million people, subject to tribute. These nine thousand towns were *encomiendas* of the king and some four thousand *encomenderos*.

The *encomienda* system then, by intention, was benevolent. It was designed for the conversion and the civilization of the native, as well as for the exploitation of his labor. But the flesh is weak, and the system was abused. The obligations to protect, convert, and civilize were forgotten, and the right to exploit was perverted into license. Practical slavery soon resulted, and the *encomienda* system became the black spot in the Spanish-American code. Philanthropists, led by Las Casas, begged for reform; abuses were checked, and *encomiendas* were gradually, though slowly, abolished.

This improvement was made easier by the decreasing attractiveness of *encomiendas*, as the conquest proceeded to the outlying districts. The semi-civilized Indians of central Mexico and Peru had been fairly docile, had had a steady food supply and fixed homes, were accustomed to labor, and were worth exploiting. The wilder tribes encountered later—the Chichimecos, as they were called—were hostile, had few crops, were unused to labor, had no fixed villages, would not stand still to be exploited, and were hardly worth the candle. Colonists were no longer so eager for *encomiendas*, and were willing to escape the obligation to protect and civilize the wild tribes, which were as uncomfortable burdens, sometimes, as cub-tigers in a sack. Moreover, the sovereigns, with increasing emphasis, forbade the old-time abuses of exploitation, but as strongly as before adhered to the ideal of conversion and civilization. Here, then, was a larger opening for the missionary, and to him was entrusted, or upon him was thrust, consciously or unconsciously, not only the old work of conversion, but a larger and larger element of responsibility and control. On the northern frontier, therefore, among the roving tribes, the place of the discredited *encomendero* was largely taken by the missionary, and that of the *encomienda* by the mission, the design being to check the evils of exploitation, and at the same time to realize the ideal of conversion, protection, and civilization.

These missionaries became a veritable corps of Indian agents, serving both Church and State. The double capacity in which they served was made easier and more natural by the close union between Church and State in Spanish America, where the king exercised the *real patronato*, and where the viceroys were sometimes archbishops as well.

Under these conditions, in the seventeenth and eighteenth centuries, on the expanding frontiers of Spanish America, missions became well-nigh universal. In South America the outstanding examples were the Jesuit missions in Paraguay. Conspicuous in North America were the great Franciscan establishments in Alta California, the last of Spain's conquests. Not here alone, however, but everywhere on the northern frontier they played their part—in Sinaloa, Sonora, and Lower California; in Chihuahua, Coahuila, Nuevo León, and Nuevo Santander; in Florida, New Mexico, Texas, and Arizona. If there were twenty-one missions in California, there were as many in Texas, more in Florida, and twice as many in New Mexico. At one time the California missions had over thirty thousand Indians under instruction; but a century and a half earlier the missions of Florida and New Mexico each had an equal number.

The missionary work on the northern frontier of New Spain was conducted chiefly by Franciscans, Jesuits, and Dominicans. The northeastern field fell chiefly to the Franciscans, who entered Coahuila, Nuevo León, Nuevo Santander, New Mexico, Texas, and Florida. To the Northwest came the Jesuits, who, after withdrawing from Florida, worked especially in Sinaloa, Sonora, Chihuahua, Lower California, and Arizona. In 1767 the Jesuits were expelled from all Spanish America, and their places taken by the other orders. To Lower California came the Dominicans, to Alta California the Franciscans of the College of San Fernando, in the City of Mexico.

The missions, then, like the presidios, or garrisons, were characteristically and designedly frontier institutions, and it is as pioneer agencies that they must be studied. This is true whether they be considered from the religious, the political, or the social standpoint. As religious institutions they were designed to introduce the Faith among the heathen. Having done this, their function was to cease. Being designed for the frontier, they were intended to be temporary. As soon as his work was finished on one frontier, the missionary was expected to move on to another. In the theory of the law, within ten years each mission must be turned over to the secular clergy, and the common mission lands distributed among the Indians. But this law had been based on experience with the more advanced tribes of Mexico, Central America, and Peru. On the northern frontier, among the barbarian tribes, a longer period of tutelage was always found necessary.

The result, almost without fail, was a struggle over secularization, such as occurred in California. So long as the Indians were under the missionaries, their lands were secure from the land-grabber. The land-grabber always, therefore, urged the fulfillment of the ten-year law, just as the "squatters," the "sooners," and the "boomers" have always urged the opening of our Indian reservations. But the missionaries always knew the danger, and they always resisted secularization until their work was finished. Sooner or later, however, with the disappearance of frontier conditions, the missionary was expected to move on. His religious task was beside the soldier, *entre infieles*, in the outposts of civilization. . . .

The missions, then, were agencies of the State as well as of the Church. They served not alone to Christianize the frontier, but also to aid in extending, holding, and civilizing it. Since Christianity was the basic element of European civilization, and since it was the acknowledged duty of the State to extend the Faith, the first task of the missionary, from the standpoint of both State and Church, was to convert the heathen. But neither the State nor the Church—nor the missionary himself—in Spanish dominions, considered the work of the mission as ending here. If the Indian were to become either a worthy Christian or a desirable subject, he must be disciplined in the rudiments of civilized life. The task of giving the discipline was likewise turned over to the missionary. Hence, the missions were designed to be not only Christian seminaries, but in addition were outposts for the control and training schools for the civilizing of the frontier.

Since they served the State, the missions were supported by the State. It is a patent fact, and scarcely needs demonstrating, that they were maintained to a very considerable extent by the royal treasury. The Franciscan missions of New Spain in the eighteenth century had four principal means of support. The annual stipends of the missionaries (the *sínodos)* were usually paid by the government. These *sínodos* varied in amount according to the remoteness of the missions, and on the northernmost frontier were usually $450 for each missionary. In 1758, for example, the treasury of New Spain was annually paying *sínodos* for twelve Querétaran friars in Coahuila and Texas, six Jaliscans in Coahuila, eleven Zacatecans in Texas, ten Fernandinos in the Sierra Gorda, six Jaliscans in Nayarit, twenty-two Zacatecans in Nuevo León and Nueva Vizcaya, seventeen Zacatecans in Nuevo Santander, five San Diegans in Sierra Gorda, and thirty-four friars of the Provincia del Santo Evangelio in New Mexico, or, in all, 123 friars, at an average of about 350 *pesos* each. This report did not include the Provincia de Campeche or the Yslas de Barlovento, for which separate reports had been asked. Other appropriations were made for missionaries in the Marianas and the Philippine Islands, dependencies of New Spain.

Besides the *sínodos,* the government regularly furnished the missionaries with military protection, by detaching from the near-by presidios from two to half a dozen or more soldiers for each mission. In addition, the royal treasury usually made an initial grant *(ayuda de costa)* of $1000 to each mission, to pay for bells, vestments, tools, and other expenses of the founding, and in cases of emergency it frequently made special grants for building or other purposes.

These government subsidies did not preclude private gifts, or alms, which were often sought and secured. In the founding of new missions the older establishments were expected to give aid, and if able they did respond in liberal measure. And then there were endowments. The classic examples of private endowments on the northern frontier were the gifts of Don Pedro de Terreros, later Conde de Regla, who offered $150,000 to found Apache missions in Coahuila and Texas, and the Jesuit Fondo Piadoso, or Pious Fund, of California. This latter fund, begun in 1697, grew by a variety of gifts to such an amount that the missions of Lower California were largely supported by the increase alone. With the expulsion of the Jesuits in 1767 the fund was taken over by the government, and became the principal means of support of the new Franciscan missions of Alta California, besides being devoted in part to secular purposes. Even in Alta California, however, the royal treasury paid the wages *(sueldos)* of the mission guards, and gave other financial aid.

Finally, the Indians of the missions were expected soon to become self-supporting, and, indeed, in many cases they did acquire large wealth through stock-raising and agricultural pursuits. But not a penny of this belonged to the missionaries, and the annual *sínodos*, or salaries, continued to be paid from other sources, from the Pious Fund in California, and from the royal treasury generally elsewhere.

While it is thus true that the missions were supported to a very considerable degree by the royal treasury, it is just as plain that the amount of government aid, and the ease with which it was secured, depended largely upon the extent to which political ends could be combined with religious purposes.

The importance of political necessity in loosening the royal purse-strings is seen at every turn in the history of Spanish North America. Knowing the strength of a political appeal, the friars always made use of it in their requests for permission and aid. While the monarchs ever used pious phrases, and praised the work of the padres—without hypocrisy no doubt—the royal pocketbook was not readily opened to found new missions unless there was an important political as well as a religious object to be gained.

Striking examples of this fact are found in the histories of Texas and California. The missionaries of the northern frontier had long had their eyes on the "Kingdom of the Texas" as a promising field of labor, and had even appealed to the government for aid in cultivating it. But in vain, till La Salle planted a French colony at Matagorda Bay. Then the royal treasury was opened, and funds were provided for missions in eastern Texas. The French danger passed for the moment, and the missions were withdrawn. Then for another decade Father Hidalgo appealed in vain for funds and permission to re-establish the missions. But when St. Denis, agent of the French governor of Louisiana, intruded himself into Coahuila, the Spanish government at once gave liberal support for the refounding of the missions, to aid in restraining the French.

The case was the same for California. Since the time of Vizcaíno the missionaries had clamored for aid and for permission to found missions at San Diego and Monterey. In 1620 Father Ascensión, who had been with Vizcaíno eighteen years before, wrote, "I do not know what security His Majesty can have in his conscience for delaying so long to send ministers of the Gospel to this realm of California," and, during the next century and a half, a hundred others echoed this admonition. But all to no purpose till the Russian Bear began to amble or to threaten to amble down the Pacific Coast. Then money was forthcoming—partly from the confiscated Pious Fund, it is true—and then missionaries were sent to help hold the country for the crown. . . .

The value of the missionaries as frontier agents was thus clearly recognized, and their services were thus consciously utilized by the government. In the first place, they were often the most useful of explorers and diplomatic agents. The unattended missionary could sometimes go unmolested, and without arousing suspicion and hostility, into districts where the soldier was not welcome, while by their education and their trained habits of thought they were the class best fitted to record what they saw and to report what should be done. For this reason they were often sent alone to explore new frontiers, or as peace emissaries to hostile tribes, or as chroniclers of expeditions led by others. Hence it is that the best of the diaries of early exploration in the Southwest—and, indeed, in most of America—were written by the missionaries.

As illustrations of this kind of frontier service on the part of the missionaries we have but to recall the example of Friar Marcos, who was sent by Viceroy Mendoza to seek the rumored "Seven Cities" in New Mexico; the rediscovery of that province, under the viceroy's patronage, by the party led by Fray Agustín Rodríguez; the expeditions of Father Larios, unattended, into Coahuila; the forty or more journeys of Father Kino across the deserts of Sonora, and his demonstration that California was a peninsula, not an island, as most men had thought; the part played by Kino in pacifying the revolt of the Pimas in 1695, and in making the frontier safe for settlers; the diplomatic errands of Fathers Calahorra and Ramírez, sent by the governors of Texas to the hostile northern tribes; the lone travels of Father Garcés, of two thousand miles or more, over the untrod trails, in Arizona, California, and New Mexico, seeking a better route to California; and the expedition of Fathers Domínguez and Escalante, pathfinders for an equal distance in and about the Great Basin between the Rockies and the Sierras.

The missions served also as a means of defense to the king's dominions. This explains why the government was more willing to support missions when the frontier needed defending than at other times, as in the cases, already cited, of Texas and California. It is significant, too, in this connection, that the Real Hacienda, or Royal Fisc, charged the expenses for presidios and missions both to the same account, the Ramo de Guerra, or "War Fund." In a report for New Spain made in 1758 a treasury official casually remarked,

> Presidios are erected and missions founded in *tierra firme* whenever it is necessary to defend conquered districts from the hostilities and invasions of warlike, barbarian tribes, and to plant and extend our Holy Faith, for which purposes *juntas de guerra y hacienda* are held.

It is indeed true that appropriations for missions were usually made and that permission to found missions was usually given in councils of war and finance.

The missionaries counteracted foreign influence among their neophytes, deterred them from molesting the interior settlements, and secured their aid in holding back more distant tribes. Nearly every army that was led from San Antonio, Texas, in the eighteenth century, against the hostile Apaches and Comanches, contained a strong contingent of mission Indians, who fought side by side with the Spaniards. Father Kino was relied upon by the military leaders of Sonora to obtain the aid of the Pimas, his beloved neophytes, in defense of the Sonora settlements. When he was assigned to California, in company with Salvatierra, the authorities of Sonora protested, on the ground that, through his influence over the natives, he was a better means of protection to the province than a whole company of soldiers. When a Spanish expedition was organized to attack the Apaches, Kino was sent ahead to arouse and enlist the Pima allies. When the Pimas put the Apaches to flight, it was Kino to whom they sent the count of the enemy's dead, recorded by notches on a pole; on the same occasion it was Kino who received the thanks of citizens and officials of the province; and, when doubt was expressed as to what the Pimas had accomplished, it was Kino who rode a hundred miles or more to count the scalps of the vanquished foe, as evidence with which to vindicate his Pima friends.

The very mission plants were even built and often served as fortresses, not alone for padres and neophytes, but for near-by settlers, too. Every well-built mission was ranged round a great court or patio, protected on all sides by the buildings, whose walls were sometimes eight feet thick. In hostile countries these buildings were themselves enclosed within massive protecting walls. In 1740 President Santa Ana wrote that Mission Valero, at San Antonio, Texas, was better able to withstand a siege than any of the three presidios of the province. This of course was only a relative excellence. Twenty-two years later the same mission was surrounded by a wall, and over the gate was a tower, equipped with muskets, ammunition, and three cannon. At the same time the mission of San José (Texas) was called "a castle" which more than once had been proof against the Apaches.

Not only were the missionaries consciously utilized as political agents to hold the frontier but they often served, on their own motion, or with the co-operation of the secular authority, as "promoters" of the unoccupied districts. They sent home reports of the outlying tribes, of the advantages of obtaining their friendship, of the danger of foreign incursions, of the wealth and attractions of the country, and of the opportunities to extend the king's dominion. Frequently, indeed, they were called to Mexico, or even to Spain, to sit in the royal councils, where their expert opinions often furnished the primary basis of a decision to occupy a new outpost. As examples of this, near at home, we have but to recall Escobar, Benavides, and Ayeta of New Mexico, Massanet, Hidalgo, and Santa Ana of Texas, Kino of Lower California, and Serra of Alta California. Thus consciously or unconsciously, directly or indirectly, with or without secular initiative, the missionaries served as most active promoters, one might even call them "boosters," of the frontier.

But the missionaries helped not only to extend and hold and promote the frontier; more significantly still, they helped to civilize it. And this is the keynote of my theme. Spain possessed high ideals, but she had peculiar difficulties to contend with. She laid claim to the lion's share of the two Americas, but her population was small and little of it could be spared to people the New World. On the other hand, her colonial policy, equalled in humanitarian principles by that of no other country, perhaps, looked to the preservation of the natives, and to their elevation to at least a limited citizenship. Lacking Spaniards to colonize the frontier, she would colonize it with the aborigines. Such an ideal called not only for the subjugation and control of the natives, but for their civilization as well. To bring this end about the rulers of Spain again made use of the religious and humanitarian zeal of the missionaries, choosing them to be to the Indians not only preachers, but also teachers and disciplinarians. To the extent that this work succeeded it became possible to people the frontier with civilized natives, and thus to supply the lack of colonists. This desire was quite in harmony with the religious aims of the friars, who found temporal discipline indispensable to the best work of Christianization.

Hence it is that in the Spanish system—as distinguished from the French, for example—the essence of the mission was the *discipline*, religious, moral, social, and industrial, which it afforded. The very physical arrangement of the mission was determined with a view to discipline. The central feature of every successful mission was the Indian village, or pueblo. The settled tribes, such as the Pueblo Indians of New Mexico, or the Pimas of Arizona, could be instructed in their native towns, but wandering and scattered tribes must be assembled and established in pueblos, and kept there, by force if necessary. The reason why the missions of eastern Texas failed was that the Indians refused to settle in pueblos, and without more soldiers than were available it was impossible to control them. It was on this question that Father Serra split with Governor Neve regarding the Santa Barbara Indians in California. To save expense for soldiers, Neve urged that the friars should minister to the Indians in their native rancherías. But the missionaries protested that by this arrangement the Indians could not be disciplined. The plan was given up therefore, and instead the Indians were congregated in great pueblos at San Buenaventura and Santa Barbara. Thus, the pueblo was essential to the mission, as it had been to the *encomienda*.

Discipline called for control, and this was placed largely in the hands of the missionaries. The rule was two friars for each mission, but in many instances there was only one. The need of more was often urged.

As a symbol of force, and to afford protection for missionaries and mission Indians, as well as to hold the frontier against savages and foreigners, presidios, or garrisons, were established near by. And thus, across the continent, from San Agustín to San Francisco, stretched a long and slender line of presidios—San Agustín, Apalache, Pensacola, Los Adaes, La Bahía, San Antonio, San Juan Bautista, Rio Grande, San Sabá,

El Paso, Santa Fé, Janos, Fronteras, Terrenate, Tubac, Altár, San Diego, Santa Barbara, Monterey, and San Francisco—a line more than twice as long as the Rhine-Danube frontier held by the Romans, from whom Spain learned her lesson in frontier defense.

To assist the missionaries in their work of disciplining and instructing the neophytes, each mission was usually provided with two or more soldiers from the nearest presidio. To help in recovering runaways—for the Indians frequently did abscond—special detachments of soldiers were furnished. The impression is often given that the missionaries objected to the presence of soldiers at the missions, but as a rule the case was quite the contrary. What they did object to was unsuitable soldiers, and outside interference in the selection and control of the guard. It is true, indeed, that immoral or insubordinate soldiers were deemed a nuisance, and that since the presidials were largely half-breeds—mestizos or mulattoes—and often jailbirds at that, this type was all too common. But in general military aid was demanded, and complaint of its inadequacy was constantly made. On this point the testimony of Fray Romualdo Cartagena, guardian of the College of Santa Cruz de Querétaro, is valid. In a report made in 1772, still in manuscript, he wrote,

> What gives these missions their permanency is the aid which they receive from the Catholic arms. Without them pueblos are frequently abandoned, and ministers are murdered by the barbarians. It is seen every day that in missions where there are no soldiers there is no success, for the Indians, being children of fear, are more strongly appealed to by the glistening of the sword than by the voice of five missionaries. Soldiers are necessary to defend the Indians from the enemy, and to keep an eye on the mission Indians, now to encourage them, now to carry news to the nearest presidio in case of trouble. For the spiritual and temporal progress of the missions two soldiers are needed, for the Indians cannot be trusted, especially in new conversions.

This is the testimony of missionaries themselves. That protection was indeed necessary is shown by the martyrdom of missionaries on nearly every frontier—of Father Segura and his entire band of Jesuits in Virginia in 1570; of Father Saeta in Sonora; of Fathers Ganzábal, Silva, Terreros, and Santiesteban in Texas; of Fathers Carranco and Tamaral in Lower California; of Father Luis Jayme at San Diego (Alta California); of Father Garcés and his three companions at Yuma, on the Colorado; and of the twenty-one Franciscans in the single uprising in New Mexico in 1680. But these martyrdoms were only occasional, and the principal business of the soldiers was to assist the missionaries in disciplining and civilizing the savages.

As teachers, and as an example to new converts, it was the custom to place in each new mission three Indian families from the older missions. After a time the families might return to their homes. As Father Romualdo remarked: "It is all the better if these families be related to the new, for this insures the permanence of the latter in the missions, while if they do flee it is easier to recover them by means of their relatives than through strangers."

Notable among the Indians utilized as teachers and colonists in the northern missions were the Tlascaltecans, of Tlascala, the native city of Mexico made famous by Prescott. Having been subdued by Cortés, the Tlascaltecans became the most trusted supporters of the Spaniards, as they had been the most obstinate foes of the "Triple Alliance," and, after playing an important part in the conquest of the Valley of Mexico, they became a regular factor in the extension of Spanish rule over the north country. Thus, when San Luis Potosí had been conquered, colonies of Tlascaltecans were set to teach the more barbarous natives of that district both loyalty to the Spaniards and the elements of civilization. In Saltillo a large colony of Tlascaltecans was established by Urdiñola at the end of the sixteenth century, and became the mother colony from which numerous offshoots were planted at the new missions and villages further north. At one time a hundred families of Tlascaltecans were ordered sent to Pensacola; in 1755 they figured in the plans for a missionary colony on the Trinity River, in Texas; two years later a little band of them was sent to the San Sabá mission in western Texas to assist in civilizing the Apaches; and twenty years afterward it was suggested that a settlement, with these people as a nucleus, be established far to the north, on the upper Red River, among the Wichita Indians of Texas and Oklahoma. To help in civilizing the mission Indians of Jalisco, Sinaloa, and Sonora, the Tarascans of Michoacán were utilized; farther north, the Opatas, of southern Sonora, were sent into Arizona as teachers of the Pimas; to help in civilizing the Indians of California, Serra brought mission Indians from the Peninsula.

Discipline and the elements of European civilization were imparted at the missions through religious instruction, through industrial training, and, among more advanced natives, by means of rudimentary teaching in arts and letters.

Every mission was, in the first place, a Christian seminary, designed to give religious discipline. Religious instruction, of the elementary sort suited to the occasion, was imparted by a definite routine, based on long experience, and administered with much practical sense and regard for local conditions.

Aside from the fundamental cultural concepts involved in Christianity, this religious instruction in itself involved a most important means of assimilation. By the laws of the Indies the missionaries were enjoined to instruct the neophytes in their native tongues, and in the colleges and seminaries professorships were established to teach them. But it was found that, just as the natives lacked the concepts, the Indian languages lacked the terms in which properly to convey the meaning of the Christian doctrine. Moreover, on some frontiers there were so many dialects that it was impossible for the friars to learn them. This was pre-eminently true of the lower Rio Grande region, where there were over two hundred dialects, more than twenty of which were quite distinct. . . .

For these reasons, on the northern frontier instruction was usually given in Spanish, through interpreters at first, and directly as soon as the Indians learned the language of the friars. In the case of children, who were the chief consideration, this was quickly done. And thus incidentally a long step toward assimilation was accomplished, for we all know the importance of language in the fusing of races and cultures. The firmness of the hold of the Spanish language upon any land touched by Spain, however lightly, has often been noted. It was partly, or even largely, due to this teaching of the native children at the missions.

The routine of religious discipline established by the Franciscans in the missions taken over from the Jesuits in Sonora, in 1767, was typical of all the Franciscan missions, and was not essentially different from that of the other orders. It was described by Father Reyes, later Bishop Reyes, as follows:

> Every day at sunrise the bells call the Indians to Mass. An old Indian, commonly called *mador*, and two *fiscales*, go through the whole pueblo, requiring all children and unmarried persons to go to the church, to take part in the devotion and silence of the Mass. This over, they repeat in concert, in Spanish, with the minister, the prayers and the Creed. At sunset this exercise is repeated at the door of the church, and is concluded with saying the rosary and chanting the *salve* or the *alavado*. The *mador* and the *fiscales* are charged, on Sundays and feast days, to take care to require all men, women, and children to be present at Mass, with their poor clothes clean, and all washed and combed.

The very act of going to church, then, involved a lesson in the amenities of civilization. There was virtue then as now in putting on one's "Sunday clothes". . . .

The civilizing function of the typical Spanish mission, where the missionaries had charge of the temporalities as well as of the spiritualities, was evident from the very nature of the mission plant. While the church was ever the centre of the establishment, and the particular object of the minister's pride and care, it was by no means the larger part. Each fully developed mission was a great industrial school, of which the largest, as in California, sometimes managed more than 2000 Indians. There were weaving rooms, blacksmith shop, tannery, wine-press, and warehouses; there were irrigating ditches, vegetable gardens, and grain fields; and on the ranges roamed thousands of horses, cattle, sheep, and goats. Training in the care of fields and stock not only made the neophytes self-supporting, but afforded the discipline necessary for the rudiments of civilized life. The women were taught to cook, sew, spin, and weave; the men to fell the forest, build, run the forge, tan leather, make ditches, tend cattle, and shear sheep.

Even in New Mexico, where the missionaries were not in charge of the temporalities—that is, of the economic interests of the Indians—and where the Indians had a well-established native agriculture, the friars were charged with their instruction in the arts and crafts, as well as with their religious education. And when the custodian, Father Benavides—later Bishop of Goa—wrote in 1630, after three decades of effort by the friars in that province, he was able to report fourteen monasteries, serving fifty-odd pueblos, each with its school, where the Indians were all taught not only to sing, play musical instruments, read, and write, but, as Benavides puts it, "all the trades and polite deportment," all imparted by "the great industry of the Religious who converted them."

In controlling, supervising, and teaching the Indians, the friars were assisted by the soldier guards, who served as *mayor domos* of the fields, of the cattle and horse herds, of the sheep and goat ranches, and of the shops. In the older missions, even among the most backward tribes, it sometimes became possible to dispense with this service, as at San Antonio, Texas, where, it was reported in 1772, the Indians, once naked savages who lived on cactus apples and cotton-tail rabbits, had become so skilled and trustworthy that "without the aid of the Spaniards they harvest, from irrigated fields, maize, beans, and cotton in plenty, and Castilian corn for sugar. There are cattle, sheep, and goats in abundance," all being the product of the care and labor of the natives.

The results of this industrial training at the missions were to be seen in the imposing structures that were built, the fertile farms that were tilled, and the great stock ranches that were tended, by erstwhile barbarians, civilized under the patient discipline of the missionaries, assisted by soldier guards and imported Indian teachers, not in our Southwest alone, but on nearly every frontier of Spanish America.

The missionaries transplanted to the frontiers and made known to the natives almost every conceivable domestic plant and animal of Europe. . . .

The laws of the Indies even prescribed and the missions provided a school for self-government, elementary and limited, it is true, but germane and potential nevertheless. This was effected by organizing the Indians of the missions into a pueblo, with civil and military officers, modelled upon the Spanish administration. When the mission was founded the secular head of the district—governor, captain, or alcalde—as representative of the king, formally organized the pueblo, appointed the native officers, and gave title to the four-league grant of land. In constituting the native government, wisdom dictated that use should be made of the existing Indian organization, natives of prestige being given the important offices. Thereafter the civil officers were chosen by a form of native election, under the supervision of the missionary, and approved by the secular head of the jurisdiction.

The civil officers were usually a governor, captain, alcaldes, and alguacil, who by law constituted a cabildo, or council. The military officers were a captain or a *teniente*, and subalterns, and were appointed by the secular head, or by a native captain-general subject to approval by the secular head. The military officers had their own insignia, and, to give them prestige, separate benches were placed in the churches for the governor, alcalde, and council. In Sonora there was a *topil*, whose duty was to care for the community houses—a sort of free hostelry, open to all travellers, which seems to have been of native rather than of Spanish origin. The Indians had their own jail, and inflicted minor punishments, prescribed by the minister. Indian overseers kept the laborers at their work and, indeed, much of the task of controlling the Indians was effected through Indian officers themselves. Of course it was the directing force of the padres and the restraining force of the near-by presidio which furnished the ultimate pressure.

This pueblo government was established among the more advanced tribes everywhere, and it succeeded in varying degrees. It was often a cause for conflict of jurisdiction, and in California, where the natives were of the most barbarous, it was strongly opposed by the missionaries. It has been called a farce, but it certainly was not so intended. It was not self-government any more than is student government in a primary school. But it was a means of control, and was a step toward self-government. It is one of the things, moreover, which help to explain how two missionaries and three or four soldiers could make an orderly town out of two or three thousand savages recently assembled from divers and sometimes mutually hostile tribes. So deeply was it impressed upon the Indians of New Mexico that some of them yet maintain their Spanish pueblo organization, and by it still govern themselves, extra-legally. And, I am told, in some places even in California, the descendants of the mission Indians still keep up the pueblo organization as a sort of fraternity, or secret society.

In these ways, then, did the missions serve as frontier agencies of Spain. As their first and primary task, the missionaries spread the Faith. But in addition, designedly or incidentally, they explored the frontiers, promoted their occupation, defended them and the interior settlements, taught the Indians the Spanish language, and disciplined them in good manners, in the rudiments of European crafts, of agriculture, and even of self-government. Moreover, the missions were a force which made for the preservation of the Indians, as opposed to their destruction, so characteristic of the Anglo-American frontier. In the English colonies the only good Indians were dead Indians. In the Spanish colonies it was thought worthwhile to improve the natives for this life as well as for the next. Perhaps the missions did not, in every respect, represent a twentieth-century ideal. Sometimes, and to some degree, they failed, as has every human institution. Nevertheless, it must not be forgotten that of the millions of half-castes living south of us, the grandparents, in a large proportion of cases, at some generation removed, on one side or the other, were once mission Indians, and as such learned the elements of Spanish civilization. For these reasons, as well as for unfeigned religious motives, the missions received the royal support. They were a conspicuous feature of Spain's frontiering genius.

5

The Presidio: Fortress or Farce?*

Odie B. Faulk

Editor's Introduction

Whereas Bolton emphasized the positive contributions of the mission system to frontier expansion and Indian control, Odie B. Faulk suggests that the missions failed to pacify the frontier. By the late eighteenth century, Spanish officials relied more heavily on the presidio than on the mission as an instrument of Indian control. Yet, the presidio, too, Faulk concludes, was largely a failure. Although it served as an effective bastion to defend those who took refuge within its walls, as an offensive element of Spanish military operations, the presidio was a "farce." (It should be noted that Faulk is not discussing coastal presidios, which had as their chief function defense against foreign invasion.)[1]

Professor Faulk's article shows the sure hand of an experienced and talented writer. Former chairman of the department of history at Oklahoma State University, and currently director of the Memphis State University Press, Faulk holds a doctorate from Texas Tech University. He is the most prolific living writer on southwestern history. He is author of

---

Journal of the West, 8 (1969): 22–28. Reprinted with permission of the author and the publisher.

numerous popular books, such as *Destiny Road: The Gila Trail and the Opening of the Southwest* (New York: 1973) as well as a textbook survey: *Land of Many Frontiers. A History of the American Southwest* (New York: 1968). Faulk is also known for such scholarly studies as *The Last Years of Spanish Texas, 1778–1821* (The Hague: 1964). With Sidney B. Brinckerhoff, he edited *Lancers for the King. A Study of the Frontier Military System of Northern New Spain* (Phoenix: 1965). The last work develops more fully some of the themes in the present essay.

NOTE

1. Leon G. Campbell, "The Spanish Presidio in Alta California during the Mission Period, 1769–1784," *Journal of the West*, 16 (1977): 63.

The Presidio: Fortress or Farce?

The Presidio was but one of three separate yet related colonial institutions employed by Imperial Spain in its drive northward from Central Mexico into what is now the American Southwest. The other two were the mission and the civil settlement. On paper these institutions seemed excellent devices for conquering, civilizing, and Hispanicizing the natives of the region. Missionaries venturing into the wilderness would spread the gospel of Christianity; those Indians converted would be gathered into missions where Franciscan or Jesuit padres would instruct them. The missionaries would be protected by soldiers, who would be housed in presidios near the religious establishments. The troops would provide the physical strength needed to over-awe the natives, but force would be used only when necessary to coerce the heathens into a receptive attitude toward the teachings of the missionaries. And the families of the soldiers would go with them to the frontier, merchants would come to sell them goods, while farmers and ranchers would be given land in the vicinity. Thus civil settlements, recognized by law, would grow near the presidios and missions. This three-pronged attack on the wilderness, it was felt, would gradually bring the northern frontier under complete Spanish domination and rule.

For the most part, however, the mission system was a failure. In Arizona, the Western Apaches did not take to mission life, nor did their eastern kinsmen in New Mexico and Texas or the lordly Comanches of the latter province. The only successes enjoyed by the missionaries were among sedentary tribes such as those in California, the Pimas and Opatas of Sonora, the Papagos of Arizona, the Pueblo Indians of New Mexico, and the Hasinai Confederacy of East Texas. Yet even these normally peaceful tribes occasionally rebelled, martyred their missionaries, burned the religious establishments, and fled to wilderness hide-outs. In 1751, for example, the Pimas staged a bloody uprising in Sonora and Arizona, as had New Mexican natives in 1680 and the Tejas Indians in 1693. Even in California there were disturbances from time to time. In addition, the mission Indians used every possible pretext to flee from the rigid confines of the padres' care; the missionaries were continually requesting governmental aid in securing the return of run-away neophytes. As a result of such vexations, the Spanish government, with very few exceptions, was unwilling to finance new efforts to convert the natives during the last years of the colonial era.

Nor did the civil settlements work as planned. At the end of the Spanish years of control, there were only a few scattered towns on the northern frontier. For the most part, these existed in the shadows of the presidios where the civilians could quickly gather whenever raids occurred. These civilians, in theory a source of strength as a standing militia, usually were timorous, impoverished peasants. They would not join in forays against the enemy, and yet they had to be protected.

Thus by the end of the Seven Years War, Spanish officials knew that the system then being used was in need of overhaul. The Marqués de Rubí and José de Gálvez were sent to inspect and make suggestions, a task they accomplished by 1768. Their recommendations[1] led to the issuance of the Royal Regulation of 1772,[2] a compilation of laws intended to bring about a pacification of the Indians by force of arms. The mission and the civil settlement would continue to play a part in frontier colonization, but their roles henceforth would be secondary.

According to the Royal Regulations, the provinces of Nueva Vizcaya, Sonora, Sinaloa, California, New Mexico, Coahuila, Chihuahua, Texas, Nuevo León, and Nuevo Santander were placed under a commandant-inspector, who was to function under the supervision of the viceroy. The officer selected for this post was Colonel Hugo O'Conor, an Irish mercenary long in Spanish service and experienced on the frontier of New Spain. Manfully and energetically O'Conor worked to effect the changes ordered. Principal among these alterations was the relocation of presidios into a cordon of twenty—stretching from the Gulf of California to the Gulf of Mexico. In the process some presidios, such as those in East Texas, were abandoned; some, such as the one at Tubac (Arizona), were moved; and some new ones were constructed, such as the one at San Buenaventura (Chihuahua).[3]

These presidios varied but little in design and construction. Located most often near good farming land and built on high ground, they were constructed on a pattern learned from the Moors. Using local materials (principally adobe bricks), the presidios were built in a square or rectangular shape with walls at least ten feet high; the length of the sides ranged from two to eight hundred feet each. On two diagonal corners, round bastions *(torreones)* were constructed, rising above the wall and pierced with firing ports. This arrangement allowed the soldiers to fire down the length of all four walls at attackers. On the inside of the walls, buildings were constructed, the roofs of which were high enough to serve as parapets from which men could fire over the walls. Included inside the presidio were storage facilities, a chapel, and rooms for the officers and men. The only outside opening was the main gate.

Variations in this basic design were used at such places as Los Adaes in the province of Texas, where wooden palisades and diamond-shaped bastions were constructed, and at Tubac, where there was one square tower instead of two round bastions. At Santa Cruz de Terrenate, there was only one diamond-shaped tower. The new systems of fortification being developed in Europe by such men as Preste de Vauban and Menno van Coehoorn had only slight influence on these Spanish frontier posts. Such changes were predicated on an enemy with artillery; as the Indians of the Interior Provinces had no such weapons, the presidial commanders could rely on inexpensive, traditional designs and materials. The adobe walls were built up to thicknesses of three feet—enough to stop any arrow or bullet. While the Indians were able to penetrate these stout walls by stealth on occasion,[4] they never overcame one by direct attack. In fact, the design of these presidios was so practical that many American traders and military leaders at a later date chose to build their forts in the Southwest on the same pattern. Bent's Fort in Colorado is an excellent example.

Although O'Conor achieved some positive results in his campaigns against the natives committing raids, the Interior Provinces continued to decline.[5] Therefore, in 1776, the king concluded that even more sweeping changes were necessary. That year he established the Interior Provinces separate from the viceroyalty of New Spain. The area was placed under a commandant-general, who combined in his office civil, judicial, and military powers. Yet his effectiveness was limited from the start by a royal decision that he would be dependent upon the viceroy for troops and supplies. As there were always more demands on the royal treasury than there were funds—and because the viceroy would not be sympathetic to the pleas of a commander not under his jurisdiction—the Interior Provinces never received sufficient funds to undertake an effective pacification of the Indians by military means.

First to occupy the position of comandante-general was Brigadier Teodoro de Croix, a native of France who had entered the Spanish army at the age of seventeen.[6] As commanding general it was Croix's formidable task to halt the shrinkage of the area under Spanish control on the northern frontier. Arriving in Mexico City in 1776, Croix spent several months studying reports, then set out to inspect personally the area under his control. What Croix discovered was that the presidio as a military structure was not at fault. The failure of the military to contain the enemy was two-fold: (1) the philosophy of building presidios was predicated on European concepts of warfare, and (2) the soldiers garrisoning the presidios were not adequately trained, supplied, or equipped for containing the type of enemy faced in the Interior Provinces.

The Royal regulations stipulated that the cordon of presidios be built "approximately forty leagues apart one from another" so that they could "give mutual aid to one another and to reconnoiter the intervening terrain."[7] Such a string of forts was in the best European tradition, yet was useless against Indians of the Interior Provinces, whose code of honor held it was stupid to stand and be killed in open battle when the odds were against them; they preferred hit-and-run and favorable odds, rarely choosing to fight in the accepted European mode. In addition, the presidios generally were understaffed, and their soldiers were spread thinly to cover a multitude of tasks. Nearby missions generally required a small force of soldiers for police duties; troops also served as escorts for the supply trains, as mail riders, and as guards for the presidial horse herds. Picketed away from the presidios because of space limitations and because of shortages of grain for feeding, these herds were favorite targets for Apache and Comanche raiders.

Basic flaws in the concept of the presidios—poor location, inadequate numbers of troops, and herding horses away from the forts—do not explain the numerous reverses suffered by Spanish forces on the frontier, however. Far more important during the battles fought than the precise location of presidios was the discipline, equipment, and morale of the soldiers involved. It was in this area that Spain made its greatest mistakes.

Actually the lower-class citizen of New Spain who enlisted in the army for service in the Interior Provinces came to his post with great potential. In most cases he had been born on the frontier and thus was accustomed to the harsh desert climate and was an expert horseman.[8] He had been so subjected to governmental discipline that he could regard soldiering as the best life open to him. A soldier had retirement benefits, a pension for his widow in case of his death, and access to skilled medical attention. There also was the hope of promotion, for most junior officers in the Interior Provinces had risen through the ranks. Additionally, the soldier could easily obtain land near the presidio for himself and his family.[9]

For his services the newly enlisted soldier received 290 pesos annually. From this he received one-fourth peso daily for his and his family's subsistence. The remainder was kept by the paymaster to be used to purchase the horses, articles of uniform, armament, and equipment needed; and twenty pesos were withheld from his pay annually for five years as a contingency fund to be given him at discharge.[10]

Unlike the regular Spanish army, the troops of the Interior Provinces were enlisted into presidial garrisons and had no regimental or larger unit designations. The viceroy at Mexico City was not inclined to release soldiers of the regular army for frontier service, although infantrymen of the Catalonian Volunteers were sent to California in 1769 and some dragoons of Mexico served in Sonora in the 1780s. By royal decree the men of the frontier army were to be accorded the ranks and privileges of the regular Spanish army. This practice, as well as the benefits mentioned, should have produced a high *esprit de corps*, a pride in the local unit unattainable in any other way. Yet such was not always the case.

The training of new soldiers was rigidly prescribed in the Royal Regulations of 1772, but in actuality it varied from presidio to presidio. The captains were expected to drill their men in the handling of firearms, in target practice, in mounted tactics, and in military discipline and procedures. Weekly reviews were to be held to inspect equipment and to see that unserviceable items were replaced.[11] But in many cases these regulations were disregarded, and the new soldier learned his profession from his fellow enlisted men in barracks discussions or, even worse, on the actual field of battle.

Besides the poor training he received, the new soldier quickly discovered that the isolation of his post meant that he was subject in many ways to the whims of his officers. This practice of paying soldiers partly in cash and partly in goods accrued to the benefit of paymasters, presidial officers, and local merchants, many of whom connived together to set exorbitantly high prices for goods of inferior quality. The temptation for officers to engage in this practice was strong since inspections were rare, punishment for those caught was light, and the example of others getting rich was ever at hand. Paymasters on occasion even spent all the money entrusted to them for pay purposes, so that deficits were common and salaries often in arrears.[12] Because of these abuses, the soldiers received so little money that they and their families lived on the edge of starvation, their equipment deteriorated, and they developed morale, as one inspector declared, "shot through with insubordination."[13]

Corporal punishment was still observed in the garrisons, inflicted by the same officers against whom an offense was committed and who sat in judgment of the culprits.[14] And there were vexing interferences in the private lives of the soldiers.[15] Nor could a discontented soldier transfer to another presidio without the consent of his commanding officer, and approval was difficult to secure since most posts were short on personnel.[16] The army was thus only as good as it officers, and Commandant-General Croix characterized his officers as poor: "Very few give any hope of improving their behavior and conduct. They openly embrace all the abominable excesses . . ., do not observe orders, [and] hide the truth . . . I have no others to whom to turn."[17]

Just as the concept of the presidio was European in origin—and ill-suited to conditions in the Interior Provinces— so were the weapons carried by the common soldiers. Each was armed with a lance, a wide sword *(espada ancha)*, a short-barreled, miguelet-lock, smoothbore carbine *(escopeta)*, and two large-caliber, heavy pistols.[18] Both the sword and the lance were excellent against an army that stood and fought hand-to-hand, as was traditional in Europe, but useless against the Indians of the Interior Provinces. The firearms proved almost useless in the Interior Provinces because of inadequate training in their use and maintenance. Also, Spanish regulations provided that each soldier be issued only three pounds of gunpowder annually; as he was charged for all powder in excess of this amount, he had little interest in target practice.

For defensive purposes, the soldier carried a shield *(adarga),* wore a leather coat *(cuera),* and leather-leggings *(botas).* All were bulky, cumbersome, hot—and practically useless. General Croix urged that the shield, the leather jacket, and the lance be discarded; he urged the use of lightly-equipped, mounted troops employing the latest firearms and the best horses in order to pursue and defeat the Indians.[19] Although the regular Spanish cavalry units in the New World had already adopted such tactics, Croix's suggestions were not implemented in the Interior Provinces to a large extent. Many officers on the frontier still believed in the lance and the leather armor, and few changes were made.

Unable to meet the Indian enemy on the open field with any great hope of victory, the troops preferred to stay behind the security of presidial walls. Finally in 1786 the new viceroy, Bernardo de Gálvez, who had seen service on the northern frontier and had later governed Louisiana, put a new plan into effect in the Interior Provinces. He decreed a vigorous war on those Indians not at peace with Spain. Once the savages asked for peace, he ordered that they be settled in villages in the shadow of a presidio where they would be given presents, inferior firearms, and alcoholic beverages. Gálvez reasoned that the presents should be of such value that the Indians would prize peace more than war, and that the arms supplied them would quickly become inoperative and could be repaired only by Spaniards.[20] The Gálvez policy worked sufficiently well to bring about a period of relative peace from 1787 to 1810 and the outbreak of the Mexican Revolution; when that conflict began, and the annual distribution of presents ceased, the Indians again took to the warpath.[21]

The presidio, therefore, was both fortress and farce. It could withstand siege, but it could not halt Indian incursions into the interior of New Spain. It served as a refuge during raids for both civilian and soldier, but it rarely was the staging area for a successful campaign against the marauding natives. As a weapon of defense, it was a fortress; as an offensive weapon, it all too often was a farce. Yet considering the shortage of supplies and funds, the paucity of support from higher echelons of government, the poor training of the soldiers, and the barbaric ferocity of the natives, the wonder is not that the presidio largely failed in its military objectives as a frontier institution but that it succeeded as well as it did.

NOTES

1. For the Rubí report, see "*Digttamen, que de orden del Exmo Señor Marqués de Croix, Virrey de este Reyno expone el Mariscal de Campo Marqués de Rubí, en orden a la mejor Situazion de los Presidios, para la defensa, y extension de su Frontera* . . . ," Tacubaya, April 10, 1768 (Archivo General de Indias, Audiencia de Guadalajara, 1768–1772, 104–6–13, Sevilla; Dunn transcripts, Archives, University of Texas Library, Austin); see also Lawrence Kinnaird (trans. and ed.), *The Frontiers of New Spain: Nicolás de Lafora's Description, 1766–1768* (Berkeley, 1958). For Gálvez, see Herbert I. Priestley, *Jose de Galvez, Visitor-General of New Spain, 1765–1771* (Berkeley, 1916).

2. For a copy of the Royal Regulations of 1772 in both Spanish and English, see Sidney B. Brinckerhoff and Odie B. Faulk, *Lancers for the King* (Phoenix: Arizona Historical Foundation, 1965).

3. For O'Conor's work during this period, see *Informe de Hugo de O'Conor Sobre el Estado de las Provincias Internas del Norte, 1771–76*, ed. by Enrique González Flores and Francisco R. Almada (Mexico City: Editorial Cultura, 1952); for biographical details on O'Conor, see David M. Vigness, "Don Hugo Oconor and New Spain's Northeastern Frontier, 1764–1766," *Journal of the West*, Vol. VI (Spring, 1966), pp. 27–40.

4. For examples, see Sidney B. Brinckerhoff, "The Last Years of Spanish Arizona, 1786–1821," *Arizona and the West*, Vol. IX (Spring, 1967), pp. 5–20.

5. See Flores and Almada (eds.), *Informe de Hugo de O'Conor*, and Alfred B. Thomas, *Teodoro de Croix and the Northern Frontier of New Spain, 1776–1783* (Norman, 1941).

6. For details on Croix's career, see Thomas, *Teodoro de Croix*.

7. Royal Regulations, Brinckerhoff and Faulk, *Lancers for the King*, p. 49.

8. For example, at La Bahía del Espíritu Santo in 1780, only four of the presidial troops had been born outside the Interior Provinces; see Domingo Cabello y Robles, "*Real Presidio de la Bahía de el Espíritu Santo. Extracto General de la Tropa* . . . ," January 12, 1780, San Antonio (Béxar Archives, University of Texas Archives, Austin). Other presidian returns show a similar condition prevailing.

9. Various land laws were in effect to grant land near the presidios to both soldiers and civilians. These laws were designed not only to encourage enlistments, but also to bring civilians to the area who, in theory, were automatically part of the militia. The presidio of Tubac, for example, grew to a population of five hundred in its first fifteen years of existence through a liberal land policy; see Ray H. Mattison, "Early Spanish and Mexican Settlements in Arizona," *New Mexico Historical Review*, Vol. XXI (October, 1946), pp. 281–282.

10. "Distribution of Funds and the Pay of Soldiers," in the Royal Regulations as quoted in Brinckerhoff and Faulk, *Lancers for the King*, pp. 23–25.

11. *Ibid.*, p. 41.

12. For an excellent study of presidial supply, see Max L. Moorhead, "The Private Contract System of Presidial Supply in Northern New Spain," *Hispanic American Historical Review*, Vol. XLI (February, 1961), pp. 31–54.

13. Quoted in Thomas, *Teodoro de Croix*, pp. 13–14.

14. For an example, see Francisco Amangual, "*Diario de las Novedades y Operaciones ocurridas en la Expedición que se hace* . . . ," March 30-December 23, 1808, San Antonio (Béxar Archives, University of Texas Library, Austin). Officers who went astray, however received only token punishments; for example, see "*Año de 1792, Num[o] 126. Expediente promovido por el Teniente D[n] Fern[do] Fernz sobre quexa contra del Alferez D[n] Manuel de Urrutia*," January 28, 1792, San Antonio (Béxar Archives, University of Texas Archives).

16. For example, see Cortes to Manuel Muñoz, September 9, 1795 (Béxar Archives, University of Texas Archives).

17. Thomas, *Teodor de Croix*, p. 42; see also Kinnaird (ed.), *Frontiers of New Spain*, pp. 214–217.

18. "Armament and Mounts," in the Royal Regulations, quoted in Brinckerhoff and Faulk, *Lancers for the King*, pp. 21–22.

19. Thomas, *Teodoro de Croix*, pp. 57, 152; Kinnaird, *Frontiers of New Spain*, p. 216.

20. Bernardo de Gálvez, *Instructions for Governing the Interior Provinces of New Spain, 1786*, trans. and ed. by Donald E. Worcester (Berkeley: The Quivira Society, 1951).

21. See Brinckerhoff, "Last Years of Spanish Arizona," Odie B. Faulk, *The Last Years of Spanish Texas, 1778–1821* (The Hague: Mouton and Company, 1964); and Joseph F. Park, "Spanish Indian Policy in Northern Mexico, 1765–1810," *Arizona and the West*, Vol. IV (Winter, 1962), pp. 325–344, for examples.

6

The Ranching Frontier: Spanish Institutional Backgrounds of the Plains Cattle Industry*

Sandra L. Myres

Editor's Introduction

In New Mexico, according to Marc Simmons, a *rancho* might be a small farm with orchards, but on the Great Plains, ranches were for grazing cattle. The cattle ranch, Sandra Myres argues, deserves a place alongside the mission and the presidio as a key institution on the northern frontier of New Spain. Unlike the mission and the presidio, however, the ranch survived the Anglo-American conquest of Mexico's far northern frontier. Ranching became a key to America's westward movement and spawned America's most celebrated folk hero, the cowboy. As Myres tells us, "the Anglo adopted the techniques, equipment, even the mores and folklore of

*Originally a paper read at the Walter Prescott Webb Memorial Lectures at the University of Texas, Arlington, this article first appeared in *Essays on the American West*, ed. Harold M. Hollingsworth and Sandra L. Myres (Austin: 1969), pp. 19–39. It is reprinted here with permission of the author and the Webb Lectures Committee.

the Spanish ranchers." If Myres is correct, it is ironic that cowboys, who often despised Mexicans, owed much of their craft to Spanish-Mexican ranching traditions.

Myres' able exposition of this thesis is not new. Historians such as Walter Prescott Webb and Odie B. Faulk have advanced a similar argument.[1] In recent years, however, writers such as Terry Jordan and John Guice have challenged and modified that thesis. They do not question the importance of ranching to the northward spread of the Spanish frontier, but they do exhort us to look eastward as well as southward to understand the origins of the Anglo-American range cattle industry. Indeed, some writers would have us look to Scotland; Professor Jordan looks to the cowpens of the Carolinas; and Professor Guice to the Floridas and Louisiana where Spanish influence was also strong.[2]

Professor of history at the University of Texas, Arlington, Sandra Myres did her undergraduate work at Texas Tech and her Ph.D. in Latin American history at Texas Christian University. Her publications reflect her wide-ranging interests: *S. D. Myres: Saddlemaker* (Kerrville, Tex.: 1961); *The Ranch in Spanish Texas, 1691–1800* (El Paso: 1969); and *Cavalry Wife: The Diary of Eveline Alexander, 1866–1867* (College Station, Tex.: 1977). She is currently editing several diaries of overland journeys made by women on the American frontier. In addition to these studies of the West, she has published in the fields of government and urban history and served as interim director of the Texas Committee for Humanities and Public Policy.

NOTES

1. See Webb's *The Great Plains* (Boston: 1931) and Odie Faulk's able article, "Ranching in Spanish Texas," *Hispanic American Historical Review*, 44 (1965): 257–66.

2. The best summary of the literature surrounding this controversy is John D. W. Guice's sprightly, "Cattle Raisers of the Old Southwest," *The Western Historical Quarterly*, 8 (1977): 167–87. Terry Jordan's most recent contribution to the debate is "Early Northeast Texas and the Evolution of Western Ranching," *Annals of the Association of American Geographers*, 67 (1977): 67–87.

The Ranching Frontier: Spanish Institutional Backgrounds of the Plains Cattle Industry

"One of the marvels in the history of the modern world is the way in which that little Iberian nation, Spain, when most of her blood and treasure were absorbed in European wars, with a handful of men took possession of the Caribbean archipelago, and by rapid yet steady advance spread her culture, her religion, her law, and her language over more than half of the two American continents where they still are dominant and still are secure—in South America, Central America, and a large fraction of North America. . . ."[1]

With these words, Herbert Eugene Bolton began his famous essay on the mission as a frontier institution. Bolton believed that Spain's success in colonizing a vast New World reflected the vigor and virility of her frontier institutions. To illustrate this thesis, he contributed valuable studies of the presidio and mission, frontier agencies that helped to establish and extend Spanish military, political, and religious control beyond the boundaries of pacified and settled areas.

The Spaniards also utilized the ranch as a frontier institution. Like the mission and the presidio, the ranch was a multifaceted, multipurpose pioneering agency with economic, political, social, and cultural features. Long before the discovery of America, the effectiveness of pastoral establishments as a means of securing, holding, and developing large tracts of semiarid land had been tested along the Moorish-Iberian frontiers on the Mesa Central of Spain. Afterwards, as the Spaniards moved out from the Caribbean Islands onto the continent and northward into New Mexico, Texas, Arizona, and California, ranchers, accompanied by their flocks and herds, took their own place beside the soldiers and churchmen in the forefront of Spanish advance.

Unlike the mission and presidio, the ranch did not disappear with the passing of the Spanish frontier and the coming of Anglo-Americans to the Southwest. Instead the Anglos adopted the techniques, equipment, even the mores and folklore of the Spanish ranchers. The ranching frontier reappeared, modified and adapted to new circumstances, but basically intact, in the post–Civil War American West. The Anglo-American ranching kingdom not only contributed to the opening and taming of the West, but it also became famous as a unique development peculiarly adapted to the needs of the frontier. Furthermore, the Western ranch was different from any similar institution east of the Mississippi. Even today, the history, literature, economics, and politics of the Anglo cattle kingdom remain a source of interest and study for scholars and laymen seeking to explain the development of the westward movement. Yet if we are to understand the genesis of this institution, we must look not eastward toward the Appalachians but southward toward the Spanish borderlands. For it was here, in the areas conquered and pacified by Spain, that the cattle kingdom had its roots. It was the Spaniards who introduced the first animals, developed the techniques for working vast herds, and established the basis for widespread and profitable pastoral industries in the New World.

During the first decades of Spanish conquest, the livestock, organization, methods, and customs of the Iberian ranching system reached the Indies and became the foundation of all American ranching. Christopher Columbus brought the first animals to Santo Domingo. They multiplied rapidly, and soon the Caribbean Islands supported numerous stock farms that provided the basis for a self-sustaining economy. Island ranches also furnished the meat and animals necessary for the conquest of the mainland. Sheep, cattle, horses, and hogs accompanied the conquistadors from the Indies into Panama, Mexico, Peru, and later northward and southward into all the lands of Spanish America.

Historians have frequently misunderstood or misinterpreted the documents relating to the progenitors of the famous Longhorn cattle of North America. The cows the Spaniards imported to their overseas colonies constituted a breed unique in both Europe and colonial America. These animals varied in color from yellows and duns to deep browns, reds, and blacks. They were distinguished by their long, low-swinging heads, formidable horns, narrow sides, and long legs. The Spanish cattle, unsuited for dairy or draft purposes, were valued chiefly for their tough hides and stringy beef, and they were perfectly adapted to a frontier existence. They were tough, strong stock, characterized by marked feral instincts and often complete wildness. They were able to survive and maintain themselves in country that would have decimated or destroyed herds of weaker and less self-sufficient animals. Conditioned to the semiarid plains of Castile, accustomed to roam untended and uncared for from roundup to roundup, the Spanish cattle made perfect specimens to survive in the unpopulated areas of the Americas—from the pampas of Argentina to the plains of Texas.

These animals were not the famous black cattle *(ganado prieto),* which were carefully bred, nurtured, and trained for the bull ring. Some black cattle were raised in the New World, and some were even introduced into the northern borderlands, but they never constituted more than a single small branch in the family tree of the North American range cow. The Spanish cattle that went into northern Mexico with Ibarra and Rodríquez, into New Mexico with Coronado and Oñate, into Texas with Alonso de León and Escandón, and later up the trail to Kansas with the Texas cowboys were the hybrid result of centuries of selection by survival, a breed developed by and for frontier conditions.

Although in other pastoral industries, notably in raising sheep and horses, the Spaniards introduced new bloodlines and attempted to upgrade their stock, they allowed the range cattle to remain unchanged until the late nineteenth century. The Spanish rancher found his tough, stringy animals remarkably well suited to the frontier environment, and he did little or nothing to improve the quality of his stock. This is not really surprising when one remembers that the Anglo cowmen did little to upgrade their herds until the introduction of Shorthorn and Hereford bulls in the late 1870s. Selective breeding practices could not become widespread until the end of the frontier period, when ranching gave way to stock farming. Only when free grass was exhausted and the open range was closed did ranchers build fenced pastures and corrals where breeding selection could be carefully supervised and controlled.

The Spaniards provided the livestock necessary for the establishment of pastoral industries, and they also developed the equipment and techniques essential to ranching. Cattle and other livestock were raised almost everywhere in Europe and America, but it is important to note that cattle raising and cattle ranching are *not* the same thing. As Charles Bishko pointed out in his study of peninsular stock raising, ranching "implies the ranging of cattle in considerable numbers over extensive grazing grounds for the primary purpose of large scale production of beef and hides."[2] Ranching was an extensive productive enterprise, and it required larger tracts of pasture land and different methods than did the care of a few dairy cows and small herds as an adjunct to agriculture. During the Middle Ages, cattle ranching in western Europe was confined to the Iberian Peninsula. The ranching techniques developed in Spain were transplanted to the Western Hemisphere, where they were modified to meet new conditions imposed by the vast grasslands and sparse population of the North American plains. A few examples will show the Spanish impact on American ranching.

One of the most distinctive features of Spanish ranching was the mounted herdsman. Even before the conquest of the New World, the Spaniards began to carry out most of their ranching activities from horseback. This custom was continued and refined on the American plains. On the other hand, French and English herders were rarely mounted. East of the Appalachians, English colonial stock raisers usually worked their herds on foot, sometimes with the aid of well-trained sheep or cattle dogs. When the Anglo stockman crossed the Mississippi and ventured onto the plains, he discovered that the long distances he had to travel and the mean, cantankerous nature of stock raised on open range required that he copy the Spanish ranching methods.

When the Anglo learned to work cattle from horseback, he also borrowed Spanish riding equipment. Since the Spaniards were mounted herdsmen, it is not surprising that the basic tool of the range industry—the Western stock saddle—was modeled on Spanish prototypes. Each part of the Spanish work saddle or *silla de campo* was designed to aid the vaquero in his ranching chores. The curved cantle and long stirrups provided a comfortable seat for the rider during long hours in the saddle. The high pommel and thick, strong horn served as a roping post and gave additional stability to the horseman. The large, flat Spanish stirrups furnished a firm foothold for the rider chasing cattle across the countryside.

In addition to copying the Spanish saddle and claiming it as his own, the Anglo cowboy also borrowed the *reata* or lariat, a braided rope used to catch and tie cattle and other livestock. Spanish herdsmen experimented with several techniques before they learned the best method for roping the large wild cattle of the American plains. At first the vaqueros tied the end of the lariat to the horse's tail, but they quickly realized that for roping wild cattle the tail rope was both awkward and dangerous. They therefore transferred the lariat to the pommel of the saddle. After throwing his loop, the rider wrapped his rope around the saddle horn, secured the animal, and allowed the saddle to absorb the weight and pull of the captured bull or cow. In Spanish this method of roping was called *da la vuelta*. When the Anglos learned the technique, they shortened and corrupted the Spanish phrase and called it "dally" roping. Some Anglos learned to dally, but many a novice cowhand lacked the necessary speed and dexterity to make fast his rope and still get his hand free of the rope and saddle horn. Most Anglos preferred to tie-fast. They secured the lariat to the saddle with a "tie" or knot. This Anglo system of roping was not as flashy or skillful a procedure as the dally, but it did prevent a generation of Texas cowboys from going through life minus a thumb. Mexican vaqueros continued to dally, however, and their skill in using the lariat to bring down wild stock was a constant source of amazement and admiration to visitors on Spanish-American ranches.

In addition to roping skills, other Spanish ranching methods became common throughout the Americas. Essential to working large numbers of livestock were the roundup and the drive, techniques that Walter Prescott Webb termed the "twin spectacles of the Range."[3] Both the roundup and the drive were perfected by the Spanish *ganaderos* ("cowmen") long before the first Texas cowboy ever tossed a rope over a Longhorn steer. As Webb noted, the roundup was to cattle what the harvest is to wheat, "a gathering of the products of the Plains grass."[4] It was invented to facilitate the sorting of herds that had become mixed on the common pastures and to bring in young stock. The mounted cowhands fanned out in a circle and drove the cattle toward some previously designated central point. There they sorted the cattle according to their brands. Strays or *mostrencos* were turned over to the king's representatives as property of the royal domain. Unbranded animals or *orejanos* were divided among the stockmen.

Spanish laws regulating the livestock industry specified that roundups must be held weekly between the middle of June and the end of November, but there were frequent violations of the rule. In the northern borderlands, Indian raids and unpredictable climate often made weekly roundups impractical. Therefore the Spanish ranchers—and later the Anglos—organized one or two big roundups a year, usually in the spring and fall.

Unfortunately, we have few descriptions of roundups in the Spanish Southwest. Evidently the practice was so common and the procedure so familiar that Spaniards saw no need to explain it. The few descriptions we do have, principally from the journals of foreign travelers, make it clear that the techniques used during the seventeenth and eighteenth centuries were surprisingly similar to those employed by Mexican and Anglo ranchers in the late nineteenth and early twentieth centuries. It is interesting to picture the scene that occurred on the Texas plains in 1788 when missionaries and ranchers combined forces to round up the unbranded stock in the pastures south of San Antonio. Imagine blue-robed Franciscans, cassocks flapping in the breeze; half-clothed Indian herdsmen crouched over the necks of sturdy mustangs; Spanish rancheros, attired in the long leather coats and *botas de ala* ("leggings") typical of the eighteenth-century cowman—all attempting to chase down and brand wild cattle that roamed free and unrestricted over the open countryside.

Spanish ranchers also perfected techniques for moving large numbers of livestock from one place to another. In Spain, sharp contrasts in climate and topography made semiannual changes in grazing lands desirable. Long before coming to the Western Hemisphere, the Iberian herdsmen worked out methods for livestock migration that included a system of communal livestock trails and seasonal pastures. In the New World, too, changing pasture conditions and distant market centers required transmigration of herds and flocks, and peninsular practices were transferred to the Spanish colonies. Throughout the Americas, Spanish ranchers shifted their herds from one grazing area to another. They also took their animals to market "on the hoof," driving them hundreds of miles to fairs, slaughtering pens, and distribution points. The Spanish livestock trade was not so well publicized as the "rivers of beef" that flowed northward out of Texas after the Civil War. Nonetheless, the Spaniards did build up an extensive commerce and perfected the methods and equipment used by the Texas cowboys along the trail to Abilene.

Cattle driving posed a number of problems. Because the Spaniards rarely castrated their stock, they faced the unenviable task of moving large herds of bulls. Spanish ranchers, therefore, relied on trained oxen to tame the cattle and break them to the trail. The vaqueros used a hair rope or halter called a *cabresto* to harness the bulls to the oxen. These huge, plodding beasts patiently led—or dragged—the recalcitrant bulls until they were broken to the trail. Although Anglo cowmen rarely employed the *cabresto,* they frequently used a lead ox or steer on drives. Both Spanish and Anglo ranchers used trained oxen to bring cattle in from the open range.

Another problem arose during livestock migrations. Herds overran plowed and planted fields and caused extensive damage to crops. This brought forth loud protests from the farmers who retaliated by slaughtering stray animals and selling the meat in local markets. In some areas, settlers claimed the migratory herds were more dangerous to life and property than unpacified Indian tribes. In Texas, citizens of San Fernando de Béxar constantly complained about loose stock that roamed the streets and fields of the town. The Spanish viceroys issued a series of regulations requiring every rancher to provide an adequate guard for his stock, but the laws were rarely enforced. Such problems were not very different from those encountered by Texas trail herds in Kansas and Nebraska during the 1860s and 1870s, and the Anglos had little more success than the Spaniards in solving them.

Another important technique utilized by the *ganaderos* was the identification of livestock by the use of brands and earmarks. In frontier areas, where animals were rarely kept in fenced enclosures, herds easily became intermingled and ownership confused. To meet this problem, Spanish ranchers used branding as a simple and effective means for separating and identifying their animals. In the Iberian Peninsula, livestock branding was an old custom dating back to the tenth century, and Iberian sheep and cattle brands became the antecedents of symbols and monograms common to ranches throughout the New World.

In the early sixteenth century, cattle bearing the brand of Hernán Cortés grazed in the Valley of Oaxaca, and a large number of brands owned by early settlers were registered with the *cabildo* of Mexico City. To protect brands and regulate their use, an elaborate code of brand ordinances evolved. The laws required that each stockman have a distinct brand so that his animals could be easily recognized. Anyone who did not have a ranch could not have a branding iron, nor was he permitted to mark stock in any way. Later, ranchers were assigned two brands. One was the permanent range brand *(el fierro para herrar los ganados)* burned into the animal's hide with a hot iron. The second was a sale brand *(el fierro para ventear)* similar to the Anglo-American trail brand. This second mark was usually applied with pitch or other temporary substances, and it was used only at the time of sale or in moving livestock from pasture to market. Numerous laws were enacted in an attempt to discourage thefts, brand alterations, and mavericking. Other ordinances regulated hide hunting, slaughtering, the semiannual roundups, and the use of common pasture and grazing land.

Enforcement of these various ordinances was necessary to the orderly regulation of ranching. This function was carried out by the Mesta—a quasi-governmental organization with responsibility for both formulation and enforcement of livestock laws. Soon after the conquest, the *cabildo* of Mexico City and the leading stockmen of the area established the Mexican Mesta or stockowner's guild. The primary purpose of the Mesta was to further the interests of the ranchers and to deal with problems associated with the rapid growth of the livestock industry. Alcaldes de Mesta were appointed to assign and register brands, supervise roundups, enforce the livestock laws, and adjudicate disputes between cattle and sheep owners. As ranching expanded northward and the pastoral industries increased in importance, new livestock regulations were included in the codes, and additional officials were appointed to enforce them. In many borderlands areas, Mesta officers served as itinerent justices of the peace with authority to investigate murders, thefts, and other crimes.

Laws and ordinances for the regulation and control of ranching activities added significantly to the development of Spanish legal codes. These laws also provided examples for the Anglo-Americans. Western ranchmen of the nineteenth century borrowed liberally from Spanish rules governing branding, slaughtering, and grazing rights; and the Mesta served as a pattern for the powerful stockmen's associations of the trans-Mississippi West.

Spanish ranchers added a colorful and romantic chapter to the history of the Americas. The distinctive dress of the modern cowboy—big hat, boots, spurs, chaps—still reflects the clothing designed by the vaqueros to aid them in their work. Ranching terms such as reata, dally, vaquero, and rodeo enrich the Spanish and English vocabulary. The games and sports of the West are based on ranching practices. Fiestas still feature demonstrations of proficiency with lasso and horse, and the professional rodeo as a form of competitive sport and entertainment is based on the skills and abilities of the cowboy.

Far more important than the strictly technical and social aspects of ranching was the use of the ranch as a frontier institution. Throughout the Americas, ranching served as an effective tool for the settlement and exploitation of frontier areas. Unlike the English, the Spaniards had considerable frontier experience before coming to the Western Hemisphere. They had experimented with various institutions to hold and control frontier areas in medieval Spain, and they transferred many of these agencies to the New World, adapting and modifying them to meet the conditions they found. Thus the frontier fortresses of the Iberian Peninsula became the presidial garrisons of the northern borderlands, the Church modified its methods for conversion and established the mission system, and the ranch became an institution for economic and political development.

In many parts of the New World, opportunities for economic growth were severely limited. For example, in northern Mexico and the southwestern United States, the Spaniards found the flat, semiarid grassland poorly suited to agriculture. Mineral resources were largely undiscovered or unexploitable. Yet the Spaniards, accustomed to the dry plains of Castile, understood the geographical limitations of the region. They quickly adapted to the conditions of climate and topography that they found, and they turned to ranching as a means for utilizing the available natural resources. Cattle, horses, and the by-products of the ranching industry furnished food, tallow, and leather, thus providing a livelihood for those pioneers willing to endure the hardships of frontier life.

In many places, ranching constituted the major economic activity of the settlers. Those who came, or were sent, to the farflung outposts of Empire along New Spain's northern borders had little to invest. The Indians were difficult to civilize, and labor was scarce. Ranching offered a partial solution to these problems. With a few animals for breeding stock and access to grazing land, the rancher was in business. The half-wild Spanish stock required little care, and throughout the Southwest the frontier ranchers became owners of huge herds and masters of seemingly interminable stretches of grassland.

To aid ranching development, the Spanish monarchs issued land grants that recognized the need of the livestock industry for large tracts of pasture and grazing lands. In determining the size of land grants, the Anglo thought in terms of acres. The Spaniard thought in terms of land utilization, and Spanish land grants reflected either agricultural or pastoral use. In Spanish America, land suitable for irrigation and farming was divided into small units called *labores.* Like the Anglo quarter section, the *labor* was intended as a land unit sufficient to produce food crops for a single family. Grasslands were alloted in blocks large enough to provide adequate grazing for livestock. The *sitio de ganado menor*, a grant of approximately 2,000 acres, was used for raising sheep, goats, and other small animals. A more extensive tract, the *sitio de ganado mayor* or league, was designed for large animals, such as cattle and horses. The league varied in size from 4,300 to 4,500 acres.

Throughout the Spanish colonies, livestock owners frequently received three or four leagues of land, and it was not uncommon for them to acquire or lease additional acreage. Some ranchers put together vast landholdings based on livestock grants. In Texas, for example, Enrique Villareal owned land that included most of the present-day city of Corpus Christi. José Narcisco Cabazos held title to more than 600,000 acres in what are now Cameron, Willacy, and Kenedy counties, and José de la Garza claimed 59.5 leagues of land in the Río Grande Valley.

In addition to individual grants, the Spaniards provided for communal or collective holdings. In ancient times, the towns of Castile owned or controlled extensive territory. These municipal lands included *baldíos* or *dehesas*—vacant pasture and grazing land in the open countryside. Stockmen pastured animals on the *dehesa* under license from the government until such time as the land was granted to an individual. This system was continued in the New World. Throughout the American Southwest, most of the unclaimed grazing land was made available to all stockowners. Hemmed in by restrictions imposed by Eastern legislatures, the Anglo, like his Spanish predecessor, turned to this open range or free grass in order to obtain sufficient forage for large-scale ranching activities. On both the Spanish and Anglo frontiers, common pasture provided grass for large herds of livestock on the semiarid plains, while the river valleys and well-watered areas were reserved for farming and agriculture.

Ranching did not always dominate the economic life of the borderlands. In many places, Hispanic-American frontier development followed the pattern later outlined by Frederick Jackson Turner for the Anglo-American West: exploration, mining, ranching—each frontier served as guide and stimulus to the next. Gold and silver rushes in nineteenth-century Colorado, Nevada, and Montana resembled earlier mining ventures in sixteenth-century New Spain, where the discovery of mineral resources attracted ranching enterprises for the support of the camps and towns. Not all stockmen, of course, responded to the lure of easy riches and new markets. Great ranches developed in areas of Mexico that were completely lacking in mines. In the United States, much of the cattle country was not mining country—for example, Kansas, Nebraska, Oklahoma, and the Texas Panhandle. At the same time, the symbiotic relationship between mining and ranching on both the Spanish and Anglo-American frontiers should not be overlooked.

In northern New Spain, the livestock industry usually expanded in conjunction with the advance of the mining frontier. Wherever mines opened, towns grew up, and the demand for meat, hides, and tallow increased. Soon large ranches or *estancias* appeared throughout the mining districts. For instance, in 1564, reports from Nombre de Dios showed 250,000 head of sheep and cattle grazing on the pasture lands surrounding the mines, and the number in other areas was much the same.

Ranching not only supported mining and other industries, but it also helped sustain Spanish imperial policy throughout the frontier regions. Although not designed as political or religious institutions, the ranches contributed to the development of the presidios and missions in their attempts to conquer, convert, and civilize the American Indian. Political and economic control of the natives was essential to Spanish expansion in the New World. Hindered by a relatively small population, numerous European commitments, and a vast area to dominate, Spaniards felt they must exploit the Amerindian, Hispanicize him, and make him a useful, productive laborer. This was fairly easy among the civilized tribes of Mexico and Peru, but, on the frontiers, this obligation—undertaken primarily by the missionaries and military commanders—was more difficult.

Ranching proved to be an important complement to the work of conversion by enabling the Church fathers to offset some of the expenses of mission upkeep through profits derived from ranch products. Every mission from Florida to California had extensive pasture lands stocked with sheep, goats, oxen, horses, and cattle. These animals supplied hides, wool, and tallow for mission industries. The padres taught their charges to tan and weave and to make shoes, harness, candles, and other items for use in the mission or for sale to nearby settlements and garrisons. The ranches furnished meat for the Indian to hunt and eat and thus somewhat lessened the chance he would "take off for the hills" in search of deer, buffalo, and other game. Stock raising also aided in the difficult task of civilizing and Hispanicizing the neophytes. Since the techniques were similar to the chase and hunt, ranching utilized skills the natives already possessed and made it easier for the nomadic Indian to adjust to a new and more sedentary way of life.

In other ways, too, the ranch advanced the work of political expansion and control. Ranching was a valuable asset to the presidios, those tiny outposts of empire charged with responsibility for protecting the borders and holding back the flood of foreign intruders. These frontier fortresses were located in areas far removed from main communication and supply routes. Throughout the colonial period, presidial commanders and provincial governors complained of difficulty in obtaining food, clothing, and equipment. The ranchers helped alleviate these shortages by providing not only meat but also oxen for plowing, mules for hauling supplies, and, most important, horses for mounting the presidial troops. On the frontier, mounted men were essential to maintain communications between widely separated points, to patrol the extensive boundaries, and to wage war against the Plains tribes. The horse was necessary to the maintenance of Spanish authority, and local ranches were the main source of supply.

It might be noted that the Anglo-Americans also used the ranch to implement government policy. Unlike the Spaniard, the Anglo did not attempt to exploit or civilize the Amerindian. Rather, the Anglo hoped to eliminate the native or at least to contain and control him. To this end, the United States established a series of Indian reservations. But, as a ward of the government, the Indian had to be fed and cared for, and he had to be kept on the reservation. Western ranches supplied horses for mounting the United States cavalry patrols and also furnished beef for government food issues. Finally, when government aid stopped and farming failed, the reservation Indian turned to ranching in an attempt to wrest a living from the inhospitable plains.

The Spaniards, and later the Anglo-Americans, found the ranch ideally suited to frontier conditions, and they made the ranch a weapon for the conquest and taming of the frontier. The ranchers' migratory wealth could be removed from the raids and incursions of enemies. Ranch products could be transported to market without the use of highly developed or sophisticated transportation facilities. Ranching adapted itself to the lack of both human and natural resources in the sparsely populated area along the frontier. Throughout the Americas—from Argentina to Texas—Spanish frontiersmen left a rich legacy in equipment and techniques for working livestock, in legal codes and stockmen's associations, and in vocabulary and folklore. But, more important, the Spanish ranchers were the first to exploit the American plains and make them not only habitable but also productive and profitable. In the nineteenth century, Spanish livestock and ranching techniques spread northward from Texas into the trans-Mississippi West and served to create new fortunes, a new society, a whole new way of life—the legendary Western cattle kingdom. Until the Industrial Revolution provided the tools to bring farming and industry, ranching dominated the economic, political, and cultural life of both the Spanish and Anglo-American West. The ranch outlasted the mission and presidio and became the only Spanish frontier institution to survive intact into the modern age.

Bibliographical Note

In comparison to the hundreds of studies of Anglo-American ranching, little has been written on Spanish-American ranching practices. Most of the material for this essay has been drawn from manuscript records and printed documentary sources. The principal manuscript collections utilized were the Béxar, Laredo, and Saltillo archives (manuscripts, photostats, transcripts, and microfilm) housed at The University of Texas at Austin. Particularly valuable was a long treatise prepared by the ranchers of San Fernando de Béxar, "Representación que la República de la villa de San Fernando ha puesto a los pies de Rafael Martíinez Pachuco," which traces the development of the livestock industry at San Antonio from 1718 to 1787.

Documents relating to the livestock industry of northern Mexico and Spanish Texas and Louisiana are to be found in Herbert Eugene Bolton, ed., *Athanase de Mézières and the Louisiana Texas Frontier, 1768–1780*, 2 vols. (Cleveland: Arthur H. Clark Co., 1914); *Documentos para la historia eclesiástica y civil de la provincia de Texas* (Madrid: Ediciones J. Porrúa Turanzas, 1961); Lawrence Kinnaird, ed., "Spain in the Mississippi Valley, 1765–1794," American Historical Association *Annual Report for 1945*, 3 parts (Washington, D.C.: Government Printing Office, 1946); Pierre Margry, ed., *Découvertes et établissements des français dan l'ouest et dans le sud de l'Amérique Septentrionale, 1614–1754, Mémoires et documents originaux*, 6 vols. (Paris: Impr. D. Jouaust, 1875–1886); and A. B. Thomas, *Teodoro de Croix and the Northern Frontier of New Spain, 1776–1783* (Norman: University of Oklahoma Press, 1941).

Journals, travel accounts, and diaries for the colonial period also contain valuable material, particularly Fray José Francisco López, "The Texas Missions in 1785," translated by J. Autry Dabbs in *Preliminary Studies*, III, No. 6 (Austin: Texas Catholic Historical Society, 1934); Fray Juan Agustín de Morfi, *Diario y derrotero, 1777–1781*, Edición de Eugenio del Hoyo y Malcolm D. McLean (Monterrey: Biblioteca del Instituto Tecnológico de Estudios Superiores de Monterrey, 1967); Morfi, *Viaje de Indios y diario del Nuevo México*, Edición de Vito Alessio Robles (Mexico City: Antigua Librería Robredo de José Porrúa e Hijos, 1935). Descriptions of horse and cattle roundups in the eighteenth century are found in Marie François Pierre de Pagès, *Travels Round the World in the Years 1767, 1768, 1769, 1770, 1771*, 2 vols. (London: J. Murray, 1791), and Donald Jackson, ed., *The Journals of Zebulon Montgomery Pike*, 2 vols. (Norman: University of Oklahoma Press, 1966).

Some secondary sources contain useful information on the development of Spanish ranching methods. For the Iberian backgrounds, see Julius Klein, *The Mesta: A Study in Spanish Economic History, 1274–1836* (Cambridge, Mass.: Harvard University Press, 1920), and Charles J. Bishko, "The Peninsular Background of Latin American Cattle Ranching," *Hispanic American Historical Review*, XXXIII (November, 1952), 491–515. The introduction of Spanish livestock into the Caribbean area is discussed in Carl O. Sauer, *The Early Spanish Main* (Berkeley: University of California Press, 1966). Livestock raising in New Spain (Mexico) is the subject of three authors: Donald D. Brand, "The Early

History of the Range Cattle Industry in Northern Mexico," *Agricultural History*, XXXV (July, 1961), 132–139; José Mantesanz, "Introducción de la ganadería en Nueva España, 1521–1535," *Historia Mexicana*, XIV (April, 1964), 522–566; and Richard J. Morrisey, "The Establishment and Northward Expansion of Cattle Ranching in New Spain," Ph.D. thesis, University of California at Berkeley, 1949. The most valuable works on institutional aspects of Mexican colonial ranching are François Chevalier, *Land and Society in Colonial Mexico–the Great Hacienda* (Berkeley: University of California Press, 1963), and William H. Dusenberry, *The Mexican Mesta: The Administration of Ranching in Colonial Mexico* (Urbana: University of Illinois Press, 1963).

Spanish riding styles and equestrian equipment are discussed in Nicolás Rangel, *Historia del toreo en México, época Colonial, 1529–1821* (Mexico City: Imprenta Manuel León Sánchez, 1924); Juan Suárez de Peralta, *Tratado de la jineta y de la Brida* (Mexico City, 1580; reprint Mexico City: José Alvarez de Villar, 1950); and Arthur Woodward, "Saddles in the New World," *Quarterly of the Los Angeles County Museum*, X (Summer, 1953), 1–5. Leovigildo Islas Escárcega, *Vocabulario campesino nacional, objeciones y ampliaciones al vocabulario agrícola Nacional* (Mexico City: Instituto de Investigaciones Lingüísticas, 1935), is invaluable for definitions of equestrian and ranching terminology and some illustrations of the use of equipment.

Ranching in the Spanish borderlands is briefly discussed by Odie B. Faulk in *The Last Years of Spanish Texas, 1778–1821* (The Hague: Mouton & Co., 1964), and "Ranching in Spanish Texas," *Hispanic American Historical Review*, XLIV (May, 1965), 257–266. LeRoy Graf, "The Economic History of the Lower Río Grande Valley, 1820–1875," 2 vols., Ph.D. thesis, Harvard, 1942, includes a chapter on colonial Spanish ranching practices. A popular writer, Jo Mora, presents some interesting material and illustrations for Spanish California in *Californios: The Saga of the Hard Riding Vaqueros, America's First Cowboys* (Garden City: Doubleday & Co., 1949), and *Trail Dust and Saddle Leather* (New York: Charles Scribner's Sons, 1946), but unfortunately Mora gives no references or bibliography and the authenticity of some of his material is questionable. The introduction of Spanish livestock into Texas and an outline of areas for further research are presented by Sandra L. Myres in "The Spanish Cattle Kingdom in the Province of Texas," *Texana*, IV (Fall, 1966), 233–246.

NOTES

1. Herbert Eugene Bolton, "The Mission as a Frontier Institution in the Spanish American Colonies," *American Historical Review*, XXIII (October, 1917), 42.

2. Charles J. Bishko, "The Peninsular Background of Latin American Cattle Ranching," *Hispanic American Historical Review*, XXXIII (November, 1952), 494.

3. Walter Prescott Webb, *The Great Plains* (New York: Grosset and Dunlap, 1957), p. 255.

4. Ibid.

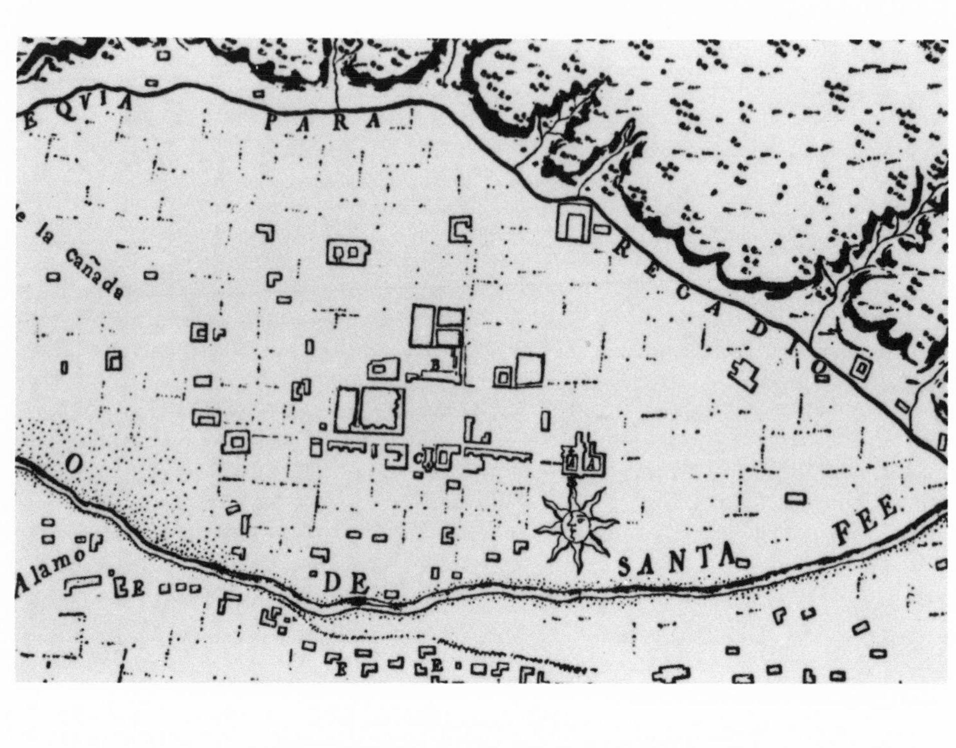
EQVIA
PARA
RECADIO
e la cañada
O
DE
SANTA
FEE
Alamo

7

Settlement Patterns and Village Plans in Colonial New Mexico*

Marc Simmons

Editor's Introduction

Along with the mission and the presidio, the civilian settlement constituted one of the basic institutions of Spanish-Mexican frontier life. As Marc Simmons explains, frontier conditions, both in time and place, altered Hispanic settlement patterns. Thus, the hacienda of seventeenth-century New Mexico gave way to the small farm or *rancho* by the eighteenth century. Despite Hispanic municipal tradition and government efforts to concentrate people in towns, frontiersmen in New Mexico found it more advantageous to settle away from urban centers. One result of the tendency of Hispanos toward dispersal, Simmons suggests, was that the most defensible towns in New Mexico may have been those of the Pueblo Indians.

The student who understands the nature of settlement patterns in New Mexico should understand that those same patterns may not have existed

*Reprinted with the permission of the author and the publisher from the *Journal of the West*, 8 (1969): 7–21.

in New Spain's other frontier provinces. We need further study of this question, especially of its comparative dimensions. In the case of the Californios, for example, it seems clear that they, like their New Mexico counterparts, preferred to settle outside of towns. That distressed the Franciscans, who saw those settlers as retarding the growth of towns, shirking civic duties, and setting a bad example for Indians by living in "remote regions without King to rule or Pope to excommunicate them."[1] Here, however, the similarity seems to end. California's *pobladores* found it more difficult to acquire land than did the New Mexicans. At the end of the Spanish period in California, Franciscan missions controlled nearly all of the arable coastal land from San Diego to San Francisco and Franciscans had successfully opposed the granting of lands to private individuals.[2]

Marc Simmons, who earned a B.A. at the University of Texas and the Ph.D. at the University of New Mexico, works as a historian and a farrier on his isolated, colonial-style *lugar* near Cerrillos, New Mexico. Writing by daylight and gas lamp, Simmons has written a prodigious quantity of books and articles and established himself as one of the leading authorities on northern New Spain and New Mexico in particular. Among his books are *Spanish Government in New Mexico* (Albuquerque: 1968), *The Little Lion of the Southwest: A Life of Manuel Antonio Chaves* (Chicago: 1973), *Witchcraft in the Southwest: Spanish and Indian Supernaturalism on the Rio Grande* (Flagstaff: 1974), and *New Mexico: A History* (New York: 1977).

NOTES

1. Fr. José Señán to the Viceroy, the Marques de Branciforte, Mexico City, May 14, 1796, in *The Letters of José Señán, O. F. M. Mission San Buenaventura, 1796–1823.* Trans. Paul D. Nathan and Lesley Byrd Simpson ([San Francisco]: 1962), p. 5.

2. Manuel P. Servín, "The Secularization of the California Missions: A Reappraisal," *Southern California Quarterly*, 2 (1965): 135–37.

Settlement Patterns and Village Plans in Colonial New Mexico

Patterns of settlement in New Mexico fluctuated during the two and one-quarter centuries of Spanish rule. Expansion and contraction of the European population was determined by availability of arable land, territorial requirements of the Pueblo Indians, and pressures of hostile nomadic tribes. Study of the influences which shaped settlement patterns in New Mexico and review of attempts by government officials and others to regulate the settling of new lands and towns offer insights into some of the economic and social problems of colonial times.

When the Spaniards reached the Southwest in 1540, they found the largest concentration of Pueblo Indians along the upper Río Grande and its tributaries with outlying nuclei of settlement to the west at Acoma, Zuñi and Hopi and to the east at Pecos Pueblo and the villages beyond the Manzano Mountains. The Río Grande drainage offered suitable home sites for the Pueblo people with sufficient land to meet their agricultural needs. The Spanish colonists as well, found the environment attractive, so they fixed their earliest farms, ranches, and towns on lands adjacent to the Pueblos. To the present day heavy population clusters occur in this same area.

Extensive exploration in the early colonial period quickly dashed hopes that New Mexico would yield treasure in gold, silver, or other profitable minerals. The fading of prospects for a mining boom meant that population growth and economic development would lack the spectacular quality which attended the colonization of some of the other frontier provinces. New Mexico, in fact, to the end of the colonial era remained thinly populated and dependent upon royal subsidies to meet her expenses. Land served as the principal source of what little wealth she possessed.

The Legal Basis of Settlement

The ultimate proprietorship of all lands in New Mexico belonged to the Spanish sovereign. By royal concession, private individuals or groups of persons might apply for lands, and after fulfilling certain legal requirements, receive a grant called a *gracia* or *merced real.*[1] All properties not conveyed in an official grant remained in the possession of the crown and were known as *tierras realengas y baldías* (royal and vacant lands). These served as a kind of reservoir from which new grants were made and to which lands whose grantees could not acquire final title were returned.[2]

Land grants in New Mexico were generally of three categories: (1) municipal concessions made by the crown to an individual *(poblador principal)* or to a group of settlers who wished to found a new community;[3] (2) private grants to farmers, stockraisers and others who agreed to develop rural property; and (3) Pueblo Indian grants, which awarded title and guaranteed full possession to the Indians of all lands they occupied or used.[4]

The laws regarding the laying out of new towns throughout the Spanish realm were extensive and precise. Municipal planning was to follow the grid-system, which required straight parallel streets with rectangular blocks and one or more rectangular plazas, the principal one to be designated as the *plaza mayor.*[5] Lots were distributed to the citizens *(vecinos)* or were reserved for government and church buildings. Lands on the fringe of the municipality were set aside as commons *(ejidos),* pasture lands *(dehesas)* and municipal lands *(propios),* revenues from which helped defray community expenses.[6] Carefully composed ordinances provided that town sites be selected after consideration had been given to matters of health, climate and defense. With regard to the last of these, settlers were instructed to erect jointly and with the greatest possible haste some kind of palisade or dig a ditch around the main plaza so that Indians could not harm them. In addition, they were encouraged to fortify their own houses.[7]

The royal regulations regarding conditions for the fulfillment of terms for private grants were somewhat less specific, since local conditions often determined particular requirements. A concession of land, however, was sure to include a demand that the recipient place it under cultivation and reside on it for a specified number of years. Restrictions ordinarily included the following: no grant could be made which was prejudicial to the rights of the Indians or which caused injury to a third party; a grant of land conveyed no judicial powers; and mineral rights were retained by the crown.[8]

New Mexico Land and Settlement Procedures

The colonial governors possessed broad powers with regard to the founding of new towns and the assignment of lands and water rights. The contract awarded to New Mexico's founder, Juan de Oñate, set forth in explicit terms his prerogatives in this area. It is apparent that the Ordinances of 1573 concerning the laying out of towns and other laws of the time served as the basis for the authority assigned to him. In addition to determining the location and boundaries of new communities, Oñate was empowered to decide whether the settlement should be designated a *ciudad, villa,* or *pueblo* and to organize the municipal government.[9]

Instructions to Don Pedro de Peralta, who assumed the governorship of New Mexico in 1609, provided for the establishment of the villa of Santa Fé, and the terms contained therein also seem to be in conformity with the current legislation.[10] The conduct of succeeding governors furnishes evidence that they were fully cognizant of the laws of the Indies that pertained to the establishment of towns and the distribution of lands.[11] Upon founding the villa of Albuquerque, Governor Francisco Cuervo y Váldez certified that he acted in accordance with royal regulations contained in title seven, book four of the *Recopilación*.[12]

Unfortunately in practically all instances the official records of the actual founding of New Mexico colonial towns are missing. The *instrumentos de la fundación*, which conveyed legal status to a new community, often contained the petition of the person or persons seeking to establish a settlement, the authorization of the governor, and an account of the formal proceedings whereby the petitioners were placed in possession.[13] Were these instruments available today, doubtless they would shed much light on the motives of Spaniards who participated in expanding New Mexico's frontier and would also aid in solving certain legal problems of modern towns whose foundations date back to Spanish colonial times.[14]

In viewing Spain's land grant policy and the influence it had on settlement patterns, it is important to keep in mind that ultimate title to all lands was retained by the king. Grants were made for occupation and use, the subject taking the rents and profits.[15] If an individual failed to meet the requirements of his grant, or if a grant was abandoned because of the Indian menace, as was often the case, the lands reverted to the crown. Even lands designated as belonging to municipalities remained subject to close royal supervision. This may be noted particularly for town lots or outlying lands which the town corporation failed to assign to citizens.[16] Occasionally after lots had been assigned, the government found it necessary to reclaim them for official use. Such a case occurred in the villa of Santa Fé in 1788 when construction work and expansion of the presidio necessitated the retaking of the lots and houses of three citizens, who were compensated for their loss out of the *tierras realengas y baldías*.[17]

The Seventeenth-Century Pattern

The statements above provide necessary background for an understanding of the introduction and spread of settlement in colonial New Mexico. The initial attempt to found a Spanish community was made by

Oñate at San Gabriel near San Juan Pueblo. By the spring of 1610, however, the effort at this site had been given up, and under viceregal orders the colonists moved southward to establish the villa of Santa Fé.[18] Governor Pedro de Peralta, who was entrusted with carrying out the transfer to the new location, received instructions on the creation of a municipal government and the manner in which lands were to be distributed to citizens. Settlers who received lots in the new villa were required to live upon them for ten years, and if they should absent themselves for three months continuously without permission of the municipal authorities, they were to forfeit all property and rights of citizenship.[19]

Down to the Pueblo revolt of 1680, Santa Fé remained the only formally organized community in the province, as the old San Gabriel settlement was totally abandoned.[20] During this period a trend was established which was carried over and reinforced in the following century: the tendency for the majority of the population to become dispersed throughout the rural areas in isolated farms, ranches and hamlets.

By tradition the Spaniard was a town dweller, accustomed to residing in communities welded into a unit by the practical necessity of defense and the common need to produce an adequate food supply. In New Mexico, as in other remote districts of northern New Spain, the municipal tradition or "sense of community" was greatly weakened and in some cases broke down altogether. This occurred, paradoxically, when the needs of defense and economic coöperation appeared the greatest.

During the seventeenth century, the small European population labored to sustain and defend the missionary friars and to extract what meager rewards it could from the province's limited resources. Land grants were made to a number of Spanish families, the more affluent of which founded fairly prosperous haciendas. In other cases simple farmsteads strung along river or stream courses were developed by the rural folk. The principal areas of occupation were the valleys north of Santa Fé and the middle Río Grande flood-plain from the Santo Domingo plains southward through the Albuquerque and Belen valleys. The Spaniards favored these regions because the best agricultural lands were situated here as were the heaviest concentrations of the Pueblo Indian population.

The native towns were distributed in *encomienda* to the leading colonists, who received from them an annual tribute, principally in maize and cotton mantas. Of greater economic significance to the majority of the settlers was Indian labor required on farms and ranches. The going wage was half a *real* a day until 1659, at which time it was increased to a full *real* a day by Governor López de Mendizábal.[21] There is abundant evidence, however, that even this nominal sum was not always maintained, the colonists preferring to squeeze labor out of the Indians while neglecting to compensate them.

The Spaniards sought to locate themselves close to exploitable labor and within easy range of their *encomienda* grants. During the first two-thirds of the seventeenth century, the ratio of Spaniard to Indian was such that the number of potential workers probably exceeded the labor demands of the colonists. After 1665, however, famine, pestilence, and raids by nomadic tribes on the Pueblo people so depleted their numbers that the village Indians were hard-pressed to meet the labor requirements of the colonists. In fact, one of their chief complaints at the time of the Pueblo revolt was that the Spaniards so burdened them with tasks, that they had little time left to care for their own fields.

The more prosperous ranches might have developed in New Mexico a settlement pattern similar to that which soon appeared in the neighboring province of Nueva Vizcaya, with widely-scattered large properties supported by the labor of dependent Indians or poor mestizos. The Pueblo revolt of 1680, however, extinguished the Spanish settlement clusters in the upper Río Grande Valley and forced a withdrawal of surviving colonists to the El Paso district down-river. When colonization was resumed some twelve years later, new patterns emerged.[22]

New Trends of the Eighteenth Century

In the years following the Pueblo revolt and the reconquest of New Mexico by the Spaniards, the character of settlement underwent a significant change. From 1700 to the end of the Spanish period, loose agglomerations of small farmsteads termed *ranchos* became the typical unit of colonization, in marked contrast to the seventeenth century during which the *hacienda* had predominated. In considerable measure, this shift from large land holdings to farms of more modest size may be attributed to the decrease in Pueblo Indian population, which greatly reduced the labor supply, and to the increase in the numbers of Spanish colonists, whose arrival created a heavy demand for farmlands in the old core area of the Río Grande Valley.[23]

By 1695 Diego de Vargas had reclaimed New Mexico for the Spanish crown, missions had been reestablished, the villa of Santa Fé had been put in some order and a large number of colonists concentrated there in anticipation of the reoccupation of outlying areas. A survey shortly was made of abandoned farms and ranches, and lands were distributed to both new and old settlers. In some cases it was discovered that Indians had built pueblos on the foundations of former Spanish settlements. Tano people, for example, had moved into such a location in the valley of the Santa Cruz River. As recolonization proceeded they were evicted and the new villa of Santa Cruz de la Cañada was created on the site.[24]

Governor Vargas was eager to found new towns, although orders from the superior government instructed him to keep the settlers together for better defense.[25] Within a brief time, new communities appeared and advances were begun into regions which had not previously known European settlement. Since the population expanded far beyond previous limits, it becomes possible to place in sharper focus the distribution patterns for the later colonial years.

Description of Life

New Mexico was essentially a rural province dominated by a rural population living in dozens of small communities. Even in the several villas there is little evidence of true urbanism since the people did not group their houses compactly but scattered them over the neighboring countryside to be near their fields. An examination of the several categories of "village types" which can be defined for the late colonial period will serve to illustrate the direction and character which the pattern of settlement assumed. New Mexican communities may be categorized as *villas* and *poblaciones* or *plazas* for the European population, and for the Indians, *pueblos* and *reducciones*.

The Villas

No New Mexican municipality ever attained the rank of *ciudad*. The formal villas, however, numbered four and included Santa Fé, Albuquerque, Santa Cruz de la Cañada, and El Paso del Norte. All were poorly organized and had populations of probably under 2,500, conditions which elicited the following terse comment from Fray Francisco Domínguez in 1776. Regarding Santa Fé, he declared, "Its appearance, design, arrangement, and plan do not correspond to its status as a *villa*." And he observed that in New Spain there were *pueblos* (a less pretentious title than *villa*) which had far more to recommend them than Santa Fé, a town that "in the final analysis lacked everything."[26]

According to George Kubler, the original plan of Santa Fé had embodied the royal regulations of 1573 for the laying out of new towns, so that this *villa* "of all Hispanic cities in the New World is a paradigm of these ordinances."[27] This statement, however, represents something of an exaggeration. There may have been more regularity to the *villa* in the seventeenth century than in the period after the Pueblo revolt, but at no time did it conform in more than a rudimentary way to the grid-system or to the requirement that adequate fortifications be provided. True, there was a *plaza mayor* fronting on the governor's residence and offices, and perhaps a secondary plaza existed to the west of San Miguel Church, but as to carefully marked streets required by the grid-pattern there were none.[28] Domínguez reported only the semblance of a single street for the entire *villa* in 1776.[29]

This lack of order in the municipal plan developed, not because of the negligence of local government officials, but through the willful determination of Santa Fé citizens to place their residences close to their fields, which were spread along the narrow valley of the Santa Fé River. They desired not only convenient access to farm plots, but wished to keep a constant surveillance over them to prevent the loss of crops to thieves and wild animals. As a result of this scattering, the limits of the *villa* measured about three leagues in circumference by the third quarter of the eighteenth century.[30]

Apparently the formlessness of the community of Santa Fé was repeated in the remaining *villas*. Bishop Tamarón in 1760 reported that at Santa Cruz de la Cañada there was no true town, the settlers being distributed over a wide area.[31] The people of El Paso preferred to live near their vineyards located several leagues above and below the *villa*,[32] while at Albuquerque only twenty-four houses were situated in the vicinity of the church, the rest being scattered for a league up-stream.[33] Each *villa* did possess a plaza adjacent to the main church with "town houses" of prominent families and perhaps a government building or two on the square or nearby. Otherwise, homes and small businesses were randomly placed according to the needs of their owners, and in defiance of colonial legislation which demanded adherence to an orderly plan of municipal development.

Poblaciones and Plazas

In New Mexico the loosely-grouped Spanish *ranchos* were generally referred to as *poblaciones*, or if the population consolidated for mutual defense, as *plazas*. The term "plaza," and its derivative "placita," thus were employed in this province to mean a town or village. A very small place was sometimes called merely a *lugar*.[34]

A *rancho* consisted of one or more Spanish households located adjacent to farm and orchard lands. The agricultural plots were small and generally long and narrow as a result of the Spanish custom of subdividing among all the heirs.[35] Land grants were usually apportioned along ditch or stream frontage—those made to Ojo Caliente settlers in 1793 were 150 *varas* wide—with the strip extending sometimes as much as one mile back from the water.[36]

In frontier zones *ranchos* were often established informally, that is, without government sanction, by poor family heads who owned no lands in the more settled central regions and who simply did not wish to abide by the proper legal forms. In 1772, Governor Mendinueta suggested that perhaps the majority of those living on *ranchos* were "intrusive owners of their lands or voluntary holdings."[37] If the farms prospered and survived Indian attack, the original settler or his descendants later might apply for a formal grant.

Scattered *ranchos* or "houses of the field," as they were occasionally termed, were the most characteristic units of rural New Mexico.[38] Even when the farmsteads were dispersed over several leagues, however, a church built by the settlers served as a focal point for community activity. Under pressure of severe Indian raids in the late eighteenth century, rural people increasingly forsook their isolated *ranchos* and congregated in small fortified towns or *plazas*. In such instances, permission was usually sought from the governor through a formal petition, and regulations regarding construction of fortifications were received and executed.

Walled towns were no novelty to the Spaniard. Fortified villages were a common feature on the Moorish frontier in Spain, and at least one authority asserts that the fortifications for the military camp of Santa Fé de Granada constructed by Ferdinand and Isabella served as the forerunner of defensive establishments in the New World.[39] Cities protected by walls arose in the Antilles and in those districts of New Spain subject to enemy attack. The villa of Santa Fé had an eight-foot wall with parapets, portions of which survived well into the nineteenth century. And as a defensive measure, the lieutenant-governor at El Paso in 1780 proposed that a wall be constructed around that town, though it seems nothing was done.[40]

On the New Mexico frontier, the settlers usually preferred not to construct a separate wall to shield communities from Indian assault; rather, the common practice was to place houses contiguously about a central plaza. The outer walls were left devoid of windows, livestock could be corralled in the square during attack, and the single gate barred. Often there were towers or *torreones* constructed in a circular or polygonal fashion. Defensive *plazas* of this kind were known at Chimayó, Truchas, Las Trampas, Taos, Ojo Caliente, Cebolleta and elsewhere.[41]

The type of *plaza* just described was comparatively large, was composed of a number of families, and possessed the aspect of a true town. Similar to it was the "restricted plaza" or fortified dwelling of a single extended family. Such residential clusters of kin were often known by the lineage surname, and those of more imposing nature were designated haciendas.[42] The hacienda or *casa grande* frequently had extensive walls, towers, parapets, and other defensive features similar to those found on the wealthy estates of northern New Spain.[43]

Fortified *plazas* and haciendas in varying degrees conformed to the royal ordinances which laid down measures to be taken for defense. As indicated, the same could not be said for the individual *ranchos* which were located haphazardly according to no particular plan. In certain instances, however, it seems the owners of these humble farmsteads did give some attention to the protection of their families and property. The result was a unique arrangement known as the *casa-corral* unit. As described by Conway it consisted of

> a dwelling—usually the conventional one-story adobe structure—with a corral or yard for holding livestock adjoining it in the rear. The walls of the corral were frequently as high as the walls of the house and of one piece with them. A door led directly from the dwelling into the corral . . . and the general impression was of a small fortress with stout, high walls, few openings and a compact, economical design.[44]

This kind of family unit clearly derived from the Ordinances of 1573 which required "houses to be constructed so that horses and household animals can be kept therein, the courtyards and stockyards being as large as possible to insure health and cleanliness, . . . and to be planned so they can serve as . . . a fortress."[45] Admittedly however, as a defensive structure, the New Mexican *casa-corral* unit was far less ambitious than the original laws intended.

Settlers on the edges of the province in the late eighteenth and early nineteenth centuries frequently petitioned the superior authorities for license to desert their homes and retreat to relative safety in the Río Grande Valley. In almost every case, their petitions were denied. Many left the frontier anyway, unmindful of threats of dire penalties. Cases of this kind were common in the Ojo Caliente-Chama district and at other points.[46] In 1805, for example, settlers at Cebolleta beyond the Río Puerco abandoned their community because of Navajo incursions, but they soon were ordered to return by Commandant General Nemesio Salcedo, who promised to send troops to punish the Indians.[47]

Indian Towns

These were of three kinds: (1) those of the Pueblo Indians; (2) the settlements of *genízaros;* and (3) the *reducciones* for members of nomadic tribes. As suggested, the colonial era saw a general reduction in the area occupied by the Pueblo peoples. This trend, which had begun as early as A.D. 1300, was greatly accelerated after the Spanish conquest, so that the Pueblo population and number of villages steadily declined. Remaining Indians concentrated into ever larger communities which were closely integrated and carefully organized for defense.[48]

The strategic value and secure shelter afforded by the pueblos was obvious, even to the Spaniard. Governor Mendinueta in 1772 urged a law with teeth in it which would require settlers to live in compact towns like the Indians.[49] The colonists, however, appear to have been less perturbed by enemy raids than were the Pueblo people; at least, they could be induced to take defensive measures only under the most severe pressure.

Many settlers in the Taos Valley, one of the areas most vulnerable to Comanche and Ute attack, spent a great deal of time in the eighteenth century living inside Taos Pueblo.[50] A *plaza* and fortified houses of their own had proven inadequate, so they took up more secure homes with the Indians. Father Domínguez in 1776 said of the pueblo, "Its plan resembles that of those walled cities with bastions and towers that are described to us in the Bible."[51] And he mentions heavy gates, fortified towers, a very high wall and solid blocks of houses. While all the pueblos were not as well-defended as this one, nevertheless, they served as a far more effective refuge for their people than did the loose communities of the Spaniards.

The settlements of *genízaros* represent a special case, and as a village type they may be classed as a variant of the Indian pueblo. Originally the *genízaros* were Indian captives or slaves of nomadic tribes who were ransomed by the Spanish government. Parceled out among the colonists, they became domestic servants or laborers. As neophytes they were given Christian names and religious instruction. Unfortunately many were mistreated by their Spanish masters and became apostates. Others, however, with the support of Franciscan missionaries petitioned for permission to found their own settlements on the frontier. Believing in the justice of the *genízaro* complaints, the Governor of New Mexico ordered that all who were abused might apply to him for relief and receive assignment to a new town. One of the earliest of such communities was created at the Cerro de Tomé south of Albuquerque.[52] Other *genízaros* later were placed at Abiquiú and the Pecos River towns of San José and San Miguel del Bado.

Since most of these people were of nomadic ancestry, they proved useful to the Spaniards as scouts, spies, and auxiliary soldiers. More significant for the discussion here, their towns, located on the fringes of European settlement, constituted an important barrier between the Spanish farmers and the hostile tribes on the frontier.

During colonial times repeated efforts were made to reduce the nomadic native people to community life under supervision of proper religious and civil authority. The *reducción*, an instrument of Spain's Indian policy from the days of earliest settlement in the New World, aimed at nothing short of full social and cultural reorientation of native ways. In many parts of Spanish America, congregation of wandering Indians into a community had been achieved through the use of force. But in New Mexico the several tribes of nomads remained unsubjugated, so that establishment of *reducciones* or formal settlements for them depended upon their voluntary submission. At various times in the eighteenth century, the Spaniards responded to pleas from Navajos, Apaches, and Comanches for aid in establishing their own towns, but in the end the Indians returned to a roving life. Since the experimental *reducciones* were situated on the far frontiers, had they succeeded, the jurisdiction of the New Mexican government would have been appreciably expanded and new areas might have been made safe for Spanish colonization.

Attempts to Regulate Settlement Patterns

A recurrent theme in official reports of the colonial years centered upon the problems raised by dispersal of the New Mexican population and the need to consolidate for defense. As early as 1609, the people of New Mexico were described as being "scattered over [that country] so that they are destitute of administration because very few reside in each place. . . ." As a result, orders were issued to gather the colonists together so they could stand united against the Indian menace.[53] No significant action was taken, however, and consequently the Spaniards suffered heavy casualties in the 1680 revolt—the isolation of individual families or small settlement clusters permitting the Indian forces to sweep the countryside.

In spite of this tragic experience, the same patterns of dispersal appeared on an even grander scale in the eighteenth century. The case was clearly put by Antonio de Bonilla, who, in 1776, remarked that in New Mexico

> The settlements of the Spaniards are scattered and badly defended . . . and quite exposed to entire ruin. Because the greater number of them are scattered ranches, among which the force of the settlers is divided, they can neither protect themselves nor contribute to the general defense of the country. This, in consequence, results in the abandonment of their weak homes and the terror of seeing themselves incessantly beset by the enemy.[54]

Of course, the government was concerned at the loss of life and the extra expense entailed in trying to protect an area in which patterns of settlement lacked regularity. But from a long view, of even more fundamental importance was the fact that erratic colonizing practices resulted in loss of entire blocks of territory to enemy raiders and a shrinking rather than an expansion of the frontier at various places. At least one historian has called attention to the Miera y Pacheco map of 1779, which shows there were more abandoned towns in New Mexico than there were occupied towns.[55]

The scattering of *ranchos* and settlements was, in part, an out-growth of the region's peculiar agricultural requirements—in a country where plowland was scarce, farms, as pointed out, were ribboned along stream valleys, and the people insisted on living near their fields, considerations of defense aside. Critics of the dispersal pattern claimed that the obstinacy and inertia of the colonists were the principal barriers to fulfillment of numerous government orders regarding establishment of organized communities. The issue was stated most forcefully by Father Juan de Morfi, writing sometime in the 1780s, who declared that the settlers like to live apart so that, far from the prying eyes of neighbors and the restraining influence of the authorities, they could commit with impunity all manner of immoral and criminal acts. He reported that some isolated colonists "were not ashamed to go about nude so that lewdness was seen here more than in the brutes, and the peaceful Indians were scandalized."[56] While moral looseness does seem to have been common in colonial society—decrees were issued with frequency condemning concubinage, indecent dances and excessive gambling—other causes, as already noted, were chiefly responsible for population dispersal.

This problem, which Bonilla and others regarded as of considerable magnitude, was finally met head-on by the Spanish government. Action came, nevertheless, only when it was realized that consolidation of the settlers was essential to the defense of the province, and that it was less costly to issue orders to that effect than to accede to repeated requests for additional presidios to supply protection.

Governor Mendinueta in a report of 1772 to Viceroy Bucareli advocated compelling "settlers of each region who live . . . dispersed, to join and form their pueblos in plazas or streets so that a few men could be able to defend themselves."[57] The viceroy was in full agreement, but some delay arose before orders could be issued and the task of concentrating the New Mexican settlers begun.[58]

On July 4, 1778, a council was held in Chihuahua which recommended prompt measures for the unification of the New Mexico population. Commandant General Teodoro de Croix then issued orders to Governor Juan Bautista de Anza calling upon him to "regularize" the settlements of his province by collecting scattered families and obliging them to dwell in compact units.[59] By 1779 the villas, except Santa Fé, were reduced to some order, and in the following year considerable success was achieved in concentrating the rural folk.[60] It was in this period of activity that many of the fortified or walled towns on the frontier had their beginnings.

The problem of concentrating the residents of the provincial capital remained unresolved for some time. The authorities, aware of "the churlish nature of Santa Fé's inhabitants" and of "the perfect freedom in which they always lived," decided to tread slowly and to seek alternative ways to strengthen defenses of the villa.[61] A formal presidio was begun adjacent to the governor's residence on the *plaza mayor* and was brought to completion in the early 1790s. Its purpose was to provide quarters near the center of town for officers and men of the garrison. Heretofore, some of the soldiers had lived as much as a league away from the plaza, and often it required several hours merely to assemble the troops. It is not certain what other measures may have been employed at this time to pull in the limits of the capital and congregate the residents, but in the long view it is doubtful if any fundamental change in the established pattern was achieved.

Conclusion

As may be seen from the foregoing, informality and a general lack of planning characterized New Mexican settlements through much of the colonial period. Economic necessity, a strong spirit of frontier individualism, a sense of fatalism about the Indian danger, and perhaps a wish to escape the paternal eye of civil government and the Church—these all influenced the settler and nourished in him the desire to build and farm on land of his own choosing, disregarding laws which were aimed at maintaining the collective welfare of the populace.

Of all causes contributing to the dispersal pattern, that which required the small farmer to live near his fields to give them proper care and protection was of uppermost importance. In this regard, it is interesting to note that the closely integrated villages of the Pueblo Indians began to break up as soon as the hostile nomads were subdued by the United States Government in the second half of the nineteenth century. With that event, it became safe for individual farmers and their families to reside permanently near more distant fields, returning to the main pueblo only on ceremonial occasions.[62] Thus, it appears that only the threat of enemy raiders had prevented the Pueblo people from scattering as the colonial New Mexicans had always done.

Overall, then, it may be said that settlement patterns in this province during the period of Spanish rule were shaped primarily by economic needs of the rural folk and only secondarily by considerations of defense. The strong tendency toward dispersion of the population was probably characteristic of most of northern New Spain, but may well have been more pronounced in New Mexico owing to greater isolation and looser enforcement of governmental decrees.

NOTES

1. J. M. Ots Capdequí, *El estado Español en las Indias* (4th ed.; Mexico, 1965), p. 34.

2. *Ibid.*, p. 36; and Julio Jiménez Rueda, *Historia de la cultura en México, El virreinato* (Mexico, 1951), p. 42.

3. Professor Clark S. Knowlton sharply distinguishes the "proprietary grant" (that of a *poblador principal*) from a community grant (one extended to a petitioning group of at least ten families seeking to establish a community). "Land Grant Problems Among the State's Spanish Americans," *New Mexico Business*, Vol. XX (1967), p. 2.

4. The existence of actual grants for the Pueblos must be inferred, since no original title papers are known today. The "Cruzate Grants" for the Pueblos have been proven to be largely fraudulent. See Myra Ellen Jenkins, "The Baltasar Baca 'Grant': History of an Encroachment," reprinted from *El Palacio*, Vol. LXVIII (1961), pp. 51–52.

5. See Dan Stanislawski, "The Origin and Spread of the Grid-Pattern Town," *The Geographic Review*, Vol. XXXVI (1946), pp. 105–120, and by the same author, "Early Spanish Town Planning in the New World," *ibid.*, Vol. XXXVII (1947), pp. 94–105.

6. O. Garfield Jones, "Local Government in the Spanish Colonies as Provided by the Recopilación de Leyes de los Reynos de las Indias," *The Southwestern Historical Quarterly*, Vol. XIX (1916), p. 68. Municipal plans which might show the *ejidos*, *propios* and *dehesas* for New Mexico communities are generally lacking. A colonial plan of the villa of San Fernando de Béxar in Texas, however, clearly manifests these features. Reproduced in Herbert Eugene Bolton, *Texas in the Middle Eighteenth Century* (new ed.: New York, 1962), p. 6.

7. Zelia Nuttall (trans.), "Royal Ordinances Concerning the Laying Out of New Towns." *Hispanic American Historical Review*, Vol. V (1922), p. 252.

8. Ots Capdequí, *El estado Español en las Indias*, p. 35; and Agustín Cue Cánovas, *Historia social y económica de México, 1521–1854* (Mexico, 1963), pp. 114–16.

9. George P. Hammond and Agapito Rey. *Don Juan de Oñate, Colonizer of New Mexico, 1595–1628* (2 vols.; Albuquerque, 1953), Vol. II, p. 599. The classification of a municipality as *ciudad*, *villa* or *pueblo* (city, town or village) was more than a mere formality since these terms implied definite ranking according to prestige and importance. Also the number of municipal magistrates and councilmen allowed by law depended upon the status of the community. See especially Ralph Emerson Twitchell, "Spanish Colonization and the Founding of *Ciudades* and *Villas* in the Time of Oñate," New Mexico Bar Association Minutes, 32nd Annual Session, Albuquerque, August, 1918, pp. 27–43.

10. "Ynstrucción a Peralta por vi-rey," *New Mexico Historical Review*, Vol. IV (1929), pp. 178–80.

11. See, for example, the remarks of Pedro Fermín de Mendinueta in Alfred B. Thomas, "Governor Mendinueta's Proposals for the Defense of New Mexico, 1772–1778," *New Mexico Historical Review*, Vol. VI (1931), p. 33.

12. Charles Wilson Hackett, *Historical Document Relating to New Mexico, Nueva Vizcaya, and Approaches Thereto, to 1773* (3 vols.; Washington, 1937), Vol. III, p. 379.

13. Lansing B. Bloom (ed.), "Albuquerque and Galisteo, Certificate of Their Founding, 1706," *New Mexico Historical Review*, Vol. X (1935), pp. 49–50.

14. Richard E. Greenleaf, "The Foundation of Albuquerque, 1706: An Historical Legal Problem," *New Mexico Historical Review*, Vol. XXXIX (1964), pp. 1–15.

15. Frank W. Blackmar, *Spanish Institutions of the Southwest* (Baltimore, 1891), p. 319.

16. The general theory of Castilian law on the subject indicates that citizens received allotments for their use and enjoyment, "but the domain itself remained in the person of the sovereign," Ralph E. Twitchell, "Spanish Colonization in New Mexico in the Oñate and De Vargas Periods," Historical Society of New Mexico, *Publications*, No. 22, p. 9.

17. Jacobo Ugarte y Loyola to Fernando de la Concha, Chihuahua, July 22, 1788, Archivo General de la Nación, México, Provincias Internas, Vol. 161, pt. 4. (From a photocopy in the Coronado Room, University of New Mexico Library, Albuquerque. Archivo General de la Nación hereinafter cited as AGN.)

18. Lansing B. Bloom, "When Was Santa Fé Founded?" *New Mexico Historical Review*, Vol. IV (1920), p. 194.

19. "Ynstrucción a Peralta," *New Mexico Historical Review*, Vol. IV (1929), p. 180.

20. France V. Scholes, "Civil Government and Society in New Mexico in the Seventeenth Century," *New Mexico Historical Review*, Vol. X (1935), p. 94.

21. France V. Scholes, *Troublous Times in New Mexico, 1659–1670*, Historical Society of New Mexico, *Publications in History*, Vol. XI (1942), p. 25.

22. Wilfred D. Kelley, "Settlement of the Middle Rio Grande Valley," *The Journal of Geography*, Vol. LIV (1955), p. 393.

23. Pueblo population in 1600 has been estimated at 35,000. According to Hubert Howe Bancroft, by 1600 it had dropped to about 20,000 and in 1760 it was down to some 9,000. *History of Arizona and New Mexico* (new ed.; Albuquerque, 1962), pp. 172, 279.

24. J. Manuel Espinosa, *Crusaders of the Rio Grande* (Chicago, 1942), pp. 221–25.

25. *Ibid.*, p. 227.

26. Fr. Francisco Atanasio Domínguez, *The Missions of New Mexico*, trans. by Eleanor B. Adams and Fr. Angélico Chávez (Albuquerque, 1956), p. 39.

27. *The Religious Architecture of New Mexico* (Colorado Springs, 1940), p. 18.

28. Vargas mentions two *plazas* for Santa Fé in 1695 (Espinosa, *Crusaders of the Rio Grande*, p. 225), and the Urrutía map of ca. 1766–68 shows an open space in front of San Miguel Church in the Indian *barrio* of Analco. Mr. Bruce Ellis of the Museum of New Mexico suggests that the present plaza was the *plaza mayor* or *plaza de armas* of the colonial documents, and that the secondary *plaza* may have existed immediately to the east in front of the parish church.

29. Domínguez, *The Missions of New Mexico*, p. 40.

30. Fernando de la Concha to Jacobo Ugarte y Loyola, Santa Fe, November 10, 1787, AGN, Prov. Int., 161.

31. Eleanor B. Adams (ed.), *Bishop Tamarón's Visitation of New Mexico, 1760*, Historical Society of New Mexico, *Publications in History*, Vol. XV (1954), p. 63.

32. Petition of Residents of El Paso, April 13, 1780, Spanish Archives of New Mexico, State Records Center and Archives, Santa Fé. (Spanish Archives of New Mexico hereinafter cited as SANM).

33. Domínguez, *The Missions of New Mexico*, p. 151.

34. The designation of "pueblo" for a Spanish community was usually avoided in New Mexico since the village Indians from a very early time were called Pueblos. The term "rancho" should be translated as small farm rather than ranch. For a definition of this word as it was used in colonial New Spain see Roberto Mac-Lean y Estenós, *Indios de América* (Mexico, 1962), pp. 79–80.

35. Kelley, "Settlement of the Middle Rio Grande Valley," *The Journal of Geography*, Vol. LIV (1955), p. 394.

36. E. Boyd, "Troubles at Ojo Caliente, A Frontier Post," *El Palacio*, Vol. LXIV (1957), pp. 349, 359.

37. Thomas, "Governor Mendinueta's Proposals," *New Mexico Historical Review*, Vol. VI (1931), p. 33.

38. *Ibid.*, p. 27.

39. Robert C. Smith, "Colonial Towns of Spanish and Portuguese America," *Journal of the Society of Architectural Historians*, Vol. XIV (1955), p. 4. It is curious to note that early documents and maps occasionally designate the capital of New Mexico as "Santa Fé de la Granada."

40. Petition, April 13, 1780, SANM

41. Bainbridge Bunting and John P. Conron, "The Architecture of Northern New Mexico," *New Mexico Architecture*, Vol. VIII (1966), p. 16. There existed abundant precedent in New Spain for this type of community. For example, an early plan called for a *casa-muro*, or wall of houses, to be built in Mexico City soon after the conquest. George Kubler, *Mexican Architecture of the Sixteenth Century* (2 vols., New Haven, 1948), Vol. I, p. 78. Also, fortified towns had been common on the Chichimec frontier. Philip Wayne Powell, *Soldiers, Indians and Silver* (Berkeley, 1952), pp. 153–55.

42. Hugh and Evelyn Burnet, "Madrid Plaza," *Colorado Magazine*, Vol. XLII (1965), p. 224. This article includes the sketch of a "restricted plaza" of the nineteenth century.

43. For a description of the *casa grande* of Pablo de Villapando near Taos, see the legend on the Miera y Pacheco map, translated by Adams and Chávez in Domínguez, *Missions of New Mexico*, p. 4.

44. A. W. Conway, "Southwestern Colonial Farms," *Landscape, Human Geography of the Southwest*, Vol. I (1961), p. 6. According to the author, the *casa corral* unit was distributed throughout the Southwest and the north Mexican provinces.

45. Nuttall, "Royal Ordinances Concerning the Laying Out of New Towns, *Hispanic American Historical Review*, Vol. V (1922), p. 252.

46. Boyd, "Troubles at Ojo Caliente," *El Palacio*, Vol. LXIV (1957), *passim*. Regarding a petition of Chamita settlers to leave their residences, and a refusal of permission by Governor Vélez Cachupín see Ralph Emerson Twitchell, *The Leading Facts of New Mexican History* (2 vols.; Albuquerque, 1963), Vol. II, p. 317n.

47. Salcedo to Chacón, Chihuahua, January 11, 1805, SANM.

48. Fred Wendorf, "Some Distributions of Settlement Patterns in the Pueblo Southwest," in Gordon R. Willey (ed.), *Pre-historic Settlement Patterns in the New World*, Viking Fund Publications in Anthropology, No. 23 (New York, 1956), pp. 21–22.

49. Bancroft, *History of Arizona and New Mexico*, p. 259.

50. Myra Ellen Jenkins, "Taos Pueblo and Its Neighbors, 1540–1847," *New Mexico Historical Review*, Vol. XLI (1966), pp. 98–99.

51. Domínguez, *The Missions of New Mexico*, p. 110.

52. Declaration of Fr. Miguel de Menchero, Santa Bárbara, May 10, 1744, in Hackett, *Historical Documents*, Vol. III, pp. 401–2.

53. "Ynstrucción a Peralta," *New Mexico Historical Review*, Vol. IV (1929), p. 184.

54. Alfred B. Thomas (ed. and trans.), "Antonio de Bonilla and Spanish Plans for the Defense of New Mexico, 1777–1778," in *New Spain and the West* (2 vols.; Lancaster, Pa., 1932), Vol. I, p. 196.

55. Cleve Hallenbeck, *Land of the Conquistadores* (Caldwell, Idaho, 1950), p. 243.

56. Fr. Juan Agustín de Morfi, Desórdenes que se advierten en el Nuevo México, AGN, Historia, 25.

57. Thomas, "Governor Mendinueta's Proposals," *New Mexico Historical Review*, Vol. VI (1931), p. 29.

58. Luis Navarro García, *Don José Gálvez y la comandancia general de las Provincias Internas del Norte de Nueva España* (Sevilla, 1964), p. 244; and Thomas, "Bonilla and Spanish Plans for the Defense of New Mexico," *New Spain and the West*, Vol. I, p. 201.

59. Concha to Ugarte, Santa Fe, June 20, 1788, AGN, Prov. Int., 161.

60. *Ibid.*; and Alfred B. Thomas, *Forgotten Frontiers: A Study of the Spanish-Indian Policy of Don Juan Bautista de Anza* (Norman, 1932), pp. 94; 101.

61. Concha to Ugarte, Santa Fe, June 20, 1788, AGN, Prov. Int., 161.

62. Wendorf, "Some Distributions of Settlement Patterns," in Willey (ed.), *Pre-historic Settlement Patterns*, p. 22.

8

California's Hispanic Heritage: A View into the Spanish Myth*

Manuel Patricio Servín

Editor's Introduction

Servín calls for a reexamination of the role of persons of mixed blood, or mestizos, in the history of the Borderlands. Focusing on California, he accuses historians who have overlooked the mestizo contribution of an anti-Mexican bias. In this case, Servín uses the word "Mexican" as a synonym for a mestizo, as opposed to an *español,* whose ancestry can be traced directly back to Spain without any mixture with Indians or Blacks in the New World. The *españoles* in California and the Franciscans in particular, according to Servín, discriminated against persons of mixed blood. In making this assertion, Servín suggests that the origins of prejudice toward Mexicans in California can be traced to the period before Anglo Americans arrived.[1]

When it appeared in 1973, Servín's article prompted a lengthy rejoinder by Professor Ralph Vigil who argued that "Professor Servín

---

*Taken from *The Journal of San Diego History,* 19 (1973): 1–9, this article is reprinted with permission of the author and the San Diego Historical Society.

never defines what the difference is between a 'Spaniard' and a 'Mexican' except in terms of race." Vigil charged Servín with overemphasizing the importance of racial distinctions. Those distinctions, Vigil said, were blurred on the frontier and overshadowed by a common nationality and culture. Indeed, for Vigil "ultimately what remains is culture." Drawing heavily on examples from New Mexico, Vigil concluded:

> Miscegenation is of limited interest biologically, and only socially important when it produces a society of castes or a society like that of the United States which is characterized by an intricate complex of tensions arising from interracial mixture or fear that this may come about. This did not happen in New Mexico specifically, nor did it occur in the borderlands generally. The reason for this is that society on the frontier was relatively open. Verticle mobility existed socially and by the early nineteenth century, all those colonists in New Mexico not obviously Indian were Spaniards.[2]

Servín would disagree, for he sees racially mixed peoples as the victims of discrimination in California. On the other hand, Servín would probably agree with Vigil that verticle social mobility existed on the California frontier. To achieve that mobility, however, Servín seems to argue that lighter-skinned mixed-bloods passed themselves off as whites or *españoles*, thereby denying their racial heritage.

Born in El Paso, Texas, Manuel Servín earned the Ph.D. in history at the University of Southern California and taught there for a decade before moving to Arizona State University (1970) and the University of New Mexico (1975) where he is currently professor of history. His early research focused on Hispanic California. More recently he has turned to Mexican-American history. Among his publications is an anthology, *An Awakened Minority: The Mexican-Americans* (Beverly Hills: 1974), to which he contributed articles on the eighteenth, nineteenth, and twentieth centuries. Professor Servín served as editor of the *California Historical Quarterly* (1961–70), and of the *New Mexico Historical Review* from 1975 until his illness in 1976.

NOTES

1. Servín expressed his views on this subject at greater length in the article which he cites in note 11.

2. "The Hispanic Heritage and the Borderlands," *Journal of San Diego History*, 19 (1973): 33, 38–39.

California's Hispanic Heritage: A View Into the Spanish Myth

No aspect of Borderlands history has been more distorted than that of the Spanish colonization of the Southwest. Despite the writings of eminent historians on the racially mixed background of the Spanish-speaking pioneers, the myth that the early settlers, and consequently the old families, were preponderantly of Spanish stock persists in many quarters.

Members of old families, whose mixed-blood ancestors early adopted the Spanish ideals of success, proudly extol their Spanish lineage and background. Viewing history through special lenses, the descendants of early settlers, as well as their Anglo-American friends and relatives, seem to focus only on the Spanish *conquistadores*, explorers, and settlers of the Borderlands. Overlooking their unbleached mestizo, mulatto, and Indian ancestors, these self-anointed Spanish-speaking pioneers see themselves as the descendants of intrepid Castilian gentlemen.

This act of self-deception appears to afflict almost the entire Borderlands area. New Mexico, perhaps because of its long history and galaxy of noble-like *conquistadores*, more than any other area suffers from this Spanish fever. The names of Don Francisco Vásquez de Coronado, Don Antonio de Espejo, and Don Juan de Oñate dominate the history of the state. Consequently, New Mexico is generally considered Spanish and its Spanish-speaking inhabitants are consequently Hispanos—not Mexicans of mixed Spanish, Indian, and African stock. Texas, with its so-called Spanish founders of San Antonio, also suffers from a similar affliction. The Spanish-speaking *rico*, the person of status, is consequently the descendant of either the notoriously indolent Canary Islander or of an alleged Spaniard or *criollo*. California, where earlier American historians overglorified the Spanish period of the province as well as the names of Junípero Serra and Gaspar de Portolá, relishes in its Spanish origins and traditions. Its distinguished families, suffering from an acute case of color blindness, call themselves *californios*, descendants of supposed Spaniards.

The recognition of the role that colonial Mexicans—that is, the role that the persons of mixed-blood—played in settling the Borderlands and especially California does not reject the essential part that Spaniards performed in the exploration, colonization, and missionization of the Southwest. Spanish *peninsulares* overwhelmingly were the *adelantados*, the officials, and the priests who explored, governed, and served settlers.

But to claim that the settlers were preponderantly Spaniards—as the *californios* assert—must be rejected as historically untenable. These settlers, as the study of California's settlement shows, were not Spanish, but overwhelmingly mixed-bloods from Indian, Spanish, and also Negro stock.

Alta California was a most unattractive province to the success-seeking colonist of New Spain. Although California was discovered in 1542 by Juan Rodríguez Cabrillo and explored in the late 1500s and early 1600s, its colonization did not occur until 1769, over two hundred years after its discovery.

Although California today has attracted the greatest number of Americans pursuing the great American Dream, it failed to lure its true founder, Don José de Gálvez, to its productive and lucrative soil. This former Spanish shepherd, seminarian, and struggling lawyer—like many a struggling unsuccessful lawyer—was dominated by a success-seeking desire for political power and status. Gálvez's inordinate ambition and quest for success, plus his ability and good fortune, made it possible for him to rise in the political sphere. Through his marriage to a French woman, he became a legal councillor at the French Embassy in Madrid; then he moved up as a secretary to the Spanish Minister of State; and, in 1765 in his forty-fifth year, the former shepherd and unsuccessful lawyer was appointed Inspector General of New Spain and thus became the most powerful man in Spanish North America.[1]

As Inspector General, Gálvez was to reorganize and reform New Spain by such measures as revising the fiscal policies, expelling the Jesuits, and establishing the frontier defense of the northern provinces. Gálvez, however, as a devoted follower of the Spanish Gospel of Success, sought a more exalted position than Inspector General. Consequently, he seized upon the imagined Russian threat to Alta California as a means of furthering his political career—a career that reached its height when he was named Marqués de Sonora and Ministro Universal de las Indias.[2]

Since the occupation of Alta California was of utmost importance to the ambitious Inspector General, he directed its entire preparation. In charge of the Alta California expedition he placed the newly arrived Catalán Captain Gaspar de Portolá. As president of the Fernandino Franciscan missionaries from the overwhelmingly Spanish Apostolic College of San Fernando of Mexico, he chose the Mallorcan Fray Junípero Serra without consulting him "whether the post would be acceptable and without any chance to refuse."[3]

The expedition, which in reality consisted of four distinct phases—two voyages by ships and two separate treks by land—was a Spanish-led enterprise. Only one leader, Captain Fernando de Rivera y Moncada, the commander of the *soldados de cuera*, the leather jackets, was not a Spaniard.[4]

Although the founding expedition has gone down in California history as the "Portolá Expedition" and both Portolá and Serra have been overly extolled, Rivera played a very significant, but almost unappreciated, role in the founding of Alta California. Rivera, whose work was virtually ignored by North American historians of California until the research of the scholarly Jesuit Ernest J. Burrus appeared in print,[5] did much more than just lead the first overland division of twenty-five *soldados de cuera*, three muleteers, and some forty Hispanicized former Jesuit-trained Indians to San Diego in Alta California. Actually Rivera not only paved the way for Portolá and Serra into Alta California but also into Baja California.

Whereas the Catalán Portolá "was a new-comer of the preceding year" of 1767[6] and Serra had only set foot on Baja California in 1768,[7] Captain Rivera had had a distinguished career as a soldier, officer, and as military commander prior to the replacement of the expelled Jesuits by the Franciscan missionaries from the College of San Fernando of Mexico.

Despite Rivera's excellent record in Jesuit Baja California and his later laudable colonizing record in Alta California, California historians—except for the Jesuits Peter Masten Dunne and Ernest J. Burrus—have been critical, if not hostile, toward Rivera.[8] Whether this attitude toward Rivera is the result of the pro-Franciscan position of most California historians or whether it originates in their unconscious prejudice of extolling Spaniards and things Spanish and of deprecating Mexicans and Mexican activities is impossible to decide. Whatever the reason may be—and I am inclined to believe that it is a latent, unrecognized anti-Mexican attitude that permeated California historians—Rivera, the Mexican pioneer and governor of Spanish California, has suffered undue and unwarranted criticism at the hands of Anglo-American chroniclers who prided themselves on their objectivity.

Rivera, although the best known, was not the only non-Spaniard or *gente de razón*[9] who came as a founder in the so-called Portolá Expedition of 1769. In addition to the twenty-five *soldados de cuera* and the three muleteers who accompanied Rivera to Alta California, the Portolá phase included Sergeant José Francisco Ortega of Guanajuato, ten *soldados de cuera* under him, four muleteers, and Portolá's and Serra's two servants. On board the *San Antonio*, the first ship of the expedition to reach Alta California, there were "a few carpenters and blacksmiths," but the true number of *gente de razón* on board is still unknown. On the *San Carlos*, whose records are available, there were "four cooks and two blacksmiths," probably none of whom was a Spaniard or a *criollo*. Therefore, the expeditions—both the two sea phases and the two land divisions—contained some sixty Mexican mixed-bloods. If the Hispanicized, Baja California, Jesuit-trained Indians, who numbered forty-two with Rivera and forty-four with Portolá, are counted as non-Spanish settlers—as they certainly deserve to be counted—the mixed-blood and Indian element arriving and remaining as colonists in Alta California is overpowering.[10] And, when the historian considers that of all the Spaniards who made and helped make the four-pronged expedition, only eight remained in California and that three of these (the distinguished Miguel Costansó, the overpopularized Gaspar de Portolá, and the relatively unknown Fray Juan Vizcaíno) soon returned to Mexico, he realizes that the Mexican mixed-blood and Indian contribution to the founding of Alta California has been woefully understated or almost ignored by North American historians of California.

Although the Mexican mixed-bloods and the Baja California Indians constituted the vast majority of the permanent soldiers and colonists of Alta California, the Spaniards—with extremely few exceptions—planned and encouraged the development of the new colony. The Spanish Franciscans not only established twenty missions but also insured California's permanent settlement and economic development. Spanish officers erected presidios, presidial towns, and civilian pueblos. It was also these officers who originated the rancho system by making the first land grants to retired Spanish soldiers. Yet, as important as Spanish leadership was, without those of mixed-blood, Alta California could neither have been occupied nor colonized.

The Mexican mixed-bloods, in addition to being the pioneer soldier-settlers who garrisoned presidios, guarded missions, carried the mail, erected buildings, farmed, and even took care of flocks, soon became the main source of "Spanish" population for securing the territory. In 1775 Captain Juan Bautista de Anza, the distinguished frontier commander who was in all probability a mestizo, left Tubac, Arizona, with some two hundred forty persons. The military colonists of the trek, most of whom were poverty ridden *gente de razón* recruited in Sinaloa, were the welcome founders and settlers of San Francisco's presidio and mission. Thus, the Mexican population was predominant in settling and populating Alta California from San Diego in the south to San Francisco in the north.

Not all Mexican mixed-bloods and Hispanicized Indians, however, were as welcome and appreciated as the first settlers of the "Portolá Expedition of 1769" and the "Anza Trek of 1775." The first lack of enthusiasm for Mexican settlers was demonstrated by the Fernandino Franciscans. These Franciscans from the beginning were opposed to the establishment of towns whose unruly inhabitants turned out to be *mestizos*, *mulattoes*, *lobos*, and other racial amalgamations. Actually, the opposition to the founding of pueblos appears to have been born not solely from racial prejudice but from other reasons, especially from the fun-loving and unchaste behavior of the religiously lax soldiers and settlers, a behavior that was far from edifying to the California mission Indian.[11] Perhaps another significant reason for the Franciscan opposition is that the towns were to be located in what the friars erroneously considered mission lands. At any rate, the opposition by the Fernandino friars was positive and determined:

> Notwithstanding Viceroy Antonio Bucareli's instructions (1773) regarding the erection of pueblos, Neve's *Reglamento* (1779), . . . the missionaries, beginning with Father Junípero Serra opposed such projects. Thus, Serra opposed the founding of San José on the basis "that the government should wait until the missions developed more. Then they could supply the presidios with produce and more land would be available for settlers by reason of the enrollment of Indians in the missions." Apparently that day never came, for on August 30, 1797, the guardian of Fernandinos "requested a suspension of the Villa de Branciforte," the third and last Spanish municipality founded in Alta California. As had happened in San José, the friars opposed Branciforte on the legality of proximity to the mission.[12]

The Fernandino Franciscans of California, when compared to the Franciscan missionaries of other Apostolic Colleges and Provinces, were unique in their opposition to the establishment of pueblos of *gente de razón* or Mexicans. Following the expelled Jesuits' example in Baja California, the Fernandino missionaries were adamant against having civilian pueblos in both of the Californias. This, however, was not by any means the general practice of the Franciscans from other missionary colleges. Professor John Walton Caughey, dean of California historians, presents a cogent picture of the situation when he writes that "Prior to [Governor] Neve's time Alta California had no pueblos. Baja California had none and, for that matter, no presidios either. But in Sonora, New Mexico, Texas, and most other Spanish frontiers the town was present alongside the mission and military post."[13]

Governor Neve, with his intense anticlerical and antifriar sentiments, broke the Fernandino Franciscan antisettler practice. Without waiting for approval from the especially proclerical Viceroy Antonio de Bucareli, Neve established the Pueblo of San José in 1777. Gathering "four soldier-settlers brought by Anza, the widow of another soldier and a vaquero" from San Francisco, and nine soldiers from Monterey, the governor initiated active hostility not only to the civilian pueblos but to the mixed-blood *poblanos*—the founders of California's first municipality.

Los Angeles, whose settlers were recruited by Rivera in northwestern Mexican states, was the second civilian pueblo of Alta California. Governor Neve, the anticlerical Spaniard, founded it on September 4,

1781, "with twelve settlers and their families, forty-six persons in all, whose names are given and whose blood was a strange mixture of Indian and negro with here and there a trace of Spanish." According to H. H. Bancroft, California's early distinguished historian,

> The settlers were as follows: José de Lara, Spaniard, 50 years of age, wife Indian, 3 children; José Antonio Navarro, mestizo, 42 years, wife mulattress, 3 children; Basilio Rosas, Indian, 68 years, wife mulattress, 6 children; Antonio Mesa, negro, 38 years, wife mulattress, 2 children; Antonio (Félix) Villa-vicencio, Spaniard, 30 years, wife Indian, 1 child; José Vanegas, Indian, 28 years, wife, Indian, 1 child; Alejandro Rosas, Indian, 19 years, wife coyote (Indian); Pablo Rodríguez, Indian, 25 years, wife Indian, 1 child; Manuel Camero, mulatto, 30 years, wife mulattress; Luis Quintero, negro, 55 years, wife mulattress, 5 children; José Moreno, mulatto, 22 years, wife mulattress; Antonio Miranda, chino, 50 years, 1 child. The last named was at first absent at Loreto. He was not a Chinaman, nor even born in China, as has been stated by some writers, but was an offspring probably of an Indian mother by a father of mixed Spanish and negro blood. . . .[14]

Governor Neve, who established the pueblos to provide an adequate food supply and to populate the almost barren province, unlike Serra and the Franciscans, saw the pueblo founders as Spanish regardless of racial origins.[15]

While Neve actually saw the Mexican mixed-bloods as Spanish subjects who would secure California for the Crown, Serra and friars generally saw them both in the pueblos and in the presidios as problems.[16] The *gente de razón* corrupted the Indian by their irreligious and unchaste behavior. They reduced the friars' influence over the Indians by their independence and lack of obedience. Furthermore, they were an "unruly element who," as Humboldt opined, "do not submit so easily to blind obedience as Indians." Yet, as disrespectful as some of the *Mestizos*, *Mulattoes*, or *Lobos* may have been, they certainly were not as hostile to the friars as Governor Neve. According to Father Guardian Francisco Pangua, Superior of all the Fernandinos, "So pronounced [was] Neve's aversion to the friars that soldiers were warned not to become *fraileros* [friends of the friars], not to perform any service for the missionaries, and not to aid in the bringing back of fugitives."[17]

Neve, however, was not the only Spanish official whose hostility undermined the friars' influence and authority over the Indians and the *gente de razón*. Such outstanding Spanish officials, as Governors Pedro Fages and Diego de Borica, were equally as critical and uncooperative. Despite the attitude of the Spanish officials toward the Fernandino friars, both at the highest and lowest echelons, it was the mixed-blood and not the Spaniard who was singled out as the problem of the Franciscan.

Nowhere were the mixed-bloods so opposed, so criticized, and so uncharitably described as in the 1797 founding of the Villa de Branciforte near present-day Santa Cruz. According to Francis Florian Guest, the leading authority on the founding of Branciforte,

> Strenuous efforts were made in New Spain to recruit settlers for California but with small success. On March 3, 1796, the king approved the plan of populating California with families who might volunteer for the project. The intendancies of Guadalajara, Zacatecas, Potosí, Guanajuato, and Valladolid were searched for families, poor, honorable, and of pure blood, who might be sent to California to increase the population and who, far from corrupting the Christian Indians, would give them good example. . . . The results were almost nil. . . . Ultimately, two groups were organized to make the voyage to the new province. The first, from Guadalajara, consisted of nine men condemned for petty crimes. The second, from Guanajuato, comprised sixteen men of the same class, and three volunteers.[18]

The colonists, as might be expected from former convicts, proved to be a serious problem to the Spanish officials, the Spanish friars, and Spanish settlers. Yet, it is difficult to see why the behavior of the mixed-blood colonists should scandalize the Spaniards when the moral decadence of Spain and of its rulers, Charles the IV and María Luisa, was at least as pronounced as that of the convict-settlers. Father Guest presents a graphic picture of scandalous conduct of the Branciforte colonists and insight into the attitude toward the mixed-bloods in some California circles.

> The trouble the convicts caused the government was more than legal in character. Their reputation for good conduct was not an enviable one. Their immorality and disorderly behavior were a scandal to the troops, the settlers, and the Indians. Sometimes their offenses were more than minor. . . . In another letter to the viceroy [Governor] Arrillaga describes the convicts as insolent, vicious, brutal, and immoral and asks that the sending of any more be suspended. Father Fermín Francisco de Lasuén portrays them as lovers of idleness and ease, half-clothed and hungry, wandering around in presidios, ranchos, and pueblos, serving one and now another but not fitting in anywhere. Raymundo Carrillo complained that, with their vices and bad example, the convicts were corrupting the Christian and pagan Indians and the children of the *gente de razón*. José Argüello declared it would be a great benefit, a distinct

gain, if the convicts did not encumber the earth. . . . José de la Guerra's comment was that it would be most favorable to the interests of the province if the convicts were distant a million leagues for a couple of centuries, an occurrence which would be of advantage to both God and king. . . .[19]

Yet, not all Spaniards were as critical of the mixed-blood *gente de razón* as the somewhat poorly educated friars, the Spanish Peninsular immigrants, and the bleaching successful *mestizo.* Some Spaniards, like the remarkable, well-educated Miguel de Costansó of the elite Corps of Engineers appreciated both the mixed-bloods and the contribution which they could make for preserving Alta California. Costansó, California's first historian and New Spain's greatest architect and military engineer, ignoring the friars' antipathy to civilian establishments and to mixed-bloods, as early as 1794 recommended that

> In order to avoid the problems and setbacks that have developed [in Alta California] and to have the missions prosper, to instruct the Indians in arts which are demanded by society to civilize and to make them more useful vassals to the Monarchy, there are no means more efficacious than from the beginning of a new establishment to introduce among them *gente de razón* [European, Spaniards, and people of mixed blood are identified as such in order to differentiate them from the native Indians][20] provided they are hardworking and useful. The governors, who are above the missionary priest, and the captains of the presidios of the provinces of this New Spain have clamored, and are clamoring for it—especially those of the Californias, Upper and Lower, or Old and New. . . .[21]

In addition to the benefits that would accrue to the Province and consequently to Spain, Costansó then presents a rather favorable description of the birthrate and integration of the mixed-blood in New Spain. Accordingly, he continues his *Report of 1794*,

> Experience has demonstrated the fertility of the Spaniards and of the persons of mixed blood of this kingdom is much greater than that of the Indians. Perhaps this is so because when they are reduced to a civilized life or a less wild existence, they [the Indians] procreate much less; or because when they intermarry with Spaniards or white persons, there is generally produced from the second or third generation some individuals who barely have a trace of Indian since they are reared among Spaniards and their language, habits and customs no longer differ from ours.[22]

Unfortunately for the mixed-bloods, too few Spaniards, particularly the Fernandino Franciscans, were as accepting and as appreciative of them as

California's Forgotten Founder, Costansó. Most mixed-bloods, because of their racial mixture, especially if they possessed a natural tan and were *póblanos* (townspeople) were stigmatized in varying degrees. Consequently, to escape discrimination or to achieve status, the second generation (the *hijos del país* or *californios*), especially the *rancheros* (ranch owners) and the *políticos* (governmental officials), started to revert to the centuries-old custom of New Spain of becoming bleached Mexicans; namely, the *criollos* of Mexico and the *californios* of Alta California. Therefore, it is not surprising that even in the Spanish period, the early California mixed-blood settlers who considered themselves as whites, and soldiers, demonstrated a spirit of superiority over the newer immigrants (the *cholos*) who arrived from Mexico. While some of this discrimination may be attributed to the fact that the immigrants of the 1780s and 1790s were convict-artisans and those of 1800 happened to be foundlings, the element of status-seeking and racial self-deception on the part of the early California mixed-blood *poblanos* cannot be ignored.

Actually, very few of the mixed-bloods, especially the *poblanos*, became acceptable or managed to pass as *españoles* (Spaniards) in the period before 1821. Such mobility appears to have been at first restricted to a great degree to the *rancheros*. Furthermore, it does not appear to have taken root until either very late in the Spanish period or early in the Mexican regime. Actually, the *poblanos*—because of their lack of the gospel of success—remained during the Spanish period as just plain Mexicans or *gente de razón*.

Consequently, it is neither startling nor amusing to read the description which the late Professor Charles E. Chapman (the teacher of so many California historians, university and college-level professors, and public and parochial school teachers) perpetuated of the *poblano* in his widely used volume, *History of California: Spanish Period* (1921). Chapman, reflecting the prejudice or perhaps the honesty, of his generation and of previous generations of Americans, wrote that

> The inhabitants [of *pueblos*] were of poorer quality than those of the presidial towns, and were of mongrel racial type. The original settlers of Los Angeles, for example, had far more Indian and negro blood than white, though all were part Spanish. None of them could read or write. By all accounts they were a dissolute, immoral, lazy, gambling lot. Between 1792 and 1795 the *pueblos* received an increase in population through the sending of a number of artisans from Mexico; these artisans were criminals. Present-day Californians need not feel in the least shocked by these details. No pioneer country in real life is ever very lovely, especially if the inhabitants are unwilling settlers. Nor should the modest character

> [the lack of a gospel of success] of certain of the Spanish Californians lessen one's pride in the greatness of their service. . . . Many of the English settlers of the West Indies and what are now the southern states of this country were as poor as the Spanish Californians.[23]

Chapman was more understanding, or perhaps less biased, regarding the Spanish period *rancheros.* Although acknowledging that the "least important of the types of settlement in Spanish days were the private ranches," he nevertheless raised the status of the grantees by asserting that "some twenty such grants were made in the Spanish period, however, usually to retired presidial officers."[24]

Actually, the first grant made in Alta California was made by Rivera in 1775. Two years prior, as W. W. Robinson states,

> Viceroy Bucareli authorized the military commanders of San Diego and Monterey, the two existing presidios, to assign lands to Indians and colonists, at the same time cautioning such recipients of land not to move away from the town or mission where they were established.
>
> Under his authority, Manuel Butrón, a soldier of the Monterey company, married to an Indian girl, Margarita, a Carmel Mission neophyte, was the first man in Spanish-ruled Upper California to get a plot of land he could call his own. . . .[25]

Butrón, however, was not destined to initiate a family of *rancheros* (and California Dons.) Unlike the veteran Mexican mixed-blood *soldados de cuera,* who later received grants and who sired distinguished and even "pure Spanish" families, Butrón failed. His small plot, less than some 140 square yards, was abandoned as he settled in the Pueblo of San José.

The first real rancheros of California were the Mexican *inválidos*—the retired soldiers. Governor Pedro Fages, on his own initiative, originated the rancho movement in Alta California in 1784 by making provisional grants to at least three *soldados de cuera* who came to the province with the founding expedition. "In that year," writes W. W. Robinson, "several retirement-minded, land-hungry veterans got permission from Governor Fages, their own commander, to put cattle on lands of their own choosing." Fages, however, was unsure of his action, and referred the matter to higher authorities in New Spain. His actions were confirmed, but with some restrictions.[26] Thus, it was as a result of Fages' actions that lowly mixed-blood frontier soldiers first became *rancheros*—the *rancheros* whose children in many cases would become Spanish *californios* and who would later disclaim Mexico and things Mexican.

Probably the first to profit from Fages' action was sixty-five-year-old Juan José Domínguez, founder of a renowned family of Mexican and American period *californios.*[27] Domínguez, despite his descendants' rise to status as *californios* in the later Mexican and United States periods, appears to have been a man of very modest background and heritage.[28] Yet his lowly station in life and his liaison with an Indian neophyte who bore him a child did not prevent Governor Fages from granting him "a site near the mouth of the Los Angeles River," where "on the slope of a hill he built several huts and corrals and established . . . Rancho San Pedro. As finally surveyed there were 43,000 acres in this rancho, though originally it had included Rancho Los Palos Verdes."[29] But even without Palos Verdes, the Domínguez family rise from frontier soldiers to dons in the Mexican period was not only rapid but lasting.

A second soldier-grantee, whose family became recognized *californios*, was Corporal José María Verdugo.[30] Born in the Villa de Sinaloa like Domínguez, Verdugo became a *soldado de cuera,* accompanied Rivera to Alta California, served at San Diego and at Mission San Gabriel, and received Rancho San Rafael on October 20, 1784, before retirement.[31] According to Robinson, Verdugo "remained in the army." Thirteen years later, however, he was so weary of military life, according to his own statement, suffered so much from dropsy, and felt so keenly the burden of his family, which included six children, that Governor Diego de Borica let him retire to his rancho. Verdugo's Rancho San Rafael comprised more than 36,000 acres, and within its boundary are today Glendale and part of Burbank. With 36,000 acres of property, his descendants had slight difficulty in attaining racial, social, and political status in Mexican California.[32]

Manuel Pérez Nieto, also a native of the Villa de Sinaloa and compadre of Juan José Domínguez, upon retiring petitioned Governor Fages for a grant to graze his cattle and horses. While he humbly petitioned the governor and meekly signed his name with a cross, his request for the grant of the acreage at La Zanja was far from humble. "Rancho Los Nictos was almost twice the size of the Domínguez grant (75,000 acres). . . . Altogether, these tracts [of Domínguez and his compadres Verdugo and Nieto] comprised almost one-third of the coastal plain now included in Los Angeles County, or in the excess of four hundred square miles."[33]

Nieto, despite being an "old man" when he retired as an enlisted man from the Presidio, was easily the giant of the *Big Three Grantees.* As Robinson states,

> he was described as an "old man," but he was not too old to raise cattle and horses successfully, nor too old to plant wheat and corn, nor too old to avoid having title disputes with the priests of San Gabriel. His adobe hut was built southwest of the present city of Whittier and within what later became Rancho San Gertrudes. By 1800 it was the center of a colony of white [*sic*] settlers. Nieto died

> in 1804, his vast holdings—Los Nietos—later forming five ranchos regranted during the Mexican period to his heirs and members of his family. These five ranchos were San Gertrudes, Los Coyotes, Los Cerritos, Los Alamitos, and Las Bolsas. A number of cities were to arise within their boundaries, the largest of which is today Long Beach.[34]

These three ranch-grants, although there were perhaps some thirty such grants made in Spanish Alta California, clearly indicate how the mixed-blood retired soldiers could and did become landowners. It also indicates how their families became prominent *hijos del país* or *californios* in the Mexican period when they, like the Mexican period grantees, minimized their Mexican ancestry and heritage.

Probably, there would have been many more "Spanish" *californios* and "Pure Spaniards" tracing their roots to Spanish and not the Mexican grants had it not been for the antipathy of the Fernandino friars to rural establishments. Fray José Antonio Señán, a distinguished, future Father-President of the Alta California Mission System, clearly voiced the Franciscan opposition to Spanish grants and ranchos when he wrote to Viceroy Branciforte in 1796:

> Towns cannot exist without people; as the number of inhabitants increases, so do the opportunities for their well being. I therefore believe that under no circumstances should retired soldiers or others with special credentials who wish to settle in the Province be permitted to establish themselves separately in remote areas or in villages outside the towns, a practice that I have tolerated these past few years. Such persons should rather be required to reside in towns, . . . otherwise we shall never have towns. The consequences to be expected from scattered and isolated colonization are distressing to contemplate. Colonists thus openly exposed are likely to suffer mischief at the hands of gentiles [pagan Indians] . . . . In short, they will live in those remote regions without King to rule or Pope to excommunicate them. . . .[35]

Obviously, the King did rule and the Pope had an opportunity to excommunicate. *Rancheros* in the Spanish period, unlike the Mexican era, barely increased in number. Yet, it was in this period that the California mixed-blood soldier-settler first sought and laid the foundation for attaining a Spanish-type success. He secured large grants by honestly requesting them at retirement. Although he himself did not become a nonworking aristocrat or a *californio* of Spanish descent, his offspring would as they inherited his lands in the post-1821 Mexican period.

Despite his own denial of his racial heritage, it was the mixed-blood and not the Spaniard, who settled and populated California. To deny this fact, and continue the myth of the Spanish settlers and settlement, is to perpetuate a deception, a deception which is not history, but in many cases, prejudice of an earlier era.

NOTES

1. See Herbert Ingram Priestly, *José de Gálvez, Visitor-General of New Spain (1765–1711)* (Berkeley: University of California Press, 1916), pp. 1–8; Charles E. Chapman, *A History of California: The Spanish Period* (New York: The Macmillan Company, 1930), pp. 207–209.

2. Charles Edward Chapman, *The Founding of Spanish California* (New York: The Macmillan Company, 1916), pp. 68–91; Priestly, *José de Gálvez, passim;* "José de Gálvez," *Diccionario Porrúa: Historia, Biografía y Geografía de México* (3rd ed., México: Editorial Porrúa, 1970), I, 806–807; Chapman, *A History of California*, pp. 209–215; "José de Gálvez," *Enciclopedia Universal Ilustrada Europeo-Americana* (Madrid: Espasa-Calpe, 1921), XXV, 557.

3. For an excellent account of Portolá's brief stay in California see Donald A. Nuttall, "Gaspar de Portolá: Disenchanted Conquistador of Spanish Upper California," *Southern California Quarterly* LIII (September 1971), 185–198. For Gálvez's imperious selection of the president of the Alta California missions see Chapman, *A History of California*, pp. 220–221; Priestly, *José de Gálvez*, pp. 253–254.

4. Rivera was born around the year 1725 in Compostela, Mexico, or its vicinity. See Ernest J. Burrus, *Diario del Capitán Comandante Fernando de Rivera y Moncada* (2 vols.; Madrid: Ediciones José Porrúa Turanzas, 1967), I, xx.

5. Ernest J. Burrus, "Rivera y Moncada, Explorer and Military Commander in Both Californias, in the Light of His Diary and Other Contemporary Documents," *The Hispanic American Historical Review* L (November 1970), 682–692; Burrus, ed., *Diario del Capitán Comandante Fernando de Rivera y Moncada*.

6. Nutall, "Gaspar de Portolá" *SCQ*, LIII, 185–186.

7. For Junípero Serra's life and achievements see Maynard Geiger's scholarly and objective *The Life and Times of Fray Junípero Serra, O.F.M.* (2 vols.; Washington: Academy of American Franciscan History, 1959).

8. For an insight into Rivera's career see Burrus, "Rivera y Moncada, Explorer and Military Commander in Both Californias," *HAHR*, L, 682–692; Burrus, *Diario del Capitán Comandante Fernando de Rivera y Moncada, passim;* and Manuel Patricio Servín, *The Apostolic Life of Fernando Consag, Explorer of Lower California* (Los Angeles: Dawson's Book Shop, 1968), pp. 67; Peter Masten Dunne, *Black Robes in Lower California* (Berkeley, University of California Press, 1952), pp. 327, 333, and 418.

9. According to John Kessell, *gente de razón* were "free rational persons subject to the laws of the land and to the jurisdiction and tithe of the secular clergy. They were, in other words, not wards of a mission. But because they lived so far from the nearest secular priest, the settlers and their families turned for spiritual needs to the missionary of Guevavi." See John L. Kessell, *Mission of Sorrows: Jesuit Guevavi and the Pimas, 1691–1767* (Tucson, 1970). Father Maynard Geiger states that *gente de razón* are "all non-mission people of whatever racial strain or mixture." See Maynard Geiger, O.F.M., "Mission San Gabriel," *Southern California Quarterly*, LII (September 1971), 219, note 3. In accordance with usage of the truly Spanish settlers, I define *gente de razón* as Hispanicized non-Spaniards who were generally a mixture of Indian, African and Spanish stock. Spaniards referred to

themselves as "Spaniards" and not as *gente de razón*—a term that would equate them to mixed-bloods.

10. Bancroft, *History of California*, I, 127–136, is the statistical source for the number of persons who arrived in the colonizing expedition.

11. Manuel P. Servín, "The Beginnings of California's Anti-Mexican Prejudice," in *An Awakened Minority: The Mexican Americans*, ed. by Servín (Beverly Hills: Glencoe Press, 1974).

12. Manuel P. Servín, "The Secularization of the California Missions: A Reappraisal," *Southern California Quarterly*, XLVII (June 1965), 136.

13. John W. Caughey, *California: A Remarkable State's Life History* (3rd ed.: Englewood Cliffs, 1970), p. 76.

14. Bancroft, *History of California*, I, 345.

15. For Governor Felipe de Neve's views on the pueblos and settlers see Bancroft, *History of California*, I, 314; Felipe de Neve, "Sobre tierras y fundación de Sn. José de Guadalupe," 15 April 1778, MS. C-A, BL; Felipe de Neve to the Comandante General, Monterey, 10 August 1778, C-A 22, BL; Felipe de Neve to the Comandante General, Monterey, 3 April 1779, C-A 22, BL; Instrucción que da [Felipe de Neve al parecer a Pedro Fages] sobre el gobierno interino de la Peninsula, 7 September 1782, MS. C-A 2, BL.

16. For Serra's and the Fernandinos' views toward the settlers see Servín, "The Secularization of the California Missions," *SCQ*, XLVII, *passim;* Bancroft, *History of California*, I, 314; Geiger, *Life and Times of Serra*, II, *passim;* Florian F. Guest, "The Establishment of the Villa de Branciforte," *California Historical Quarterly* XLI (March 1962), *passim.*

17. Bancroft, *History of California*, I, 381.

18. Guest, "The Establishment of the Villa de Branciforte," *CHSQ*, XLI, 37.

19. Guest, "The Establishment of the Villa de Branciforte," *CHSQ*, XLI, 40–41.

20. Costansó here uses the term *gente de razón* as the missionaries did, but not as the Spanish settlers of California. The Spanish settlers always referred to themselves as "Spaniards" and not as *gente de razón* which to them connoted an Hispanicized mixed-blood.

21. Manuel P. Servín, tr., "Costansó's 1791 Report on Strengthening New California's Presidios," *CHSQ*, XLIX, 226. It is interesting to note that Costansó, a Peninsular, referred to the criollos as *gente de razón*, while the latter would have called themselves "Spaniards."

22. Servín, "Costansó's 1791 Report," *CHSQ*, XLIX, 227.

23. Chapman, *A History of California*, pp. 391–392.

24. Chapman, *A History of California*, pp. 392 and 393.

25. W. W. Robinson, *Land in California* (Berkeley: University of California Press, 1948), pp. 45–46.

26. Robinson, *Land in California*, p. 46. For confirmation of Fages' action by the Commandant General see Galindo Navarro to the Commandant General, Chihuahua, 21 June 1786, C-A 52, BL.

27. See Robert Cameron Gillingham, *The Rancho San Pedro* (Los Angeles: Domínguez Estate Company, 1961). For documentation and testimony on Domínguez's Rancho presented to the Board of Land Commissioners see L-C 398, SD, BL.

28. Hubert Howe Bancroft, *Register of Pioneer Inhabitants of California, 1542–1848* (Los Angeles: Dawson's Book Shop, 1964), pp. 782–783; Gillingham, *Rancho San Pedro*, pp. 67–89.

29. Robinson, *Land in California*, pp. 46–47.

30. Leonard Pitt, *The Decline of the Californios* (Berkeley: University of California Press, 1966), pp. 251–252.

31. Gillingham, *Rancho San Pedro*, p. 70; Hubert Howe Bancroft, *California Pioneer*

Register and Index, 1542–1848 (Baltimore: Regional Publishing Company, 1964), p. 369. For documentation and testimony on Rancho San Rafael see L-C 381, SD, BL.

32. Robinson, *Land in California*, p. 48.

33. Gillingham, *Rancho San Pedro*, pp. 70, 41; Robinson, *Land in California*, pp. 48–50. For documentation and testimony on Rancho los Nietos see L-C 290, SD, BL.

34. Robinson, *Land in California*, pp. 49–50.

35. Fray José Señán to Viceroy Marqués de Branciforte, Mexico, 11 May 1796, in *The Letters of José Señán, O.F.M., Mission San Buenaventura, 1796–1823*, tr. Paul D. Nathan, ed. Lesley B. Simpson (San Francisco: John Howell Books, 1962), p. 5.

9

Comparative Demographic Analysis of Texas, 1777–1793*

Alicia Vidaurreta Tjarks

Editor's Introduction

Many writers have generalized about the racial and social fluidity of society on New Spain's far northern frontier, but none have based their generalizations on as much empirical data as Alicia Tjarks. Dr. Tjarks belongs to a generation of historians who, under the influence of French social historians, are making greater use of quantitative techniques to understand peoples of the past. She has made excellent use of census records to answer a variety of elusive questions about common people in eighteenth-century Texas: What was their average life expectancy? What percentage of the population were children? What percentage of the adult population was male? female? single? married? widowed? lived out of wedlock? How common were illegitimate children?

*This article appeared originally in the *Southwestern Historical Quarterly*, 77 (1974): 291–338. It is reprinted here in condensed form with permission of the publisher and the author. Although some material has been deleted where indicated, for the convenience of researchers notes and tables retain the same numbers which appeared in the original article.

Ms. Tjarks provides fascinating answers to these questions. Her method of arriving at those answers was necessary. Unlike historians who study literate elite groups, those historians who wish to understand more about the average frontiersman are handicapped by a shortage of literary sources—letters, government documents, diaries, and wills. Census data, on the other hand, have enabled Tjarks to compose demographic profiles of illiterate groups. Census data also have many limitations, as she suggests. Tjarks found, for example, that settlers in Texas resembled the *californios* described by Servín in their tendency to "whiten" themselves—to misrepresent their racial ancestry to the census taker. Demographic analysis, then, requires much more than counting. Like other modes of historical analysis, the demographer needs to approach documents with skepticism and sensitivity and use them in conjunction with a variety of sources.

In the article that follows, Tjarks discusses her methods and her conclusions. This article has been shortened substantially because of space limitations in this anthology. Students doing research on this question should consult the original.

Alicia Vidaurreta Tjarks has studied on three continents. She completed her undergraduate work in Argentina, the country of her birth, and did graduate work in Spain (Ph.D., University of Madrid), and in the United States (Master of Library Science, University of Denver). Dr. Tjarks, who has taught at universities in Spain and Argentina, has been Ibero-American bibliographer at the Zimmerman Library, University of New Mexico since 1973. Her numerous publications range over a wide variety of subjects, from a book on *El comercio inglés y el contrabando* (Buenos Aires: 1962), to a bibliography of Brazilian travel literature (*Revista de Historia de America*, 1978). The piece reprinted in this anthology forms part of a book-length manuscript entitled "Economic and Social Life in Colonial Texas, 1770–1790." Dr. Tjarks has published a related study in the *Revista de Indias* (1973–74), "Evolución urbana de Texas durante el siglo XVIII," and a similar work on New Mexico: "Demographic, Ethnic and Occupational Structure of New Mexico, 1790," *Americas*, 35 (1978): 45–88.

Comparative Demographic Analysis of Texas, 1777–1793

Demographic analysis has been a very much neglected area in the history of Spanish Texas. A few historians and scientists have provided scattered information based on some census reports from the late eighteenth and the early nineteenth centuries.[1] This limited statistical information leaves, however, an important gap, as these general data are insufficient for a thorough demographic and social study of the Spanish period of Texas, and are at times even contradictory. Perhaps the political history of Spanish Texas—accurately called the "key of New Spain"—has exerted too strong an attraction on the researchers or perhaps those census reports have been inaccessible because widely scattered over the world, in collections like the Archivo General de Indias in Seville, the Archivo Histórico Nacional in Madrid, the Biblioteca Nacional of Mexico City, or the Archives Division of the Texas State Library and the Bexar Archives at the University of Texas, both in Austin. For whatever reason, the fact is that a more profound and objective study of the demographic aspect of Spanish Texas history, of the racial and social characteristics and movements of the population has been delayed and avoided up to the present. What is presented here is not a complete detailed analysis, but some appraisals that can guide future research in this area, so that historians, as suggested by Harley L. Browning, "at least those concerned with economic and social history, can benefit from a better understanding of the demographic perspective."[2]

The social structure of colonial Texas, like that of many other frontier areas, possessed several traits that made it different from the Mexican society of the eighteenth century. Lyle N. McAlister's classification of the Mexican population, based on their economic characteristics, holds some validity relative to Texas in general terms. McAlister viewed the Mexicans as divided into three classes: the upper class, consisting of the owners of haciendas and mines, rich merchants, the higher echelons of the clergy, and the bureaucracy; the middle class, consisting of smaller ranchers and mine owners, small merchants, clerks and civil servants, artisans, and the lower clergy and bureaucrats; and the lower or proletarian class, including poor artisans, peasants, peddlers, servants, and vagabonds, all people without land and property.[3] At first glance this classification seems applicable to Texas, but closer scrutiny reveals that its generalities are inadequate because of numerous exceptions.

The northern borderlands of New Spain became the assembly point for a quite heterogeneous population, coming from all walks of life and places. Such a frontier society can be identified with the relatively open society of the Conquest much more easily than with the cohesive and hierarchical structure later imposed by Spain on its American possessions.

This is not an isolated or casual fact. Texas was incorporated into the Spanish realm when the colonization of Central Mexico had been already completed. San Antonio, originally just a tiny garrison town, was settled by peasants from the Canary Islands, who, fortified by their own rural past and their innate toughness, adapted themselves perfectly to the new environment, despite isolation and need. The social stratification of the vicekingdom, which reached its most significant momentum in the second half of the eighteenth century, was not completely absent, however, from this new frontier society. It unquestionably existed, but only in such an extenuated and permeated way that it presents—unlike the situation in some other regions of America—a clear case of acculturation of the European, a process which at the beginning of the nineteenth century would turn into a complete identification with the natives and the environment.[4]

It is pretentious, however, to define that Texan culture as a democratic society in the current sense. The new province was formed under the influence of the social order ruling in New Spain, but without the presence of really closed ethnic or economic groups. This circumstance was primarily determined by the scarcity of the original European population, which was readily followed by larger contingents of settlers from Mexico. Racial miscegenation was strong in this second wave of immigrants. They came to the borderlands looking for social and economic improvement, particularly after 1749, when the vicekingdom underwent a great agrarian crisis, resulting in an intense internal migration. The sequels of the dramatic economic crisis suffered by New Spain in 1785–1786 were even more largely effective in the increase of the borderland population. These effects were principally felt in agricultural and mining areas, where the scarcity of food and work, as much as the extremely high cost of living, triggered the "giant migrations"—as they were appropriately called by Enrique Florescano—which enticed some groups of people from northern Mexico to move in search of a better way of living, even to such isolated areas as Texas.[5] According to Silvio Zavala, "the frontier was not a safety valve, but it was a land of opportunity."[6]

As a consequence of the mixture of races and classes, Texan society experienced an increasing upward mobility, a phenomenon about which census reports and parochial registers frequently bear witness. It is remarkable that, along with the continuing concept of a caste society, differences due to skin color and other related circumstances were reduced to such a point that a society definitely heterogeneous, both in its origin and in its composition, emerged in Texas.

The information relative to the population of Texas available in printed sources, which refer to that province or to the vicekingdom of New Spain in general, is relatively abundant, although quite contradictory. The period considered was recorded through one of the initial stammerings of statistical techniques, since the first general census was carried out to fulfil the Royal Order of November 10, 1776, which demanded periodic census reports for all inhabitants of America and the Philippines.[7] Examining the census reports *(padrones)* from Texas one will occasionally find satisfactory answers to his questions, and the demographic information gathered permits some conclusions pertaining to the population of Texas, which do not always agree with those already accepted. The roaming Indian tribes cannot be included in the general estimate of the Texan population. Some information about them exists, such as the estimates supplied in 1778 by Athanase de Mézières, lieutenant governor of the town of Natchitoches in Louisiana, to the commander general of the Interior Provinces, the Chevalier de Croix, or the data provided by a few tribal censuses, like those taken by Nicolás de la Mathe and Esteban de Vaugine, in 1783, and by Governor Domingo Cabello, in 1785. These figures, however, are merely approximate or rough estimates, notwithstanding that they resulted from commendable efforts.[8] Consequently, the present analysis will consider only the Indians of the missions and those who lived permanently in the Spanish towns. To proceed otherwise—that is, trying to add into the calculations a minimum of 6,000 pagan Indians (Croix mentioned 7,280 in 1778) to some 3,000 inhabitants of the three Spanish towns—would lead to an extreme ambiguity and lack of precision.[9]

The present study had to adopt the methodology suitable to prestatistic and protostatistic periods, applied by the French School and the Berkeley Group.[10] All existing sources, even if in many cases very incomplete, have been used to cross-check data, particularly in the racial aspect. The baptism registers from the parish of San Fernando de Béxar and from the missions are primary demographic and social sources, invaluable for the study of the dynamic social structure; they not only provide quantitative information about birth, but also supply rich collateral material about racial groups, miscegenation, and illegitimacy. Matrimonial registers are very fragmentary, invalidating a thorough analysis of this aspect, but the census of 1793 allows the identification of exogamic and endogamic marriages, at least among the civilian population. Gaps in information created by the lack of obituary books have been partially filled by marginal notes in baptismal registers, which indicated the demise of those who had been baptized. Even if the monthly reports of the governors to

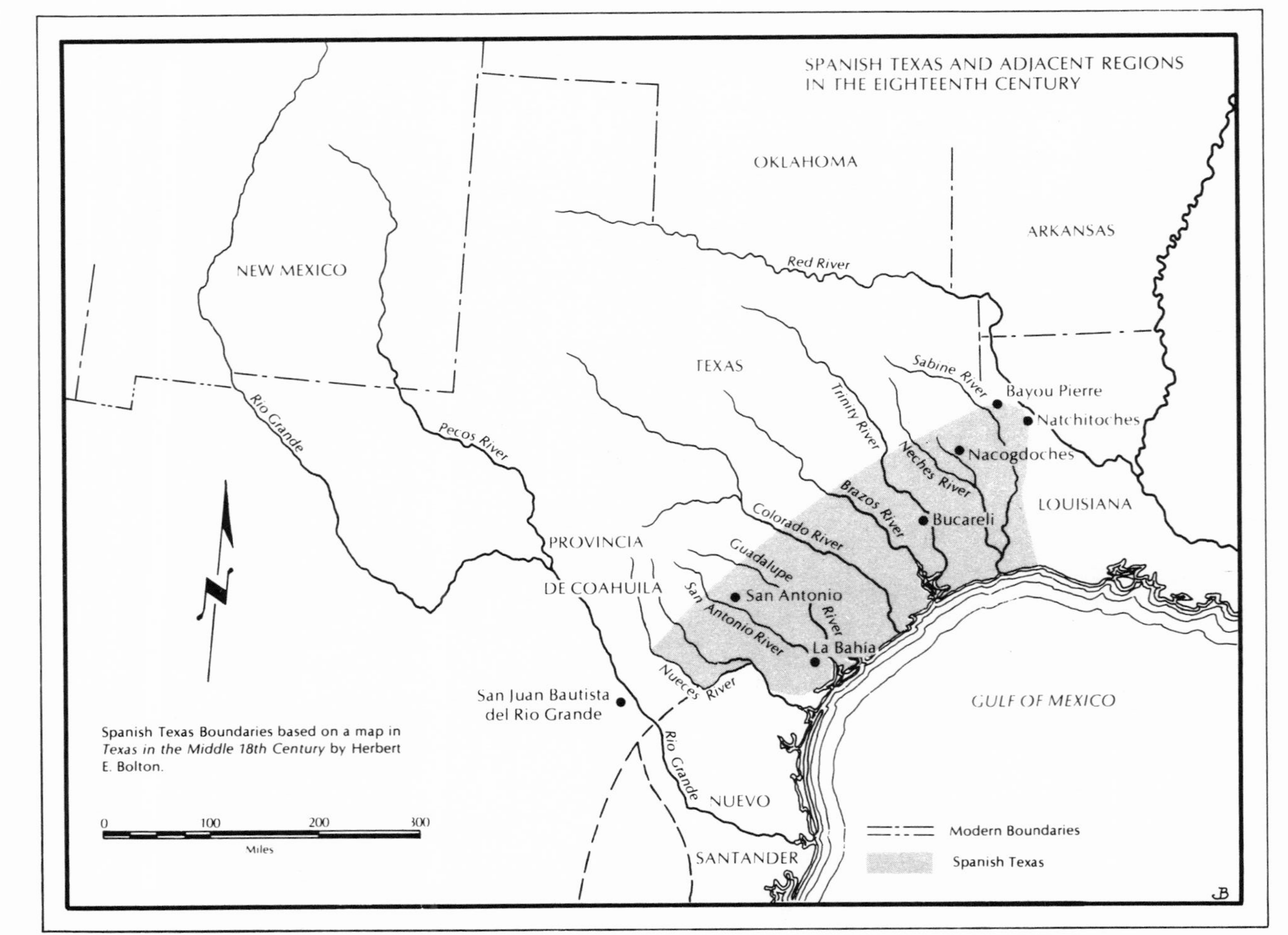
SPANISH TEXAS AND ADJACENT REGIONS
IN THE EIGHTEENTH CENTURY
OKLAHOMA
ARKANSAS
NEW MEXICO
Red River
TEXAS
Sabine River
Bayou Pierre
Natchitoches
Nacogdoches
Trinity River
Neches River
LOUISIANA
Brazos River
Bucareli
Colorado River
PROVINCIA
DE COAHUILA
Guadalupe
San Antonio
San Antonio River
River
La Bahía
Pecos River
Rio Grande
Nueces River
San Juan Bautista
del Rio Grande
GULF OF MEXICO
Rio Grande
NUEVO
SANTANDER
Modern Boundaries
Spanish Texas
Spanish Texas Boundaries based on a map in
Texas in the Middle 18th Century by Herbert
E. Bolton.
0
100
200
300
Miles
JB

the commander general seldom contain quantitative information, they cannot be discarded as reference sources relative to sanitary conditions, epidemics, harassment by Indians, and similar factors that influenced the growth of the population. Finally, no demographic model was applied in the analysis of age and fertility, as there is no way to assure that they could validly apply to Texas at that time.

From the first census in 1777 to that of 1793, twelve general and local censuses were taken in Texas. In some cases only partial information is available, not only because of loss of documents (as in 1793, a year for which only data from the civilian population of San Antonio, Nacogdoches, and the new settlement of Bayou Pierre could be found), but also because of the census takers' occasional omission of the population of the missions from the count. In spite of the multitude of reports on hand, it is obvious that the orders of José de Gálvez were not received with enthusiasm by those in charge of taking the population census. In San Antonio, for example, Governor Domingo Cabello had to threaten the alcaldes of the Cabildo with fines and imprison two former members of this corporation to force them to carry out their duty.[11]

In 1790, as a consequence of the creation of the intendance system, and also for taxation purposes, the viceroy, Conde de Revillagigedo, ordered the first general census in New Spain.[12] With detailed instructions and a printed model on hand, municipal, parochial, and district authorities, between 1791 and 1793, carried out this census. Now called the "Revillagigedo Census," its results were in part disclosed by Alexander von Humboldt, although many of the data he published have been later questioned.[13] The reports included data on the population, including such characteristics as age, sex, place of birth, race, occupation, and marital status, information which supplemented the data provided by the preceding local census sheets.[14]

In Texas the most important antecedents are the two censuses taken by Governor Cabello in San Antonio in 1779 and in La Bahía (presently Goliad) in 1780. Even if these reports do not furnish significant details like the age of each member of the family, or even if they mistakenly classified as "Spaniards" all the inhabitants of both presidios of Texas—while many of the soldiers were mestizos, and some even mulattoes—they provide such other interesting facts as details on real estate and other property or information relative to the occupational structure of the population. These census reports can therefore be considered the first economic census of Texas and the only sources furnishing such information before the 1790s.[15]

The inadequacies of these earlier population counts brought about the preparation of the general census of Texas. The deficiencies of the methods used in this 1791–1792 census are clearly revealed in the correspondence of Governor Manuel Muñoz with Bruno Díaz de Salcedo, then intendant of San Luis Potosí.[16] The confusion and incompleteness of the figures and the inadequacy of those in charge of the census operation, make analysis of the data from the general census practically useless, both because of its irregularities and because of the exaggerated data it presents, which must be rejected after a simple comparison with data offered by the reports of the preceding and later years. The authorities of Nacogdoches clearly testified to this inaccuracy when they confessed to the governor that they omitted many classes of information because they did not know how to procure it or how to present it in writing.[17] The rules set down by Revillagigedo prescribed that the census should not be taken among the people belonging to the military garrisons of the vicekingdom, a deplorable decision in the case of Texas, where a considerable part of the population was concentrated in the presidios of San Antonio and La Bahía, as dependents. The military and their families, however, were included in the census of 1790, making that year's report one of the most complete, together with the already mentioned reports on 1779–1780.[18]

In the late eighteenth century, Texas was certainly one of the least-inhabited territories of New Spain. The Interior Provinces had an average of six inhabitants per square league; Texas and Coahuila showed scarcely two; and only desert Baja California had a lower ratio—one inhabitant per square league.[19] If, for mere reason of comparison, one takes into account the whole population of New Spain at that time, estimated by Humboldt for 1793 at 4,483,569 souls, the population of Texas was so small that it could not make up 1/10,000 of that total.[20]

The first exact statistic on the total population of Texas can be found in the report of 1777. This report, called here the "Croix Census," was undertaken by Teodoro de Croix (then commander general of the Interior Provinces) upon the orders of José de Gálvez, as Viceroy Antonio María de Bucareli y Ursúa did in the other provinces of New Spain.[21] In Texas, it shows a population of 3,103 souls for that year, including the inhabitants of the missions.

The only retrospective data available for the eighteenth century are the following: 3,090 souls in 1742 (1,290 Indians and 1,800 Spaniards and *Gente de Castas)* given by Peter Gerhard; 1,500 persons in 1744, as estimated by Henderson Yoakum—a total quite reduced for that time, particularly when Yoakum indicates that this population was centered largely in San Antonio; and a final estimate of 1,846 people living in Texas in 1760, elaborated by Sherburne F. Cook and Woodrow Borah on information furnished by the Bishop of Guadalajara for that year.[22]

Even for later periods the data are fluctuating and doubtful. In his general report of 1781, the Chevalier de Croix gave an approximate total of 4,000 persons living in Texas in 1780. Vicente Riva Palacio estimated a population of 3,394 inhabitants in the early nineteenth century, a figure that seems to be much closer to the real population in the last decade of the eighteenth century than the one provided by a contemporary account of Governor Juan Bautista de Elguezábal in 1803, who reported that the population of Texas was 4,800 people, 2,500 of whom lived in San Antonio.[23] With manifest lack of realism Humboldt indicates 21,000 inhabitants for that same year, while for 1810 Fernando Navarro y Noriega goes back to a reduced total of 3,334 souls. If the information of these contemporaries offers so many variations, the data supplied by later scholars are in no way more uniform; thus for the beginning of the nineteenth century, Bancroft comes up with a total of 3,900 people, a figure which is increased by *The Handbook of Texas* to 7,000 inhabitants.[24] All these evaluations, with the exception of the moderate estimates of Navarro y Noriega and of Bancroft, lose validity and precision through confrontation with the actual data of the census reports. To prove this one can simply take into account the report of Governor Manuel de Salcedo, who indicates a total population of 3,122 persons in 1809, a sum that, if compared with the one given in 1777, proves that no sensible change had occurred in thirty years.[25]

As a matter of fact, the population of Texas remained stagnant when it did not decrease, as it did during the period 1778–1783. A slight increase in later years can be attributed much more easily to the migratory flow from the north of New Spain than to natural demographic expansion. Life was shorter in the borderlands; permanent warfare against the Indians, the fight for subsistence in a hostile environment, a deficient and limited diet, and, above all, epidemic diseases like smallpox and *matlazahuatl* fever, which specially ravaged Texas (as most of New Spain) during the years 1785–1786, resulted in the loss of many lives, particularly among the infant population.[26] Since 1790 one can observe a tendency toward slow demographic expansion, even though a momentary retrogressive slump of more than 100 people occurs two years later.

The demographic development will be different in each of the Spanish towns. All through this period San Antonio maintained the traits of a typical border town, where the ups and downs of the population were more conspicuous, mostly because the capital of Texas had become the rallying point for the migrants from other areas.[27] The expansive trend was much more pronounced in La Bahía. It started there around 1792 and reached its summit in 1796, with 1,138 inhabitants. From then on, economic stagnation reversed the trend, reducing the population to 405 persons by 1810. This development is easy to explain: La Bahía offered little incentive to civilian settlers, mainly because of the lack of irrigation for agriculture and because of the threat of raids from the Indians of the Gulf Coast. Nacogdoches, the town of the eastern border, doubled its population between 1778 and 1810, when it reached a total of 655 inhabitants. The demographic expansion here was based on the slow but constant immigration of settlers from Louisiana and of other foreigners, mostly French and Englishmen. If the census of 1792, so imperfectly carried out, could be considered valid, this would have been the year of the largest population of Texas in the eighteenth century, with 3,210 inhabitants. But it is wiser to use the more realistic report of 1790, which shows a total of 3,169 (Table 1).

The stagnation and demographic weakness of the population of Texas are more noticeable in a comparison of Texas and Louisiana data. Louisiana, in the very short period of sixteen years, between 1769 ("O'Reilly Census") and 1785, more than doubled its population. In 1788 the city of New Orleans alone had 5,338 inhabitants, or approximately 66 percent more than all the residents of Texas.[28]

The chronic situation of depopulation and little development had not yet changed in 1811, when Miguel Ramos Arizpe, deputy of the Eastern Provinces of New Spain at the Spanish Cortes in Cádiz, denounced the lack of official support in stimulating the colonization of Texas, and recommended that such a task should not be neglected at a crucial time when preservation of the area to Spain was vital because foreign pressure was mounting on its frontiers.[29]

Analysis of the census reports between 1777 and 1793 on the basis of sex indicates a constant predominance of the male population—another characteristic trend in the borderlands, particularly in those areas guarded by military garrisons—even though this established ratio of male predominance is not so pronounced as to warrant description as sexual imbalance (Table 2). In some particular cases, as at the mission of San Antonio de Valero on the eve of secularization, the female almost matched the male population. Still with reference to the missions, one should not be deceived by a slight increase of the masculine rate in the last decade of the century, notwithstanding the continuous depopulation of the Franciscan establishments. This change did not result from an increase of the Indian male population, but from a migration of mestizos, mulattoes, and even Spaniards to the mission lands, where they went to live as *agregados, arrimados,* or servants.

The census of 1792 registers the highest rate of female population in the century, resulting probably from a distortion of data through the exclusion, since 1791, of the inhabitants of the military garrisons from the reports. At the mission of Espíritu Santo, in La Bahía, one finds in 1785 the only case of clear female predominance, but a relative sexual balance will be the norm in the following years. A logical explanation of this fact can be found in the lack of success of the missions in La Bahía, where desertion of the male Indian neophytes was all too frequent.

TABLE 1
Total Population of Texas
(1777–1793)

Year	Béxar			La Bahía			Nacog-doches	Bayou Pierre	General Total
	Military and Civilian	Missions	Total	Military and Civilian	Missions	Total			
1777	1,351	709	2,060	515	181	696	347	—	3,103
1780	1,463	—	—	544	—	—	—	—	—
1782	—	—	—	—	—	—	—	—	2,840[a]
1783	1,248	554	1,802	454	214	668	349	—	2,819
1784	1,224	599	1,823	496	110	606	399	—	2,828
1785	1,248	617	1,865	503	118	621	433	—	2,919
1786	1,288	673	1,961	513	100	613	(438)	—	(3,012)[b]
1787	—	—	—	488	104	592	—	—	—
1789	1,295	566	1,861	—	116	—	—	—	—
1790	1,383	495	1,878	633	134	767	524	—	3,169
1791	1,530	269	1,799	598	243	841	570	—	3,210
1792	1,302	470	1,772	728	—	728	505	—	3,005[c]
1793	1,321	—	—	—	—	—	457	85	1,863[d]

**Sources:* AHN, Estado, legajo 3883; AGI, Guadalajara, legajo 283; Biblioteca Nacional (Mexico City), Archivo Franciscano, legajo 100; BA, reels 15, 17, 20, 21, 22, 24; Nacogdoches 2-23/443, (Archives Division, Texas State Library, Austin). The same sources were used in the following tables.

[a]Total shown in the census of 1783.

[b]Totals between parentheses estimated on the base of geometric progression.

[c]Does not include the population of the garrisons of San Antonio and La Bahía. The soldiers and their families made a total of 720 persons. Consequently, they have to be added to the census figure of 3,005 souls to produce the real total of the province for 1792, which was 3,725 for that year. This census, ordered by the Viceroy Count of Revillagigedo for all New Spain, excluded the populations from the garrisons in all provinces. In La Bahía the population of the missions was added to the civilian population of the town. The Nacogdoches figure includes inhabitants of Bayou Pierre (31) and surrounding ranches (another 31).

[d]Includes civilian population only of San Antonio, Nacogdoches, and Bayou Pierre.

TABLE 2
MASCULINE INDEX OF THE TOTAL POPULATION (1777–1793)

Year	Total Population of Census	Male		Female		Index of Masculinity
		Total	Percent of Total Population	Total	Percent of Total Population	
1777	3,103	1,708	55.05	1,395	44.95	1.25
1782	2,840	1,561	54.96	1,279	45.04	1.22
1783	2,819	1,549	54.95	1,270	45.05	1.22
1784	2,828	1,567	55.41	1,261	44.59	1.24
1785	2,919	1,584	54.26	1,335	45.74	1.185
1786	2,574[a]	1,406	54.63	1,168	45.37	1.21
1787	592[b]	323	54.56	269	45.44	1.20
1789	1,861[c]	990	53.19	871	46.81	1.14
1790	3,169	1,763	55.63	1,406	44.37	1.25
1792	3,005[d]	1,354	45.05	1,651	54.95	0.82
1793	1,863[e]	1,005	53.94	858	46.06	1.17

[a]Excludes Nacogdoches.
[b]Only La Bahía and corresponding missions.
[c]Only San Antonio (garrison, civilian population, and missions).
[d]Does not include the garrisons of both presidios and their dependents.
[e]Only civilian inhabitants of San Antonio, Nacogdoches, and Bayou Pierre.

TABLE 3
MASCULINE INDEX OF THE TOTAL ADULT POPULATION (1777–1793)

Year	Total Adult Population	Male		Female		Masculine Index
		Total	Percent of Total Population	Total	Percent of Total Population	
1777	2,063	1,147	55.59	916	44.41	1.25
1783	1,748	952	54.46	796	45.54	1.20
1785	1,977	1,068	53.05	909	46.95	1.13
1790	2,314	1,285	55.63	1,029	44.47	1.24
1792	2,024[a]	917	45.30	1,107	54.70	0.82
1793	1,292[b]	711	55.03	581	44.97	1.22

[a]Not including garrisons and dependents.
[b]Only civilian inhabitants of San Antonio, Nacogdoches, and Bayou Pierre.

In brief, the total estimates of the census reports indicate that the rate of masculine predominance remains almost stable over the period, and that even in 1790 it shows the same proportion as twelve years before (1.25 : 1). The sudden decrease observed in 1792 is due to the fact that the population of the military garrisons was omitted from the census. In some way, a similar process must be reported for 1793, when the inhabitants of the missions were also excluded. The resulting year's ratio of 1.17 : 1 can be deemed only provisional and of relative value, because it includes the population of Bayou Pierre, the new settlement on the eastern border, which was largely male.[30]

In the analysis of the sexual characteristics of the adult population, all inhabitants fourteen years of age and older are considered. This pragmatic age limit, used also by the Spanish census takers, is not always coincident with puberty, as the study of fertility rates presents numerous cases in which women married at the age of fourteen, thirteen, and even twelve had children. The same sexual ratio prevails among adults as among the total population. The decrease of the masculine rate for 1785 can be ascribed to the already mentioned epidemic of that year and to the war against the Comanche Indians, which brought about a severe loss of lives in 1784–1785 (Table 3).

There are no reports analyzing the population by age, not even for family heads, until the "Revillagigedo Census." The only useful precedents are the "Croix Census" and the censuses of 1779–1780 taken by Governor Cabello, which record the age of the family head, the sex of his descendants, and their age as over or under fourteen years. The "Revillagigedo Census" classified by age all the inhabitants of the vicekingdom, but in some areas of Texas the census takers unfortunately omitted to register all children younger than seven years of age, thus making these reports inaccurate. The final printed forms or summaries, therefore, were discarded for this study, and the local handwritten drafts, which painstakingly indicate the age of each of these infants, were used instead.

Adults made up two-thirds of the population of Texas and in San Antonio they were an overwhelming majority. The trend is predominant and unchanging (Table 4). Parochial baptism registers bear witness to an actively normal rate of births, while other sources also inform as to an extremely high rate of infant mortality, which explains such a marked adult predominance.[31] A detailed study, comparing parochial records and census reports for San Antonio and depending missions, shows that numerous families decreased in size over the years and that practically no family failed to lose at least one child during its first year of life.

Despite such a detrimental factor in population increase, a classification of the civilian population of Texas in 1793 by age, in the three towns

TABLE 4
PERCENTAGE RATIOS OF ADULT AND MINOR POPULATION WITH INDICATION OF SEXES (1777–1793)

Year	Male				Female				Total			
	Adults		Minors		Adults		Minors		Adults		Minors	
	No.	Percent of Male Population	No.	Percent of Male Population	No.	Percent of Male Population	No.	Percent of Male Population	No.	Percent of Male Population	No.	Percent of Male Population
1777	1,147	67.15	561	32.85	916	63.84	519	36.16	2,063	65.63	1,080	34.37
1783	952	61.45	597	38.55	796	62.67	474	37.33	1,748	62.01	1,071	37.99
1785	1,068	67.42	516	32.58	909	68.08	426	31.92	1,977	67.72	942	32.28
1789[a]	749	75.65	241	24.35	638	73.24	233	26.76	1,387	74.52	474	25.48
1790	1,285	72.88	478	27.12	1,029	73.18	377	26.82	2,314	73.01	855	26.99
1792[b]	917	67.72	437	32.28	1,107	67.05	544	32.95	2,024	67.35	981	32.65
1793[c]	711	70.74	294	29.26	581	65.38	277	34.62	1,292	69.35	571	30.65

[a]Only for San Antonio.
[b]Not including garrisons and dependents.
[c]Only civilian population of San Antonio, Nacogdoches, and Bayou Pierre.

TABLE 5
AGE OF THE POPULATION
(1793)[a]

Age	Men	Women	Total
Under 10 years	261	236	497
11 to 20 years	189	180	369
21 to 30 years	200	167	367
31 to 40 years	153	126	279
41 to 50 years	97	67	164
51 to 60 years	56	56	112
61 to 70 years	20	17	37
Over 70 years	6	6	12
Undetermined	23	3	26
Total	1,005	858	1,863

[a]Only minors of civilian families of San Antonio, Nacogdoches, and Bayou Pierre. The handwritten census of 1793 was used because the census of 1792, analyzing the population from the age of seven years up, excludes and ignores those inhabitants below that age.

where the census was taken that year (San Antonio, Nacogdoches, and Bayou Pierre), reveals that minors up to ten years of age still constituted the largest relative group of inhabitants (Tables 5 and 6). A great part of the population was less than thirty years old and the age of forty seems to have been the normal life expectancy, especially among the feminine population. Very few inhabitants (only 161 of them) were fifty years of age or older (Figure 1).

About two-thirds of the adult Texan population was married, and that was a normal trend. Single men greatly outnumbered single women,

TABLE 6
AGE OF MINORS UP TO TWELVE YEARS OF AGE
(1793)[a]

Age	Males	Females	Total
Under 1 year	14	23	37
1 year	17	21	38
2 years	16	22	38
3 years	32	30	62
4 years	24	23	47
5 years	23	26	49
6 years	20	18	38
7 years	32	23	55
8 years	40	30	70
9 years	18	11	29
10 years	25	9	34
11 years	11	15	26
12 years	22	26	48
Total	294	277	571

[a]Only minors of civilian families of San Antonio, Nacogdoches, and Bayou Pierre.

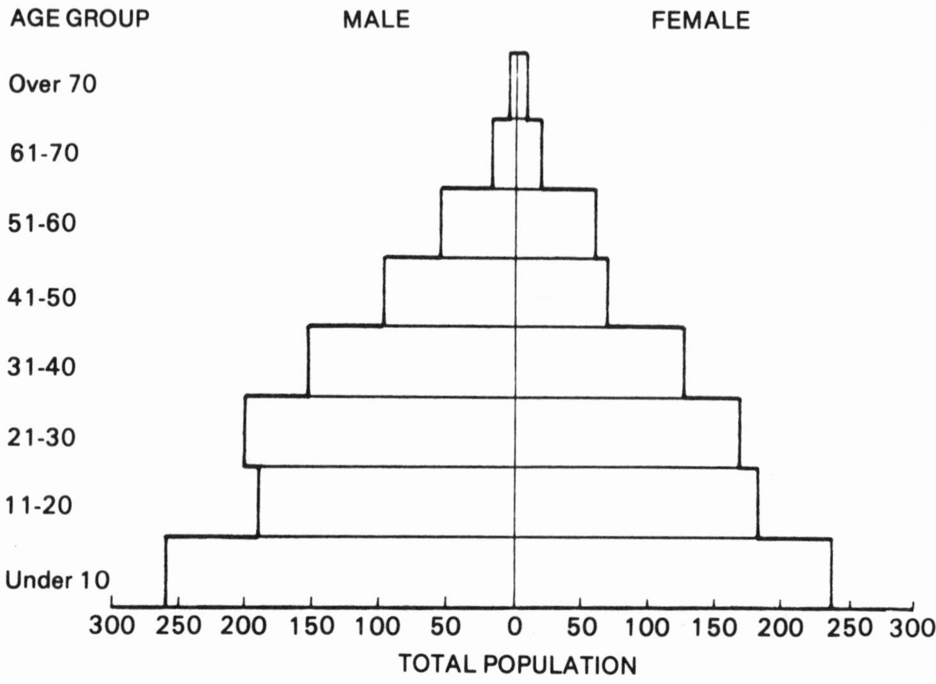

a very typical and common situation in frontier settlements and still more outstanding in towns with military garrisons. Most of the immigrants and soldiers, however, married women from the local community, thus providing a certain stability to such a developing society. But the information collected and the social characteristics of the frontier, in so many instances beyond the surveillance of the law, bear witness to the existence of frequent irregular unions and illegitimate descendancy. It is a known fact that the *barraganía* or concubinage, an institution which took deep roots in medieval Spain, was transplanted to America, where it acquired peculiar shades and became a defining element of racial miscegenation.[32] In many communities—and in Texas, primarily in San Antonio and Nacogdoches—it reached high rates and the persistence of such a custom worried some of the authorities, and above all the Chevalier de Croix, whose social prejudices rejected many norms which governed the lives of the frontiersmen. Consequently, as abundant evidence proves, many couples living together, were registered as singles. Classification of single inhabitants on the basis of sex indicates a predominance of males, not because of a higher masculine birthrate, but because of women's tendency to marry as soon as they reached the age of puberty. This fact determines a sexual imbalance among the singles, which achieved its highest point during the century in 1790 (Table 7).

The percentage of widowed persons is also high, particularly among women, as a consequence of the premature death of soldiers and neighbors in the wars against the Indians.[33] Although this is a preeminent reason for the large number of widows, mainly in San Antonio, one should not exclude other factors, already mentioned, like epidemics and fevers, so easily contracted during long trips and the campaigns against the Indians. The sexual imbalance among widowers and widows is particularly high in 1790 and in 1792, and the detailed local reports for 1793 warrant the conclusion that most of the younger widows remarried soon, as the majority of those recorded that year were more than forty years of age (Table 8).

Information relative to the birthrate has proven to be incomplete and otherwise not fully satisfactory, as the sources are very deficient and limited to the area of Béxar, providing no data on births in La Bahía and the eastern border towns. Baptismal registers, particularly those from the parish of San Fernando de Béxar, recorded the baptism of infants among the garrison and the civilian populations of San Antonio. Data for the missions are fragmentary and relevant only to San Antonio de Valero and San José. The disappearance of documentary sources from other missionary establishments turns the analysis into a provisional attempt and reduces to only relative values the data on birthrate.[34] Baptisms registered in San Antonio reached their highest level in 1774 and in 1784, while they were much less frequent in the missions, except for the year 1779 in San Antonio de Valero and the year 1784 in San José (Table 9).

Because of the zeal of the friars, who tried to consecrate all marital unions, no records of illegitimate births were made in the Franciscan establishments. On the contrary, the parochial books of San Fernando bring forward a relative abundance of baptisms of *expósitos* (foundlings), *hijos de la Iglesia* (sons of the Church), *espurios* (spurious), bastards, or children of unknown parents—all names used to indicate the illegitimate origin of children. The already mentioned illegality of many temporary or permanent unions and the relative licentiousness in which the population of Texas lived roused no little criticism from the Chevalier de Croix when he visited there in 1778, a year when the percentage of illegitimate births started to show an increasing trend. Such a trend reached its highest levels at the end of the century, that is in 1799, when 20 percent of all births were illegitimate.

These rising birthrates in San Antonio and the two missions would normally predict a constantly developing population trend, if other statistical data on the total population did not belie them. In other words,

TABLE 7
Marital Status of the Adult Population of Texas
(1777–1793)

Year	Place or Area	Total of Census Popula- tion	Married		Widowed Persons				Singles		Classification of Singles		
					Widowers		Widows						
			No.	Per- cent	No.	Per- cent	No.	Per- cent	No.	Per- cent	Priests	Unwed Males	Unwed Females
1777	Béxar	759	414	54.54	91[a]	11.98	—	—	254	33.84	—	—	—
1777	La Bahía	257	154	59.92	14[a]	5.45	—	—	89	34.63	—	—	—
1780	Béxar	834	514	61.63	19	2.29	52	6.23	249	29.85	—	—	—
1780	La Bahía	348	222	63.79	8	2.31	18	5.17	100	28.37	—	—	—
1783	Texas	1,712	1,310	76.51	61	3.58	122	7.12	219	12.79	11	—	—
1784	Nacogdoches	240	176	73.33	10	4.16	7	2.93	47	19.58	1	41	5
1784	Texas	1,785	1,346	75.40	63	3.55	84	4.70	292	16.35	13	216	63
1785	Texas	1,934	1,422	73.52	58	3.02	69	3.56	385	19.90	10	270	105
1786	Béxar	1,282	934	72.85	30	2.34	45	3.52	273	21.29	7	174	92
1786	La Bahía	468	304	64.95	15	3.22	31	6.62	118	25.21	2	92	24
1789	Béxar	1,371	1,028	74.98	24	1.76	56	4.08	263	19.18	7	192	64
1790	Texas	2,314	1,432	61.88	76	3.28	140	6.05	666	28.79	14	491	161
1791[b]	Texas	—	—	—	—	—	—	—	—	—	—	—	—
1792	Texas	2,024	1,350	66.70	70	3.45	150	7.41	454	22.44	13	188	253
1793	San Antonio[a]	933	514	55.09	17	1.82	88	9.43	314	33.66	6	220	88
1793	Nacogdoches	291	183	62.88	8	2.74	16	5.49	84	28.89	2	65	17
1793	Bayou Pierre	68	26	38.23	—	—	1	1.48	41	60.29	—	37	4

[a]Both sexes without discrimination.

[b]An existing summary shows discriminated total population for 1791, but the figures are so out of proportion with those given for 1790 and 1792 that they do not offer any credibility whatsoever. Consequently they were not included.

[c]Civilian population.

TABLE 8
WIDOWERS AND WIDOWS BY AGE AND SEX
San Antonio, Nacogdoches, and Bayou Pierre
(1793)[a]

Age	San Antonio		Nacogdoches		Bayou Pierre	
	Widowers	Widows	Widowers	Widows	Widowers	Widows
Under 20	—	1	—	—	—	—
21 to 30	—	14	5	1	—	—
31 to 40	2	11	1	7	—	—
41 to 50	8	16	—	2	—	—
51 to 60	5	29	2	5	—	1
61 to 70	1	10	—	1	—	—
Over 70	1	7	—	—	—	—
Totals	17	88	8	16	—	1

[a]Includes only civilian population. The 1793 census was used, even though the data for La Bahía are missing, because it offers the most precise and detailed information.

although the birthrate was high, it did not affect the demographic development of Texas because of the accompanying extremely high infant mortality (Table 10). Most of those baptized were registered as Spaniards, followed in order of importance by the mestizos; but a scholar has to be too gullible to accept such racial classification without reservations. In many cases it was possible to verify that children of the same parents were registered as belonging to different, and sometimes surprisingly clashing, racial groups. These errors were partly due to the ignorance of the local parish priests or to the absence of rules for such a classification, but mainly the responsibility for such "mistakes" is the outcome of racial prejudice, whose pressure to attain the "whitening of the skin" was so strong that it sensitized the parish registrars or misled them, as when they recorded as mestizos the offspring of Spaniard and mulatto interracial marriages. Some of these and other mistakes have been corrected in this analysis,[35] in which, however, racial identification of most of those illegitimately born was impossible, since a specific indication of their race or caste was lacking (Table 11). . . .

The ethnic structure of Texas became a melting pot of races in the second half of the eighteenth century, when the initial group of European settlers was followed by a second wave of colonizers, mostly coming from the north of New Spain, from all ways of life and racial combinations. The medieval caste system had taken deep root in Spanish America, but one cannot believe that in the borderlands it could follow the same strict rules which were applied to other areas, where the social hierarchy was strongly correlated with racial origins.[41] Such a principle, which may fit "rich" societies like those of Mexico and Peru, loses consistency if one tries to adjust it to peripheral areas, especially in the borderlands. Although that strict correlation existed in the early years of the

TABLE 9
IDENTIFIED ILLEGITIMATE BIRTHS REGISTERED IN THE JURISDICTION OF BÉXAR (1770–1799)*

Years	San Antonio			Mission Valero	Mission San José	Years	San Antonio			Mission Valero	Mission San José
	Total Births	Illegitimate Births	Percent of Total				Total Births	Illegitimate Births	Percent of Total		
1770	45	5	11.11	3	—	1785	56	6	10.71	—	6
1771	57	4	7.01	4	—	1786	66	7	10.60	—	13
1772	52	3	5.76	2	—	1787	59	5	8.47	—	14
1773	75	5	6.66	4	—	1788	65	6	9.23	—	6
1774	88	4	4.54	3	—	1789	69	4	5.79	—	12
1775	60	2	3.33	1	—	1790	62	6	9.66	—	9
1776	54	3	5.55	8	—	1791	65	6	9.23	—	6
1777	60	4	6.66	4	2[a]	1792	55	6	10.90	—	2
1778	71	7	9.85	4	13	1793	72	8	11.11	—	1
1779	56	7	12.50	14	2	1794	70	6	8.57	—	5
1780	70	6	8.57	3	3	1795	69	10	14.49	—	2
1781	43	4	9.30	6	6	1796	55	8	14.54	—	4
1782	69	4	5.79	4	11	1797	62	7	11.29	—	4
1783	70	8	11.42	10[b]	10	1798	54	9	16.66	—	4
1784	73	4	5.47	—	15	1799	58	12	20.69	—	3

**Sources:* CSF, BCA, Baptismal Books 3 and 4, and Baptismal Books of the Missions San Antonio de Valero and San José. The same sources were used for Table 10. No records for the other missions are extant.

[a]The Baptismal Book of the Mission San José starts in 1777.

[b]The Baptismal Book of the Mission San Antonio de Valero concludes in June, 1783.

TABLE 10
Birthrate Indexes for San Antonio and Corresponding Missons (1778–1790)[a]

Year	San Antonio			Mission Valero			Mission San José		
	Total Adult Population	Total Births	Birthrate Per Total Population (Percent)	Total Adult Population	Total Births	Birthrate Per Total Population (Percent)	Total Adult Population	Total Births	Birthrate Per Total Population (Percent)
1778	821	71	8.64	52	4	7.69	117	13	11.11
1780	835	70	8.38	—	—	—	—	—	—
1783	663	70	10.55	84	10	11.90	72[b]	10	13.88
1784	756	73	9.65	—	—	—	105	15	14.28
1785	838	56	6.68	—	—	—	115	6	5.21
1786	913	66	7.22	—	—	—	115	13	11.30
1788	—	—	—	—	—	—	88	6	6.81
1789	993	69	6.94	—	—	—	147	12	8.61
1790	983	62	6.30	—	—	—	133	9	6.76

[a]The three missions where no records have been found are not included.

[b]Births of mestizos are recorded from 1783 on; from 1784 on one also finds the birth of mulattoes registered. The latter are children of servants or *agregados* (attached) from the mission.

TABLE 11
Recorded Births in the Parish of San Antonio According to Race (1770–1799)

Year	Spaniards	Indians	Mestizos	Mulattoes	Lobos and Coyotes	Negroes	Unclassified	Total
1770	33	3	4	4	—	—	1	45
1771	43	3	7	1	1	—	2	57
1772	43	2	4	3	—	—	—	52
1773	55	2	11	5	—	—	2	75
1774	67	—	18	1	—	1	1	88
1775	46	—	9	4	—	1	—	60
1776	40	2	7	3	—	—	2	54
1777	40	2	10	2	5	—	1	60
1778	46	2	11	2	1	1	8	71
1779	36	—	12	2	1	—	5	56
1780	43	4	13	3	—	—	7	70
1781	26	1	13	—	—	—	3	43
1782	45	—	8	—	5	—	11	69
1783	50	1	—	—	1	1	17	70
1784	59	1	2	2	1	—	8	73
1785	40	1	1	1	4	1	8	56
1786	43	1	—	1	16	—	5	66
1787	46	—	—	1	8	—	4	59
1788	41	—	—	2	17	—	5	65
1789	52	—	—	1	13	—	3	69
1790	38	3	3	—	12	—	6	62
1791	51	—	5	6	—	—	3	65
1792	33	1	3	4	3	—	11	55
1793	32	4	18	3	10	1	4	72
1794	42	10	5	7	5	—	1	70
1795	36	2	14	7	9	—	1	69
1796	26	3	13	3	10	—	—	55
1797	33	1	6	9	12	—	1	62
1798	22	7	6	2	16	1	—	54
1799	29	2	11	4	12	—	—	58

[a]According to the classical treatise by Nicolás León, *Las castas del México Colonial Nueva España: Noticias etno-antropológicas* (Mexico City, 1924), passim, a "coyote" was a person of mixed Indian and mestizo descent (25 percent white and 75 percent Indian), while the offspring of a Spaniard and a mestizo was called "castizo" (75 percent white and 25 percent Indian). In Texas and in New Mexico, however, the terms "castizo" or "tresalbo" were practically never used for this lighter skin color, which was always registered as "coyote." Even today in New Mexico, when people of Spanish surname and origin want to indicate that they have a trace of Indian blood, they call themselves "coyotes." Similarly, according to León, a "lobo" was of Indian and Negro descent (50 percent of each), although in other parts of Spanish America this caste was more popularly known as "zambo." In Texas, nevertheless, both the offspring of Indian and mulatto and, less frequent, those of Indian and Negro were indiscriminately called "lobo."

colonization of Texas, when the first pioneering settlers from the Canary Islands concentrated in their hands most of the land, after the 1770s several Spanish Americans acquired the proprietorship of such land and became ranch owners and members of the leading class. The influential Menchaca family provides the best example of this social uplift of the newcomers. The creoles are strongly identified with the "aristocracy" of Texas, if the European pioneers and their descendants, notwithstanding their rural and peasant origin, can be so considered. Soon access to the ownership of the land was opened also to darker castes and the census of 1779–1780 reveals that several mestizo, coyote, and mulatto *vecinos* of Béxar and La Bahía were owners of farms, ranches, and cattle.[42]

In spite of the racial and social discrimination which existed in colonial society, sometimes accompanied by heavy shades of intolerance, these traits did not show up so intensively among the racial groups of the Northern Interior Provinces of New Spain. This region included Texas, where the color of the skin did not carry with it implied social standing. On the contrary, as explained above, the society of Texas became heterogeneous, as much by its origin as by its composition or perhaps as a sequel to the easy social and ethnic upward mobility conditioned by its borderland characteristics.

Several castes developed as a consequence of this ethnic mixture, turning Texas in some ways into a miniature projection of the Mexican society, which meticulously classified its colored people into fifty-two different castes.[43] White people, that is European or American Spaniards, were the most numerous in Texas, followed in importance by the Indians, the castes known as *color quebrado* (brittle or frail color), which included the mestizos, coyotes, mulattoes, and lobos, and finally the Negroes. Here another ethnic distortion in the census classification, besides the ones already found in the parochial registers, can be observed: in proportion to their actual number, mestizos were so classified very infrequently, probably because such a name still carried with it, at least in the popular mind, a meaning of illegitimacy. It is known, however, that many of the soldiers of the Spanish garrisons were mestizos, and some were even mulattoes, a fact rejected by the census reports, which enrolled all military personnel as "Spaniards."[44]

The Indians, even though many of them were pagans and enemies of the Spaniards, always had a high racial ranking in Texas. Not so the mulattoes; to use that name was an insult or sure defamation.[45] Such a strong prejudice promoted repeated racial "migrations" of mulatto settlers from the old garrison town of Los Adaes, when they were forced to relocate in San Antonio. Over the years they became "mestizos" and even "Spaniards" in the military documents and parish books, an example of racial ambiguity which soon found many followers among the local colored castes. Instances of such racial migration are numerous, but perhaps the most significant example is Antonio Gil Ibarvo, the founder and lieutenant governor of Nacogdoches. Naturally he is always mentioned in the census reports as a Spaniard, but everybody knew him as a mulatto, and his enemies used this circumstance to revile him. This questionable status, however, did not prevent his becoming the most powerful person on the eastern frontier, or his accumulating considerable wealth.[46] But if being a mulatto, or worse still a lobo, did lower a person's status, membership with the coyotes did not have the same effect. Their number increased considerably at the end of the century and their caste implied a closeness to the white man or Spaniard, not only in the racial, but also in the social sense, because of the status acquired through possession of a skin lighter than the complexions of the Negroes, the Indians, and even their own mestizo mothers.

The racial analysis of the population of Texas (Table 18) proves the large quantitative predominance of the Spaniards throughout the period and the province, as they constituted more than half of the total population (Figure 2). Because of the irregularities in the racial classification as it was carried out in Texas, the term "Spaniard" can be used only as a classifying

Figure 2
ETHNIC STRUCTURE OF TEXAS (1777—1793)

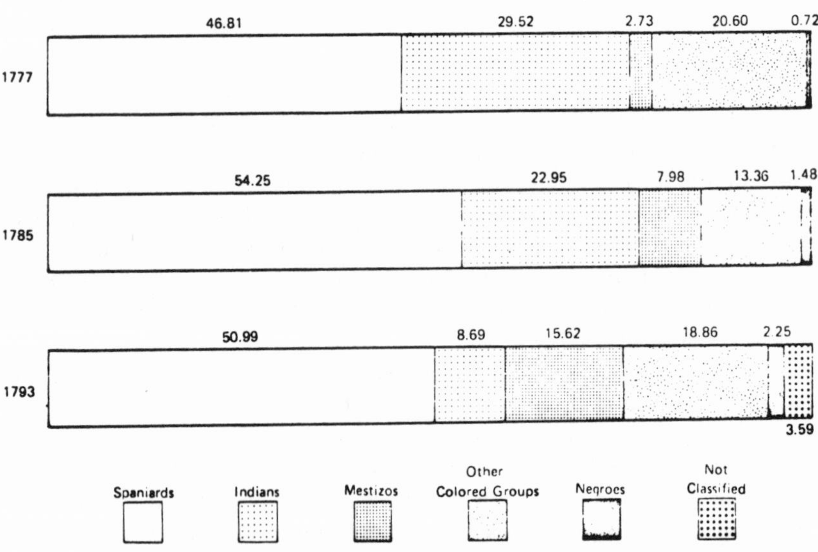

category, and not as a pure racial identification. When the initially small contingent of European settlers married women from the local community they started the process of miscegenation. The same can be said of the Frenchmen from Louisiana who established themselves in East Texas. They came from a land where the creole and the Afro-American were much more numerous than in northern Mexico; therefore they acculturated more easily and eliminated all forms of racial segregation or discrimination. The census sheets frequently report Frenchmen married to or living with Indian, mestizo, mulatto, or Negro women.[47]

The highest percentages of Spanish population show up in La Bahía in 1787 and in Bayou Pierre in 1793. The first case should be attributed more to a sudden decrease among the Indian and colored populations (from such causes as desertion and epidemics) than to a real natural increment of the white settlers. The Bayou Pierre's case is still more misleading: most of the 85 persons living in the new settlement were foreigners (British, Irishmen, European, Canadian, and Louisiana Frenchmen); in Nacogdoches, besides the people of those nationalities, was also an Italian. Many times the foreigners were classified as "Spaniards" from the European country of origin, as "Spaniard from France," or, as in the last case, "Spaniard from Italy." The same happened with the Navarro brothers of San Antonio ("Spaniards from Córsica") and a "Spaniard born in Canada" in the census of 1779. It was probably due to the color of their skin. In the case of the Frenchmen from Louisiana, even though many of them were born French, the province had belonged to Spain since 1763.

The reasons for the constant demographic ebb and flow among the Indian population originated in their reluctance to live under surveillance of the missionaries, in their frequent mass flights from the Spaniards, and in their high mortality rate, particularly during the epidemics of 1780 and 1785. These fluctuations would have been much greater if the census reports had not included among the Indians many natives who lived in the Spanish towns, most of them coming from northern Mexico, who were completely assimilated into the Spanish population, and who worked there as artisans, farmers, or servants.

Upward social and ethnic mobility can be proven by the increase of the caste population, particularly in the census reports for 1792 and 1793, where one finds more truth and less concealment as to the real racial identification of the registered persons. Nevertheless, already in 1780, of 100 registered householders who were family heads in La Bahía, 52 were mulattoes, and in the same year that racial group, with 86 families was the second largest in San Antonio.

The infusion of pure African blood, coming from the eastern border, is

TABLE 18
ETHNIC STRUCTURE OF TEXAS
(1777–1793)

Year	Place	Spaniards		Indians		Mestizos		Other Colored Groups		Negroes		Total Population
		No	Percent	No	Percent	No	Percent	No	Percent	No	Percent	
1777	San Antonio and Missions	924	44.85	654	31.74	54	2.62	413	20.04	15	0.72	2,060
1777	La Bahía and Missions	370	53.16	185	26.58	24	3.45	117	16.81	—	—	696
1777	Bucareli[a]	62	47.69	13	10.00	1	0.77	49	37.69	5	3.84	130
1777	Total Texas	1,356	46.81	852	29.52	79	2.73	579	20.60	20	0.69	2,886
1780	San Antonio (garrison and town)[b]	885	61.00	85	6.00	51	3.50	361	24.00	—	—	1,463
1780	La Bahía (garrison)	340	62.50	—	—	21	3.86	183	33.64	—	—	544
1785	Total Texas	1,583	54.23	670	22.95	233	7.98	390	13.36	43	1.48	2,919
1786	San Antonio and Missions	1,006	51.30	479	24.42	167	8.51	287	14.63	22	1.14	1,961
1787	La Bahía and Missions	429	72.50	104	17.56	13	2.19	45	7.59	1	0.16	592
1789	San Antonio and Missions	862	46.26	505	27.18	203	10.90	275	14.77	16	0.89	1,861

1790	San Antonio											
1790	La Bahía and Missions[d]	519	67.67	170	22.17	11	1.43	61	7.95	1	0.13	767
1790	Nacogdoches	258	49.24	117	22.33	75	14.31	58	11.07	16	3.05	524
1790	Total Texas [e]	1,785	56.32	671	21.14	226	7.13	342	10.79	94	2.96	3,169
1792	Total Texas[f]	1,194[g]	39.73	816	27.16	179[h]	5.96	782	26.02	34	1.13	3,005
1793	San Antonio (town)	790[i]	59.80	126	9.55	172	13.02	215	16.27	18	1.36	1,321
1793	Nacogdoches[j]	109[k]	23.85	29	6.34	117	25.60	130	28.47	10	2.18	457
1793	Bayou Pierre[l]	56[m]	65.88	7	8.23	2	2.35	6	7.05	14	16.49	85
1793	Total Texas[n]	950	50.99	162	8.69	291	15.62	351	18.86	42	2.25	1,863

[a]Only family heads. The figures show 89 women and 128 children of both sexes which have not been racially distinguished.

[b]No data given for the Negro population. These and other unclassified sevants total 81 persons (5.50 percent of the total population)

[c]Forty-six persons racially unclassified (2.45 percent of the total population).

[d]Five persons racially unclassified (0.65 percent of the total population).

[e]Fifty-one persons not classified (1.66 percent of the total population).

[f]Population of the garrisons and missions not included.

[g]Fifteen Europeans, both Spaniards and foreigners, are included here.

[h]These figures show an evident distortion. Many mestizos were included in the column of Other Colored Groups *(color quebrado)*.

[i]Included here are 5 EuropeanSpaniards, 2 Frenchmen from Louisiana,and 1 Corsican.

[j]Sixty-two inhabitants are not classified (13.56 percent of the total population).

[k]Five Spaniards and 6 Frenchmen from Europe, 2 Englishmen, 2 Irishmen, 1 Italian, 3 Frenchmen from Louisiana, and 2 French-Canadians are included here.

[l]Five are not classified inhabitants (5.88 percent of the total population).

[m]This number includes 23 Frenchmen (3 from Europe, 12 from Canada, and 8 from Louisiana, 2 Englishmen, and 2 Irishmen.

[n]Only civilian population of San Antonio, Nacogdoches, and Bayou Pierre. Sixty-seven persons are not classified (3.59 percent of the total population).

also significant. The Negro, although fewer in number than other races, immigrated as a slave or as a freeman. Twice as many Africans as in the rest of Texas in the same period lived in the town of Bucareli, and later in Nacogdoches, where the inhabitants of Bucareli were transferred. Most of the slaves were bought in New Orleans or in the French settlements along the Louisiana border by Texan cattlemen, who often used them as barter currency in their cattle business.[48] Many fugitive slaves from Louisiana came as freemen to Texas, living their lives under three flags, as they were born French, became subjects of Spain, and later lived as citizens of Mexico, having Spanish names and command of that language.[49] . . .

The most positive deduction arising from all these trends, however, is a marked racial diversification, combined with and induced by an active biological and cultural miscegenation.

As an immediate consequence, these factors encouraged a strong social and ethnic mobility, tending toward a free and heterogeneous society, which a few decades later was ready to break away from the old order.

NOTES

1. Joseph Antonio de Villa-Señor y Sánchez, *Teatro Americano, Descripción general de los Reynos, y Provincias de la Nueva España, y sus jurisdicciones* (2 vols.; Mexico City, 1746–1748), contains general data relative to the population of New Spain, taken from the census ordered by Royal Decree of July 19, 1741. This census was carried out between 1742 and 1746 under the supervision of the Viceroy Conde de Fuenclara. It is now usually called the "Fuenclara Census." Even if royal cosmographer Villaseñor covers most of the Interior Provinces, he omits all data relative to Texas. Further analysis and a summary of the "Fuenclara Census," supplemented by additional data on areas not covered by Villaseñor, can be found in Peter Gerhard, *México en 1742* (Mexico City, 1962), 30. With reference to Texas, Gerhard presents an approximate estimate of total population, based on a 1740 report from the Franciscan missions in Texas, including the civilian population of the towns and the inhabitants of the presidios. Juan Agustín de Morfi, *Viaje de Indios y Diario del Nuevo México,* edited by Vito Alessio Robles (Mexico City, 1935), 275–280, presents a demographic, ethnic, and occupational structure of the presidios of San Antonio and La Bahía, of the villa of San Fernando de Béxar, of the ranches and missions, and also of the new settlement of Nuestra Señora del Pilar de Bucareli, based on the census taken by Governor Baron de Ripperdá in 1777. Vito Alessio Robles, *Coahuila y Texas en la época colonial* (Mexico City, 1938), 525–526, using the same information, comments on Texas's racial and economic ties with the rest of northern New Spain. The data of the census of 1777, with more details for the population of the Texas missions, were also used by Juan Agustín de Morfi in his "Memorias para la Historia de la Provincia de Texas," of which, besides the original, four manuscript copies are available. The copy consulted for this study is that held by the Real Academica de la Historia (Madrid), Colección Juan Bautista Muñoz, Mss. 9/1930–1931, which includes this valuable demographic information (I, ff. 35–40). See Real Academia de la Historia, *Catálogo de la Colección de Juan Bautista Muñoz. Documentos*

interesantes para la Historia de América (3 vols.; Madrid, 1956). See also Hubert Howe Bancroft, *History of the North Mexican States and Texas* (2 vols.; San Francisco, 1886–1889), II, 2; Edward W. Heusinger, *Early Explorations and Mission Establishments in Texas* (San Antonio, 1936), 193; Carlos E. Castañeda, *Our Catholic Heritage in Texas, 1519–1936* (7vols.; Austin, 1936–1958), IV, 317, and V, 32–34, 400; J. Autrey Dabbs (ed. and trans.), "The Texas Missions in 1785," *Mid-America*, XXII (January, 1940), 38–58; Alfred Barnaby Thomas (ed. and trans.), *Teodoro de Croix and the Northern Frontier of New Spain, 1776–1783* (Norman, 1941), 72–73; Alejandro de Humboldt, *Ensayo político sobre el Reino de la Nueva España* (5 vols.; Mexico City, 1941), II, 14, 170–171, 311–317; Ernest Wallace and David M. Vigness (eds.), *Documents of Texas History* (Austin, 1963), 29–35; Odie Faulk (ed. and trans.), "A Description of Texas in 1803," *Southwestern Historical Quarterly*, LXVI (April, 1963), 513–515; Luis Navarro García, *Don José* de Gálvez y la Comandancia General de las Provincias Internas del Norte de Nueva España (Seville, 1964), 406; Nettie Lee Benson (ed. and trans.), "A Governor's Report on Texas in 1809," *Southwestern Historical Quarterly*, LXXI (April, 1968), 611; Sherburne F. Cook and Woodrow Borah, *Essays in Population History: Mexico and the Caribbean* (Vol. 1; Berkeley, 1970), 168.

2. Harley L. Browning, "Mr. Historian, Meet Mr. Demographer," *Investigaciones Contemporáneas sobre la Historia de México* (Mexico City, 1971), 619. Mr. Browning objectively mentions the scarcity of critical demographic studies which make an accurate evaluation of the sources: "I think the main reason for the uncritical acceptance of population figures and the often weak and unsatisfactory analysis of these data is due mainly to the fact that historians simply are unfamiliar with demographic procedures and therefore are ill-equipped to evaluate and effectively utilize demographic data. It is highly unlikely that most historians have been exposed to any sort of formal training in demography and they seldom give the reader any evidence of familiary with demographic literature." *Ibid.*, 620.

3. L. N. McAlister, "Social Structure and Social Change in New Spain," *Hispanic American Historical Review*, XLIII (August, 1963), 362. For more recent discussion, see D. A. Brading, *Miners and Merchants in Bourbon Mexico*, 1763–1810 (Cambridge, England, 1971), 247–270; Brading, "Grupos étnicos, clases y estructura ocupacional en Guanajuato, 1792," *Historia Mexicana*, XXI (January-March, 1972), 460–480; and Brading, "Government and Elite in Late Colonial Mexico," *Hispanic American Historical Review*, LIII (August, 1973), 389–414.

4. Relative to frontier dynamics in northern Mexico, see among others: Silvio Zavala, *New Viewpoints on the Spanish Colonization of America* (Philadelphia, 1943), and "The Frontiers of Hispanic America," in *The Frontier in Perspective*, edited by Walker D. Wyman and Clifton B. Kroeber (Madison, 1957), 43–58; Francois Chevalier, *La formación de los grandes latifundios en México* (Mexico City, 1956), 226–229; Enrique Florescano, "Colonización, ocupación del suelo y 'frontera' en el Norte de Nueva España, 1521–1750," *Tierras Nuevas*, edited by Alvaro Jara (2nd. ed.; Mexico City, 1973), 43–76.

5. Additional information relative to demographic movements and tendencies, epidemic diseases, and agrarian crisis periods in New Spain, is provided in Enrique Florescano, *Precios del maíz y crisis agrícolas en México, 1708–1810* (Mexico City, 1969), 151–152; Elsa Malvido, "Factores de despoblación y de reposición de la población de Cholula (1641–1810)," *Historia Mexicana*, XXIII (July-September, 1973), 52–58, 67, and 96–101.

6. Zavala, "The Frontiers of Hispanic America," 45

7. "Estado general que manifiesta el número de vasallos y habitantes que tiene el Rey en esta provincia de Texas, con distinción de clases, estados y castas de todas las personas de ambos sexos, sin excluir los párvulos," Bexar, November 6, 1777 (Biblioteca Nacional, Mexico City), Archivo Franciscano, legajo 100, n. 5, f. 24. The same census report with additional information relative to the economic and populational characteristics of Texas was sent by the commander general of the Interior Provinces, Teodoro de Croix, to the Minister

of the Indies, José de Gálvez, Chihuahua, September 23, 1778, including the "Plan que manifiesta el número de vasallos que tiene el Rey en esta Provincia de los Texas o de Nuevas Filipinas con distinción de clases, castas y destinos, armamento y bienes que poseen, expresándose por notas lo correspondiente al estado, situación y circunstancias de dicha provincia" (Archivo Histórico Nacional, Madrid; hereafter cited as AHN), Estado, legajo 3883. See also Morfi, *Viaje de Indios*, 275–280; Castañeda, *Our Catholic Heritage in Texas*, IV, 317.

8. "Acta de la junta de guerra convocada por el Comandante General D. Teodoro de Croix, San Antonio de Bexar, January 5, 1778" (Archivo General de la Nación, Mexico City; hereafter cited as AGN), Provincias Internas, Volume 64, ff. 66 v.–71 v.; Vincente Cortés Alonso, "Noticia sobre las tribus de las costas de Tejas durante el siglo XVIII," *Trabajos y Conferencias*, IV (1954), 3–6; Indian census report by Governor Domingo Cabello, San Antonio, October 25, 1785 (Archivo General de Indias, Seville; hereafter cited as AGI), México, legajo 1536.

9. Marcello Carmagnani, "Colonial Latin American Demography: Growth of Chilean Population, 1700–1830," *Journal of Social History*, I (Winter, 1967), 181, analyzes the population of southern Chile and finds there conditions similar to those prevailing in Texas. Carmagnani could not incorporate the roaming Araucanianas and other Indian groups, which lived in the south of Chile and did not recognize the Spanish rule, into his estimates of the Chilean population.

10. The French School was made up of Ernest Labrouse, Ferdinand Braudel, Pierre Gaubert, Etienne Gautier, Louis Henry, and Ruggero Romano; while the Berkeley Group consisted of Sherbourne F. Cook, Woodrow Borah, and Leslie B. Simpson.

11. Cabello to the Cabildo of San Fernando de Bexar, San Antonio, January 26, 1784, Bexar Archives (Archives, University of Texas Library, Austin; reference to the Bexar Archives are hereafter cited as BA), microfilm, reel 15; Croix to Cabello, Arizpe, February 3, 1780, ibid., reel 13; Phelipe de Neve to Cabello, Arizpe, October 2, 1783, ibid., reel 15, frames 536–539. The last two documents expressly recommend the governor to order the alcaldes, the parish priest of San Fernando, the missionaries, and other pertinent authorities to fulfil their obligations by taking every year the census of the civilian population, of the military garrisons' personnel, and dependents living in their respective districts.

12. Conde de Revillagigedo to Manuel Antonio Valdés, minister of the Indies, Mexico City, December 27, 1789; circular letter of Revillagigedo to the intendants, Mexico City, January 1, 1790 (printed), AGI, México, legajo 1230; Revillagigedo to Governor Rafael Martínez Pacheco, Mexico City, February 16, 1790, BA, reel 20; Bruno Díaz de Salcedo, intendant of San Luis Potosí, to Marfinez Pacheco, San Luis Potosí, March 1, 1790, ibid.

13. Victoria Lerner, "Consideraciones sobre la población de la Nueva España (1793–1810); Según Humboldt y Navarro y Noriega," *Historia Mexicana*, XVII (January-March, 1968), 327–348.

14. Humboldt, *Ensayo Político*, II, 9–34; S. F. Cook, "The Population of Mexico in 1793," *Human Biology*, XIV (December, 1942), 499–515; Cook and Borah, *Essays in Population History*, I, 44–45.

15. Bexar and La Bahía census reports, July 1, 1779, January 1, 1780, AGI, Guadalajara, legajo 283; Croix to Gálvez, Arizpe, December 23, 1780, ibid., legajo 277. The latter is a valuable proof of the social reality of the frontier areas, and particularly of the heterogeneous racial makeup of the military garrisons, Croix clearly states there: "En su admisión de reclutas sólo se procura que el color del rostro disimule su naturaleza. Esta, por lo común, les constituye en la esfera de mulatos o de otra de las castas impuras que abundan en este continente."

16. Manuel Muñoz to Bruno Díaz de Salcedo, San Antonio, August 4, 1793, BA, reel 23. The governor pointed out the defects and irregularities of most *padrones*, due to the inefficiency of the census takers and the lack of uniformity and norms. So erroneous were the

data of the Texas general report of 1792 that the intendant ordered Muñoz not to fill out the columns of total population and caste classification in the census sheets for the following year. He also gave precise and detailed instructions as to how to proceed in taking the census of 1793. Díaz de Salcedo to Muñoz, San Luis Potosí, December 16, 17, 1793, ibid., reel 24; Pedro de Nava to Muñoz, Chihuahua, October 23, 1793, ibid., reel 23.

17. The lieutenant governor of Nacogdoches, Cristóbal de Córdoba, confessed that he was incapable of making calculations and classifying the population of his district. Córdoba to Muñoz, Nacagdoches, November 2, 1792, ibid., reel 22; April 26, May 4, 1793, ibid., reel 23.

18. Census reports of Bexar, La Bahía, and Nacogdoches, December 31, 1790, ibid., reel 21.

19. Humboldt, *Ensayo Político*, II, 170–171, points out that in 1803 there were 49 inhabitants per square league, giving an estimated total of 5,837,000 inhabitants for the whole vicekingdom. Lerner, "Consideraciones sobre la población de Nueva España," 329, criticizes the demographic information given by Humboldt and points out his error in calculating the population density on the basis of 2,335,628 square kilometers of total surface for New Spain. Modern estimates indicate that at the end of the eighteenth century the total was really 4,146,483 square kilometers, practically 2,000,000 more than those estimated by Humboldt, therefore making his population-density calculations obsolete. In the Interior Provinces, according to Humboldt, the ratio of population varied from 2 per square league in Coahuila and Texas to up to 10 per square league in Nuevo León and Nueva Vizcaya.

20. Humboldt, *Ensayo Político*, II, 14.

21. Cook and Borah, *Essays in Population History*, I, 137–159.

22. Texas census report (1777) cited in note 7 above. The data given by Morfi agree with this census, from which they were taken, but his total of 3,803 souls is mistaken, undoubtedly a copying error. See Morfi, *Viaje de Indios*, 275. See also Berhard, *México in 1742*, p. 30; H. Yoakum, *History of Texas from Its First Settlement in 1685 to Its Annexation to the United States in 1846* (2 vols.; New York, 1885), I, 87; Cook and Borah, *Essays in Population History*, I, 168.

23. Croix to Gálvez (general report of the Interior Provinces), Arizpe, July 29, 1781, AGI, Guadalajara, Legajo 279 (other copy in AGI, Guadalajara, 281 B); Thomas, *Teodoro de Croix*, 72; Navarro García, *Don José de Gálvez*, 406; V. Riva Palacio, *México a través de los siglos* (5 vols.; Mexico City, 1890), II, 890; Odie Faulk (ed. and trans.), "A Description of Texas in 1803," pp. 513–515.

24. Humboldt, *Ensayo Político*, II, 171; Fernando Navarro y Noriega, *Catálogo de curatos y misiones de la Nueva España, seguido de la memoria sobre la población del Reino de la Nueva España* (Mexico City, 1943), 62; Bancroft, *History of the Northern Mexican States and Texas*, II, 2; Walter Prescott Webb and H. Bailey Carroll (eds.), *The Handbook of Texas* (2 vols.; Austin, 1952), I, 321. Humboldt estimated a total surface of 10,948 square kilometers for Texas with the already mentioned population density of two inhabitants per square league. A critical discussion of Humboldt and Navarro y Noriega's figures in Lerner, "Consideraciones sobre la población de Nueva España," 329–332, indicates that Humboldt's estimates are always too high, a fact already criticized by his contemporaries. For example, in 1803 he gives Texas a population of 21,000 (Navarro y Noriega estimates 3,334 souls for 1810), while he calculates that the total population of the intendancy of San Luis Potosí—to which Texas was incorporated—was 230,000.

25. Benson (ed. and trans.), "A Governor's Report on Texas in 1809," 611. According to the report of Manuel de Salcedo, 1,700 persons inhabited San Antonio and its jurisdiction, while 405 people lived in La Bahía and its neighboring missions, 655 in Nacogdoches, 189 in Bayou Pierre, 82 in San Marcos, and 91 in Trinidad.

26. Angel Rosenblat, *La población indigena de América desde 1492 hasta la actualidad* (Buenos Aires, 1945), 69–70; Esther A. Wagner Stearn, *The Effect of Smallpox on the*

Destiny of Amerindian (Boston, 1945), 42–51; Donald B. Cooper, *Epidemic Disease in Mexico City, 1761–1813: An Administrative, Social, and Medical Study* (Austin, 1965), 7–85; Florescano, *Precios del maíz*, 129, 133, 148. For the effects of the 1780–1781 smallpox epidemic in northern New Spain, see these sources: S. F. Cook, "Smallpox in Spanish and Mexican California, 1770–1845," *Bulletin of the History of Medicine*, VII (February, 1939), 154–155; Francis, R. Packard, *History of Medicine in the United States* (2 vols.; 2nd. ed.; New York, 1963), II, 938, with reference to Texas; Marc Simmons, "New Mexico's Smallpox Epidemic of 1780–1781," *New Mexico Historical Review*, XLI (October, 1966), 319–326.

27. Ripperdá to Julián de Arriaga, San Antonio, February 15, 1770, AGI, Guadalajara, legajo 302. Unofficially, San Antonio became the capital when Governor Baron de Ripperdá took office February 4, 1770, following the instructions received from Viceroy Marqués de Croix, in Mexico City. Until then the town and presidio of Los Adaes had been the seat of government. San Antonio was officially designated the capital of Texas by the Reglamento de Presidios (1772), which came into effect in Texas in 1773. Consequently Ripperdá ordered the forcible evacuation of Los Adaes (June, 1773). Most of the inhabitants reluctantly migrated to San Antonio, although a few families took refuge in Louisiana. See *Instrucción para formar una línea o cordón de quince presidios sobre las fronteras de las Provincias Internas de este Reino de Nueva España y Nuevo Reglamento del número y calidad de los oficiales y soldados que éstos y los demás han de tener, sueldos que gozarán desde el primero del año próximo de mil setecientos setenta y dos, y servicio que deben hacer en sus guarniciones* (Mexico City, 1771). The original manuscript is in AHN, Estado, legajo 3882, expediente 9. It was published in Madrid (1772) and republished in Mexico City (1773, 1790, and 1834). About the reforms introduced in Texas see Herbert E. Bolton, "The Spanish Abandonment and Re-Occupation of East Texas, 1773–1779," *The Quarterly of the Texas State Historical Association*, IX (October, 1905), 79–89; H. E. Bolton, *Texas in the Middle Eighteenth Century: Studies in Spanish Colonial History and Administration* (reprint; New York, 1962), 113–117; Navarro García, *Don José de Gálvez*, 268–273.

28. Alejandro O'Reilly's census report, New Orleans, March 1, 1770 (Biblioteca Nacional, Madrid), Manuscritos de América, number 17617; Charles Gayarré, *History of Louisiana* (4 vols.; New York, 1854–1866), II, 352, mentions approximately 13,538 persons as the total population for 1769. John Walton Caughey, *Bernardo de Gálvez in Louisiana, 1776–1783* (Berkeley, 1934), 77–78, estimates a total of 17,926 persons (8,381 whites, 273 free mulattoes, 263 free Negroes, 545 mulatto slaves, and 8,464 Negro slaves) for 1777. According to the data furnished by Alcée Fortier, *A History of Louisiana* (4 vols.; New York, 1904), II, 110, 119, in 1785 Louisiana had 32,115 inhabitants and in 1788 the population was 36,235 (a 12.8 percent increase in three years).

29. Miguel Ramos de Arispe, *Memoria, que el Doctor D. Miguel Ramos de Arispe, Cura de Borbón, y Diputado en las presentes Cortes Generales y Extraordinarias de España por la Provincia de Coahuila, una de las cuatro internas del Oriente en el Reyno de México, presenta á el Augusto Congreso, sobre el estado natural, político, y civil de su dicha provincia, y las del Nuevo Reyno de León, Nuevo Santander, y los Texas, con exposición de los defectos del sistema general, y particular de sus goviernos, y de las reformas, y nuevos establecimientos que necesitan para su prosperidad*, translated with introduction and notes by Nettie Lee Benson (Austin, 1950), 47–48. See also Miguel Ramos Arizpe, *Discursos, Memorias e Informes*, edited by Vito Alessio Robles (Mexico City, 1942), 29–36.

30. Lerner, "Consideraciones sobre la población de Nueva España," 345, points out that an example of the few points of agreement between Humboldt and Navarro y Noriega in their estimates for the vicekingdom during the period 1793–1810 is their analysis of the proportion of the sexes, which Humboldt calculates at the rate of 100 men per 95 women and Navarro y Noriega at the rate of 100 per 98.

31. Information on infant mortality may be found in these sources: Baptismal Books 3 and

4, and Burial Books of the missions San Antonio de Valero and San José y San Miguel de Aguayo, Cathedral of San Fernando Records (Bexar County Archives, San Antonio; hereafter cited as CSF, BCA), microfilms; Cabello to Croix, San Antonio, October 20 (frames 630–631), November 20, December 6, 1780, BA, reel 14; Cabello to José Antonio Rengel, San Antonio, May 20, 1785, ibid., reel 16; Cabello to Jacobo Ugarte y Loyola, San Antonio, November 5, 1786, ibid., reel 17. Among the infants who died were four of the six children of the Baron de Ripperdá, all born in San Antonio between 1770 and 1777. Their deaths are registered in each case next to the baptismal record. CSF, BCA, Baptismal Book 3, microfilms. For imformation on the spread of venereal diseases among the mission Indians of Texas, and their consequences (for example, feminine sterility, natural and induced abortions, birth defects, retardation, and premature death of infants), see José Antonio Alcocer, *Bosquejo de la historia del Colegio de Nuestra Señora de Guadalupe y sus Misiones. Año de 1788* (Mexico City, 1958), 172–174. Another possible reason mentioned for the decline in birth rates in the missions is the diminishing number of women of age to conceive. See S. F. Cook, *Population Trends among the California Mission Indians* (Berkeley, 1940), 17, whose generalizations apply also to Texas. An example relative to the worries created by the licentious life in the frontier areas can be found in the correspondence of the Bishop of Durango, Esteban Lorenzo de Tristán, to Viceroy Revillagigedo, in 1794. See Guillermo Porras Muñoz, *Iglesia y Estado en Nueva Vizcaya* (1562–1821) (Pamplona, Spain, 1966), 635–636.

32. The *barraganía* was an irregular union, without the consecration of the Church. Rosenblat, *La Población indígena de América*, 258; Richard Konetzke, "El mestizaje y su importancia en el desarrollo de la población hispano-americana durante la época colonial," *Revista de Indias*, VII (1946), 28, 220–224; [Magnus Mörner (ed.)], *El mestizaje en la historia de Ibero-América* (Mexico City, 1961), 32; W. Borah and S. F. Cook, "Marriage and Legitimacy in Mexican Culture: Mexico and California," *California Law Review*, LIV (May, 1966), 949–952, and 954–965.

33. The monthly reports of the governors, particularly those presenting great detail such as the reports of Colonel Domingo Cabello and those from the captains of the presidio of La Bahía, frequently cited encounters with Indians, in which soldiers and *vecinos* were killed by the enemy. See, for example, reports from Cabello to Croix, 1780–1781, BA, reel 14; Croix to Gálvez, Arizpe, March 26, May 23, June 23, 1780, January 23, February 23, March 23, 1781, AGI, Guadalajara, legajo 271; Croix to Gálvez, Arizpe, June 30, July 30, 1781, ibid., legajo 267. One of the bloodiest episodes was the attack on the Cibolo Fort on February 6, 1781, by the Comanches. Only two soldiers survived. Cabello to Croix, San Antonio, February 28, 1781, BA, reel 14.

34. Baptismal Books 3 and 4, San Antonio de Valero and San José missions, CSF, BCA. Baptized convert adults are not included in the count. Herbert E. Bolton, "Spanish Missions Records at San Antonio," *The Quarterly of the Texas State Historical Association*, X (April, 1907), 297–307, was the first to point out their importance. For information on the importance of parochial registers in sociodemographic analysis, see Richard Konetzke, "Documentos para la historia y crítica de los registros parroquiales en las Indias," *Revista de Indias*, VII (July-September, 1946), 581–586; Elio Lodolini, "Los libros parroquiales y de estado civil en América Latina," *Archivum*, VIII (1958), 95–113; Nicolás Sánchez Albornoz, "Les registres paroissiaux en Amérique Latine. Quelques considérations sur leur exploitation pour la démographie historique," *Revue Suisse d'Histoire*, XVII (1967), 60–71; Cook and Borah, *Essays in Population History*, 49–52; Woodrow Borah and Sherburne F. Cook, "La demografía histórico de América Latina; necesidades y perspectivas," *Historia Mexicana*, XXI (October-December, 1971), 312–327; Claude Morin, "Los libros parroquiales como fuente para la historia demográfica y social novohispana," *Historia Mexicana*, XXI (January-March, 1972), 389–418. Two recent and excellent examples of the results of the analysis of parochial registers are Marcello Carmagnani, "Demografía y

sociedad: La estructura social de los centros mineros del norte de México, 1600–1720," *Historia Mexicana*, XXI (January-March, 1972), 436–445, and Elsa Malvido, "Factores de despoblación y de reposición de la población de Cholula (1641–1810)," 52–110. See also Claude Morin, "Santa Inés Zacatelco, 1643–1813: contribution a la démographie du Mexique Colonial" (Ph.D. dissertation, University of Montreal, 1970).

35. Confusion in the recording of castes are so frequent that in each case a check on the racial group of both parents was necessary before acceptance of the caste assigned to the baptized infant, or for rectification of a wrong classification. Application of the same procedure was necessary with the castes indicated for several soldiers of the garrison of San Antonio. The census report of 1779 registered them as Spaniards, while the parochial registers classified them as mulattoes or mestizos. Perhaps the most surprising cases of "racial disguise"—perpetrated by Father Pedro Fuentes y Fernández—are those regarding the offspring of a mestizo couple, registered arbitrarily as coyotes, mulattoes, or tresalbos (the only cases in Texas during this period), and regarding the children of an emigrated couple from Los Adaes, who were registered as mestizos in the 1779 census, but who were recorded as Spaniards in the baptismal books of San Fernando. See Baptismal Books 3 and 4, CSF, BCA.

41. Magnus Mörner, *Race Mixture in the History of Latin America* (Boston, 1967), 53–54, 60.

42. Bexar and La Bahía census reports, 1779–1780, AGI, Guadalajara, legajo 283. Among the mestizo landowners María Josefa Cadena was the most important; among the mulattoes Marco Cepeda, Marcos Guerra, Alberto Morales, Matías Pérez, José Miguel Serna, Felipe de Luna, Francisco Xavier Rodríguez, Juan Bautista de Luna, Manuel Mascorro, and María Micaela Carrasco; and among the coyotes Blas de Avila and Diego Menchaca.

43. Nicolás León, *Las castas del México Colonial*, passim; Hensley C. Woodbridge, "Glossary of names used in Colonial Latin America for crosses among Indians, Negroes, and Whites," *Journal of the Washington Academy of Sciences*, XVIII (November 15, 1948), 353–362; Magnus Mörner, *Race Mixture*, 53–70. For a discussion of the zoological origin of the names given to several "impure" castes, see Gonzalo Aquirre Beltrán, *La población negra de México, 1519–1810: Estudio etno histórico* (Mexico City, 1946), 172.

44. See note 15. When the theft of a considerable sum of money from the funds of the presidio of La Bahía was discovered, Captain Luis Cazorla, the local commander, accused one of the officers, the quartermaster *(habilitado)* of being the author of the embezzlement, and described him as "mulato de casta, soltero, y no natural de este presidio." L. Cazorla to R. Martínez Pacheco, La Bahía, January 18, 1788, BA, reel 18.

45. "Año de 1785. Diligencias practicadas por el Coronel D. Domingo Cabello Gobernador de esta Provincia, á instancia de Fernando Arocha carabinero de la compañía de caballería de este Presidio contra la Persona de D. Luis Maríano Menchaca por haberle dicho que era un Mulato Indígino ási el como todos de su familiar. . . ." San Antonio, November 5, 1785, ibid., reel 17; "Francisco Xavier Rodríguez, regidor decano del Ayuntamiento contra Manuel Padrón, por haber golpeado e insultado a su esposa, Juana Travieso, gritándole mulata," San Fernando, October 20, 1783, ibid., reel 15. Perhaps the most interesting case by which racial prejudice against mulattoes can be proved is the lawsuit "Diligencias practicadas sobre la oposición hecha por José Miguel y Francisco de Sales Games; Carlos, y Pedro Hernández; tíos y hermanos de Ana Maria de la Trinidad Games, para que no Efectúe Matrimonio con Urbano Inojosa, Indio de la Misión de San Antonio," June 4, 1781, ibid., reel 14. The bride was a mulatto, thirteen years old. Finally the marriage did not take place, but not because of opposition from the bride's family. Inojosa reacted against the mulattoes' prejudice against Indians, and accused the girl's relatives of being "mulatos por todos sus cuatro costados, y siendo Mulatos, con ser soldados, ni son españoles ni de mejor condición, o de mejor, y más limpia sangre que la de un Indio." ("Mulattoes on all four sides and being mulattoes, even if they are soldiers, they are not

Spaniards nor of better position, nor do they have a better and cleaner blood than an Indian.")

46. Documents related to the conduct of D. Antonio Gil Ibarvo, AGN, Historia, Volume 100; Bolton, "The Spanish Abandonment and Re-Occupation of East Texas, 1773–1779," 84; Nyal C. King, "Captain Antonio Gil Ybarbo: Founder of the Modern Nacogdoches, 1729–1809" (M.A. thesis, Stephen F. Austin State University, 1949). Although his descendants signed their name as Ybarbo and the name has been spelled in several different ways, the spelling Ibarvo used in signing many documents, including his own will, is employed here. See will of Antonio Gil Ibarvo, San Fernando de Bexar, May 19, 1800, BCA, VIII, Wills and Estates, 119.

47. Nacogdoches census reports by families (1792, 1793, 1794, 1796, 1797, 1799), BA, reels 22, 24, 25, 26, 28, 29. All are dated December 31 of the corresponding year. See Woodrow Borah and Sherburne F. Cook, "Sobre las posibilidades de hacer el estudio histórico del mestizaje sobre una base demográfica," *Revista de Historia de América*, n. 53–54 (June-December, 1962), 181–190.

48. The practical nonexistence of metallic currency and the high price of slaves in Texas and of cattle in Louisiana justified this type of barter-trade. The same cow valued at six pesos and four reales in Texas brought in twenty pesos when sold in Louisiana. The Menchaca family, who owned the San Francisco Ranch, were very active both in the legal and in the contraband cattle trade. During a lawsuit for illegal export of cattle it was proven that the Menchacas had received slaves, tobacco, French fabrics, and other goods imported from New Orleans as part of the price for their cattle. Cabello to Croix, La Bahía, May 9, June 14, and San Antonio, September 20, 1780, BA, reel 14. Other examples of this trade are revealing: Toribio Fuentes, brother of the parish priest of San Fernando, bought a slave from Nicolás de la Mathe, from Louisiana, and paid the full price of 220 pesos in cattle. Even Ibarvo, in his will, declares to have purchased a slave from his former partner José María Armand, paying for him a mule, a horse, and a gun. In 1789, in Natchitoches, three horses were exchanged for an adult female mulatto slave and two slave boys of four and fifteen years of age respectively. See Testimonio de venta de un esclavo por Nicolás de la Mathe a Toribio Fuentes, San Fernando de Bexar, June 10, 1778, ibid., reel 12; Will of Ibarvo, BCA; Testimonio de venta efectuado por Luis Le Blanc a Manuel Soto, Natchitoches, May 30, 1789, BA, reel 19.

49. Harold Schoen, "The Free Negro in the Republic of Texas," *Southwestern Historical Quarterly*, XXXIX (April, 1936), 292–293.

10

The California Frontier*

C. Alan Hutchinson

Editor's Introduction

The essays by Simmons, Servín, and Tjarks which appear in this volume raise the important question of the impact of the frontier on Spanish-Mexican society. Many historians have remained convinced that Frederick Jackson Turner's frontier thesis was essentially correct: that the frontier—an area of abundant land and natural resources—provided opportunities for the hard-working individual to better himself. The frontier environment made Americans more democratic, nationalistic, individualistic, and inventive.[1] C. Alan Hutchinson finds that the Turner thesis has little applicability to California. It was not a land of opportunity, he argues. Free land was not readily available and lower-class Mexicans could not easily emigrate to California because of distance and cost. Mexican frontiersmen in California did not exercise much initiative and authoritarianism intensified rather than diminished on the California frontier.

**Frontier Settlement in Mexican California: The Híjar-Padrés Colony and Its Origins, 1769–1835* (New Haven, Connecticut: 1969), pp. 393–99. (Reprinted with permission of the author and the publisher.

Professor of history at the University of Virginia, C. Alan Hutchinson was born in England, and educated at Cambridge and the University of Texas, where he received his doctorate. A specialist in early nineteenth-century Mexican history, he is author of several articles and has been writing a biography of President Valentín Gómez Farías. One result of his work on Gómez Farías was the major study from which this essay is drawn, *Frontier Settlement in Mexican California: The Híjar-Padrés Colony and Its Origins, 1769–1835* (New Haven: 1969). He analyzes the abortive attempt of the Gómez Farías administration to colonize northern California with Mexican artisans and farmers; in the process he sheds considerable light on California politics, missions, and land use. Professor Hutchinson's most recent book is a splendid translation and editing of José Figueroa's *Manifesto to the Mexican Republic* (Berkeley: 1978).

NOTE

1. For a splendid explication of the Turner thesis and the views of its critics, see Ray Allen Billington, *America's Frontier Heritage* (Albuquerque: 1974).

The California Frontier

On the eve of what the Mexicans were to call the War of the American Invasion, Manuel Payno, the distinguished writer and statesman, looked despairingly at California and asked, "Is it not probable that the Californias will have the same fate as Texas? Is there no remedy that can be applied? Shall we resign ourselves to lose those fertile and spacious lands without getting even the slightest benefit from them?" It was not that Payno did not know what Mexico should do; he had seen American settlers moving west in the United States in their long trains of covered wagons, and in his view Mexicans should do likewise. Finding nothing of this kind in recent Mexican annals except the Farías colony, which he duly saluted, he came to a depressing conclusion: "It is an unquestionable truth that the honorable man who wishes to work makes his fortune, but the Mexican character is not fitted for colonization."[1]

There is a striking contrast between the relative inability of Spain and Mexico to colonize California and the inexorable westward movement of the American frontiersmen, who were finally to overwhelm it. Payno's theory that Mexicans were prevented by some national characteristic from being colonizers is belied by their Spanish forebears and is, in any case, too vague a statement for useful discussion; but a consideration of what may perhaps be called the California frontier, in the sense that Frederick Jackson Turner used the term, may serve to bring together some of the views previously put forward in this study.

Certain differences between the California frontier and the American westward movement are sufficiently obvious: the drive to colonize California was not due to any pressure of population on Mexico, which was itself badly in need of more settlers, but to the Spanish and Mexican fears of encroachment from Russia and the United States. Since California was, in effect, an overseas colony of Mexico after the closing of overland communication in 1781—even in 1834 traveling from California to Mexico was sometimes referred to as returning "to the continent"—the expense of going there was too great for the poverty-stricken individual even if he had wanted to go.[2] Successive Spanish and Mexican governments, spurred on by fear of Russian aggression, were willing to recruit colonists and give them free passage to California, together with promises of free land, free farm animals, and free farming tools. In spite of these inducements, only a trickle came forward. Both governments then took to sending what Adam Smith picturesquely calls "felons and strumpets" to California, with equally poor results.

Colonization of California, it will be noted, was promoted and paid for by the state, as under the Romans, and not a matter of individual initiative, as on the American frontier. Even the Farías colony, sponsored by the egalitarian government of the time, was paternally controlled by its directors of colonization. Its major difference from previous colonization programs was that it planned to colonize mission lands and to permit Indians to be colonists on an equal basis with the whites.

Interest in making colonists out of the Indians, however, was not a new idea. It is evident that the Spanish government's support for the missions in California was due, among other considerations, to the fact that there simply were not enough Spaniards available to settle it, let alone cultivate it. Yet according to the highly esteemed Swiss arbiter of eighteenth-century international law, Emmerich von Vattel, a nation must actually populate a country which it takes as its own, and its settlers should preferably not merely run cattle on it but cultivate it. Vattel also disapproved of nations that took more land than they needed. Missions solved these problems by turning the Indians into civilized beings and setting them to cultivate the land. Also, the fact that they made Christians out of pagans and protected their proselytes against the white man would help to offset Spain's vulnerability, from Vattel's point of view, as a country that was engrossing a "much greater extent of territory than it is able to people or cultivate."[3] But trying to convert Indians into Spanish farmers proved a baffling and frustrating experience. While they were willing to accept the presents the missionaries gave them and would even labor in the fields for their food and clothing, Indians always seemed to want to return to their old primitive way of life. As time went by and ideas of the equality of man began to spread, opinion about the worth of the missions changed. The intellectual capacity of the Indians became a subject for debate rather than a cause for the shaking of heads. Observers began to criticize the missionaries for their slowness in civilizing their Indians, and some advanced the idea that segregating the Indians from society in missions was a poor way of making them into members of that society. The attempts of the Mexican government to secularize the missions and integrate the Indians with the other inhabitants of California, however, came to grief. The Indians who were freed from the missions were at the mercy of the whites, who wanted to make use of their labor and take their land.

One of the keys to the problem of the difference between the Hispanic frontier in California and the American frontier lies in this question of land. The dynamic force behind Turner's concept of the moving frontier is free land, and Adam Smith's eighteenth-century prescription for successful colonies was "plenty of good land." Although the Spanish and Mexican governments talked about granting land to colonists, remarkably few settlers seem to have acquired full rights to their land in California.

Land was not generally surveyed, and it was often granted in enormous acreages to single individuals. By the time Governor Manuel Victoria came to California in 1830, all the best coastal land had been engrossed by the missions, who spread their cattle domains around them as if to protect themselves from undesirable settlers in the few existing towns. Before the country was populated by more than a handful of people, therefore, there was little land left, unless the settler moved into pagan Indian country. This was where the Farías colony went for strategic reasons; but although the colonists were provided with weapons, which they might have used against Indians if they were attacked, Governor Figueroa saw a threat to himself in these arms and ordered them removed. Only the experienced, independent American frontiersmen in California seem to have been in a position to take exposed lands.

The magnet of free land in California hardly existed as far as Mexico was concerned, and when the Farías government attempted to divide mission lands among the mission Indians and various groups of white men, both Californians and Mexicans, it provoked defiance on the part of Governor Figueroa and his Territorial Deputation. The Californians were unwilling to see the best lands of their territory go to newly arrived immigrants from Mexico; they worked out a secularization plan for the missions which kept them going as productive haciendas—on which most people in California depended—while reserving some land for selected mission Indians. If their experience with freed Indians was to be repeated, the whites might confidently expect that in due course they would fall heir to Indian owned land, if they could not share it on the ground that they, too, were natives of California. Thus the neophytes, who supposedly owned the mission lands they worked, were eventually to lose them.

If "plenty of good land," the most essential ingredient for a movement to the frontier, was lacking in California under Mexico, what about the other requirement put forward by Adam Smith for a successful colony: "liberty to manage their own affairs their own way"?[4] There is no doubt that Mexico neglected California. In spite of constant reminders by successive ministers of relations, the Mexican Congress failed to provide a code of laws for the territory, which was forced to guide its affairs by reference to parts of Spanish laws, Mexican laws, the Spanish Constitution of 1812, and the Mexican Constitution of 1824. On the other hand, neglect by the government in Mexico meant more power for the governor and Territorial Deputation in Monterey. When Mexico did nothing, Monterey had to act, if only provisionally. Governor Figueroa, in the crisis over mission land policy, even went further than this and invoked the traditional, "I obey but I do not comply" of the colonial viceroys when faced with unacceptable legislation made in Spain.

Can it be said that these signs of autonomy were in any sense due to a burgeoning of democracy on the California frontier? There would seem to be little evidence for such an idea. In one of his speeches to the Territorial Deputation, Governor Figueroa lauds the virtues of democracy, by which he seems to mean freeing the governor from the petty affairs of government, which should be taken care of by lower officials.[5] But Figueroa himself acted more like a caudillo than a representative of the people, and in their turns, the other military commanders in California's outlying regions behaved like lesser caudillos. The attempts of many Californians to have the military command separated from the civilian governorship went unheeded until the Farías administration made a vain attempt to inaugurate it. Their demands for more democracy were made to look like treason.

Adam Smith put forward a frontier thesis which provides insight into the situation in California and other Latin American areas. "The absolute governments of Spain, Portugal, and France," he says, "take place in their colonies; and the discretionary powers which such governments commonly delegate to all their inferior officers are, on account of the great distance, naturally exercised there with more than ordinary violence. Under all absolute governments there is more liberty in the capital than in any other part of the country."[6] While a Paraguayan living in Asunción with Dr. Francia might not have entirely agreed with this, perhaps it may be modified to read that life on the frontier, under a dictatorship, is likely to be just as dictatorial, or even at times more dictatorial, than it is at the seat of government. The frontier, in this case, simply gives more free rein to the local official, who becomes a petty despot. In turn, the subordinates of the petty despot, far removed from his eyes, tend to become lesser tyrants. In other words, the frontier reproduces, in somewhat more visible fashion, what is already present in the homeland from which the settlers came. Turner's thesis that the American frontier promoted democracy follows this idea, and it seems to fit the situation in Hispanic California. Híjar and Padrés, at any rate, regarded the actions of Governor Figueroa and Ensign Vallejo in this light. They went back to Mexico City with the intention of revealing to the government how these men, protected by the distance of the frontier, had overstepped their authority. By the time they reached the capital, however, the Farías government had been removed and Santa Anna had taken over; dictatorship was to be firmly seated at Mexico City itself.

At this point, perhaps, one further question may be raised. Were the liberals in Mexico at this time trying to promote their ideas on the frontier, far from the power of orthodox conservative opinion in Mexico City? More precisely, were they consciously trying to make the frontier a seedbed for their democratic views? There were those at the time who thought that this was their intention and that it accounted for Santa Anna's actions against the Farías colony. But if this was so, it will be noted that Mexico City was the source of the democratic moves, not the California frontier.

If the California frontier reveals little sign of promoting democracy, which Turner held to be the most important effect of the frontier on the United States, it also shows little evidence of other attributes commonly associated with the American frontier. For example, the Californians, sufficiently provided with Indian labor, did little or no work themselves. Commodore Charles Wilkes, on his visit to California in 1841, reported that he had heard a story about a Californian "who had been known to dispense with his dinner, although the food was but a few yards off, because the Indian was not at hand to bring it to him." The Californians are not credited with such frontier virtues as independence or resourcefulness, and they were not self-sufficient. In fact they may be compared with planters in the Old South, if hides and tallow are substituted for cotton and mission Indians for Negro slaves.[7] . . .

California under Mexico does not appear to have been a frontier in the same sense that Turner used the word,. . .

NOTES

1. Manuel Payno, "Alta California," *Revista científica y literaria de Méjico*, 1 (1845), 83, 84.
2. Buenaventura Araujo, Service Record, Archivo de Defensa, México, D.F.
3. Bolton, "The Mission as a Frontier Institution," *American Historical Review*, 23 (1917), 52; Emmerich von Vattel, *The Law of Nations* (Philadelphia: 1849), items 208, 209.
4. Adam Smith, *An Inquiry into the Nature and Causes of the Wealth of Nations* (New York: 1937), p. 538.
5. Legislative Records, 2, 39, Bancroft Library, University of California, Berkeley.
6. Smith, *Wealth of Nations*, p. 552.
7. Charles Wilkes, *Narrative of the United States Exploring Expedition* (5 vols.; Philadelphia: 1845), 5, 176; Carey McWilliams, *Southern California Country: An Island on the Land* (New York: 1946), p. 52.

11

The Frontiers of Hispanic America*

Silvio Zavala

Editor's Introduction

C. Alan Hutchinson's conclusions regarding the California frontier vary somewhat from Silvio Zavala's suggestions regarding the Mexican north, which would include the area from California to Texas. In a sweeping essay entitled "Las Fronteras de Hispanoamérica," Zavala compared frontiers in the hemisphere. He suggested that Turner's thesis did not generally apply to Spanish American frontiers. Nevertheless, because of the diversity of regions in Spanish America, the thesis might apply to some frontiers. Further research, he suggested, might show the northern Mexico frontier to be one such region. The difference in viewpoint between Hutchinson and Zavala may reflect, in part, the difference in the nature of the California frontier and other provinces in northernmost Mexico. If Hutchinson is correct that authoritarianism increased in California, then California may be an example of that kind of frontier

*Zavala's essay first appeared in *The Frontier in Perspective*, ed. Walker D. Wyman and Clifton B. Kroeber (Madison: 1965). A portion of the essay appeared in *Cuadernos Americanos*, 17 (1958): 374–84. It is published here with permission of the author and the University of Wisconsin Press.

which, Zavala says, "could become the refuge of bossism *(caciquismo)* and local abuses."

Silvio Zavala, eminent and honored historian of colonial Latin America, holds a doctorate in law and has served as Mexico's ambassador to France. He has held many distinguished positions, including founder and director of the *Revista de Historia de America* (1938–65), director of the Museo Nacional de Historia del Palacio de Chapultepec (1946–54), and president of El Colegio de México (1963–66). Among his best known published works are *La defensa de los derechos del hombre en América Latina, siglos XVI-XVIII* (Paris: 1963), *y El Mundo Americano en la época colonial* (Mexico City: 1968).

The Frontiers of Hispanic America

Background

The advance of Spanish civilization into the New World, considered in its broadest context, seems but a continuation of the struggle between the Christian and Moslem that characterized Iberian history in the days of the Reconquest. For nearly eight centuries, these two peoples had lived together, and though mutual distrust and frontiers existed, cultural borrowing and personal alliances also characterized their relationship. The struggle to drive out the Moor touched all Christendom, causing warriors from beyond the Pyrenees to go forth to stop the Moslem advance and reclaim the peninsula, and inspired historical chronicles and literature, including the twelfth-century poem in the frontier mood, *El Cantar de Mío Cid*. The Reconquest was not only a war against the infidel; it was also an experience in colonization of the conquered areas. Considering all the varied circumstances under which the Christian advance took place over the years, it now seems but a "fabric of conquests, of founding of towns, or reorganization of new provinces wrested from Islam, of expansion of the Church into the new domain; the transplanting of a race, a language, and a civilization."[1]

This crusade against the nonbeliever and this experience in colonization gave force to Spanish and Portuguese expansion down the African coast and to the Atlantic islands. It assumed new form in 1492, after the fall of Granada ended the Reconquest.

The conquistadors of the New World in the late fifteenth and early sixteenth centuries believed themselves defenders and propagators of the Christian faith and in their capacity as subjects of the crown extended the royal domain and gained honor and profit for themselves. They were charged with spying out the secrets of those new lands to see if there were mosques and Moslem priests. They became skilled at using interpreters *(farautes)*, leading expeditions, and enriching themselves through slave raiding and gaining other booty. They ruled the conquered people in seignorial style, forcing them to work and render tribute. They founded towns and, as their forefathers had done, named some of them for the frontier (e.g., Segura de la Frontera). In their conquests and colonization, these men were armed with an ideology that included the medieval theory of the "just war" of Christians against infidels and the thinking of the Renaissance about the relations of "prudent men" with barbarians.

One aspect of the Hispanic frontier is told through the introduction of the horse, the cow, the sword, the iron lance, and the harquebus. Another may be seen in the two types of colonial settlements. First, there was the domination of an area inhabited by sedentary Indians who lived in farming communities like the Aztec *calpulli* and the Peruvian *ayllu;* second, there was the expansion of Spanish rule into the hostile Indian country, as happened in northern Mexico, southern Chile, on the Río de la Plata prairies, and elsewhere. The inhabitants of this latter frontier were known, respectively, as Chichimecas, Araucanians, and Pampa Indians; but there was a wide variety of local tribes within each of these, some being hunters, others foraging for a living, some doing a little farming or, as in southern Chile, breeding llamas.

Though both of these frontier types characterize Spanish colonization in the New World, it was the first that produced the hybrid Hispanic-American society based on the acculturation of Indians and Europeans. However, this type remained frontier only in the brief moment of conquest. For example, the conquistadors built arsenals in the city of Mexico, their houses served as forts, and municipal ordinances required all citizens to keep arms and horses ready for use. In time, stability came, the cultures of the Spaniard and Indian blended, and the frontiers moved on, as they had in the Roman Empire, to the fringes of settlement that lay exposed to the attacks of unconquered natives. The Spanish conquerors understood the differences between the two types of lands, calling the Indians of the central region of Mexico "peaceful" or "sensible" *(indios de razón)* and those of the border areas "wild" or "warlike."

The densely populated provinces where the sedentary Indians lived could be won quickly in pitched battles, while the conquest of the lands of the nomads involved long and indecisive war. The former readily supported the conquering hosts in comfortable circumstances, the wealth and property varying with the province; but the latter, lacking permanent Indian settlements, made distribution of the conquered towns as seignorial grants impossible. Wars of attrition and slave raids continued for many years while efforts at pacification proceeded through the establishment of forts, the making of treaties, and the forging of alliances with principal tribes. These "lands of war" prompted a special body of legislation and, as on the Iberian peninsular frontier, their checkered history inspired various literary and historical works.

In the lands of sedentary native population, the process of acculturation was so complex and the relations between Indians and Spaniards so variegated that their study would offer ample substance for a treatise on the institutions of the Spanish-American empire. The *repartimiento* and the *puebla* of Reconquest days could be the origin of the *encomienda* and the settlers' *villa* of Mexico and Peru. The peninsular Reconquest was a historical preparation for the conquest of America. The manner in which the Christians made war, the principles by which they justified it, the way they established their rule over the conquered, the distribution of booty and land, the founding of settlements—all these were much alike on all Hispanic frontiers on both sides of the Atlantic. However, it was the second type, the expansion into the hostile Indian country that afforded not only a new experience in the American milieu but also an extension of the warlike history of the medieval Iberian frontier, a distant migration of that frontier from Europe to America as a part of the process of colonization.

The experiences faced by the Spaniards in the peninsular and the American frontiers were similar but, of course, not identical. In one instance the Christian advance confronted an Arabic civilization, while in the other it faced the native cultures of the Canary Islands and the New World. The Moslem enemy possessed a formalized and hostile faith, while the Guanches and American Indians were looked upon simply as heathen. Thus, by the time of the conquest, Christian thinkers had arrived at doctrinal distinctions among the various kinds of infidels, aside from those of anthropological nature which actual contact was revealing. The peculiarities of the New World experience made themselves felt and the frontier continuum changed as much in the conquest of "sensible" Indians as in the struggles with the "wild" ones. Variations in geography and native populations had, in every case, an influence upon the Hispanic-American frontier. Some traces of pre-Columbian history were still noticeable. The nomadic tribes of northern New Spain knew no Aztec conquest, and in South America vast territories lay beyond the scope of Inca domination. Although Chile had been an object of one of these invasions, the Inca never gained firm control south of the Bío-Bío River, a region which also proved costly to the Spaniards. There are a few cases during the colonial era in which Indians moved from one frontier to another—as in Chile in the eighteenth century, when the Araucanians, already masters of horsemanship, crossed the Andean ranges and took part in frontier fighting on the Argentine pampa. In general and for good historical reasons, however, there was more continuity on the Christian front than on the Indian side.

The Indian frontiers were still part of the scene in nineteenth-century Argentina, Chile, and Mexico, and during that period important changes came about in institutions and in the means used to expand that frontier. Ideologically, the opposition between civilization and barbarism prevailed, and this concept was already understood in terms of the philosophy of progress. National governments sent out expeditions of experienced troops, trying to bring an end to the prolonged Indian wars. The "conquest of the desert" in Argentina by General Julio A. Roca in

1878–79 was one example of such efforts. The repeating rifle, telegraph, plans for railroads, and outlook for European immigration, all helped to create the atmosphere in which such expeditions developed. These campaigns brought to an end the frontier cycle begun by the Spanish conquistadors, at about the same time the North Americans were subduing the Indian west of the Mississippi.[2]

Characteristics

Advances along the Spanish-American frontier were often caused by the discovery of precious metals. By 1550, silver lodes in northern Mexico had been found and *reales* or mining settlements were being founded. In Chile during the same period, some gold deposits both north and south of Santiago were being worked. The southern mines lay in the "lands of war" and suffered much from the attacks of powerful Araucanian Indians. The plains of the Plata region lacked mineral wealth, but they were excellent for grazing, and stock ranching established itself there.

The geographic distribution of the minerals in New Spain determined the direction of the advance taken by the prospectors. Silver was found near the first settlements established by the Spaniards, as at Taxco, Sultepec, and Pachuca, and also to the north in the lands of the nomads, in Zacatecas, Guanajuato, and Parral. These mining strikes brought settlements into the lands of the nomadic tribes. Roads pushed out from the cities and towns in Mexico to these new population centers. Silver was sent on its way to the European metropolis and served as a means of exchange in obtaining the commodities needed from abroad, especially the mercury used in extracting silver from its native ore. The mining settlements were not isolated economies but were necessarily open to trade with Spain and other parts of the realm. Farming and stock raising were essential to these mining communities *(reales de minas)* for the settlers needed hides and tallow, and animals were the principal source of power. Since local Indians rarely were numerous enough to supply the needed manpower, even if enslavement and forced labor were used, the need had to be filled by attracting natives from areas previously colonized or by using Negro slaves. When the lodes continued rich, a permanent settlement grew up, and as the settled areas expanded, roads were extended and regular and seasonal trade brought in the commodities of urban life and artistic development.

The nomadic Indians were always a threat to the youthful mining towns, particularly when they attacked communication lines that linked the mines with the central provinces of the viceroyalty. To protect the pack trains and carts en route with silver or goods, forts were built at strategic points, settlements were established along the roads, and convoys were organized. A map of the *villas* of San Miguel and San Felipe, made about 1580, shows the great, long-shafted, two-wheeled carts, drawn by oxen and surrounded by armed horsemen bearing harquebuses, their horses protected from arrows by long trappings. Indians are shown on foot attacking horsemen and killing cattle with bow and arrow. One native is shown hanging by the roadside and others beheaded, as examples of the punishments meted out by the Spaniards. As the traffic on the roads increased and the settlements along the way grew, the hostile nomadic zone retreated. Still, in Mexico this was a slow and expensive froniter expansion, one fraught with sudden disaster and constant danger. The mines by their northern location gave impetus to expansion, and the military operations that made the roads secure were direct results of the consecutive mining strikes.

The competition for land between farmers and ranchers in central New Spain contributed to the advance of the stockmen into the unsettled regions of the north, and by the middle of the sixteenth century there was a considerable movement of settlers with their cattle, horses, sheep, goats, and hogs into the wild Indian country. With stock from the Iberian Peninsula or the Spanish islands of the Antilles, these ranchers moved into the good pasture lands that had long been held in low regard by earlier frontiersmen.

The Spanish settlers were horsemen. The figure of the *vaquero* appears in several places on the Spanish frontier: the *charro* in Mexico, the *llanero* of the Venezuelan plains, and the *gaucho*, both Spanish and Portuguese, in the Río de la Plata. The authorities granted permits for roundup and slaughter of cattle that had been running wild and multiplying on the plains. Thus hides were obtained for trade. These customs, as common in Texas as in the Plata region, greatly reduced the number of herds.

Not all settlers were small operators and not all cattle were wild and unclaimed. There were also the *estancias* or ranches, composed of buildings set amid an extensive range, where the owner and his cowboys—half-breeds *(mestizos)*, creoles, and some times mulattoes—cared for branded cattle and other livestock. On these remote *estancias*, horsemanship, roundups, the use of knives and guns, and the presence of hostile Indians, all contributed to the development of boldness and skill in these men. The owners were jealous of their seignorial prestige. Possession of a vast estate, the habit of command, and the holding of military titles made them prominent leaders in the coarse insecure world of the frontier. Upon occasion, the *estancieros* succeeded in gaining political leadership, particularly during the civil wars of the nineteenth century.

The range country most hospitable to stock raising was also inhabited by nomadic tribes. From the Pampa Indians of South America, the gaucho acquired his weapon, the *boleadora*, which the native used for hunting the *guanaco*. The coming of horses and cattle into the Indian country affected the customs of those who lived there. They learned to eat meat and to use the hides of these new animals. Mare's meat was a tender morsel to the nomads of the Plata region. Thus, if the presence of white men was a threat to the wild Indians, the same white man also brought with him elements of life that helped satisfy the Indians' needs and that also provoked their attacks. When these plains tribes learned to ride and developed their own horseback style, they were fearsome enemies on both the northern and southern frontiers of the American continent.

It was the introduction of European animals among the tribes that revolutionized their way of life. La Pérouse, in his famous *Voyages*, remarked that the importation of domestic animals "has had its most striking effect on all those peoples living between Santiago and the Straits of Magellan. These folk observe practically none of their former customs, they wear different clothes, they do not eat the same foods, and today they affect a style much more like that of the Tatars, or of the people living on the shores of the Red Sea, than like that of their own ancestors of two centuries ago."[3] No matter how exaggerated this appraisal may be, there is some truth in it.

The smaller animals, sheep, goats, and hogs, as well as cattle and horses, were important on various Latin-American frontiers and contributed much to the settlement of such territories as Nuevo León and New Mexico in northern New Spain. Wool had long been famous as a commodity of export and manufacture in Spain, and by the middle of the sixteenth century wool of good quality was being produced in Mexico. The association of ranchers for moving their livestock from summer to winter range, known as the *Mesta*, was transplanted to New Spain but never evolved as it did in the homeland. Sheep ranching led to the establishment of workshops *(obrajes)* which manufactured both cotton and wool textiles for the mining towns, and this domestic trade forged another link between the central and northern provinces of New Spain.

The northward expansion in New Spain required the development of new farming centers near the mining and ranching settlements. Since parts of the northern lands were arid, farming was necessarily carried on near rivers and springs. The crops were corn, wheat, beans, peppers, fruits, other vegetables, grapes, and cotton. Cacao was brought into these lands from places like Tabasco and Soconusco in the far south.

Propertied holdings were built up by means of grants of land *(mercedes de tierra)* made by the authorities and by lump-sum payments *(composiciones)* the owners made to the crown to obtain clear titles of ownership. Some settlements were composed of Spanish farmers; others were made by sedentary Indians taken from the central parts of Mexico, e.g. the Tlaxcalans at Saltillo. Some of the northern tribes that had a farming tradition, such as the Tarahumaras, grew crops on their own lands and helped supply food to the mining communities. As will be shown later, the missions can also be considered centers of agricultural development.

As the Spanish colonizers spread into the marginal lands, important changes came about in their labor system. The practice of enslaving prisoners of war continued longer on the frontier than in heavily populated areas. Such enslavement had dated from the early days of the conquest but had been abolished by the crown. Nevertheless, the capture of natives for use as slaves continued in the wild Indian country.

The *encomienda* was able to function with no particular difficulty among the farming populations of Middle America and the Andes, but when the tribes that paid tribute and the Indians available for forced labor began to be scarce, the degeneration of the seignorial system soon followed. For example, in Nuevo León the Spanish colonist lived part of each year with his Indians, putting them to work and in return furnishing them the necessities of life. During the rest of the year these Indians were free to roam the country as they pleased. This mobile *encomienda (congrega)* was not based on stable, permanent settlements, and confusion resulted when the Spanish owner returned to put his natives to work. Disputes over the ownership and sale of Indians and their children made this social system different from the *encomienda* in permanent settlements. In Nueva Galicia and Nueva Viscaya *repartimientos* were tried, a system that used Indians in relays for forced labor in agriculture and mining. However, the scarcity of native settlements on the frontier was an obstacle to effective use of this system.

The *encomienda* system suffered the same fate elsewhere. Among the Pueblo Indians of New Mexico, who sustained themselves amid hostile nomadic tribes and lived the settled life of farmers, the Spaniards tried with great determination but without complete success to implant seignorial institutions. Reports from the second half of the seventeenth century show that the Indians in Chile lived on their lords' estates rather than in towns. In southern Chile there were hardly any *encomiendas* "with town and native chief," and the few that did exist were inhabited by a servile group who had been captured in war or had been born on Spanish cattle ranches or farms without ever having known village life. All of these *encomiendas* rendered labor service instead of tribute.

Unstable frontier conditions and wars against the tribes were means of providing the Spanish colonists with a captive labor supply. Soldiers frequently went on expeditions into the Indian country *(malocas)* to capture slaves. These men, women, and children were sold for use in Peru, Chile, and elsewhere. The minimum age for enslavements was ten and a half years for boys, nine and a half for girls; young captives were kept in temporary bondage up to the age of twenty. Those of legal age *(de ley)* were valued between two hundred and fifty and three hundred pesos each, and younger ones *(piezas de servidumbre)* from one hundred and fifty to two hundred pesos. This slave trade was opposed by some of the clergy, and royal statutes alternated between prohibiting and permitting it.[4]

The northward expansion in New Spain does not seem to have resulted from population pressure due to a sizable European immigration in the sixteenth century or from the considerable increase in population in the central region. The frontier was not a safety valve, but it was a land of opportunity. The first conquered provinces were under the seignorial tenure of the original conquistadors and settlers, not a numerous group, but one that controlled extensive Indian lands. Thus the expeditions into new lands were attractive to Spaniards who had not profited from the first distributions of property and privilege, who had arrived after the original conquest, or who were still eager for the honor and profit to be gained in such conquering expeditions. For these reasons, the Spanish colonization expanded largely in accord with the interests of both the crown and the captains of the conquest and their men, who were hungry for new opportunities. This expansion was part of the spirit of risk and adventure that dominated sixteenth-century Spanish society. It is interesting to observe the mobility of those Spanish expeditions which led to the geographic extension of the Empire in North and South America, an area that contained 160,000 people of European origin or descent before the end of the first century of conquest.[5]

Wherever an embattled frontier developed, as it did in the Chichimec and the Araucanian country, it was not easy to sustain the conquerors' enthusiasm. The demands of these frontiers, particularly of Chile, were met by offering attractive salaries and awards, by sending men there for punishment, and by using soldiers who had learned their trade in the Spanish campaigns in Europe. The frontiers of the Plata region were no more popular than those of the Chichimecs or Araucanians, exposed as they were to all the dangers and privations common to troops stationed in forts in that area.

The nomadic Indians were in many ways admirably suited to the type of warfare characteristic of the Spanish-American frontier. They had great mobility, the will to resist, and a sense of adaptation that enabled them to become formidable opponents. They knew the terrain and used it advantageously, scattered when they were hard pressed, and chose the most favorable time and place for their attack. They soon understood the importance of horses in war and upon acquiring them in numbers, they neutralized the Spanish advantage of a mounted cavalry. The gauchos of the Argentine pampa learned very early how rapidly the natives took to the saddle. However, the Christians maintained their military advantage down to the end by their possession of steel weapons and firearms, though when factions of white men tried to gain control of the savages, they often furnished their erstwhile enemies with guns and ammunition. Repeating rifles did not come into general use until the last third of the nineteenth century; this fire-power advantage was too great for the natives to overcome despite their use of the horse and their wise adaptation to the terrain.

In colonial times, the nomadic Indian could not be defeated in open battle or dominated by means of seignorial rule. Thus the conquering lord of the central region could maintain himself on that exposed frontier only by use of cavalry, construction of forts *(fortines)* and presidios, and extermination, enslavement, or deportation of the Indian. These tribesmen were not vassals, as were their sedentary brothers who were subject to forced labor and tutelage. Instead, they were enemies of the Empire, thought of as barbarians, and known to be dangerous because of their attacks upon travelers, traders, silver pack trains, muleteers, ranches, and range stock. Still, there were times when churchmen strongly intervened to impose a policy of peace which upon occasion confined military effort to strictly defensive ends. The authorities sometimes made brief alliances with the Indians, giving them the necessities of life as presents in exchange for peace. However, hostilities would soon break out again because of the colonists' greed, the mistreatment of the Indians, or the renewed attacks made by the Indians themselves in times of real need, aggression, or vengeance.

The amalgamation of races on the frontier occurred at random rather than as a general blending of societies. It is interesting to note that many Christian captives and renegades lived among the Indians of the Plata region during the second half of the nineteenth century.

Along with the miner, rancher, farmer, trader, soldier, and muleteer, the missionary took his place on the Spanish-American frontier. He played an active part in the invasion of the marginal areas of the Empire. He undertook the most arduous expeditions, established centers for the conversion of the barbarians, and at times suffered martyrdom for his labors. Prepared for his work in the religious schools, he found his Christian discipline tempered by the rigor and danger of frontier life. In the missions, his neophytes learned the rudiments of Christian faith and civil life. These missions were not exclusively religious institutions, since in most cases both social and economic affairs were under the controlling hand of the missionary priest. His Indians practiced agriculture, learned the care of livestock, and acquired a few crafts. Iron tools and domesticated animals thus became a part of the native's material life and went hand in hand with the propagation of the faith. Save for the single case of the expulsion of the Jesuits from Spanish America in 1767, the crown gave military and economic protection to the missions. The work of the missionaries was distinguished by their concept of invading the wild Indian country armed with a message of peace and the benefits of civilization. As it turned out, however, they had to adjust to the conditions prevailing on the frontier. Thus from time to time the mission played a military role. It did not significantly increase the mixing of the races *(mestizaje)*. Though many missions did not endure, the records clearly indicate the importance of these establishments and show that they were of equal importance with the mining *reales*, the Spanish towns, agricultural estates, and stock ranches as froniter institutions.[6]

Evaluations

It has been noted before that during the Middle Ages, writings about the Iberian frontier began to appear. Other such writings resulted from the overseas expansion, and then more appeared in connection with the Spanish-American frontier. Those works of any merit belong equally to two periods—the age of the post-conquest colonization and the period after independence. Some have literary merit and others are informative as to the native society, religion, or politics. In any case, these works permit an examination of the meanings of these historical experiences, their main orientation and evaluation.

Even before the end of the Spanish settlement, it was realized that the society of northern Mexico was different from that of the central region, that the North had taken on a spirit in which the prevailing dangers and hardships could be confronted. Alexander von Humboldt observed in his *Political Essay on the Kingdom of New Spain* that the struggle against Indians and insecurity had stamped the character of the northern people with a certain energy and temper all their own. He noted the lack of docile Indians whom the whites might have exploited so they could live a life of idleness and indolence. The active life, lived for the most part on horseback, helped to develop physical strength, and in that country men had to be strong to deal with hostile Indians and herds of range cattle. Those men were strong in spirit, of unexcitable nature, and possessed of clean and robust bodies. To Humboldt this picture was—and this explains his benevolent point of view: "a state of nature, preserved amid the trappings of an ancient civilization."[7] In the same tone, a native son of

Coahuila, Miguel Ramos de Arizpe, explained in his Memorial to the Cortes of Cádiz in 1811 that agriculture, source of the wealth of nations, was the common occupation of people in all the eastern inland provinces of Coahuila, Texas, Nuevo León, New Mexico, and Nuevo Santander. He said, "it shapes their general character, and for this reason, busy night and day in honest work on the land, receiving their living from it rather than from any person, they are surely immune to intrigue, are virtuously upright in morals, and are enemies of arbitrary conduct and disorder. They are worshippers of true liberty and, naturally enough, are the best fitted for all the moral and political virtues. They are much devoted to the liberal and mechanical arts."[8]

Whether because of a naturalistic bent so typical of Enlightened philosophy or whether because of physiocratic leanings or localism, the fact is that the distinguishing natural and historical character of the northern provinces was understood by local people and foreigners alike, even though their conceptions and expressions of it were different. The local conditions, the relations with the Indians, and the kind of activities typical of the region, all had contributed to making the northern frontier and its people unique in New Spain. With the coming of independence when the conservatives and radicals, the federalists and centralists were struggling over the question of the nation's political organization, the northern provinces were seen by some republicans as bulwarks of liberal principles. These regions could more easily avoid involvement in the issues of theocracy, militarism, and the hierarchic lack of equality that was holding the Indian in subjection. When the central government was in the control of the conservatives, it could be resisted by those distant provinces. Seen in this light, the northern frontier seemed to be the guardian of liberty.

Some men of affairs who regarded the northern provinces in this way and who observed the thin population of these regions came to reflect on the possibility of foreign immigration. Thinking of the progress made by the first Anglo-American colonies in Texas, Lorenzo de Zavala wrote that within two or three generations that part of Mexico would be richer, more free, and more civilized than all the rest. Because of its immigrants, Mexican Texas would be an example to other states still in a semifeudal stage and ruled by military and clerical influences, fateful inheritances from Spanish rule.[9] Thus the northern frontier was seen not merely as a different society more favorable for the growth of democratic life, but also as a hope for the regeneration of all Mexico. Precisely because these frontier regions had come through the colonial period so thinly populated did they seem particularly promising for new immigration projects in the nineteenth century.

The northern frontier had been ruled by military government, particularly after the *Comandancia de Provincias Internas* was organized in 1776. After several reorganizations, this command included the provinces of Nueva Viscaya, Sonora, Sinaloa, California, Coahuila, New Mexico, and Texas. Ramos de Arizpe petitioned the Cortes of Cádiz for the establishment of a civil government, arguing that a military commander, by his education and character, naturally seeks to execute the laws he knows and is accustomed to enforce, "demanding of the peaceful farmer, the quiet cattleman, the hard-working artisan, that blind obedience, that wordless compliance, that his soldiers must render at command—and this, sometimes, without meaning to do so. Finally, he makes himself a despot, with the worst results for the people, who would never suffer so under civil government which would hold more closely to civil and social law."[10] Thus regionalism did not signify an absolute guarantee of liberty since it could become the refuge of bossism *(caciquismo)* and local abuses.

The loyalty of Anglo-American immigrants to Mexico was not as strong as the ties that bound them to their own people, and they did not bring the hoped-for internal development of the northern provinces or the instructive example it was hoped they would offer the other states of the republic. Instead, there followed the revolt and independence of the Texans, their annexation to the United States, and the war between that nation and Mexico. These events were followed in turn by the loss of lands lying north of the Rio Grande.

For a brief moment during the revolution that began in Mexico in 1910, the northern provinces exercised great influence in national politics. The revolt gained impetus in Coahuila, Chihuahua, and Sonora. In this may be seen an extension of those historic liberal impulses already mentioned, but there were also such new factors as the help in arms and other resources obtained from north of the United States border. In any case, the cavalry and cattle of the North helped sustain the troops in their long marches and campaigns. Among these soldiers were creoles, mestizos, and even Yaqui and Mayo Indians, who went on to pitch their tents in the patios of the National Palace of Mexico City. During that long war, the northern fighter gained great fame for courage and endurance and his leaders were at the helm of a number of the revolutionary governments.

It remains to inquire, finally, whether the northern frontier may be considered a source of the Mexican national type. If a balanced mixture of ethnic stocks may be considered the symbol of what is Mexican, it is possible that the people of the old northern frontier meet this standard. On the other hand, there are scholars who hold that the great number of northerners are ethnically creole, i.e., descendants of whites. If Mexican nativism is based on the blending of the ancient civilization of the sedentary Indians and that of the Spaniards, then the central provinces rather than the northern must have originated the distinctive Mexican character. This is true if we accept a national character rather than a plurality of types that may be closer to reality. Certainly, the sedentary Indians were most numerous in the central region and presumably the greatest amalgamation of the races took place there. In accordance with this last interpretation, then, the North can be considered only a source of social peculiarities. It remains apart, however, from that nativism that stems from the pre-conquest culture of Middle America.

A diversity similar to what we have seen in Mexico—between the inland provinces *(tierra adentro)* and those of the central part *(tierra afuera)* of the viceroyalty—also appears in Chile. The division there is between the central region permanently colonized by the Spaniards and those lands to the south that remained in Araucanian hands or lay on the frontier exposed to their attacks. In the late sixteenth and early seventeenth century, Indian warfare had forced abandonment of the settlements of Arauco, Santa Cruz, Valdivia, Imperial, Angol, Villarica, and Osorno. Chillán and Concepción had been attacked, but the Christians had managed to re-establish their control in the country lying between the Rivers Maule and Bío-Bío. The policy of defensive war, begun late in the seventeenth century, consisted in holding the line of the Bío-Bío so as to protect the central part of the colony. Only missionaries were permitted to cross that line to deal with the natives. This important frontier, on which depended the conservation of Spanish power in the South Pacific, attracted the attention not only of the authorities of Chile but also of those of the Viceroyalty of Peru and of Spain.

Like the war in northern Mexico, this struggle against the Araucanians went through several stages, expending troops and funds which during the seventeenth century came as a subsidy *(situado)* from Peru. This war, like the Mexican, alternated between attack and defense and led to the capture of prisoners on both sides. There was some mixing of blood due to unions between Spanish soldiers and Indian women and of Indians and captured Spanish women. Historians and students of Chilean literature point out that the war along the Araucanian frontier contributed unique features to the national culture. Among the themes brought forth in this literature as it has developed since the sixteenth century have been the glorification of the Araucanian war, begun by Alonso de Ercilla, and the recognition of the Indian's right to defend his land. The selection of these two themes is not meant as derogatory to any of the authors who praise the expansion of the Faith and of Christian rule or who exalt the deeds of Spanish creole soldiers who fought the Indian wars.[11] As late as the nineteenth century, one can still note the dualism between the regard for the Araucanian's merits and for the final campaign that conquered him.

In the complex patterns of ideas about racial mixture, the vigor of the

Araucanian is given credit as soon as it is seen to be a part of the racial stock just as European ancestry, particularly the Basque, is a matter for pride and distinction. Authors discuss the question of whether or not there has been an amalgamation of Spanish and Indian in the great oligarchic families. They speak of the balance attained between the various racial strains in the general population. Some believe in a Gothic origin of the pioneer Spaniards who came to Chile, while others prefer to stress the influence of the German migration of the late nineteenth century. They also single out certain forces drawn from ethnic and historical backgrounds to account for traits in the national character. For example, the laziness and improvidence of the people, their stoicism and courage, their martial spirit, inconstancy, and love of adventure are accounted for through the influence of war and their frugal frontier life. These ideas about the intermingling of peoples and the unity of feeling that results from blending a warlike history with qualities imputed to the national character throw into bold relief the influence of the southern frontier on the shaping of the personality of Chile.

Numerous writings about the plains of the Plata region deserve careful literary, social, and political analysis, and a few themes from the work of Domingo Faustino Sarmiento have been selected here[12] to enable us to compare the image of this frontier with that of others in the New World. Driven by his political desire to attack the tyrannical rule of the cattleman Juan Manuel de Rosas, Sarmiento contrasted the barbarism of the pastoral provinces with urban civilization of European origin. The passion of his argument did not blur the clarity of his description of gaucho life and he was well aware of the promise, implicit in the vigorous originality of this historical development in its American setting, for those who would treat it as a literary theme. As with Francis Parkman, the historian, and James Fenimore Cooper, the man of letters, Sarmiento was attracted by the American frontier. In the United States as in Argentina, he saw the dramatic interplay of civilization and barbarism between the European immigrant and the nomadic Indian. He saw these analogies clearly and was perhaps the first of New World writers to make the connection between North American and Spanish American frontiers. However, there are in his pages some historical differences which make this parallel more complex. After all, the gauchos who inhabited the pastoral pampa and who are descendants of Spaniards, Indians, and sometimes also Negroes, were organized into a society already Europeanized during the colonial period. That society had conquered large tracts of the back country by use of cattle, horses, steel weapons, and firearms. It had founded the cities that Sarmiento pictured as oases of civilization in a cultureless plain.

Contrary to Sarmiento's point of view, we can properly speak of the existence of a historical frontier only where the Christian gauchos faced Indian enemies. That other frontier, conceived politically by Sarmiento as lying between the civilized and the barbarous, between urban and pastoral people, between European immigrants and gauchos—in short, between those who were politically disinherited as was Sarmiento and those who governed under the protection of Rosas—cannot be confused with the historical frontier that did lie between the wild Indians and the fortified line established during the colonial period. Here we see the dualism of Sarmiento's thought with respect to the urban and pastoral heritage of Spanish America. On the one hand, he saw this heritage as the fulcrum of tradition and civilized progress in Argentina, although he did try to distinguish between the Spanish colonial period with its backward society and the new policies directed toward economic progress, European immigration, religious tolerance, educational advances, and political democracy. On the other hand, he confused that older tradition with American barbarism—Indian, mestizo, gaucho, and colonial in origin—that was to be eliminated by advancing civilization. This dualism as lived and expressed by Sarmiento with dramatic intensity helps explain the historical position from which he viewed both the past and the future.

In explaining that the Argentine prairie wagons were drawn up in a circle for defense against Indian attack, he was well aware that the gauchos fought from within the defensive circle just as did the men of the western United States. Both represented to him the progress of European civilization on the American frontier in the face of the aborigines. The westward movement in the Argentine and in the United States began, however, in different centuries and followed different rhythms until a certain parallelism was reached in the nineteenth century. By that time, there already existed in South America a gaucho civilization, denoting an intermediate stage between the newly arrived European immigrant and the nomadic Indian.

The similarity between the frontiers of North and South America which Sarmiento saw derived from environmental conditions and from the tasks necessary to control these influences, that is, from factors peculiar to invasion of lands inhabited by nomads. His attention was drawn to the social and political aspects of life on the pampa, although the essential vigor of his writing stems from his poetic re-creation of the peculiar aspects of the countryside and the personality of the gaucho. He emphasized certain characteristics that may have been common to all men who pioneered in the new lands of America.[13] He was aware of the significance of the horse for the civilization of the New World, of the diversity between the mounted *vaqueros* of the pastoral regions and the peons or foot servants in the agricultural districts; and he knew the contributions made by the *llaneros* of Venezuela, for example, during the wars of independence. Nonetheless, his statements do not coincide with the thesis later formulated by Frederick Jackson Turner—this despite certain external similarities—since Turner found on the frontier not the cradle of pastoral despotism, as exemplified in the dictator Rosas of Argentina, but rather the seeds of democracy and social fluidity.[14] Sarmiento understood and admired the civilization of the United States. He knew how it differed from European society which he himself had seen, and he thought the American superior to the European. To him the frontier was the battleground between barbarism and civilization. The origin of democracy lay not on the frontier but in the European tradition transplanted there, the immigration of the Puritans, the freedom that rose out of the Reformation, and the life of the Atlantic coast and its expansion. He hoped the European immigrants would bring a reforming spirit to the Argentine and it mattered little to him that this might be done at the expense of gaucho customs which, in his general condemnation of barbarism, he inevitably treated as equivalent with the life of native nomads. Thus Sarmiento could perceive some of the problems which European immigration created for the United States and for Argentina, and in time he came to doubt the civilizing influence of these newly arrived people.[15] To achieve the goal of progressive virtues, he placed his best and final hopes in popular education.

The only Spanish-American writer I know who has tested Turner's frontier thesis for Spanish America is not Sarmiento, who died five years before Turner presented his paper of 1893, but the Peruvian, Víctor Andrés Belaúnde.[16] He is of the opinion that the frontier appeared only rarely in the Spanish colonies. He points out the importance of the beginning of colonial occupation but believes that when that early period had passed, there was no free land in which a frontier might have been opened for the many. This was because of problems created by the Amazon River valley and the Andean range. From the geographical point of view, he sees nothing comparable to the opportunities held forth by the Mississippi Valley.

After examining the landholding situation in Chile, on the plains of the Orinoco, and in Mexico, Belaúnde pauses to consider the prairies of the Plata region and southern Brazil. Here the geography was more like that of the United States. The pampa, however, was occupied during the colonial period; later, the railroads and government land cessions further impeded the development of a frontier in a social sense, since large holdings prevailed. From this lack of a frontier stemmed a rigid social structure and an absence of vitality and youthful spirit. What Belúnde emphasizes is the diversity of the situation, and he concludes that Turner's thesis does not apply.

In conclusion, I believe that the evidence is not all in, that the thesis may be examined in other regions and from other points of view. One case that deserves such study is the meeting of the Spanish-American frontier in northern Mexico with the westward-moving American frontier, not in its well-known political, military, and diplomatic aspects, but with reference to social exchanges and adjustments that occurred.

Selected Readings

Barlow, R. H. *The Extent of the Empire of the Culhua Mexica* Berkeley: University of California Press, 1949.

Belaúnde, Victor Andrés. *The Frontier in Hispanic America* ("Rice Institute Pamphlets" No. X [October, 1923]), 202–213.

Bolton, H. E. "The Mission as a Frontier Institution in the Spanish-American Colonies," *American Historical Review*, XXIII (1917), 42–61.

Gibson, Charles. *Tlaxcala in the Sixteenth Century*. New Haven: Yale University Press, 1952.

Powell, Philip W. *Soldiers, Indians, and Silver. The Northward Advance of New Spain, 1550–1600*. Berkeley: University of California Press, 1952.

Ramos de Arizpe, Miguel. *Report that Dr. Miguel Ramos de Arizpe. . . presents to the August Congress on the Natural, Political and Civil Condition of the Provinces of Coahuila, Nuevo León, Nuevo Santander, and Texas. . .*, translations, annotations, and introduction by Nettie Lee Benson ("Latin American Studies," No. XI). Austin: University of Texas, Institute of Latin-American Studies, 1950.

Sauer, Carl O. *Colima of New Spain in the Sixteenth Century*. Berkeley: University of California Press, 1950.

Simpson, Lesley B. *The Encomienda in New Spain: the Beginning of Spanish Mexico*. Berkeley: University of California Press. 2d ed. rev., enl., 1950.

West, Robert C. *The Mining Community in Northern New Spain. The Parral Mining District*. Berkeley: University of California Press, 1949.

Zavala, Silvio A. *New Viewpoints on the Spanish Colonization of America*. Philadelphia: University of Pennsylvania Press, 1943.

NOTES

1. C. Sánchez Albornoz, *España y el Islam* (Buenos Aires, 1943), 186–187.

2. See E. S. Zeballos, *Recuerdos Argentinos. Callvucurá y la dinastía de los Piedra* (2d ed.; Buenos Aires, 1890; orig. pub. Buenos Aires, 1884), 358. The President's message to Congress, August, 1878, explained that the "old system of successive stages of occupation handed down from the Conquest, obliging us to scatter our national military forces over a very broad area and to remain vulnerable to all Indian attacks, has shown itself to be powerless to guarantee the lives and goods of people living in frontier towns that are under constant threat. We must give up the old system and seek the Indian in his encampment, to defeat him or drive him out, leaving him barred not by a large man-made ditch but by the great and impassible barrier of the Río Negro, deep and navigable in its whole course from the Ocean to the Andes." Zeballos' *La conquista de quince mil leguas leguas* (Buenos Aires,

1878), 372, states that "the military power of the barbarians is wholly destroyed, because the Remington has taught them that an army battalion can cross the whole pampa, leaving the land strewn with the bodies of those who dared to oppose it."

3. Quoted in José Toribio Medina, *Los aboríjenes de Chile* (Santiago, 1882), xiii.

4. D. Amunátegui y Solar, *Las encomiendas de indíjenas en Chile* (2 vols.; Santiago, 1909–1910), II, 165 and 223.

5. See Juan López de Velasco, *Geografía y descripción universal de las Indias* . . .(Madrid, 1894).

6. For the foregoing see items in the appended list of readings; also W. Jiménez Moreno, "La colonización y evangelización de Guanajuato en el siglo xvi," *Cuadernos Americanos*, XIII, no. 1 (Jan.-Feb., 1944); J. Miranda, "Notas sobre la introducción de la Mesta en la Nueva España," *Revista de Historia de América* no. 17 (June, 1944); F. Chevalier, *La formation des grands domaines au Mexique: terre et société aux xvi-xvii siècles* (Paris, 1952); M. González Navarro, *Repartimientos de indios en Nueva Galicia* (Mexico, 1953); Silvio A. Zavala, "Los esclavos indios en el norte de México, siglo xvi," *El Norte de México y el Sur de los Estado Unidos* (Mexico, Sociedad Mexicana de Antropología, 1944); Vito Alessio Robles, "Las condiciones sociales en el Norte de la Nueva España," *Memorias de la Academia Mexicana de la Historia*, IV (April-June, 1945), and the same author's *Coahuila y Texas en la época colonial Mexico*, 1938). See also reports of inspections *(visitas)* as in Alonso de la Mota y Escobar, *Descripción Geográfica de los Reinos de la Nueva Galicia, Nueva Viscaya y Nuevo León* (2d ed., with slightly altered title, Mexico, 1940; orig. pub., Mexico, 1930); and Nicolás de Lafora, *Relación del viaje que hizo a los presidios internos, situados en la frontera de la América Septentrional* . . . (Mexico, 1939). Miguel Ramos de Arizpe's Memorial to the Cortes of Cádiz in 1811 is in Ramos de Arizpe, *Discursos, Memorias, e Informes* . . ., with notes by Vito Alessio Robles (Mexico, 1942).

7. Alexander von Humboldt, *Political Essay on the Kingdom of New Spain*, vol. II, as cited in Ramos de Arizpe, *Discursos, Memorias, e Informes* . . ., xvi.

8. Ramos de Arizpe, *Discursos, Memorias, e Informes* . . ., xix and 41.

9. See his *Ensayo Histórico de las Revoluciones de Méjico, desde 1808 hasta 1830* (2 vols.; Paris and New York, 1831–1832), II (New York, 1832), 171.

10. Ramos de Arizpe, *Discursos, Memorias e Informes* . . ., 58.

11. After Ercilla's *Araucana*, the anonymous poem given in José Toribio Medina, *Historia de la literatura colonial de Chile* (3 vols.; Santiago, 1878), I, 250; Hernando Alvarez de Toledo, *Purén Indómito* (Leipzig, 1861: written after 1597); and Pedro de Oña, *Arauco Domado* (Santiago, 1917 orig. pub., Lima, 1595), among others.

12. For the most part I follow the fine selection in *El pensamiento vivo de Sarmiento*, comp. Ricardo Rojas (Buenos Aires, 1941). Quotations that follow in the text are mostly from *Facundo, ó Civilización i Barbarie* (orig. pub. at Santiago, 1845, in the newspaper *El Progreso*, as *Facundo*, then separately in the same year as *Civilización i barbarie. Vida de Juan Facundo Quiroga . . .)*, and *Conflictos y Armonías de las Razas en América* (Buenos Aires, 1883). For a recent penetrating analysis, see Ezequiel Martínez Estrada, *Muerte y Transfiguración de Martín Fierro* (2 vols.; Mexico, 1948).

13. *El pensamiento vivo de Sarmiento*, 136: "Individualism was his very essence, the horse his exclusive weapon, and the immense pampa his theater"; on p. 132: "valor, boldness, dexterity, violence, and opposition to established justice"; and on p. 127: "The gaucho admired above all else physical force, skill in horsemanship, and courage."

14. See R. E. Riegel, "Current Ideas of the Significance of the United States Frontier," *Revista de Historia de América*, No. 33 (June, 1952), 30: "These men were optimistic, nationalistic, and expansionist. They were individualistic and materialistic, with a sprinkling of the lawless, but withal brave, hardy and ingenious, willing to experiment until they overcame the difficulties of each new region. They were the primary source of such American traits as individualism, democracy, inventiveness, and materialism." Merle E.

Curti, *Historiadores de América, Frederick Jackson Turner* (Mexico, 1949), 26, states that "the westward movement, he [Turner] argued, developed the essentially American traits of restless energy, self-reliance, voluntary co-operation on the part of individuals, practical ingenuity and versatility, inventiveness, and a masterful grasp of material things. . . ." Note that in this listing of personal qualities there are as many coincidences as discrepancies with those ascribed to the gaucho.

15. *El pensamineto vivo de Sarmiento*, 77–78, 208. See Martínez Estrada, *Sarmiento* (Buenos Aires, 1946), 99. The nativist reaction as it was in 1870 is reflected in Lucio V. Mansilla, *Una excursión a los indios Ranqueles* (Buenos Aires, 1870).

For critical opinion of Sarmiento's historical position, see Martínez Estrada, *Sarmiento*, 94, and Ricardo Rojas' prologue to *El pensamiento vivo de Sarmiento*, 24–26.

16. *The Frontier in Hispanic America* (Rice Institute Pamphlets, No. X [October, 1923]), 202–213.

José de Gálvez

EIGHTEENTH-CENTURY CHANGES

12

The North of New Spain as a Political Problem in the Eighteenth Century*

Luis Navarro García

Editor's Introduction

During the first century of her epic New World explorations, Spain was the only European power with pretensions to North America. In the eighteenth century, however, France, England, and Russia pushed into areas claimed by Spain. Meanwhile, nomadic Indian nations, their mobility enhanced by the introduction of the horse by Spaniards, challenged Spanish-Mexican intruders more effectively than ever before. In detailed studies, historians have examined the ways in which Spanish policymakers met these challenges of the eighteenth century. Foremost among the students of this subject is the Spanish historian Luis Navarro García, who studies northern New Spain from across the Atlantic, as did many Spanish officials. From that distance, Navarro García takes a broad view of Spanish policy. He has sharpened his view substantially by examining the thousands of pertinent documents which remain in the

Estudios Americanos, 20 (1960): 17–31. Reprinted with permission of the author.

famed General Archive of the Indies, located within walking distance of his office at the University of Seville.

In the present essay, Navarro García focuses on Spanish attempts to meet the threats to northern New Spain posed by foreign powers and Indians during the reign of Charles III (1759–88). He describes the evolution of the policy that made the Interior Provinces of New Spain a separate administrative unit in 1776. Navarro García provides a sharp analysis of the interplay between the divergent views of two high-ranking Spanish officials, the Marqués de Rubí and José de Gálvez. Throughout, he makes it clear that circumstances peculiar to the frontier shaped the development of policy as much as policy shaped the development of the frontier.

First published in 1960, this essay represents a distillation of some of the conclusions that Navarro García reached in his massive study, *José de Gálvez y la Comandancia General de las Provincias Internas del Norte de Nueva España* (Seville: 1964). To date, this article, along with his other work, has been available only in Spanish. It appears in English for the first time in this anthology, translated by Beth Gard of the University of New Mexico Press, and the editor.

Luis Navarro García has written many other studies which historians on both sides of the Atlantic respect. Among his books are: *Intendencias en Indias* (Seville: 1959); *Las Provincias Internas en el siglo XIX* (Seville: 1965); *Sonora y Sinaloa en el siglo XVII* (Seville: 1966); and *Hispanoamérica en el siglo XVIII* (Seville: 1975).

The North of New Spain as a Political Problem in the Eighteenth Century

It has often been written that the progression of the Spanish frontier north from Mexico was notably delayed because of the resistance of Indian peoples to subjugation. These Indians have been characterized as having a much lower level of cultural development and a much more rudimentary political structure than those of the so-called Aztec Empire. Without denying this, in my judgment it is important to point out that the sparseness of Spanish settlement in the north was caused more by the lack of mineral deposits—the classic impetus to colonization. In the north there was to be a richness of laws, and a paucity of people. Where mineral deposits were extant, human settlement reached enormous proportions and completely transformed the appearance of regions in northern New Spain. This happened, for example, in the broad zone between Zacatecas and San Luis de Potosí and, much later, in the Santa Eulalia-Chihuahua region, to cite only the most well-known instances.

These two examples of developed areas also serve to mark the beginning and the end of a process that lasted more than a century and a half, from 1540 to 1706, and resulted in the incorporation into the Spanish Empire of the extraordinarily extensive lands and peoples included in the area from a line drawn between the Santiago and Pánuco rivers and the village of Taos, and between the California Peninsula and Nacogdoches.

The conquistador, miner, and Jesuit or Franciscan missionary were the heroes of this marvelous process, which was nothing less than spectacular and which demonstrates the uninterrupted vitality of the Spanish people long after the first American conquests. After Zacatecas and San Luis de Potosí were already joined to Nueva Galicia and New Spain respectively, there came into being the independent governments of Nueva Vizcaya, Nuevo León, New Mexico, and later Coahuila and Texas. In the eighteenth century, Sonora and Nuevo Santander came into existence.

Five of these units—Sonora, Nueva Vizcaya, New Mexico, Coahuila, and Texas—are, properly speaking, the "Provincias Internas" [or Internal Provinces]. Governing them were a series of men, representatives of the Spanish government during the reign of Charles III, in whose eyes these northernmost provinces of the Mexican viceroyalty would acquire extreme importance.

These were men such as Pedro Tamarón, Bishop of Durango; the Marqués de Rubí, *visitador* of the frontier presidios; José de Gálvez, *visitador general* of the Real Hacienda and the Tribunales, who came north bearing all the authority of the viceroy. There was Viceroy Antonio de Bucareli, who saw the solution to the problems of the Provincias Internas as one of the tasks basic to his management of this part of the viceroyalty; and Hugo de O'Connor, constant fighter of the Apaches along the Rio Grande and the Pecos and Gila rivers. Bernardo de Gálvez, Teodoro de Croix, and many others in the Provincias Internas always had a great deal to say about the state of the provinces and the remedies to their problems. They were sensitive to the realities and possibilities of that frontier area and constantly designed projects for defense and conquest, unlike fathers Francisco Garcés and Junípero Serra, who struggled for the nonmilitary, Christian conquest of the Indian peoples who, up to that time, lived on the margins of Spanish influence.

The situation at the middle of the eighteenth century in the Provincias Internas is understandable if we show how, at that point, a series of long-standing problems came to a head—and were perhaps intensified by other events in the sphere of international politics or in the movements of Indian peoples in the North American West.

What I will do here is delineate the attitudes toward these problems and the results of the projects put into effect to resolve them, prompted in part by renewed interest in that cutting edge of the American empire on the part of the Spanish crown.

The primary problem along the northern border of New Spain was the hostile indigenous population, which not only made northward expansion difficult, but also threatened life itself. In this regard, the Spaniards simply fell heir to the traditional combat between nomads and settled peoples, who for centuries had waged war on the northern edge of the ancient Mexican cultures and in the area around the agricultural nucleus of the Pueblo Indians. The Spaniards found themselves at war for two centuries and it blocked their advance beyond the Gila River Basin, the middle Rio Grande, and the area around Laguna and along the Conchos. Farther east, occupation of the areas along the tributaries of the right bank of the Rio Grande, and above all, along the coast north of Tampico, came very late.

The warfare which the Spaniards inherited manifested itself for the first time when they carried out the settlement of New Mexico. This warfare acquired an endemic nature as the frontier moved from west to east, crossing the lands of the most primitive American civilizations. Seldom did Spaniards enter these lands, and when they did, they were usually motivated by political strategy (as in the case of Texas) or evangelization (as in the case of Baja California).

A New Problem

In 1686, when La Salle went down the Mississippi to the Gulf of Mexico, an age of unrest began for the authorities of the viceroyalty, the Spanish court, and the provinces of New Mexico, Nueva Vizcaya, and Coahuila. The occupation of Texas [in 1690 and again in 1716] illustrates this unrest. From that time on, the fluctuation of the frontier between the Rio Bravo and the Caddo country clearly indicated that in America a new scenario of European diplomatic struggles and warfare was to unfold.

Texas is, of course, the clearest example of indecisive Spanish action. Its settlement was motivated exclusively by strategic considerations. Conditions for settlement were clearly adverse: Texas was so far from the center of the viceroyalty; the paucity of the white population contrasted greatly with the immensity of the territory; incentives to promote immigration were lacking; and Indians either were hostile or simply showed little aptitude to be absorbed or influenced by the Spaniards. All of these circumstances foretold that the Spanish imprint on the lands to the east of the Rio Grande would not be deep. Moreover, we should take note of the government policy that required Texas to trade with the only legal port in the viceroyalty (Vera Cruz). Then, the establishment of the capital of Texas as Los Adaes, a few leagues from the French trading post of Natchitoches, makes it easy to understand how logical it was that Texas became a center for contraband and an avenue for the illegal export of silver from the Interior Provinces.

The contact with France quickly became localized on a line parallel to the Mississippi, and from the Mississippi to the Rio Grande, across the lands of the Indian peoples who maintained their independence. It soon became clear that the distance between these two rivers did not aid in defense. From New Orleans, from the post of Cavagnolles on the Missouri, from Michilimackinac on the Great Lakes, expeditions of French merchants came persistently to the Spanish frontier provinces. Ascending the tributaries of the Mississippi, the French traders also carried on an active trade with the Plains tribes. In exchange for horses, the French offered Indians firearms. The Spaniards had avoided putting arms in the hands of Indians, even of their Indian subjects.

The situation came to concern the governors of New Mexico, but this danger disappeared as abruptly as it had arrived. In a simple game of diplomacy, France donated Louisiana to Spain in 1763—the same year that France also lost her Canadian dominions.

But the uneasiness that disappeared on one side as an immediate concern, surfaced now from the opposite direction. Russia, disengaging itself from the immense extension of Siberia, began to push its men and ships toward American shores from her bases at Kamchatka. Dutch and English ships appeared on the California coast and their activities there gave birth to both the hope and the fear of the existence of the long-awaited Strait of Anian, or Northwest Passage. This could well be an undiscovered branch of the Colorado River that flows to the Pacific, or some other navigable river which drains or has its sources near the Great Lakes or Hudson's Bay.

The international turmoil that this possibility naturally produced did not fail to alarm Spain, who necessarily took measures to assure that she would not lose a game in which she considered herself to be holding the winning cards.

The Interest of the Crown

The end of the Seven Years' War (1756–63) brought true commotion to the Mexican viceroyalty, no longer bound by its detailed plan to fortify the northernmost Spanish possessions in America [against France].

The momentary circumstances of the political situation in the New World forced Charles III to take every means to defend the Empire (although that might have already been a principle point in his program upon receiving the crown [in 1759]). The presence of a homogeneous body of English possessions, from Hudson's Bay to Cape Sable, was sufficient reason to concern whoever knew the general state of weakness in which the enormous colossus, Spain, found itself.

From two points of view, then, military and monetary, agents sent to New Spain could not overlook that line along the frontier that ran from the Pacific to the Atlantic. It followed a course that, however changeable and variable, defined the farthest positions achieved by Spaniards in the Gulf of California, along the Rio Grande, and on the Texas coast. The Marqués de Rubí and José de Gálvez carried the interests of the Crown to the most remote corners of the frontier, and each one of them focused almost exclusively on one of the two major problems of that time.

In reality, the frontier by itself had required special attention for some time, due to the perplexing crisis that affected it. International events, however, provided the opportunity which caused a discussion of the frontier's urgent problems to occupy a notable place among the affairs of government.

Heightened Tensions

In the middle of the eighteenth century, a storm unleashed itself across the far northern frontier of the Mexican viceroyalty. The pressure of the barbaric Indians increased to a maximum and the defensive line was at the point of giving way. This continuous assault on the frontier establishments, which began in 1748, lasted for over four decades and demonstrated the solidity of the Spanish occupation of the territory. If the frontier overcame the danger which it faced for so long a time, it must be attributed to political as well as military considerations that made possible the endurance of the Spanish population and Spanish way of life at such a distance from the nucleus of Mexico City.

A new people had begun to spill out of the Rockies at the beginning of that century and had challenged the Apaches for the supremacy of the Plains. In great numbers the Comanches swept across the territory. They formed a second belt around the Apaches and pushed them to strike with renewed boldness against the Spanish lines. At this time, the constant incursion of new Indian groups into Nueva Vizcaya, Coahuila, and Texas began to be noticed. The frequency and intensity of the attacks created an atmosphere of terror in the frontier provinces. In New Mexico, Sonora, and Nueva Vizcaya lands began to be abandoned. Along the slopes and in the gorges of the Sierra Madre, the Apaches moved far to the south in Sonora and Nueva Vizcaya, and placed the Pima, Opata, and Tarahumara peoples under constant assault. Around Chihuahua, dead people on the roads and attacks on ranches and haciendas became everyday occurrences.

The Apaches were also terrorized. The Comanches, who were more numerous, warlike, and barbarous, held a monopoly on the firearms trade with the French along the Mississippi. The Comanches jealously guarded this trade to keep it from falling into the hands of enemies—those who would dislodge them from their hunting grounds.

The Apaches, whose population was doubling, were forced inevitably to go after the livestock of the Interior Provinces. But even the Comanches failed to achieve this—coming up against the Spaniards first in New Mexico at a very early date and later in Texas and even in Coahuila.

In 1763 western Louisiana became Spanish. It was not long before it became clear that the English colonists of the thirteen colonies were replacing the French in the trafficking of firearms to the Plains Indians.

The situation was complicated by the arrival on the scene of a new European power, Russia. Her navigators, Bering and Chiricot, appeared along the Alaskan coastline from 1741 on. Behind them came the fur traders, who carried out Russian occupation of the Northwest Pacific Coast.

Commissioned to visit the frontier presidios in 1765, the Marqués de Rubí, member of the commission charged with militarily restructuring the viceroyalty and headed by General Juan de Villalba, clearly conceived the idea of a line of small fortifications. From the Gulf of

California to the Gulf of Mexico, these would delimit Spanish territory in North America. For the Marqués, the solution to the problem of continued frontier hostilities carried out by one common enemy, the Apaches, was to coordinate all the presidios and rationalize the line. The garrisons would be established at equal intervals of forty leagues, except in the Bolson de Mapimí where it would cut across along a straight line, following the Rio Grande, from Junta de los Ríos to San Juan Bautista.

Rubí's idea was so defined that it left out New Mexico and Texas. The line went from the presidio of Altar, on the Sonoran coast, to the Bahía del Espiritu Santo, on the Texas coast of the Gulf of Mexico. To the north of this line the principal nucleus of the province of Texas, centered on the San Antonio River, had to maintain itself as an enclave. So, too, would the northern portion of New Mexico remain an enclave, as it had during the preceding two centuries.

Analyzing Rubí's idea from another point of view one finds that it presupposes two omissions. Perhaps because his instructions and his commission had nothing to do with international problems, the Marqués almost completely ignored them. It is clear that the nearest foreign presence up to that time, the French in Natchitoches, had been removed to the Mississippi—the line of contact with the British.

Also, Rubí's activities presupposed a tacit negation of any northward movement beyond the line. His efforts, then, were purely regional. They were limited to the Spanish-Indian war affecting the frontier populations and garrisons. At best, his vision did not go beyond the general state of war with Indians throughout the Provincias Internas. Thus, he sought to establish a compact front with easily defensible positions along the supposed natural frontier provided by the Rio Grande in the weakest and most harrassed part of the Provincias Internas.

Don José de Gálvez approached the problems of the frontier in a totally different manner than had Rubí. For him, the frontier was Sonora and Nueva Vizcaya, and, for special reasons, California. His clearest idea was to expand in these directions. In this sense, Gálvez inherited the ancient ambition of Father Eusebio Francisco Kino, to connect Sonora and the California Peninsula by way of the Colorado River. This expansion had to be maritime as well as overland, ascending the Pacific Coast. Naturally, as in previous stages, this meant the need to subdue the rebellious Pima and Seri Indians in Sonora and the barbaric Apaches there and in Nueva Vizcaya. It also meant the economic development of these territories, which had to serve as the take-off point for the unknown and promising north.

In a way, Gálvez's plans applied to the entire northern periphery of the viceroyalty. Perhaps he intended to establish a cordon of semimilitary centers all along the frontier visited by Rubí, but his actions focused clearly on California, Sonora, and Nueva Vizcaya. Gálvez had in mind, above all, the real or possible international tension in the North Pacific. He supposed that the vanguard of the Russian advance in America was extraordinarily close, and he appeared to accept the idea that the English (heirs to the French along the Mississippi Valley), could reach the Pacific via the Colorado River. Thus he felt expansion had to occur.

In order to carry out his project, Gálvez undertook a general reordering of government. He hoped to create an entity with a political character much like that of the viceroyalty—a *comandancia general* (with its center in Sonora) whose expansionist objectives were very obvious in the proposal he sent to the Court. Its capital would be located not on the frontier but in unconquered territory, along the Gila River or at the confluence of the Gila and the Colorado rivers.

Wanting to implement his idea immediately, Gálvez himself proceeded to visit the territories, with the intention of implanting in them a more adequate system of government: one that would allow them to enter fully a phase of intense development, and to achieve by any and all means the vitalization of their economies and growth of their populations. At the same time, he began the advance to San Diego, Monterey, and San Francisco. Land and sea expeditions painfully made their way north to fulfill his goals.

The Port of San Blas (in the district of Nueva Galicia) played a fundamental role in this expansion. A Mexican naval base in the Pacific, with a perfectly defined northward expansionist orientation, San Blas was the personal work of Gálvez. It was the first step toward complete enactment of his idea. The dockyards of San Blas made Spanish Alta California possible.

But other foundations were necessary to the success of the visitador's project. On beginning the enterprise, Gálvez counted on the ships of San Blas, the silver of California and Sonora, peace in Sonora and Nueva Vizcaya, colonization of the frontier, and the founding of town and cities. All of this, and the restructuring of the government in the Interior Provinces, would make possible the plan of development and an efficient financial organization.

Possibly the only two successes which Gálvez achieved through his personal intervention were San Blas and Alta California. These alone, of course, demonstrate the extraordinary worth of the man. But the unfortunate results of the land expeditions led by Gaspar de Portolá demonstrated clearly the impossibility of using the peninsula of Baja California as a base of support for the northward advance.

Baja California was, to all intents and purposes, a deep self-deception on the part of Gálvez. Gálvez had ignored reality: there were no mines, no pearls, no water, no fish. Returning to the mainland, now abandoned by the miners and settlers, another problem appeared where he did not expect to find one: the rebellious Indians were not easily dominated; the war with them lasted for years. Gálvez then went insane, thus freeing himself from being a conscious witness to the noisy crash of his illusions, so removed from reality.

Gálvez had taken into account only political expansion and the urgency of the international situation. Unlike Rubí, he lost sight of the basic daily problems presented by the Indian frontier. Once he had regained his mental balance, in Mexico Gálvez became the architect of a solution which was a compromise between his and that of the Marqués de Rubí, although it contained more of Rubí's plan than his own. This new plan was enacted first in Viceroy Croix's regulations for the presidios, dated 1770, and formalized by Charles III's regulations of 1772.

The formula put forth in both regulations amounted to establishing Rubí's line of frontier presidios (changing the position of some to fill gaps and locating them so they reenforced one another and strengthened the whole line). But the idea of the unity and continuity of the frontier, so typical of the Marqués, was strengthened by Gálvez's inclusion, in accordance with his own principles, of someone with authority over all the presidios, a *commandante inspector*. By taking concerns of war from the provincial governors and giving them to the comandante inspector, he gave the presidio line an independent character. Still, the comandante inspector might be a subordinate of the *comandante general* of the provinces in the event that the King decided to authorize that position. This indicates that Gálvez's plan was still under consideration. The King approved the plan a year after its formulation, but because of the doubtful success of the California and Sonora expeditions (and also, of course, because there was no one to take charge of the plan's execution), it was not put into practice.

Gálvez had undoubtedly learned something from that almost romantic adventure. Knowing the little advantage to be gained from the California Peninsula, he renounced the idea of creating an intendancy there as he had originally planned when he conceived the idea of the *comandancia general*. Both Californias, thus, would come under military jurisdictions, making up a frontier district. Gálvez had also become aware of the obstacle that Apache hostility posed to any expansion endeavor as well as to the very prosperity of the Internal Provinces.

Consequently, the man chosen to implement the new decree, Don Hugo O'Connor, first *comandante inspector* of the presidios of New Spain, received a plan of action which contained two crucial proposals: first, to establish the new defensive lines according to those proposed by Rubí and Nicolás de Lafora [a military engineer with Rubí], while at the same time, keeping the rear guard free of enemies. Then, from the new positions, he was to start a series of general campaigns which once and for all would eliminate the Apache menace and open the door to a new era of expansion.

O'Connor attempted to carry out these plans. During his four years of frontier command [1772–1776][1] he displayed exemplary interest and dedication. Essentially, O'Connor achieved the goal of straightening the line of presidios, except along the Rio Grande. There he failed because of the terrain and also, more important, because the river does not follow a straight line between El Paso and the presidio of San Juan Bautista, but has a large double curve below La Junta.

At the end of O'Connor's four years, the Apaches had infiltrated the presidial line to harrass the settlements behind it. O'Connor was not to blame: this only demonstrates what an imperfect solution this was to frontier problems.

The four years that O'Connor served as comandante inspector were ones of transition. They saw the implementation of a temporary solution to the frontier problem. At the same time, those years constituted an interval between Gálvez's personal actions in the Provincias Internas and the implementation of his idea once he joined the Secretaría de Indias.

The failings of the solution under O'Connor are obvious. O'Connor's authority did not extend to the Californias and what authority he had on the frontier was purely military. Nevertheless, at the end of his mission expansion seemed possible. And it was during O'Connor's term that the two expeditions of Captain Don Juan Bautista de Anza succeeded in going overland from Sonora to Alta California, fulfilling the mission always expected of that province: that of serving as a base for northward penetration. Some of Anza's group became the first inhabitants of San Francisco on the bay of the same name on the Pacific.

In 1776, the promotion of Gálvez to the Ministry of the Indies resulted in the immediate creation of the *Comandancia General*, proposed by him eight years before. At this time two events of little apparent interest happened. These two events would demonstrate the problems caused by vacillation.

The royal decree setting up the comandancia general allowed this new political entity to encompass the Californias, Sonora, Nueva Vizcaya, and New Mexico. But soon the jurisdiction included Coahuila and Texas. We do not know why New Mexico was included, although it may have been considered an extension of Nueva Vizcaya, the northernmost part of the Empire, and a good starting point for penetrating the unexplored areas to the west and to the north and even to the Pacific. Also, the Hopi country between Sonora and New Mexico seemed to be the next step after the settlement of the Gila. Whatever, the defining of the four provinces as the comandancia general is a true indication of the persistance of Gálvez's original project to expand northward.

In contrast, the annexation of those four provinces to the Eastern

Provincias Internas was an answer to the long-standing need for unity among the frontier provinces which faced a common danger from Indians. The consequences of this event were quite clear. The comandancia general had been designed for the unification and strengthening of the four western provinces with an eye to their northern expansion. The capital of the comandancia, located at Arizpe in Sonora, right in the center of the defined territory (and of that to be occupied) clearly denotes this tendency. The addition of Coahuila and Texas, given that they presented neither demographic nor economic benefit to the comandancia, caused the comandante to divide his interest between the primary objectives in the west and the defense of these two provinces. Coahuila and Texas were completely exposed to Apache and Comanche invasions along their long and unfortified frontiers.

For Coahuila and Texas, the inclusion in the comandancia was likewise not advantageous. The government that would have kept watch over them was in Arizpe, as far away as the former seat of government in Mexico. In short, the embryonic comandancia staggered under the burden of enormous responsibilities, which weakened Gálvez's original policy of expansion.

Certainly Gálvez's idea had weak points. Fundamentally, to have applied the comandancia project as it was designed in the beginning would have left open the eastern flank of New Mexico and Nueva Vizcaya, from Taos to Laguna, especially once the penetrability of the famous presidio line had been demonstrated after 1776. It was precisely in this area that the provinces suffered the worst combat. The annexation of Coahuila and Texas would allow their troops to work with those of New Mexico and Nueva Vizcaya. And once the unity of the line was constituted and proven, it would be neither logical nor convenient to break it. But the defensive usefulness of Coahuila and Texas did not compensate for the problems that their incorporation raised.

The Double Front and the Failure of the Comandancia

We have to ask ourselves if the comandancia had been restricted to the four western provinces, whether it would have filled the objectives for which Gálvez, as Secretario de Indias, created it: or if, on the contrary, it would have been a frustrated experiment. To do this, we ought to remember not only specific failures (like that of colonizing among the Yumas, an effort which ended tragically in 1781) but those general conditions which, in principle, blocked the success of the broad and expansive enterprise conceived by Gálvez. In effect, we have to keep in mind the insufficient demographic base of those four provinces, a base necessary to the advance of any frontier. Moreover, we have to keep in mind the lack of a truly strong motive for people to begin to move north by themselves. Expansion, to occur, had to be paid for and directed by the Crown.

Also, one must remember those characteristics peculiar to the territory to be brought under Spanish rule. In truth, nothing favored this effort. Great deserts blocked the flow of population into the four provinces. The margins of the Gila and Colorado rivers were not appropriate for settlement. The indigenous population was not slow to show hostility. These things, together with a purely defensive attitude that it had become necessary to adopt along all of the borders, definitively stopped what was to be the Spanish advance to the Colorado, the Hopis, and the Rockies.

The irregular line of the frontier from San Francisco to Taos, from Taos to Natchitoches, left numerous gaps: great open spaces between the two Californias; between the Californias and Sonora; from the district of El Paso to the Santa Fe nucleus; and from Junta de los Rios to Texas. This area resembled three arms reaching northward—Texas, California, and New Mexico—with gigantic empty pockets in between. Due to the weakness of the Spanish position, these became centers of pressure along her vast borders.

Given the way in which the comandancia was finally set up, subjugation of the Indian enemy became the primary objective of this new government and its fundamental mission of expansion (for which the comandancia was created) became hopeless. That fight took up practically all the country's energies. The comandancia could hardly expand when its own defense was a basic daily problem. Because of this dilemma, Gálvez's proposed ideal went by the wayside in deference to the defensive strategy which began with Rubí, was used by O'Connor, and achieved its purest expression with the Caballero de Croix and his immediate successors.

The principal problems that faced the comandantes generales were: readjustments of the presidio line; founding of settlements on the frontier; and subjugation of the still difficult Seri and Tarahumara Indians (who occasionally allied themselves with the Apaches). The urgency of defense impeded the initiation of any other objectives of a broader nature.

Other problems, naturally, accompanied those mentioned. All resulted in the downfall of the motivating idea of the comandancia. The difficulty of communication between Sonora and Alta California, and the scarce or complete lack of support that could be given to Alta California (especially after the Yuma revolt), left Alta California dependent on Baja California. Given the obvious inadequacy of this, Alta California actually depended on help brought by sea from the Port of San Blas. Thus, San Blas was the port of the two Californias; but it was nearer the viceroy and so came under his jurisdiction. So, too, did the Californias after 1792 and this amputation was the final blow to the comandancia's goal of expansion.

Through a series of adverse circumstances, the Provincias Internas in themselves were an inadequate base for northward expansion. The comandancia general did nothing to better the situation. After the early years, two questions were debated but never resolved: the unity or fragmentation of the comandancia, and its autonomy or subjugation in regard to the viceroyalty.

The problem of unifying the comandancia came about because of the difference between the eastern and the western provinces, their distance from the capital, and the outside danger of foreign invasion from the east after Louisiana passed into the hands of the United States. Because of the distinctive situations which arose during the forty-five-year life of the comandancia, it was divided two or three times and reunited as many, producing only confusion and instability.

The question of the independence of the Provincias Internas from the viceroy also received contradictory solutions at various times. Even though it is obvious that the particular problems of the frontier made autonomy the most desirable goal (and the one proposed by Gálvez), it must be remembered that conditions were never right for making that ideal a reality. In effect, if economic independence was a primary requisite, the Provincias Internas never achieved it. The comandancia general always depended on financing from the viceroy. A fundamental move would have been the establishment of a mint, which would have facilitated the circulation of money and promoted trade. But one was established, in an irregular manner only during the final years of Spanish rule, and it caused new problems. Similarly, the Provincias Internas had to put up with receiving European goods through the port of Veracruz almost to the end of the empire, with consequent disadvantages. When some ports were opened in Nuevo Santander and Texas, it was too late. They were of little significance.

In all of this one sees the lack of continuity of development of an idea, such as that of Gálvez. His idea was difficult at first to formulate properly. It was difficult, also, to find a person who could guide it toward success, although success was perhaps not too difficult to achieve. Instead, in analyzing the history of the comandancia general, one sees how rapidly it renounced its northwestern expansion. Once the Californias were removed from the comandancia's jurisdiction, it was not long before the capital moved to Chihuahua and even Durango. Meanwhile, wars with the heathen tribes (shortened because of the early campaigns which decimated them) gave way to a system of alliances. They sought a peace based on a balance of power between these tribes. When this peace was not achieved, life on the frontier was reduced to a desultory series of endless skirmishes and punative expeditions. All efforts to make Apaches settle down, and to assimilate them, failed miserably. Thus, the frontier endured. At the end of the Spanish empire its principal problem was United States' pressure on Texas and New Mexico.

Epilogue

If the grandiose attempt to push the Spanish frontier north into the unknown region of the Rocky Mountains was the failure we have just claimed, it was in no way Gálvez's fault. Gálvez, minister of Charles III, has the distinction of being the only person concerned with finding a sufficient and intelligent solution to the internal and external problems facing the north of Mexico during the last part of the eighteenth century. Gálvez's solution did not have to fail. It only needed time to work. In fact, before the end of the century, peace along the frontier had been achieved, and the possibility of opening a new era of expansion seemed likely. Diverse factors prevented this: the viceroy's preoccupation with other more urgent questions at times when the comandancia depended on him for support; the spector of friction with the United States after 1803; monetary setbacks; the general paralysis caused by the Napoleonic invasion of Spain [in 1808]; and the subsequent fight for freedom.

In spite of everything, during the forty-five years that the system of the comandancia general lasted under Spain, the Provincias Internas made progress on all sides, from the demographic to the cultural. Due also to certain favorable circumstances, it maintained intact the integrity of Spain's possessions and Spain's rights to neighboring territories that it did not actually occupy, but only claimed.

Certainly this success can be attributed partly to the wisdom of establishing one superior political and administrative entity to coordinate the various governments of the interior provinces—governments which earlier had been so distant from the seat of power. The creation of two more bishoprics, the restructuring of the provincias into three intendancies, the interest in evangelizing the entire area, the founding of educational centers, the care given to the development of mining and business—all are basic characteristics of this epoch, which closed with dignity the long era of Spanish presence in this region.

NOTE

1. Editor's note: Navarro García refers repeatedly to O'Connor's "six" years of frontier command. For greater clarity, I have changed this to four years, representing the time that O'Connor effectively shaped policy as commandant inspector. He was appointed on September 14, 1772, and replaced by José Rubio on February 25, 1777. Meanwhile, however, the importance of O'Connor's position had diminished with the appointment on May 16, 1776, of Teodoro de Croix to the newly created office of commandant general of the Provincias Internas.

Teodoro de Croix

13

Spanish Indian Policy in Northern Mexico, 1765–1810*

Joseph F. Park

Editor's Introduction

As Luis Navarro García makes clear in the preceding article, José de Gálvez began a serious reassessment of Indian policy on New Spain's far northern frontier. In the present article, Joseph Park outlines the evolution of that policy. In 1765, when Gálvez began to probe the question, Spanish-Mexicans led a perilous and tenuous existence on the edge of the Apache and Comanche frontiers. In the face of heightened Indian resistance, many Spanish-Mexican *pobladores* had abandoned their settlements and sought refuge farther south. By 1790 the situation had changed. New Policies had won a period of peace that stabilized the frontier. This lasted from 1790 to 1810, when the beginnings of Mexico's independence struggle diverted funds and manpower away from the frontier.

---

*This article originally appeared in *Arizona and the West*, 4 (1962): 325–44, and is reproduced here with minor corrections with permission of the author and the publisher.

In an article noteworthy for its lucid overview of the complex events of these years, Joseph Park describes frontier conditions in the 1760s and explains the role of Gálvez and the Marques de Rubí in bringing about reformed military regulations in 1772. Park outlines how officials sought to implement those regulations by realigning presidios and coordinating offensive strategies. He focuses on the efforts of Hugo Oconor (1773–77) and Teodoro de Croix (1777–83), but the greatest changes that he describes occurred when Bernardo de Gálvez, nephew of José de Gálvez, served as viceroy of New Spain (1785–86). His changes, Park suggests, won a peace on the frontier: Spanish officials combined an iron fist with a velvet glove, giving some Indians liquor and inferior firearms, settling some on reservations, and generally making peace more attractive than war.[1]

A high school dropout who worked in the aircraft industry before going to college in his mid-thirties, Joe Park entered the academic world in a roundabout manner. He has taught on the Fort Apache Indian Reservation and served as a Supply Inspector at Davis-Monthan Air Force Base in Tucson while completing course work toward the Ph.D. at the University of Arizona. Park is presently microforms librarian at the University of Arizona. In addition to the present article, he has written "The Apaches in Mexican-American Relations, 1848–1861" *(Arizona and the West,* 1961) and "The 1903 'Mexican Affair' at Clifton" *(Journal of Arizona History,* 1977), which grew out of his pathbreaking M.A. thesis, "The History of Mexican Labor in Arizona During the Territorial Period" (University of Arizona, 1961)

NOTE

1. Like all historical scholarship, Park's article is somewhat outdated. If he were to rewrite it, he would have to alter some of his conclusions in light of fresh research. For example, in his book *The Apache Frontier* (Norman: 1968), Max L. Moorhead expanded our understanding of the role of Jacobo de Ugarte and downplayed the importance of Bernardo de Gálvez. In *The Presidio* (Norman: 1975), Moorhead also comes to conclusions about the evolution of Spanish Indian policy which vary somewhat from Park's.

Spanish Indian Policy in Northern Mexico, 1765–1810

During the last quarter of the eighteenth century, Spanish authorities in Madrid and in Mexico City made a concerted effort to formulate policies that would curb the Indian menace that long had plagued the northern frontier of Mexico. For nearly two centuries in the borderlands, which stretched from the Gulf of California to eastern Texas, refractory bands had not only defied military reduction but had fomented rebellion among the nomadic tribes that had settled near the missions and presidios. The area extending from Sonora east across Chihuahua to western Coahuila—or roughly the colonial province of Nueva Viscaya—was the scene of the greatest unrest, with raiding parties from Texas, from New Mexico, and from eastern Arizona striking deep into Chihuahua and into the districts around Saltillo and Parras in Coahuila. Official attention was first directed to the seriousness of the Indian problem by José de Gálvez, who ordered an inspection of the northern defenses of Mexico in 1765; and in the thirty years that followed it was his recommendations that laid the foundation for a pragmatic Indian policy that included punitive expeditions, trade alliances, and balance of power tactics. By the end of the eighteenth century Spanish commanders had forced a majority of the hostile bands to locate near the presidios, and the northern borderlands entered a period of peace.

During the wars of succession in Europe, Spain became vitally interested in protecting her sprawling overseas empire. At the outset, Carlos III expressed particular concern regarding the Russian designs on California and the English interest in Florida. To meet these threats he sent José de Gálvez, a former court *alcalde*, to Mexico with instructions to take every measure necessary to strengthen the northern frontier. In 1765 Gálvez arrived in Vera Cruz vested with the full powers of *visitador-general* in matters of administration, finance, and defense. He swiftly dispatched secret orders calling for a rigorous investigation of fiscal irregularities, set in motion the machinery to expel the Jesuits from Mexico,[1] then turned to the problems on the northern border. Meeting in Mexico City with several military *juntas*, Gálvez discussed particularly the urgent need to pacify the nomadic tribes that prowled among the settlements at every opportunity. Financial and administrative reforms were long overdue, he conceded, but these measures would prove of little benefit to Mexico or to Spain unless the depredations were stopped immediately.[2]

To formulate an effective Indian policy for northern Mexico was a difficult task. The vast extension of this frontier constituted a major problem—the distance from Monterey, California, east to Monterrey, Nuevo León, being equal to that from London to Tripoli. The region was characterized by a wide diversity in topography and ecology. Moreover, the cultural differences among the various Indian tribes made it impossible for the Spaniards to impose the methods of reduction and assimilation they had employed in dealing with the large sedentary societies in the Valley of Mexico, in Oaxaca, and in Yucatán. Added to this was the fact that in the northern provinces administrators repeatedly found their hands tied by the benign paternalism of Spanish Indian laws which emphasized missionization rather than military campaigns as the means for pacifying hostile tribes. Even when authorized to meet uprisings with force, they often found their efforts hampered by lethargic procedures endemic to the Spanish bureaucracy. For example, before a presidio commander could exact punishment upon an Indian band, he was required to submit proof of its depredations to the viceroy.[3] At the time Gálvez arrived conditions had become extremely acute, and local officials were either ignoring the Indian inroads, avoiding direct encounters with hostile bands, or forwarding to Mexico City falsified reports of campaigns never performed.[4]

Spanish control in the north, Gálvez learned, was fast disintegrating. In Sonora the Pimas had revolted in 1751,[5] and an atmosphere of rebellion pervaded the entire region from the Seri villages on the west coast to San Xavier del Bac on the Santa Cruz River. At this remote outpost Fray Alonso Espinoza in 1763 reported that all the Indians except the sick and aged had strayed from the mission.[6] East of Sonora, the province of Nueva Viscaya was suffering continually from Apache raiding parties, while in eastern Texas the settlements were virtually isolated by hostile Lipans and Comanches. Disturbed by these conditions, Gálvez ordered a thorough investigation of the frontier line. He went north to survey personally the conditions in Sonora with an eye toward bolstering the defenses in that province and in Alta California, and he sent the Marqués de Rubí, a member of his staff, to inspect the presidios from Sonora to Texas.

In 1766 at Altar, in northern Sonora, Rubí began his tour. Traveling eastward, he saw the blackened walls of many abandoned ranches, and at his inquiry was told that Apaches annually entered the area to prey on Mexican herds and invariably took an alarming toll of lives in the isolated villages. Presidio commanders attributed most of the depredations to the Gileño Apaches, whose stronghold lay to the north and along the Gila and Mimbres rivers in Arizona and western New Mexico.[7] Farther east, Rubí found the same conditions, but learned that most of the raids originated in the country of the Mescalero and Lipan Apaches of New Mexico and western Texas.

The scattered Spanish settlements in eastern Chihuahua and western Coahuila were particularly vulnerable. Here, topography and climate presented a nightmare to the military tactician and the quartermaster. Directly below the Big Bend region of Texas, and pointing straight into the heart of the populated districts, was the Bolsón de Mapimí, a great longitudinal depression that had been the bed of an ancient sea. Along the sides of the depression ran a series of mountain ranges. Described by Fray Juan Agustín de Morfi as so fiercely arid "that even the cactus pads appeared to be toasted,"[8] the basin was the highway south for Lipans and Mescaleros. Following trails linked by water seeps and meager pasturage, they slipped undetected into the heart of Nueva Viscaya and struck in every direction. Through the spring and summer months, according to Morfi, the Bolsón became a monstrous entity that "vomited barbarous savages" through the mountain passes and into ranches and villages as far south as Parras and Saltillo.[9]

Crossing the Rio Grande, Rubí reached Texas in August of 1767. Here was a section of the Spanish frontier that differed greatly from the region through which he recently had passed. North of a line which extended roughly from San Antonio east across the Sabine River into Louisiana roamed the Kiowas, the Wichitas, and the Comanches—buffalo hunters whose culture was identified closely with that of the tribes of the Great Plains region. The Comanches, in particular, periodically attacked the Lipan Apaches, their traditional enemies, and in so doing ranged far to the south into Spanish Texas, making lateral sorties west against the mission at San Sabá and east into the isolated settlements struggling for existence near the Sabine.[10] The less hostile Caddoan tribes in eastern Texas presented a difficulty of another kind. Their allegiance lay with the French traders who, prior to the transfer of Louisiana from France to Spain in 1763, had carried on a regular traffic in firearms with them. Rubí saw immediately that Spanish curtailment of trade in weapons could either provoke the Caddoans to wrath, or encourage them to barter with the English to the east at Pensacola, Florida.[11]

Rubí's survey awakened the policy makers in Madrid to the nature and magnitude of the Indian problem in northern Mexico. With the Texas-Louisiana region in mind, he informed his superiors that Spain must distinguish between her true and her "imaginary" dominions.[12] He recommended leaving the district that included Natchitoches and Los Adaes to the jurisdiction of Louisiana, but urged the withdrawal of the settlers in eastern Texas to San Antonio, where they would be given new lands.[13] As to the Caddos, with few modifications the trade should be left in the hands of French traders such as Athanaze de Mézières, whose knowledge of the tribes along the Sabine was unsurpassed.[14] Rubí believed that the scattered garrisons of the northern froniter should be reorganized into a presidial line stretching from Texas to Sonora. He suggested that the presidios northeast and north of San Antonio be transferred to southwestern Texas, where they would constitute the eastern segment of the new presidial chain. To provide greater protection for the settlements south of the Rio Grande, he recommended that the outpost on the Rio San Sabá be reestablished at the junction of the Rio Grande and the Rio Natagés (Pecos River). The presidios situated around the Bolsón de Mapimí would be moved northward and placed at strategic intervals, so that flying companies from these bases might intercept Apache raiding parties at the northern entrance to this vast basin. West of the Bolsón, and along the northern frontier of Chihuahua and Sonora, the garrisons near the settlements also would be pushed north to reinforce the existing presidios—or to serve as intermediate outposts.[15] Rubí realized that these changes would expose the region north of San Antonio to the Comanches who hovered near the settlements to prey on the Lipan Apaches. To eliminate this menace he advocated a systematic extermination of the Apaches, and the forwarding of captive families south to be distributed in the interior of Mexico.[16]

When Rubí began his tour of the northern frontier, Gálvez remained in Mexico City to coordinate civil and military efforts toward the effective occupation of Alta California. With the support of several general *juntas*, he raised some 300,000 pesos from private and public sources, recruited an army, and constructed two brigantines to transport his "Sonora Expedition" up the west coast of Mexico. Then, sailing north to establish a base at La Paz, Baja California, for expeditions to strengthen the defenses on the Pacific coast, Gálvez instructed Colonel Domingo Elizondo to land at Guaymas and begin military operations in Sonora. On March 10, 1768, Elizondo put three hundred and fifty soldiers, including some two hundred veteran dragoons, ashore as ordered, and drew upon the garrisons and militia of Sonora for additional support. He soon was able to place in the field about 1,100 men.[17] From March through June Elizondo unsuccessfully pursued Seri and Pima factions between their strongholds in the Cerro Prieto range and the peaks of Tiburón Island, adjacent to the Sonoran coast. Although ordered by Carlos III to extend full support to the California expeditions then being organized on the peninsula at La Paz, Gálvez returned to the mainland to assume command in Sonora. In October of 1769 he arrived in Pitic (Hermosillo) sick with fever, but late in the month made a vigorous but unrewarding assault on the Pimas in the Cerro Prietos.[18] Meanwhile, the Apaches diverted their attacks from northern Sonora to Nueva Viscaya. Seriously ill and mentally depressed over the failure of the punitive expeditions in Sonora, Gálvez was forced into bed, and Viceroy Carlos Francisco de Croix returned the command to Elizondo, who reduced the operations to harassing actions to keep hostile bands on the move.[19]

The failure of the campaign in Sonora, which cost 189,000 pesos between 1767 and 1769, coupled with the spread of hostilities into Chihuahua, prompted Carlos III to conclude that it was useless to continue formal operations in one region while the rest of the frontier was virtually aflame with revolt. Preferring defensive actions only in critical areas, he suggested that colonial officials try to placate the nomadic bands with gifts and presents. Toward this end, he recommended following the presidial plan outlined by Rubí. By a royal order of April 25, 1770, the viceroy convoked a *junta* composed of Gálvez and several military experts, and they began a detailed analysis of Rubí's suggestions.[20] The decisions of this meeting were incorporated in the *Reglamento de Presidios of 1772.*

In 1773 Hugo Oconor, the governor of Texas, was placed in charge of putting into effect the provisions of the new frontier policy. Appointed *inspector-commandante* of the northern provinces with headquarters in Chihuahua, Oconor set about to reorganize the presidial line. His orders affecting the settlements in Louisiana immediately involved him in a controversy with the French and Spanish colonists at Los Adaes, a town near the east bank of the Sabine River. Following the occupation of New Orleans by General Alejandro O'Reilly in 1769, these families had established themselves in relative security at Los Adaes, and did not wish to move. When the new governor of Texas, Baron de Ripperdá, ordered the evacuation of all the settlements in eastern Texas, the "Adaesaños" assumed a rebellious mood and quickly aligned themselves behind Antonio Gil Ybarbo, who petitioned Viceroy Antonio María Bucareli that his followers be permitted to remain in Louisiana. Oconor protested that Los Adaes had long been the center of contraband trade in arms among the northern tribes, and charged that the resumption of this traffic lay behind Ybarbo's petition. The Adaesaños finally had their way. Locating on the Trinity River midway between the Sabine and San Antonio, they founded the village of Pilar de Bucareli in honor of their benefactor.[21]

The Indians called Oconor "El General Colorado" (the Red General), and he justified his reputation as a vigorous campaigner by relentlessly striking into the heart of hostile territory. Though his *entradas* into the Bolsón de Mapimí proved more destructive to his own cavalry mounts than to the Apaches, he began in December of 1773 steadily chasing scattered bands northward across the Rio Grande. In western Chihuahua, Oconor broke up an alliance between the Tarahumara and the Gileño Indians, and when the Gileños again began raiding he personally led an expedition into their stronghold in the Sierra de Huacha. In 1775 at El

Paso this Apache group, weary of eluding constant patrols, requested peace.[22] Turning to the unrest in Sonora, Oconor sent Lieutenant Colonel Antonio Bonilla of Coahuila to investigate conditions at the presidio of Tubac, where on three occasions during 1773–1774 the Apaches had driven off the presidial herd. In view of the recurring depredations there and the need to strike renegade Gileños at large in Chihuahua, Oconor decided on a joint campaign. Unable to obtain support from the troops of the Sonora Expedition, then being used by Captain Juan Bautista de Anza to escort colonists to California,[23] Oconor enlisted the aid of Governor Francisco Antonio Crespo of Sonora. With Crespo's militia forming a trap in the mountains west of Santa Fe, Oconor drove the Gileños northward, killing one hundred and thirty-eight warriors and recovering 1,966 animals. Encouraged by his success, the general in 1776 joined Governor Pedro Fermín de Mendinueta of New Mexico in an encircling operation that soon brought reports from the missionaries at Zuñi that the hostile bands wished to surrender.[24]

The events of Oconor's administration suggested the salient features of a new Indian policy that would ultimately bring peace to the northern frontier. His joint campaigns of 1775–1776, while more expensive than the local operations conducted by Gálvez in 1768, demonstrated the effectiveness of meeting sporadic and widespread hostilities with coordinated offensives capable of driving the Indians into their strongholds, where Spanish arms could deliver an object lesson in the merits of peace.

On the other hand, Oconor encountered difficulties in carrying out the presidial changes prescribed in Rubí's plan. The Marqués, a distinguished officer from Spain, had outlined a strategy that might have been effective against the colorful arrays that advanced across the open fields of Flanders or Almanza, but it was of little use against an enemy accustomed to the deserts and broken mountain ranges of northern Mexico. Separated one from another by as much as one hundred and forty leagues and located far north of the settlements, the frontier presidios were virtually lost on a vast horizon. The Apaches easily eluded the flying companies sent out from these outposts, and with impunity they levied destruction upon the unprotected settlements to the south—which might have suffered even graver consequences were it not for the counteroffensives by Oconor. Despite his efforts, however, the years from 1771 through 1776 witnessed the murder of 1,674 villagers in Nueva Viscaya alone, not counting the soldiers and travellers killed or captured in the isolated areas of the province.[25] In addition to the weaknesses that he saw develop in the system for defending the western frontier, Oconor also encountered friction in the administration of the eastern segment of the presidial line. The general took a strong stand against incorporating into Spanish Indian policy the French methods of manipulating alliances based largely on trade in firearms and liquor. Believing such a decision by Spanish authorities in Mexico City and in Texas to be contrary to Crown policy, he asserted that the village of Bucareli had been established to promote this illegal traffic, and broadened his accusations to include Governor Ripperdá and others. The feud continued until 1777, when Oconor, tired and broken in health, petitioned for a transfer to Guatemala.[26] In the summer of 1778, Ripperdá gave Ybarbo and his colony at Bucareli permission to settle among the friendly Hasinais between the Trinity and Sabine rivers. The colonists reoccupied the abandoned village of Nacogdoches, and, with Ybarbo as Indian agent, the town soon became an important center of trade.[27]

The vexing problems of defense Oconor had faced prompted Carlos III in 1776 to set off the northern frontier of Mexico as a separate military jurisdiction—the Commandancy-General of the Interior Provinces. The following year Teodoro de Croix, the *commandante-general*, arrived in Chihuahua, holding virtual viceregal powers and answerable to the Crown alone. Croix soon found that his instructions contained conflicting provisions. While endeavoring to secure his basic objectives—the conversion of the Indians and strict adherence to the *Reglamento de Presidios of 1772*—he was at the same time to "defend, stimulate, and extend" the territory under his command.[28]

From the first Croix interpreted broadly the clauses in his orders that pertained to defense and to pacifying the hostile Indians. Beginning in October of 1777, he spent eight months inspecting the northern frontier. During this tour he held war councils at Chihuahua, Monclova, and San Antonio, each of which were attended by governors, local military commanders, and prominent settlers. The strategy that resulted was a synthesis of ideas put forth at these meetings.[29] In particular did the councils approve of the suggestions which had been made by Oconor's subordinate, Antonio Bonilla. During the last year of Oconor's administration, Bonilla had questioned the value of fixed defenses, and, pointing to New Mexico as the key to frontier defense, had advised that money be allocated to support regular campaigns from Santa Fe by veteran troops against hostile bands.[30] Croix and the members of the councils accepted the plan and recommended that immediate attention be given to the western Apaches. It was agreed that expeditions would be launched north from El Paso and Sonora, and south from Zuñi, to form a trap similar to that employed by Oconor in 1776 on a smaller scale in western New Mexico.

Croix turned next to eastern New Mexico and Texas. In this region he suggested a departure from the policy of war, and advocated strategy that involved balance of power alliances with the Caddoans and the

Comanches. Hoping that the Comanches could be coaxed into war with the Lipan and Mescalero Apaches, Croix ordered Governor Juan Bautista de Anza of New Mexico to arrange an alliance with the Comanches, and in eastern Texas he instructed the Spanish agents Gil Ybarbo and Athanaze de Mézières to encourage the tribes along the Red River to join the Comanches in making war on the Apaches. Although stating clearly his disapproval of an easy peace with the Indians, Croix was sensitive to the Crown's wishes regarding pacific measures, and tempered his program with a proviso. He offered peace to the hostile tribes who would settle near specified presidios.

Croix soon lost patience with this effort, however. In 1777 several Gileño bands were defeated in western Chihuahua, and agreed to settle at the presidio of Janos, where they were supplied with food until the crops they planted matured. But the following year many of the Indians fled the encampments and began boasting that they would destroy Janos and San Buenaventura—and all the forces the "big Chief at Chihuahua" sent against them. Spanish commanders were forced to track down and defeat the renegades.[31] These events dampened Croix's interest in encouraging the establishment of Indian settlements on the frontier. Late in 1778 he began extensive preparations for a prolonged military campaign, and even issued a decree to suppress desertion then prevalent among the provincial militia.[32] But, before a large-scale operation against the Apaches could be organized, word came that Carlos III had decided to join France in supporting the rebellion in the North American colonies against England. On February 20, 1779, Croix received an order from Spain to refrain from open war with the Indians whenever possible.[33]

Forced to take the defensive, Croix issued instructions that called for retrenchment along the frontier. By authority of the new dispensation he ordered that most of the presidios recently moved north in accordance with the Rubí plan be returned to their former sites on the perimeter of the Bolsón de Mapimí, and that a secondary line of military establishments be located in an arc to swing southeast from Chihuahua, then north through Coahuila to protect Parras, Saltillo, and Monclova.[34] To garrison both presidios and secondary outposts, Croix made great use of Indian auxiliaries from Chihuahua and Sonora.[35] To the northeast, in Texas, he continued his concern with alliances. In the spring of 1779 Mézières visited the tribes along the Red River, taking with him a large stock of presents that included twenty-seven muskets and an ample supply of power and shot. At the Tuacana villages he made an impressive harangue before the council, emphasizing the long friendship between the Red River tribes and the Spaniards, and urged them to help draw the Comanches into an alliance against the Lipan Apaches in Texas.[36] But Mézières' plea was to no avail, for the Comanches not only remained aloof but increased their forays into northern Texas and eastern New Mexico. Having no other choice, Anza launched a campaign against the Comanches in August of 1779, defeating several of the bands so severely that he easily extracted a treaty calling for war on the Lipan Apaches.[37] Meanwhile, in Coahuila, Governor Juan de Ugalde had concluded a similar alliance with the Mescalero Apaches, who consented to settle on the northern frontier of that province and serve as mercenaries against the Lipans. In the spring of 1780 disorganized Lipan bands, scattered and decimated by the unrelenting Comanche onslaught from the north, appeared in the northern districts of Coahuila. Confronted by Ugalde and his Mescalero allies, they quickly made peace. The settlers of Coahuila and southern Texas breathed a sigh of relief.[38]

Selecting Santa Fe as a base for dealing with the hostile Comanches, Kiowas, Utes and other tribes making up the so-called "Nations of the North," Croix laid plans to handle these Indians individually by overlooking petty offenses and by playing upon their mutual hatreds. Above all, every precaution had to be taken to prevent an alliance between these tribes and the Apachean bands to the south. Referring to the serious consequences of such a combination, Croix had written to Gálvez on April 25, 1777: "If today an army is needed only to make war on the numerous and vagrant Apaches, what force would be necessary to curb the other nations?"[39] A year later, in March of 1778, Governor Mendinueta of New Mexico had expressed concern over a possible alliance between the Utes and the Navajos, the latter of whom were already joining the Gileños in raids south into northern Sonora.[40] Aware of the need to pacify the Indians to the west, Governor Anza in the fall of 1779 had visited the Moqui villages in the heart of the Navajo land. Though they had resisted the influence of the missionaries, the Moquis were not hostile to the Spaniards. Facing crop failure and starvation, many were abandoning their pueblos to join the Navajos, who for years had coveted the lands of these isolated people. Fully cognizant of these developments Anza requested permission to move the remnants of the Moqui tribe to the upper Rio Grande. Croix approved the plan but warned against policies that might drive the Indians into a union with the Gileños, or that might provoke the Navajos and Utes into an uprising against the Spaniards.[41] In May of 1780 Fray Andrés García moved one hundred and fifty Moquis to the Rio Grande and reported that some forty families were ready to follow. On the pretext of scouting in the Navajo country, Anza then visited Oraibe, where he obtained the consent of the Moqui chief for the removal of all families wishing to locate in New Mexico.[42] Later, in 1786, Anza flattered the Navajos into an alliance which, supplemented by liberal economic and military agreements, finally turned them against their Gileño allies.[43]

In dealing with problems in the Sonora-California region, Croix found himself drawn into the ancient controversy between the church and the military concerning jurisdiction over the Indians. On the frontier of Mexico the missionaries generally conceded that the pacification of the Apaches and other warlike tribes should be left to the army, but in California the Franciscans had found a fresh garden of souls far more docile than those they had encountered elsewhere on the northern border.[44] When confronted with military interference, they were quick to defend their missionary prerogatives. A case in point occurred in the mid 1770s when presidio commanders in California, alarmed at the outbreaks beyond the mission region, extended their powers in an effort to prevent the introduction of guns and horses among the Indians. But in 1775 after the San Diego revolt, an open break between the army and the clergy developed when Captain Rivera y Moncada insisted on punishing an Indian fugitive who had sought the sanctuary of the Church. The defiant padres promptly excommunicated the officer and his soldiers. At San Juan Capistrano in 1777 and 1778 other revolts occurred, with the missionaries accusing the local commanders of abusive treatment of the natives, while the Spanish officers, in turn, attributed the unrest among the Indians to laxness on the part of the overzealous friars.[45]

Although Spanish authority on the northwestern frontier of Mexico was characterized by a great deal of internal bickering, Croix proceeded to establish a mission on the lower Colorado River—a project that had been requested by missionaries since the days of Father Francisco Kino.[46] Because of the lack of funds, the mission was combined with a presidio and a settlement. Fathers Francisco Garcés and Juan Díaz had assured Croix that this would succeed.[47] Other missionaries, however, warned that the plan was contrary to good practice: Fray Francisco Palóu scornfully described the experiment as a "*nuevo modo de conquistar*" (a new method of conquest). These predictions soon proved true. The settlers' stock invaded the gardens of the Yumas, and quarrels flared between the Spaniards and the irate Indians over land. The storm broke on July 17, 1781, when Captain Rivera's column, en route from California to Sonora, pastured their mounts in the Indian fields near the mission. Incensed by this act, the Yumas fell upon the settlement and killed one hundred and four persons, including Rivera, Garcés, and Díaz. In September at Croix's orders, Pedro Fages led a punitive expedition north from Pitic to the Yuma villages, secured the freedom of sixty-one settlers being held captive by paying a ransom in flannel, beads, and tobacco, then escorted them to the safety of the Papago village of Sonoitac. The following month Fages returned to the Yuma villages only to learn that Chief Palma and the instigators of the massacre had fled, leaving their tribesmen to suffer retribution at the hands of the Spaniards.[48]

During the period 1783–1786 Spanish Indian policy in northern Mexico entered a new phase. Croix was transferred to Peru and the Interior Provinces were placed under the jurisdiction of the viceroy. The Crown ordered that Mexico be reorganized into twelve intendancies. Two of the new administrative divisions concerned the northern frontier: the *Provincias del Oriente* (Texas, Coahuila, Nuevo León, and Nuevo Santander) and the *Provincias del Poniente* (Nueva Viscaya, New Mexico, Sonora, and California). General Ugalde remained in command in the east, while the command in the west was given to General Jacobo Ugarte y Loyola. The most significant change in administration was the return of the northern provinces to the jurisdiction of the viceroy—then the capable Bernardo de Gálvez. Son of a former viceroy of New Spain and a nephew of José de Gálvez, he had extensive knowledge of administrative affairs and frontier problems. He had served as commander-general of Nueva Viscaya and governor of Louisiana, and as a field officer had campaigned against the Apaches in Sonora and Chihuahua and the British on the lower Mississippi River.[49] Bernardo de Gálvez died during his second year as viceroy, but he translated his years of experience in Indian affairs into a set of specific instructions which brought relative peace to the northern provinces of Mexico for the remainder of the Spanish colonial period.

Bernardo de Gálvez' program for Indian control was not new in its essential components. He drew from the experiences of many administrators, combining the best of their methods into a practical formula, and added the required degree of French duplicity and Spanish wrath to make his policy work. There would be no truce with the Indians. The choice they would have to make was simple: peace—or war. The first phase of the program involved a concerted military effort to force the Indians to settle near the presidios; the second aimed at the suppression of raiding, the obliteration of social and ceremonial traditions, and the ultimate destruction of the entire cultural core of tribal organization. In his instructions to those responsible for governing the Interior Provinces, Gálvez summarized the nature and intent of his plan:

> They [the Indians] may be attracted gently to the advantages of rational life and to commerce by discreet and opportune gifts. If peace is broken . . . we should rightly return to incessant and harsh war, alternating war and peace as often as the haughty or humble behavior of the barbarous Indian requires. These essentially are the rules on which the proposed system is based; they appear to be just, and they employ the ancient hatred, factional interest and inconsistency and perfidy of the heathen tribes to their mutual destruction.

Gálvez was aware of the economic base of the Apache raiding pattern. In his opinion the Spaniards could either feed Apaches or destroy them. He preferred the latter alternative:

> I am very much in favor of the special ruination of the Apaches, and in endeavoring to interest the other tribes and even other Apaches bands in it, because these Indians are our real enemies in the *Provincias Internas;* they cause its desolation and are the most feared because of their knowledge, cunning, and warlike customs acquired in the necessity of robbing in order to live.[50]

Gálvez's plan was put into effect, despite the misgivings of Viceroy Flores, his successor. In the northeastern provinces General Ugalde led an army of four hundred soldiers and Apache scouts on a six-month campaign into the Pecos River region, and in 1787 concluded treaties with the Lipan and Mescalero Apaches. The following year he extracted from the principal Mescalero chief an alliance for war against the Comanches.[51] On the northwestern frontier the Apaches suddenly found their freedom to roam cut short. Spanish troops drove scattered bands into the region west of Santa Fe, where in 1787 General Ugarte struck the Apaches in their *rancherías.* To induce his soldiers to greater exertions, he offered a bonus for each pair of Apache ears they took during battle or while on patrol.[52] This practice later led to the offering of scalp bounties by the civil and military authorities in Chihuahua and Sonora.[53] By 1790 the principal Gileño groups had agreed to settle near the Spanish presidios. The first phase of the Gálvez plan—the pursuit and exterminaton of hostile bands—had brought results.

With the settlement of numerous nomadic bands at the presidios, Spanish authorities now considered the second phase of the Gálvez program—the weakening of Apache culture. Provision was made to feed some 6,000 Indians congregated in *establecimientos de paz* (establishments of peace) on the frontier at an annual expense of 23,000 pesos, of which 7,000 pesos were designated for Sonora to support the Apaches settled at the town of Bacoachi and at the presidios of Fronteras, Santa Cruz, and Tucson.[54] At these centers the Indians were supplied liquor and encouraged to dote upon their old weakness for personal adornments and other luxuries which only the Spaniards could supply. Trade in inferior firearms was permitted to encourage the Indians to discard the deadly bow and arrow as their principal weapon for hunting and warfare.[55] According to one source horses even were given to the Apaches at the presidios.[56]

Although Gálvez had stressed the missionary goal of assimilation and conversion, few officials believed that the gentle methods of the padres would be effective among the Apaches at this stage of the program. For example, in 1795 when Fray Diego Bringas requested permission from the commanding general of the western provinces to send priests into the Apache settlements at Janos, Bacoachi, and Tucson, the officer replied that the padres would be welcome at the presidios, but advised that "the minister of the Apaches ought to be a captain of soldiers as well." Bringas' petition for military aid in founding missions among the western Apaches on the upper Gila was deemed unsound.[57]

Frontier commanders were reluctant to relax their control over the Apaches. Even under the most alert officers the Indians were restless. Moreover, there was constant resentment by the settlers, who were forced to pay extra taxes to feed these wards of the government; and peaceful Indians, who were often flogged and worked in chains merely for leaving their villages without permission, regarded with bitterness the special attention given the Apaches.[58] But despite the cost to the Crown and the constant vigilance the system required, the Gálvez policy soon reduced the problem of frontier defense to a matter of routine patrols and police actions. From 1790 to 1810, frontier towns experienced new life, churches were built, and prospectors began exploring for precious metal.[59]

The collapse of the system of *establecimientos* came with the outbreak of the Mexican Revolution in 1810. Spanish administrators, diverting troops and money to meet the crisis, weakened the northern defenses. Morale at the presidios deteriorated, and soldiers turned to graft and illegal trade with the Indians to compensate for reductions in pay.[60] Riots flared among the Apaches settled nearby when commanders attempted to cut the rations or assign field work. When renegade factions left the reservations, presidio commanders launched half-hearted campaigns and made patched-up treaties, allowing the Apaches to keep the plunder they had taken in adjacent provinces.[61] Emboldened by such signs of weakness in the presidial line, the Apaches openly deserted the military settlements. The twenty-year respite of peace ended in a flame of revolt that burned brightly for many years thereafter.

From 1765 to 1810 Spanish officials in Mexico had struggled continually with the problem of the Apache menace that had blunted the northward thrust of the missionary effort and made the borderlands untenable for settlers. Military campaigns, balance-of-power tactics, and trade alliances all were tried before a satisfactory solution was found. The policy of defeating, collecting, and provisioning hostile tribes on reservations near frontier outposts constituted a marked departure from the traditional missionary ideal of conversion and assimilation, but it brought an extended period of peace to the far flung frontier of northern Mexico.

NOTES

1. For background of Gálvez's assignment see Herbert I. Priestley, *José de Gálvez, Visitor-General of New Spain, 1765–1777* (U. of California Press, 1916), 5, 133–34.

2. The Indian policy employed later in the northern provinces may have been worked out in these meetings, rather than in Madrid. If the Spanish Crown considered the Indian problem as an important aspect of the defense of northern Mexico, the solution was left to Gálvez, for his original instructions did not specify a course of action in this respect. See Gálvez's instructions March 14, 1765, in Priestley, *José de Gálvez*, 404–17.

3. Hubert H. Bancroft, *History of the North Mexican States and Texas, 1531–1800* (2 vols., San Francisco, 1884–1889), I, 559–60. In 1748, an investigation of the presidial commands of Sonora revealed that the Apaches were aware of the advantage left open to them by this regulation. In some instances their raiding parties even heaped insult upon injury by sending an old woman with a cross to make peace, while the warriors went on to attack some other point. Bancroft, *North Mexican States*, I, 534–35.

4. *Ibid.*, I, 516–17; Hubert H. Bancroft, *History of Arizona and New Mexico, 1530–1888* (San Francisco, 1889), 272–73.

5. For a discussion of this revolt, see Russell C. Ewing, "The Pima Outbreak in November, 1751," *New Mexico Historical Review*, XIII (October 1948), 337–46.

6. Bancroft, *North Mexican States*, I, 560–61.

7. Though the Spanish often distinguished between the Chiricahua, Mimbres, and other bands of the western Apaches, they usually referred to them collectively as the Gileños during this period.

8. Quoted in Vito Alessio Robles, *Coahuila y Texas en la época colonial* (Mexico: Editorial Cultura, 1938), 29–30.

9. *Ibid.*, 162.

10. Seeking protection from the Comanches, the Lipans requested that a mission be established on the Llano River. They later fled, however, and the padres at San Sabá were massacred by the Comanches in March of 1758. Herbert E. Bolton, *Texas in the Middle Eighteenth Century* (U. of California Press, 1915), 86–87.

11. *Ibid.*, 35–36, 105.

12. *Ibid.*, 379.

13. *Ibid.*, 107–108.

14. Herbert E. Bolton (ed.), *Athanaze de Mézières and the Louisiana-Texas Frontier, 1768–1780* (2 vols., Cleveland: Arthur H. Clark Co., 1914), I, 70–71, 79–84.

15. Donald E. Worcester (ed.), *Instructions for the Governing of the Interior Provinces of New Spain, 1786, by Bernardo de Gálvez* (Berkeley: Quivira Society, 1951), 9–10.

16. Bolton, *Texas*, 381–82.

17. Priestley, *José de Gálvez*, 234–37.

18. *Ibid.*, 276.

19. From October through November of 1769, Gálvez was frequently ill. Obsessed with the Indian problem, he threatened his officers with death if they countermanded his orders. On one occasion he rose from his bed at two o'clock in the morning shouting that Saint Francis of Assisi had promised to bring him six hundred apes from Guatemala, and declared that he would send them in uniforms against the Pimas. *Ibid.*, 279.

20. *Ibid.*, 277.

21. Bolton, *Texas*, 113–17.

22. Alfred B. Thomas (ed.), *Forgotten Frontiers: A Study of the Spanish Indian Policy of Don Juan Bautista de Anza, Governor of New Mexico, 1777-1787* (U. of Oklahoma Press, 1932), 6–8.

23. The colonization of California was not only conducted as an exclusive project, but with little apparent coordination with other undertakings in the northern provinces. On receiving

a report from Zuñi, dated April 7, 1775, that an Indian had seen a "European village" near the Gila-Colorado junction, Oconor wrote Viceroy Bucareli on August 9, 1776, that on the completion of his campaign in New Mexico he would investigate this apparently unauthorized "poblazon de europeos." The Indian probably had seen the encampment of colonists who passed the Colorado junction in February 1774 with Anza's first expedition west from Tucson to California. Anza's second expedition passed the same point in November of the following year, leaving Fray Francisco Garcés and a small party behind to explore the region. Oconor was either unwilling to accept that the Indian's report was associated with these events, or he knew little about Anza's activities. Hugo Oconor to Antonio Maria Bucareli, August 9, 1776, Documents Relating to the History of Spain in Arizona and the Southwest [1768–1782], Film 34, in the University of Arizona Library, Tucson, Cited hereafter as Documents Relating to the Southwest.

24. Thomas (ed.), *Juan Bautista de Anza*, 9–13.

25. Bancroft, *North Mexican States*, I, 593–94.

26. Thomas (ed.), *Juan Bautista de Anza*, 13.

27. Bolton (ed.), *Athanaze de Mézières*, I, 107–108.

28. Alfred B. Thomas (ed.), *Teodoro de Croix and the Northern Frontier of New Spain, 1776–1783* (U. of Oklahoma Press, 1941), 18.

29. *Ibid.*, 35–37. For a detailed discussion of the war councils, see Bolton (ed.), *Athanaze de Mézières*, II, 152–70.

30. Bancroft, *Arizona and New Mexico*, 263.

31. Thomas (ed.), *Teodoro de Croix*, 15–18.

32. Order Indicating Rewards to those who Apprehend Deserters . . ., November 2, 1778, frames 145–48, Reel (1778), Parral Documents [Film 318], University of Arizona. Cited hereafter as Parral Documents. The original historical records of the Spanish province of Nueva Viscaya are in Parral, Chihuahua.

33. Thomas (ed.), *Teodoro de Croix*, 43–44.

34. *Ibid.*, 53–55.

35. Chart entitled Provincial Dragoons of San Carlos [October 15, 1779, Parral, Chihuahua], frames 26–27, Reel A (1779), Parral Documents.

36. For Mézières' account of the visit, see Bolton (ed.), *Athanaze de Mézières*, II, 239–87.

37. Bancroft, *Arizona and New Mexico*, 264–65.

38. Thomas (ed.), *Teodoro de Croix*, 46.

40. Bancroft, *Arizona and New Mexico*, 264.

41. Thomas (ed.), *Juan Bautista de Anza*, 169–71.

42. *Ibid.*, 27–30.

43. *Ibid.*, 345–51.

44. For a description of the California tribes, see Herbert I. Priestley (trans.), *A Historical, Political, and Natural Description of California by Pedro Fages, Soldier of Spain* (U. of California Press, 1937).

45. Hubert H. Bancroft, *History of California* (7 vols., San Francisco, 1884–1890), I, 266, 314–15).

46. Though the Crown concurred with the plan, the physical arrangement of the Yuma mission seems to be the work of Croix and Garcés. Croix's instructions indicated in detail the establishment and complement of the mission. Instructions . . . for the Establishment of the Spanish and Indian Pueblos on the Banks of the Rio Colorado . . . [March 12, 1780, Arizpe, Sonora], 202/24, Reel 2, Film 305, Fray Marcellio da Civezza Collection, University of Arizona Library. The original documents are in the Pontifica Ateneo Antoniana, Rome, Italy. Cited hereafter as the Civezza Collection.

47. Charles E. Chapman, *The Founding of Spanish California* (New York, 1916), 408–409. Also see ch. 17 [of Chapman's book].

48. On returning to the Yuma villages in November, Fages rescued thirteen additional captives, raising the total number of survivors to seventy-four. Pedro Fages to Juan Agustín de Morfi, January 22, 1782, Documents Relating to the Southwest.

49. Worcester (ed.), *Instructions*, 19–22.

50. *Ibid.*, 79–80.

51. Al B. Nelson, "Juan de Ugalde and Picax-Ande Ins-tinsle, 1787–1788, "*Southwestern Historical Quarterly*, XLIII (April 1940), 438–64.

52. In his diary of a campaign into the Gila River region in 1795, Captain José de Zúñiga mentions taking *pares de orejas*, which further indicates that the offering of premiums was a part of the extermination plan. Zúñiga's diary for 1795, Documents Covering the Years 1737–1795, VII, in University of Arizona Library. Collected in seven volumes, these are typewritten copies of original documents from the Archives of the Indies, Seville.

53. Francisco R. Almada, *Diccionario de historia, geografía y biografía sonorenses* (Chihuahua: Ruiz Sandoval, 1952), 72.

54. José Francisco Velasco, *Noticias estadísticas del Sonora . . .* (Mexico: Imprenta de Ignacio Cumplido, 1850), 240–41, gives 30,000 pesos as the total annual expense in Sonora. A copy [Film 114] of this volume is in the University of Arizona Library. For further discussion of the establishments of peace, see Bancroft, *Arizona and New Mexico*, 378–79; Laureano Calvo Berber, *Nociones de historia de Sonora* (Mexico: Librería de Manuel Porrua, 1958), 47–48.

55. Bancroft, *North Mexican States*, I, 682–84. The use of firearms by the Indians worked to their disadvantage during this period. In a sustained encounter the bow and arrow proved far more deadly, and remained so until the advent of the metallic cartridge in the mid-nineteenth century.

56. See Fray Diego Bringas to Fray Juan Francisco Rivera, May 28, 1795, 202/46, Civezza Collection.

57. Bringas to Rivera, May 28 and June 12, 1795, in *ibid.*

58. See Ugarte's decree, August 7, 1790, frame 605, Reel A (1790), Parral Documents.

59. Bancroft, *Arizona and New Mexico*, 379.

60. Ignacio Zúñiga, Rápido ojeada al estado de Sonora (Mexico: Juan Ojeda, 1835), 22–26. A copy [Film 87] of this volume is in the University of Arizona Library. Bancroft, *Arizona and New Mexico*, 402–403.

61. Bancroft, *North Mexican States*, II, 596, 600–601. José Agustín Escudero in *Noticias estadísticas del estado de Chihuahua* (Mexico: Juan Ojeda, 1834), 244–45, notes that Anglo-American traders were the ultimate recipients of cattle and property plundered by the Apaches during these years. The presidio at Janos, Chihuahua, encouraged the traffic in cattle stolen in Sonora through protective treaties with the Apaches. This provoked military commanders in Sonora into sending punitive expeditions against the Apaches congregated at Janos. For a discussion of these protective treaties and their consequences, see Joseph F. Park, "The Apaches in Mexican-American Relations, 1848–1861, "*Arizona and the West*, III (Summer 1961), 129–46.

INDIANS AS ACTORS

14

Shifting for Survival in the Spanish Southwest*

Albert H. Schroeder

Editor's Introduction

On New Spain's northern frontier Indians far out-numbered Spanish-Mexicans. California's indigenous population in 1769, for example, (estimated at 310,000)[1] was one hundred times greater than its maximum non-Indian population during the Spanish period. Nonetheless, due in large part to the availability of Spanish documents, historians know far more about the activities and institutions of Spanish-Mexicans than about Indians. Moreover, those Spanish documents have strongly influenced our perceptions of Indians. Many traditional historians have tended to see Indians from a Spanish viewpoint. On the other hand, ethnohistorians such as Albert Schroeder, try to understand Indians on their own terms.

In this article, Schroeder surveys three centuries of Indian population shifts in Arizona and New Mexico. Instead of ascribing those shifts to the impact of Spanish-Mexicans, he argues that "ecological factors and intertribal enmities played a far greater role in affecting native population shifts than did the presence of, or pressures from the Spaniards." Schroeder's focus is on the Pueblos. Along with many other anthropologists, he suggests that the Pueblos maintained the essentials of their culture by selectively accepting certain objects of European culture and rejecting others.[2]

**New Mexico Historical Review*, XLIII, 4 (October 1968), 291-310. Reprinted with permission of the author and the editors of the *New Mexico Historical Review*.

Schroeder's conclusions are by no means definitive. Does he, for example, underestimate Spanish influences? First, does he understate the impact of the horse, which Spaniards introduced? Schroeder acknowledges that it gave Plains Apaches "a very definite advantage over their enemies" in the seventeenth century. The same might be said of the Comanches in the eighteenth century. Second, should he take into account the impact of the diseases, which Spaniards unwittingly introduced, on the shifts of indigenous peoples? The Pueblo population, for example, numbered between thirty and forty thousand in 1600, then declined to about sixteen thousand in 1700, due in part to European disease. This population decline also resulted from the effects of forced labor, the migration of some Pueblos away from Spanish settlements, and the assimilation of other Pueblos into the Spanish-speaking population, according to one specialist.[3]

Sketching his ideas in broad strokes, Mr. Schroeder leaves many questions unanswered, but his essay serves as a refreshing antidote to those pieces which focus on Spanish-Mexican initiatives and reduce Indians to minor players on their own stages.

Albert Schroeder, who retired in 1976 as Chief of the Division of Interpretation, United States National Park Service, Southwestern Regional Office, has enjoyed a long and productive career as an archaeologist. He holds a B.A. in archaeology and an M.A. in anthropology, both from the University of Arizona. His numerous scholarly articles, which date back to 1943, include ventures into history as well as anthropology and archaeology. Among his books is *A Colony on the Move: Gaspar Castaño de Sosa's Journal, 1590–1591*, edited and translated with Dan S. Matson (Santa Fe: 1965), and *A Brief History of New Mexico*, co-authored with Myra Ellen Jenkins (Albuquerque: 1974). Mr. Schroeder, who signs himself "retired but busier than ever," has in press a study of climate and man in the prehistoric Southwest.

NOTES

1. Sherburne F. Cook, *The Population of the California Indians, 1796–1970* (Berkeley: 1976), p. 43. By 1820, California's non-Indian population had reached a high of about 3,000.

2. See, for example, Edward P. Dozier, "The Spanish-Mexican Impact on Pueblo Culture," in *Perspectives in American Indian Culture Changes*, ed. Edward H. Spicer (Chicago: 1961), pp. 137–42, and Spicer, "Spanish-Indian Acculturation in the Southwest," with comments by Dozier and Florence H. Ellis, *American Anthropologist*, 56 (1954): 663–84.

3. Edward P. Dozier, *The Pueblo Indians of North America* (New York: 1970), p. 63.

Shifting for Survival in the Spanish Southwest

Much has been written about the submergence by the Europeans of the American Indian and his culture, indicating that the rate of change varied according to the type, frequency, and density of contacts between the Indians and neighboring white men. Too little reference has been made to those ethnic groups which retained their way of life for several centuries, practically unaffected culturally by nearby European activities and settlements. Some of the best examples of Indian cultural survival and Indian interaction are found in the Southwest. Here, between A.D. 1540 and the 1820s, a number of inter-Indian hostilities and population shifts occurred, many of which ran their full course only indirectly influenced by the presence of the Spaniards. Ecological factors and intertribal enmities played a far greater role in affecting native population shifts than did the presence of, or pressures from, the Spaniards. This paper outlines the history of Indian population shifts in the Southwest during the Spanish period and the factors involved in the tribal moves discussed.

Indians, like most any other people, were prone to accept new ideas or traits that would ease their way of life, providing that these elements did not alter their own pattern of culture. In the Southwest some of the Indians received gifts from the early Spanish explorers, usually trinkets and an occasional metal knife or axe. These items paralleled articles of adornment and stone knives and axes already existing in their own culture. As Spanish settlement advanced into the Southwest, the Indians accepted other material goods on the same basis. Their stone tools, stone arrow-points, pottery containers, and other objects were slowly supplemented with or replaced by metal European items of like nature. Glass and metal also became desired materials for adornment and sometimes replaced native stone, bone, and shell ornaments. This process reflects substitution in, not alteration of, a basic culture pattern. The indigenous way of life remained essentially the same without any specific changes in settlement patterns, warfare practices, means of subsistence, or social or ceremonial activities.

[*Sixteenth Century*]

Between 1540 and 1598 six Spanish exploring expeditions visited the Pueblo farmers of the Rio Grande, as well as those of the Zuñi and Hopi villages, the desert irrigation Sobaipuri Pima farmers of southern Arizona, and the Yuman-speaking floodwater farmers of western Arizona. The Spaniards also encountered various nomadic Apache and Yavapai groups, as well as some factions of Plains Indians (figure 1). The exchange of a few gifts, and perhaps a few ideas, marks the extent of cultural contact that took place. So far as is known, the explorers left no equipment, no livestock, and no seeds—only the gifts, and a few zealous missionaries who chose to remain behind and quickly met the fate of martyrdom.

Of the southern Tiwa pueblos in the Bernalillo region (figure 2), Coronado's army in 1541 took over one for a base headquarters and laid siege to two others. The people of nine neighboring Tiwa pueblos left their homes but reoccupied them after Coronado departed for Mexico in 1542.[1] Spanish expeditions of the 1580s reported as many as twelve to fourteen pueblos in this same area. There is no evidence that Coronado permanently displaced these southern Tiwa pueblos.

Though Spanish exploratory contacts were brief, journals of the *entradas* contain considerable information, supported by recent archaeological investigations, showing changes in locales by Pueblo groups. The Pueblo people of the Chama River drainage, for example, whom the Spaniards mentioned but did not contact,[2] abandoned their homes in the late sixteenth century to join their Tewa-speaking linguistic relatives living along the Rio Grande between Española and Santa Fe. Others, along the Rito de los Frijoles within present Bandelier National Monument, moved south to join their Keres-speaking neighbors at Cochiti, and some perhaps east to San Ildefonso. Those of the pueblo of Gipuy, on lower Galisteo Creek, moved west to join their Keres kindred at Santo Domingo. The people of two pueblos on the north end of the Sandia Mountains which were attacked by other Indians and abandoned in 1591, probably took refuge among Tiwa relatives near Bernalillo. Almost a dozen pueblos were permanently abandoned between 1540 and 1598, but not from causes attributable to the Spaniards.[3]

Known hostilities between Indian groups, as recorded by the Spanish chroniclers of these early expeditions, account for some but not all these abandonments. The Teyas, a Caddoan-speaking farming group on the plains, destroyed pueblos in the Galisteo Basin and attacked Pecos on the eastern Pueblo frontier as early as 1526, but by the time the Spaniards came in 1540, they were friendly with Pecos.[4] Later, in the 1580s, Apaches on the plains were enemies of the Tanos of Galisteo Basin.[5] They may also have been responsible for the 1591 attack in the Sandia Mountains mentioned above. In the 1580s Piro-speakers of the Socorro region were at war with southern Tiwas on their northern border, perhaps the warfare referred to by Juan Morlete in his report of 1591,[6] but no abandonment was recorded along their common border during the late decades of the century. Some friction also existed between the Zuñi and

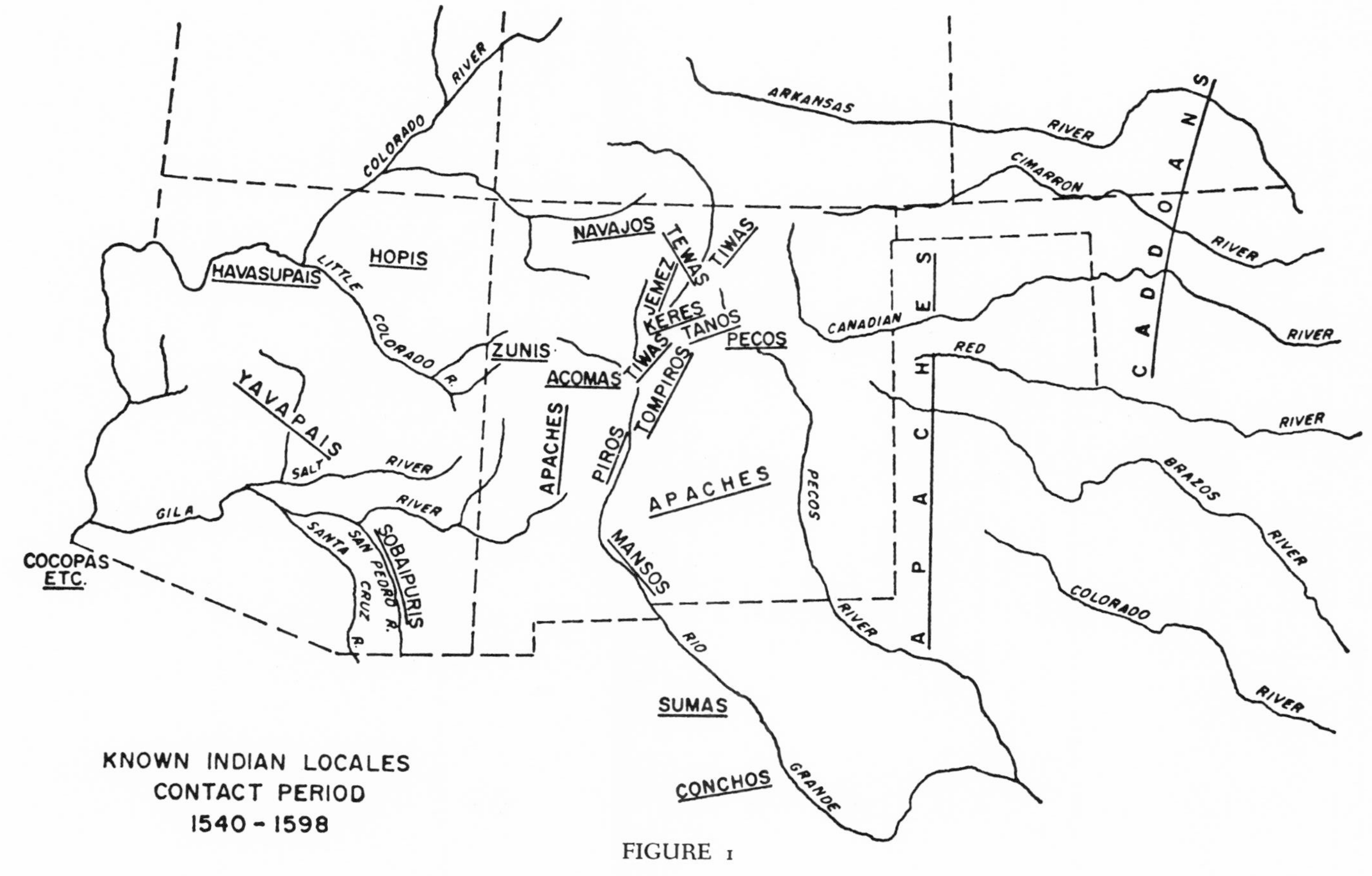
KNOWN INDIAN LOCALES
CONTACT PERIOD
1540 - 1598
COLORADO RIVER
HOPIS
HAVASUPAIS
LITTLE COLORADO R.
ZUNIS
YAVAPAIS
SALT RIVER
GILA
RIVER
SANTA CRUZ R.
SAN PEDRO R.
SOBAIPURIS
COCOPAS ETC.
APACHES
ACOMAS
NAVAJOS
TEWAS
TIWAS
JEMEZ
KERES
TANOS
PECOS
TIWAS
TOMPIROS
PIROS
MANSOS
APACHES
RIO GRANDE
SUMAS
CONCHOS
PECOS RIVER
ARKANSAS RIVER
CIMARRON
RIVER
CANADIAN
RIVER
RED RIVER
BRAZOS RIVER
COLORADO RIVER
APACHES
CADDOANS

FIGURE 1

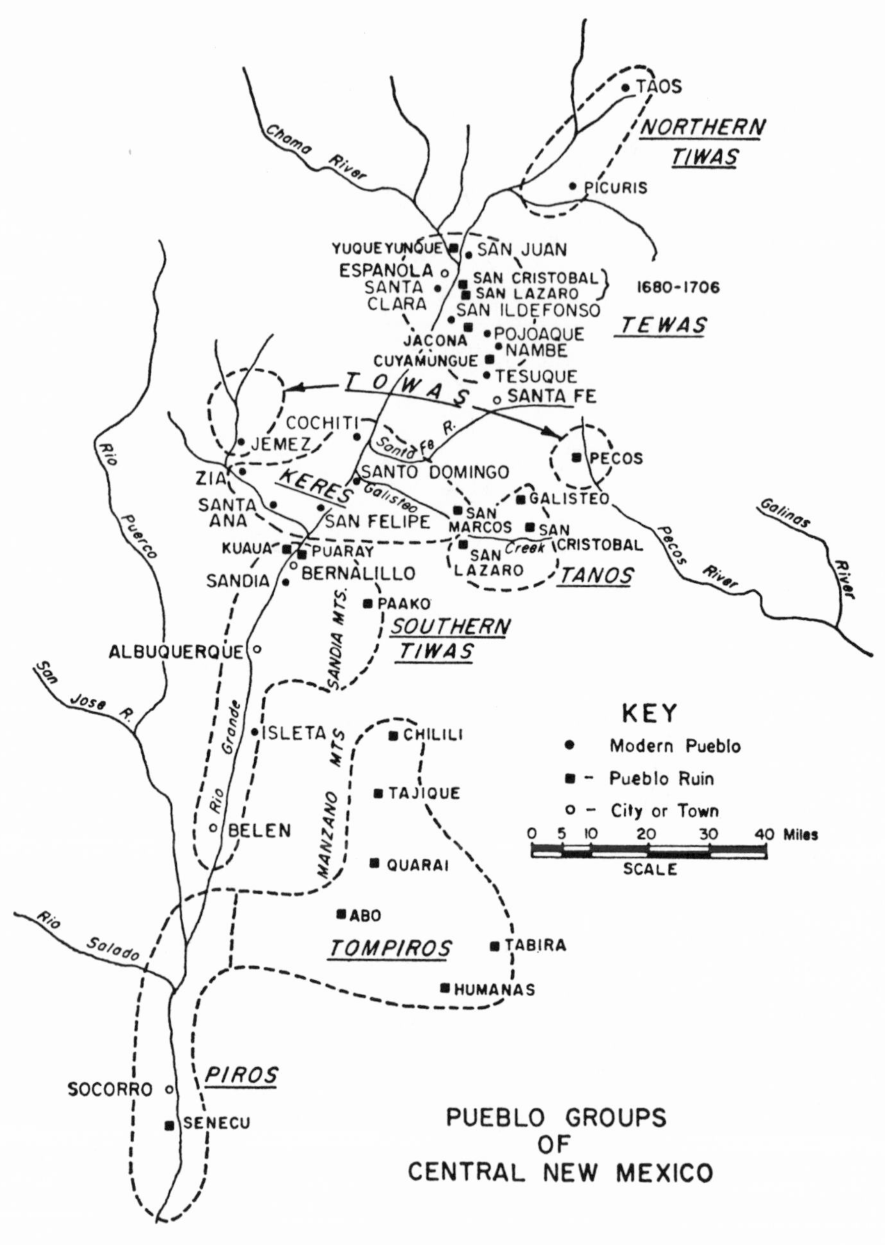
TAOS
NORTHERN TIWAS
PICURIS
Chama River
YUQUEYUNQUE
SAN JUAN
ESPANOLA
SAN CRISTOBAL
SAN LAZARO
1680-1706
SANTA CLARA
SAN ILDEFONSO
JACONA
POJOAQUE
TEWAS
NAMBE
CUYAMUNGUE
TESUQUE
TOWAS
SANTA FE
COCHITI
Santa Fe R.
JEMEZ
PECOS
ZIA
SANTO DOMINGO
KERES
Galisteo
SANTA ANA
SAN MARCOS
GALISTEO
SAN FELIPE
SAN CRISTOBAL
Creek
KUAUA
PUARAY
SAN LAZARO
TANOS
BERNALILLO
SANDIA
Pecos River
Galinas River
PAAKO
Rio Puerco
SANDIA MTS.
SOUTHERN TIWAS
ALBUQUERQUE
San Jose R.
KEY
Modern Pueblo
Pueblo Ruin
City or Town
ISLETA
CHILILI
Rio Grande
MANZANO MTS
TAJIQUE
0 5 10 20 30 40 Miles
SCALE
BELEN
QUARAI
Rio Salado
ABO
TOMPIROS
TABIRA
HUMANAS
PIROS
SOCORRO
SENECU
PUEBLO GROUPS OF CENTRAL NEW MEXICO

FIGURE 2

the Hopi pueblos throughout the same period.[7] All these hostilities, however, were far to the east, south, and west of the northern pueblos abandoned during the 1500s.

It is possible, though doubtful, that the presence of Navajo Indians northwest of the Tewa pueblos in the north might have been a disrupting factor. The first specific documentary reference to "marauding Apaches" is in the vicinity of the Spanish colony near Española, 1606–1607.[8] We know that during the early 1600s the Picuris, Taos, Pecos, and "Apaches" formed an alliance against the Tewa people because they were harboring the only Spanish settlement in New Mexico.[9] Perhaps it was this alliance that moved the Spaniards to abandon their first colony and establish the capital at Santa Fe, some twenty-five miles to the south, in 1610. The alliance against the Tewa people that developed in the early seventeenth century appears to be too late to explain the abandonment of certain Tewa, let alone Keres, pueblos in the late sixteenth century. Moreover, since Picuris, Taos, and Pecos are known to have carried on good trade relations with Apaches in eastern New Mexico,[10] the "Apaches" who joined this alliance are more likely to have been from east of the Rio Grande rather than Navajo-Apaches from west of the continental divide.

The most probable cause for the abandonment of certain northern pueblos appears to have been ecological rather than cultural. The pueblos located on tributaries of the Rio Grande were dependent on dry farming, and the area was struck by a severe drought toward the end of the sixteenth century.[11] The Tewas and the Keres were forced to contract their territory, and farmers from the tributary streams abandoned their pueblos and took refuge among their irrigation farmer relatives on the Rio Grande.[12]

[*Seventeenth Century*]

During the initial period of Spanish settlement in the Southwest, which began with the colony founded near Española by Don Juan de Oñate in 1598 and ended with the expulsion of the Spaniards during the Pueblo Rebellion of 1680, the Spaniards introduced the Rio Grande Pueblo Indians to wheat growing. Fruit trees provided welcome additions to Pueblo diet. Although the Puebloans had long raised domestic turkeys,[13] the introduction of pastoral ways was truly new. The Spaniards distributed livestock among some of the pueblos, but they kept the horse herds under guard near their own settlements because the use of horses would increase the mobility and fighting power of the Indians. In spite of this precaution, it was not long before mounted non-Pueblo Indians became a reality, and already existing intertribal hostilities accelerated. The pattern of native warfare now was changing in some ethnic groups.

The Spaniards of the seventeenth century imposed their civil system and missions on the Pueblo people. This led to considerable strife, including friction between Spanish officials of church and state. In many instances appointed Pueblo Indian officials used their authority to screen out or dilute unwanted elements of Spanish culture and to evade undesirable mandates. The church made attempts to suppress Pueblo ceremonies. Civil officials exacted payment of various items as a form of tax. Conversions among inhabitants of the various pueblos drew members away from native ceremonial societies, led to factional splits, and weakened the structure of their complex and closely knit society. By the early 1640s many of the Pueblos were rebelling against impositions which were slowly changing their way of life. Some of the Taos Indians fled east into the plains and remained among Cuartelejo Apaches in the area of present Scott County, Kansas, until they were brought back under Spanish escort in the early 1660s.[14] The practice of returning Indians to their villages became the custom of the Spaniards. The only group who fully accepted missionization during this period was the non-Pueblo Mansos of southern New Mexico, who, in 1659, moved into a mission near El Paso where they eventually lost their identity (figure 3).

While Pueblo Indians in the seventeenth century resisted much of Spanish culture unattractive to them, they were nevertheless strongly influenced. Nomadic groups, on the other hand, continued as in the past to trade at various pueblos, obtaining Spanish goods at times, and even horses. By the early 1640s the governor of New Mexico traded directly with Apaches of the plains, rather than through frontier pueblos, bartering horses and various items in exchange for hides, slaves, and other articles. The Apache masters of the plains were quick to shift from dogs as beasts of burden to horses. In short order this one addition to their culture increased their already mobile way of life, and mounted Plains Apache warriors now held a very definite advantage over their enemies. Apache raids into eastern New Mexico became a major problem in the 1660s. Their depredations, plus the severe droughts of the late 1660s, led to the abandonment of all the Tompiro pueblos east of the Manzano Mountains by the early 1670s.

Apache groups west of the Rio Grande concentrated their attacks on the Zuñi pueblos, which were isolated from the Spaniards, but maintained friendly relations with Acoma. In the 1580s Apache Indians joined Acomas in resistance against the Spaniards.[15] In 1599 Oñate sentenced a number of the old people of Acoma to the care of an Apache group.[16] As late as 1692 an Apache faction was reported in council at Acoma, an alliance the Spaniards were still attempting to break four years later.[17] These or

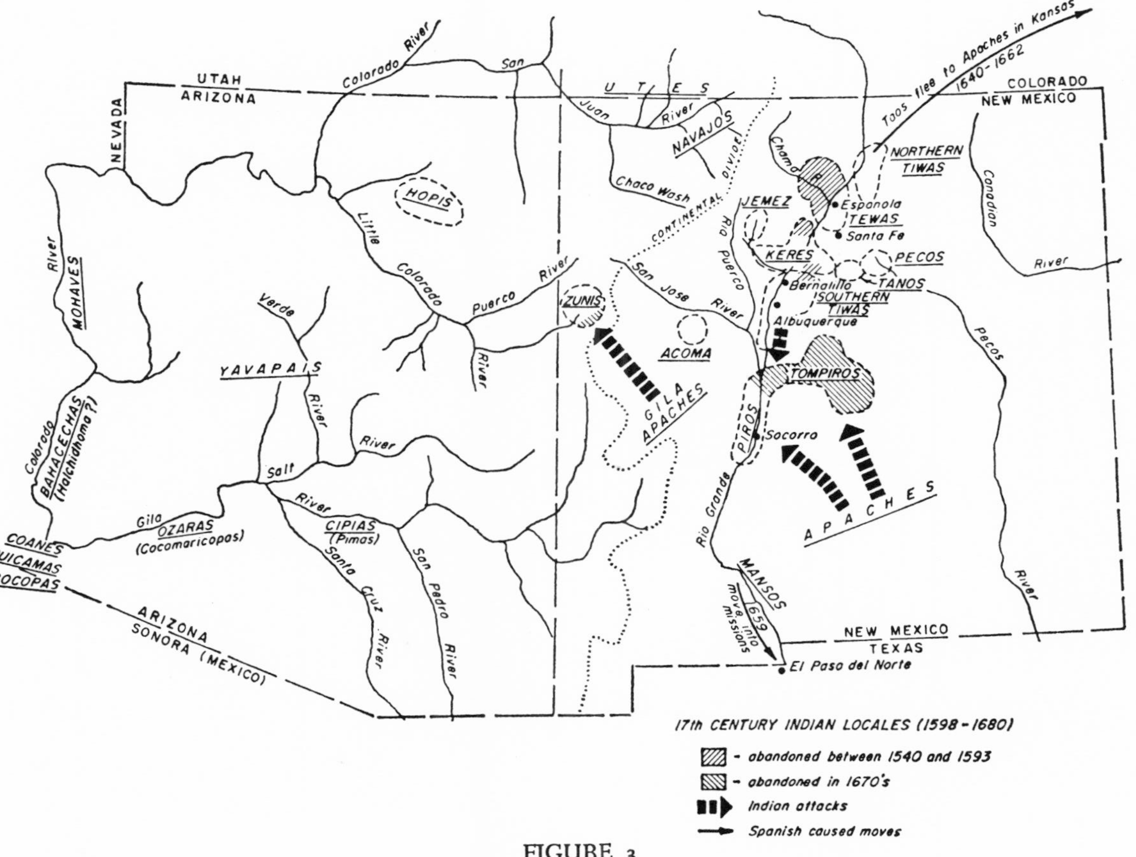
UTAH
ARIZONA
NEVADA
COLORADO
NEW MEXICO
NEW MEXICO
TEXAS
ARIZONA
SONORA (MEXICO)
Taos flee to Apaches in Kansas 1640-1662
Colorado River
San Juan River
U T E S
NAVAJOS
Chaco Wash
CONTINENTAL DIVIDE
HOPIS
Little Colorado
Puerco River
Verde River
YAVAPAIS
Salt River
Gila
OZARAS
(Cocomaricopas)
CIPIAS
(Pimas)
Santa Cruz River
San Pedro River
MOHAVES
River
Colorado
BAHACECHAS
(Halchidhoma?)
COANES
QUICAMAS
COCOPAS
ZUNIS
ACOMA
GILA APACHES
San Jose River
Rio Puerco
JEMEZ
KERES
Chama R.
Espanola
TEWAS
Santa Fe
NORTHERN TIWAS
PECOS
TANOS
Bernalillo
SOUTHERN TIWAS
Albuquerque
TOMPIROS
PIROS
Socorro
Rio Grande
A P A C H E S
MANSOS
1659 move into missions
El Paso del Norte
Canadian River
Pecos River
17th CENTURY INDIAN LOCALES (1598-1680)
- abandoned between 1540 and 1593
- abandoned in 1670's
Indian attacks
Spanish caused moves

FIGURE 3

closely related Apaches also developed an alliance with the people of Jemez who, up to the 1620s, were living in the mountains, depopulated by war and famine,[18] possibly the aftereffects of the severe drought of the late 1500s. From 1614 on these allies also plotted against the Spaniards. Some of these Apaches were reported among the Jemez as late as 1694.[19]

In the late seventeenth century Apache raids against Piro and Tompiro pueblos, as well as against those of the Zuñis on the west, met with little or no direct Spanish military opposition at these pueblos. Occasional punitive expeditions were sent into Apache country from the Santa Fe region, but few troops could be spared to protect outlying areas. The few thousand settlers of New Mexico lived in the Rio Grande Valley between Socorro and Española, with a heavy concentration in the Santa Fe area. After 1640 all available military forces were needed to cope with a series of uprisings among nearby Tewa and Keres pueblos, and threats of Apache attacks.[20]

In August 1680, after almost a century of oppression, the Pueblo Indians rose in revolt, forcing the Spaniards to withdraw south to the El Paso region where they remained for twelve years. This uprising marked the beginning of a number of population shifts (figure 4). As the Spaniards withdrew, they were joined by some Isletans and some of the weakened Piro Indians of the Socorro region who already had abandoned one of their pueblos in the 1670s because of Tiwa attacks[21] or Apache inroads throughout the 1600s.[22] Perhaps the droughts of the late 1660s and 1670s had also broken the spirit of those Piro farmers who decided to leave with the Spaniards. In November 1681 Spaniards probing north found that other Piro pueblos had been sacked and abandoned. The occupants either had followed their relatives to El Paso or had joined other Pueblos farther north or had been taken captive by them.[23]

During the absence of the Spaniards between 1680 and 1692, a number of pueblos moved to new sites. The Tanos of Galisteo Basin, the first group to arrive in Santa Fe and take part in the rebellion, remained in Santa Fe and in the area immediately to the north.[24] The Jemez left their homes, into which the Spaniards had gathered them in the early 1620s, and built new pueblos in the mountains to the north where the Spaniards had first found them in 1614, and were to find them again in 1692, still allied with Apaches.[25] The Keres speakers of San Marcos joined relatives on the Rio Grande who also took refuge in the mountains or on mesas, probably for defense against the enemy Tano and Tewa or from Apache raids coming in from the south.[26] During this period, five Zuñi pueblos were merged into one under pressure of continuing Apache attacks from the southeast. These enemies had already caused the abandonment of one Zuñi pueblo in the 1670s.[27] The Hopis, plagued by Ute attacks, moved their pueblos to the mesa tops, with the exception of Oraibi, which already had been similarly situated. Perhaps it was at this time that they also abandoned their farmlands in Canyon de Chelly.[28] The Utes also were hostile toward the northern Tiwa, Tewa, and the Jemez pueblos. The pueblo changes in locale, almost entirely measures of defense, can be related to prerebellion hostilities between tribes.

Interpueblo friction also was rife. Though Isleta did not move, leaders of the rebellion came from the north in 1680 or 1681 and burned the church and all objects within it in their attempt to stamp out everything Spanish.[29] This may explain the willingness of some Isletans to go to El Paso with the Spaniards who entered Pueblo country in 1681. Almost all Rio Grande pueblos were forced to take a stand on interpueblo strife. As a result, Pecos, Taos, Jemez, and the Keres were allied for a time against the Tanos, Tewas, and Picuris. Apaches west of the Rio Grande were allied with the Jemez, and those to the east with Pecos or with Picuris and their allies.[30]

The shift of pueblos to defensive positions between 1680 and 1692 has been thought by some to have been due to fear of reprisal by the Spaniards if they returned. The evidence cited, however, indicates that old enmities as well as new ones flared high during the absence of the Spaniards and required immediate action to handle hostilities close at hand. Though the Spaniards, far off at El Paso del Norte, had sent punitive expeditions into Pueblo country in 1681 and 1687, on their re-entry in 1692 and 1693 they found several pueblos ready to do battle, while others sought refuge elsewhere before the Spaniards approached their pueblos.[31] There is no documented case or any evidence of a pueblo changing its locale during the rebellion or at any other time because of a fear of Spaniards.

The Pueblo Rebellion also marks changes in and expansion of Apache raiding patterns. After the abandonment of the Tompiro pueblos in the early 1670s, the Apaches of southeastern New Mexico were able to extend their raids northwest against the southern Tiwas, Keres, and Tanos during the revolt period.[32] This seems to have been the reason not only for the abandonment of Tompiro pueblos east of the Manzano Mountains, but also of the few surviving Tiwa pueblos in the foothills of the Sandias; as well as of the Keres pueblo of San Marcos, and for the failure of the Tanos to reoccupy their Galisteo Basin homes after the Spaniards left in 1680 (figures 4 and 5). Northern Gila Apaches to the west of the Rio Grande continued to hammer the Zuñi pueblos, while the Apaches of southern New Mexico ranged south of the present international border in the early 1680s. In 1684 the latter formed an alliance with the Sumas, Janos, and Jocomes of western Chihuahua and eastern Sonora.[33]

During the 1690s a vanguard of southern Gila Apaches, in company with Janos and Jocomes of northern Mexico and southeastern Arizona,

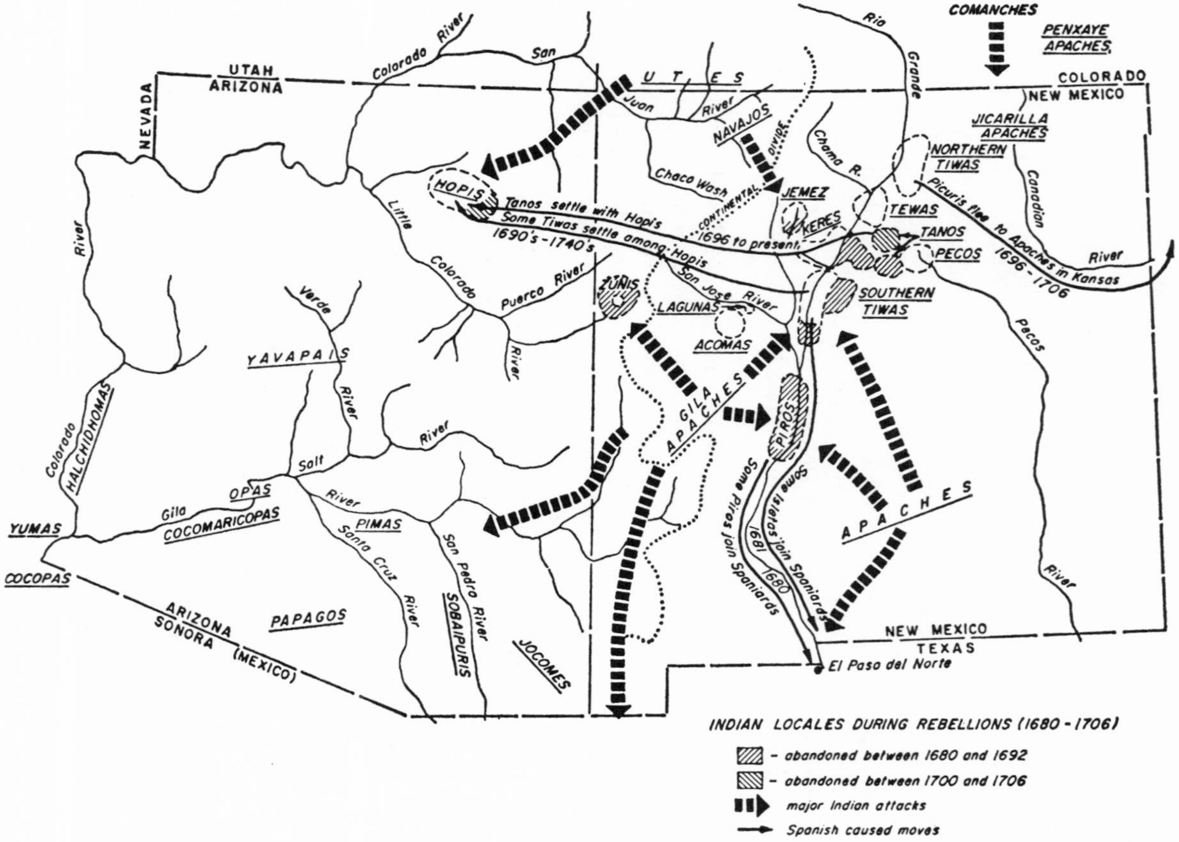

COMANCHES
PENXAYE APACHES
UTAH
ARIZONA
NEVADA
COLORADO
NEW MEXICO
TEXAS
ARIZONA
SONORA (MEXICO)
UTES
NAVAJOS
JICARILLA APACHES
NORTHERN TIWAS
TEWAS
TANOS
PECOS
JEMEZ
KERES
SOUTHERN TIWAS
HOPIS
ZUNIS
LAGUNAS
ACOMAS
PIROS
GILA APACHES
APACHES
YAVAPAIS
HALCHIDHOMAS
YUMAS
COCOPAS
OPAS
COCOMARICOPAS
PIMAS
PAPAGOS
SOBAIPURIS
JOCOMES
Colorado River
San Juan River
Rio Grande
Chama R.
Chaco Wash
Continental Divide
Canadian River
Pecos River
Little Colorado
Puerco River
San Jose River
Verde River
Salt River
Gila
Santa Cruz River
San Pedro River
Tanos settle with Hopis
Some Tiwas settle among Hopis
1690's - 1740's
1696 to present
Picuris flee to Apaches in Kansas
1696 - 1706
Some Isletas join Spaniards
Some Piros join Spaniards
1681
1680
El Paso del Norte
INDIAN LOCALES DURING REBELLIONS (1680 - 1706)
- abandoned between 1680 and 1692
- abandoned between 1700 and 1706
major Indian attacks
Spanish caused moves

FIGURE 4

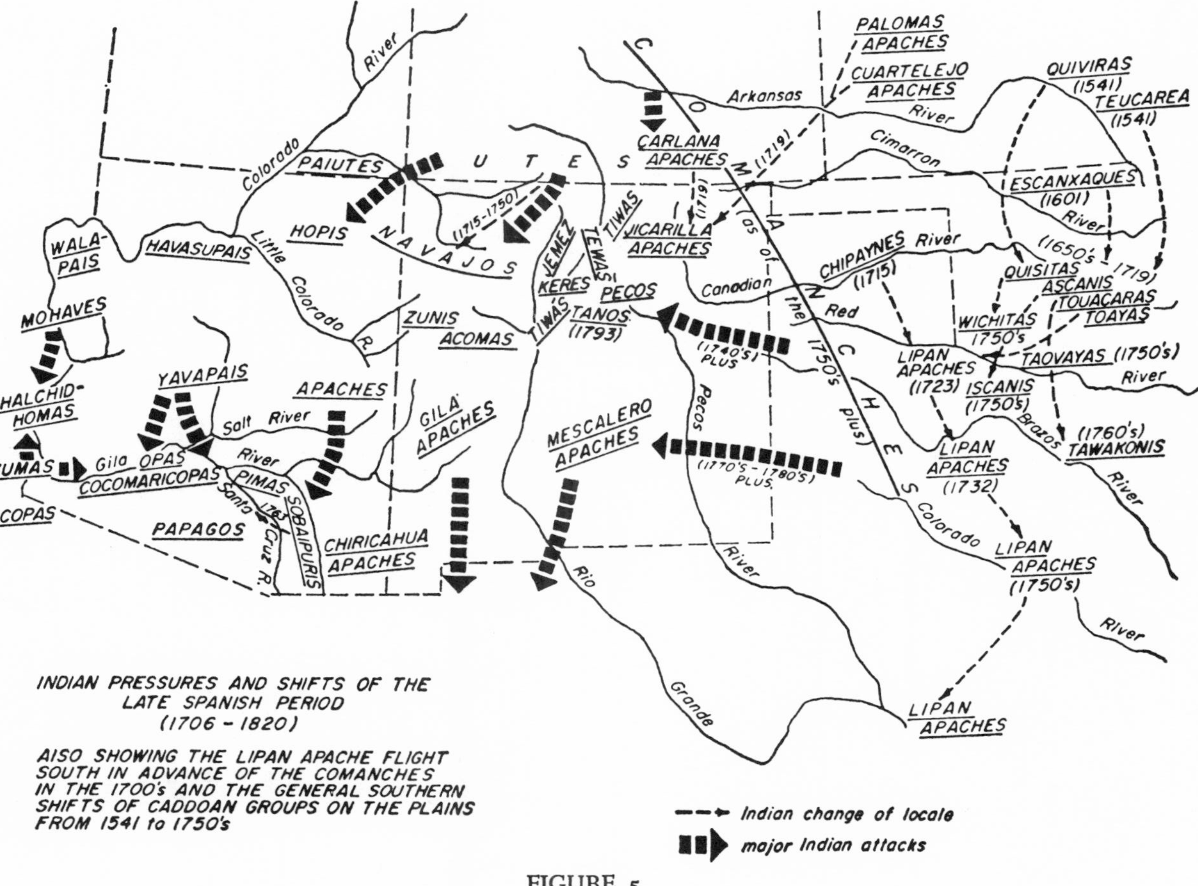
INDIAN PRESSURES AND SHIFTS OF THE
LATE SPANISH PERIOD
(1706 - 1820)
AISO SHOWING THE LIPAN APACHE FLIGHT SOUTH IN ADVANCE OF THE COMANCHES IN THE 1700's AND THE GENERAL SOUTHERN SHIFTS OF CADDOAN GROUPS ON THE PLAINS FROM 1541 to 1750's
Indian change of locale
major Indian attacks
PALOMAS APACHES
CUARTELEJO APACHES
QUIVIRAS (1541)
TEUCAREA (1541)
Arkansas River
Cimarron
CARLANA APACHES
(1719)
C O M A N C H E S (as of the 1750's plus)
ESCANXAQUES (1601)
River
U T E S
PAIUTES
Colorado
River
WALA-PAIS
HAVASUPAIS
Little Colorado R.
HOPIS
NAVAJOS
(1715-1750)
TIWAS
JICARILLA APACHES
JEMEZ
TEWAS
KERES
PECOS
TIWAS
TANOS (1793)
Canadian
CHIPAYNES (1715)
River
(1650's - 1719)
QUISITAS
ASCANIS
TOUACARAS
TOAYAS
WICHITAS 1750's
Red
MOHAVES
ZUNIS
ACOMAS
(1740's) PLUS
LIPAN APACHES (1723)
TAOVAYAS (1750's)
River
HALCHID-HOMAS
YAVAPAIS
APACHES
Salt River
GILA APACHES
MESCALERO APACHES
(1770's - 1780's) PLUS
ISCANIS (1750's)
Brazos
(1760's) TAWAKONIS
YUMAS
Gila OPAS
COCOMARICOPAS
River
PIMAS
Pecos
LIPAN APACHES (1732)
River
COCOPAS
Santa Cruz R.
1763
SOBAIPURIS
PAPAGOS
CHIRICAHUA APACHES
Colorado
River
LIPAN APACHES (1750's)
Rio Grande
River
LIPAN APACHES

FIGURE 5

began attacking Opata Indians in Sonora, Sobaipuri Indians along the upper San Pedro River of present southeastern Arizona, and mission rancherías which were expanding north at this time. By the opening of the eighteenth century these Apaches began to use the Chiricahua Mountain area as a home base, absorbing or displacing the local Jocomes in the process.[34] Even the more northern Gila Apaches opened up new routes to the south, via San Francisco River, to raid into northern Sobaipuri country.[35] By 1762 the Sobaipuris, no longer able to stem Apache onslaughts from the north, abandoned their fertile valley and joined their Piman-speaking relatives near and to the west of present Tucson,[36] where Spanish missions had begun the process of breaking down the culture of the Papagos.[37]

After the return of the Spaniards to New Mexico in 1692, Indian alignments shifted one way or another according to events. Some of the Navajos allied themselves with the pueblos of San Ildefonso and Cochiti.[38] The localized Pueblo rebellion of 1696 was ineffective and led to moves which can be related directly to dissatisfaction with the Spaniards. The Tewa pueblos of Jacoma and Cuyamungue were abandoned for all time.[39] Some dissatisfied southern Tiwa Indians, as well as Tanos from San Cristóbal and San Lázaro pueblos on the Santa Cruz near Española, took refuge among the Hopis.[40] Some of the Picuris went out among the Cuartelejo Apaches on the plains.[41] A group of Keres speakers also formed a new pueblo at Laguna in 1698 or 1699. In 1700–1701, the Hopis even sacked one of their own pueblos, Awatovi, for allowing Spanish friars to enter.[42] The period from 1680 to 1700 was one of considerable stress among the Pueblo people at a time when they were making a major attempt to retain their way of life.

Several of these Pueblo shifts were not permanent. The Picuris on the plains requested aid and were escorted back to their pueblo in 1706.[43] Most of the refugees from Rio Grande pueblos, when offered the choice, elected to leave the Hopi villages in the 1740s and settled at Sandia and other pueblos.[44] Only the Tano group who had settled in 1696 at Los Tanos, or Hano, decided to remain among the Hopis. Their descendants are still there, still Tewa-speaking, today.[45] Though the flight of some of the Pueblos in 1696–1698 was caused by the Spaniards, most of the groups returned to their original locales.

[*Eighteenth and Nineteenth Centuries*]

A new element—the coming of Comanches and their Ute allies into northern New Mexico in the opening years of the eighteenth century—set up a chain reaction that was to affect population shifts for many years. In 1706 Penxaye Apaches north of Raton Pass were involved in their last desperate fight against Comanches. Jicarillas, badly mauled by Comanche attacks, planned to move to Navajo country west of the Rio Grande, only to be talked out of it by the Spaniards. Soon more Apaches, fleeing south from north of Raton Pass, joined the Jicarillas. By 1719 Cuartelejo Apaches, pressed by Plains tribes armed with guns obtained from the French, fled west to the Jicarillas.[46] Comanches, moving south into eastern New Mexico and northern Texas, forced Lipan Apaches on the upper Canadian River south into central Texas and continued to harass the Jicarillas and their allies, who fell back into the Sangre de Cristo Mountains between Taos and Pecos in the late 1720s.[47]

While Comanches were causing a rearrangement of tribal territories east of the Rio Grande in 1715, Southern Utes began a long war against Navajos, then living just west of the continental divide, and gradually forced them to the south and west. By the 1750s the last of these Navajos abandoned their homeland. Following this victory, the Southern Utes broke their alliance with Comanches and aligned themselves with the Jicarilla Apaches.[48] This association assured Jicarilla survival in and to the east of the Sangre de Cristo Mountains. From their newly gained territory on the plains, Comanches began to raid into New Mexico from the east. The surviving Tano pueblo of Galisteo, resettled under Spanish direction in 1706 with Tano refugees from pueblos north of Santa Fe, managed to survive Comanche depredations into the Galisteo Basin until 1793, when it was abandoned. These Tanos joined the people of Santo Domingo pueblo.[49] Farther south, Comanche raids into the country of Mescalero Apaches cut them off from their buffalo-hunting grounds east of the Pecos River.[50] Repeated attacks upon the pueblo of Pecos on the eastern frontier plus the ravages of epidemics so reduced the population that in 1838 a handful of survivors walked out of the pueblo to join their linguistic relatives at Jemez.[51]

Comanche-Ute hostilities continued to the end of the eighteenth century and beyond. During the first half of the nineteenth century, Southern Utes hunting on the plains clashed not only with their former allies but also with Kiowa, Shawnee, Arapahoe, and Cheyenne Indians who frequented the upper Arkansas River, one of the regions through which these Utes passed on their way to hunt on the plains. The other major Southern Ute access to the plains was through Jicarilla country. This led to considerable trouble along the western end of the Santa Fe Trail in the 1820s and later.[52]

Indian population shifts in New Mexico during the eighteenth and nineteenth centuries were paralleled by similar movements far to the west in Arizona, where Spanish activity was confined mostly to the area south of the Gila River. Halchidhoma Indians, pressed by Mohaves and Yumas living above and below them on the banks of the lower Colorado River, abandoned their homes and fled south in the 1820s, eventually joining Pimas on the Gila River. Maricopa Indians on the Gila near Gila Bend and Yavapais of central Arizona, separated by a strip of no-man's-land which had been developed over centuries of conflict, continued their hostilities; but the Maricopas, also a target of Yuma attacks from the west, finally moved east and took refuge among Pimas by the 1840s.[53] As in New Mexico, native groups in Arizona battled among themselves, with even less or no communication or contact with the Spaniards.

Thus, over a span of almost three hundred years, Indian territories and pueblos in the Southwest shifted, contracted, or expanded—often radically. Events after the arrival of the first Spaniards indicate that most of these changes resulted from hostilities (many probably originating in prehistoric times) between Indian groups rather than from Spanish intrusion. One might well wonder how many population shifts of this nature occurred in prehistoric times. In the case of the historic period nomadic Indians of New Mexico, Spanish interference in intertribal warfare was sporadic. The warring tribes' almost constant preoccupation with intertribal friction undoubtedly reduced contacts with and influence of Spanish culture. Spanish-appointed Pueblo officials, really buffers between Spanish officialdom and Pueblo caciques and other leaders, probably played a large part in minimizing any change. In addition, the complex intertwining of Pueblo ceremonial societies and kinship groups provided a society stronger than that of the frontier Spaniards in which friction between church and state probably created a greater split than any conflict within any pueblo during the Spanish period.

These hostilities appear to have played a major role in limiting the amount of cultural exchange among the groups involved, up to the mid-nineteenth century. Spanish alliances with one-time enemies, such as Jicarillas, Utes, Navajos, and Comanches, intended to protect Spanish settlements menaced at the time they were made, seem to have had little effect on the culture of these Indians. Although Spanish punitive expeditions, undertaken with Indian allies, were sometimes victorious, they gained little more than a brief respite from aggression. Lack of central authority among the occasionally vanquished nomadic groups made it impossible to impose terms on all people of any one group, with the result that normal culture exchange had a minimum time in which to operate. It was not until the 1870s, when the United States introduced the reservation system, that Indian population shifts in the Southwest were brought to a halt. And this in turn, because of territorial and associated cultural restrictions, quickly broke down what remained of the indigenous cultures of most of the groups involved.

NOTES

1. George P. Hammond and Agapito Rey, *Narratives of the Coronado Expedition* (Albuquerque, 1940), pp. 233–34.
2. *Ibid.*, p. 244; ". . . four strong pueblos in the craggy land."
3. Albert H. Schroeder and Dan S. Matson, *A Colony on the Move* (Santa Fe, 1965), pp. 131–32, 160; H. P. Mera, "Population Changes in the Rio Grande Glaze Paint Area," *Laboratory of Anthropology Technical Series*, Bulletin 9 (Santa Fe, 1940), p. 18; Bertha P. Dutton, *Sun Father's Way: The Kiva Murals of Kuaua* (Albuquerque, 1963), pp. 22–23, 33, 204.
4. Hammond and Rey, *Narratives*, p. 258.
5. George P. Hammond and Agapito Rey, *The Gallegos Relation of the Rodríguez Expedition to New Mexico,* Historical Society of New Mexico Publications in History, vol. 4 (Santa Fe, 1927), p. 29.
6. *Ibid.*, p. 25; George P. Hammond and Agapito Rey, *The Rediscovery of New Mexico, 1580–1594* (Albuquerque, 1966), p. 303.
7. George P. Hammond and Agapito Rey, *The Espejo Expedition into New Mexico Made by Antonio de Espejo, 1582–1583* (Los Angeles, 1929), pp. 94–95.
8. France V. Scholes, "Juan Martínez de Montoya, Settler and Conquistador of New Mexico," NMHR, vol. 19 (1944), p. 340; George P. Hammond and Agapito Rey, *Don Juan de Oñate: Colonizer of New Mexico, 1595–1628* (Albuquerque, 1953), p. 1059.
9. Frederick W. Hodge, George P. Hammond, and Agapito Rey, *Fray Alonso de Benavides' Revised Memorial of 1634* (Albuquerque, 1945), p. 86; Hammond and Rey, *Oñate*, p. 1094.
10. *Ibid.*, pp. 400, 838; J. Manuel Espinosa, *Crusaders of the Rio Grande* (Chicago, 1942), p. 204; Schroeder and Matson, p. 124.
11. Harold C. Fritts, "Tree-ring Evidence for Climatic Changes in Western North America," *Monthly Weather Review*, vol. 93 (1965), fig. 3 (A.D. 1556–1590).
12. Schroeder and Matson, pp. 117–18. For irrigation at Acoma and Zuñi, see Hammond and Rey, *Espejo*, pp. 87, 92.
13. Hammond and Rey, *Gallegos*, pp. 24, 26, 36; Schroeder and Matson, pp. 115, 147.
14. France V. Scholes, "Church and State in New Mexico," NMHR, vol. 11 (1936), p. 324; Charles Wilson Hackett, *Historical Documents Relating to New Mexico, Nueva Vizcaya and Approaches Thereto, to 1773*, 3 vols. (Washington, 1937), vol. 3, p. 264.
15. Hammond and Rey, *Espejo*, pp. 111–12.
16. Hammond and Rey, *Oñate*, p. 478.
17. Espinosa, *Crusaders*, p. 297; J. Manuel Espinosa, *First Expedition of Vargas into New Mexico* (Albuquerque, 1940), p. 154.
18. Charles Lummis, "Fray Zárate Salmerón's Relacion," *Land of Sunshine*, vol. 11 (1899), p. 346.
19. Espinosa, *Crusaders*, pp. 86, 200; Albert H. Schroeder, "Navajo and Apache Relationships West of the Rio Grande," *El Palacio*, vol. 70 (1963), p. 7.
20. R. E. Twitchell, *Leading Facts of New Mexican History*, 2 vols. (Cedar Rapids, 1911–17), vol. l, pp. 346–50; Scholes, "Church and State," p. 324.
21. Hackett, *Historical Documents*, vol. 3, pp. 292, 298.

22. Hodge, Hammond, and Rey, pp. 64, 84–85, 248.

23. C. W. Hackett and C. C. Shelby, *Revolt of the Pueblo Indians of New Mexico and Otermín's Attempted Reconquest, 1680–82*, 2 vols. (Albuquerque, 1942), vol. 1, p. ccii, vol. 2, pp. 203–07; Espinosa, *Crusaders*, p. 234.

24. Erik K. Reed, "The Southern Tewa Pueblos in the Historic Period," *El Palacio*, vol. 50 (1943).

25. Espinosa, *Crusaders*, p. 86.

26. *Ibid.*, pp. 57, 60–61, 84, 139–40, 144; Espinosa, *Vargas*, pp. 98–99, 109–10; Hodge, Hammond, and Rey, pp. 260–62; Schroeder and Matson, pp. 144–45.

27. R. E. Twitchell, *Spanish Archives of New Mexico*, 2 vols. (Cedar Rapids, 1914), vol. 2, p. 269.

28. Albert H. Schroeder, "A Brief History of the Southern Utes," *Southwestern Lore*, vol. 30 (1965), pp. 56–57.

29. Hackett and Shelby, p. 208.

30. Espinosa, *Vargas*, pp. 98–99, 109–10; Espinosa, *Crusaders*, pp. 86, 137, 204.

31. Espinosa, *Crusaders*, pp. 136–37.

32. *Ibid.*, pp. 60, 140.

33. A. F. Bandelier, *Final Report of Investigations among the Indians of the Southwestern United States* (Cambridge, 1892), pt. 2, pp. 573–74; J. Manuel Espinosa, "The Legend of Sierra Azul," NMHR, vol. 9 (1934), pp. 125, 127–30.

34. Herbert E. Bolton, *Kino's Historical Memoir of Pimería Alta*, 2 vols. (Berkeley and Los Angeles, 1919), vol. 1, pp. 121, 145–46, 162, 165–66, 178–81; Juan Mateo Manje, *Unknown Arizona and Sonora, 1693–1721*, tr. by Harry J. Karns (Tucson, 1954), pp. 96–97.

35. Bolton, *Kino*, vol. 1, pp. 171–72, 199; Rufus K. Wyllys, "Padre Luis Velarde's Relación of Pimería Alta, 1716," NMHR, vol. 6 (1931), p. 139; Donald Rowland, "The Sonora Frontier of New Spain, 1735–45."

36. Karns, p. 79.

37. Edward H. Spicer, *Cycles of Conquest* (Tucson, 1962), p. 131.

38. Frank D. Reeve, "Navaho-Spanish Wars, 1680–1720," NMHR, vol. 33 (1958), pp. 210–11.

39. Hodge, Hammond, and Rey, p. 237.

40. Reed, "Southern Tewa."

41. A. B. Thomas, *After Coronado* (Norman, 1935), pp. 110 ff.

42. Hodge, Hammond, and Rey, p. 298.

43. Thomas, *After Coronado*, pp. 60–75.

44. Hackett, *Historical Documents*, vol. 3, pp. 405–06; Hodge, Hammond, and Rey, pp. 254–55.

45. Reed, "Southern Tewa."

46. Ulibarrí Journal, July 28; Valverde Journal, Sept. 22, Oct. 14 and 16, in Thomas, *After Coronado*.

47. *Ibid.*, pp. 115, 211, 218–19, 257, 337.

48. A. B. Thomas, *The Plains Indians and New Mexico, 1751–1778* (Albuquerque, 1940), pp. 29–30, 131.

49. Reed, "Southern Tewa."

50. A. B. Thomas, *Forgotten Frontiers* (Norman, 1932), pp. 15, 63–64.

51. Hodge, Hammond, and Rey, p. 273.

52. Schroeder, "Southern Utes," pp. 62–63.

53. Herbert E. Bolton, *Anza's California Expeditions*, 5 vols. (Berkeley, 1930), vol. 2, p. 376; Silas St. John to Acting Commissioner of Indian Affairs, Jan. 18, 1860, U.S. National Archives, Record Group 75; Ronald L. Ives, "Sedelmayr's Relacion of 1746," *Bureau of*

American Ethnology, Bulletin 123 (1939), p. 110; Bolton, *Anza*, vol. 5, pp. 224–45; Leslie Spier, *Yuman Tribes of the Gila River* (Chicago, 1933), pp. 9, 39; Albert H. Schroeder, "An Archeological Survey of the Painted Rock Reservoir, Western Arizona," *The Kiva*, vol. 27 (1961), no. 1, pp. 1–28; William H. Emory, *Notes of a Military Reconnaissance, from Fort Leavenworth, in Missouri, to San Diego, in California*, Senate Ex. Doc., No. 7, 30th Congress, 1st Session (Washington, 1848) p. 89.

15

Indians and the Breakdown of the Spanish Mission System in California*

George Harwood Phillips

Editor's Introduction

The preceding article by Albert Schroeder suggests that a balanced understanding of human activity in the Southwest requires looking at events from Indians' viewpoints as well as Spaniards' perspectives. In the present essay, another ethnohistorian, George Phillips, also demonstrates the importance of angle of vision in perceiving the past.

Phillips examines the Indians' roles in the Calfornia mission system.[1] He tries to understand missionization as a process involving two peoples, both of whom play a role in shaping historical events. Phillips rejects the notion of the California Indians as passive and ahistorical and offers in its place a fresh and provocative interpretation. Herbert Bolton, as we have seen in an earlier essay, regarded the mission as an institution that represented an arm of the Spanish crown reaching out onto the frontier to pacify and civilize Indians. Phillips also sees the mission as an institution,

**Ethnohistory*, 21 (1974): 291–301. This article is reprinted here with minor alterations with permission of the author and the American Society for Ethnohistory.

but to him it approximates a "plural institution," such as a penitentiary or a mental institution, in which a small staff (the padres) forcibly controls a large number of culturally distinct inmates (the Indians). Some of the mission Indians in California, Phillips suggests, responded to this arrangement just as modern inmates would. Rather than passively accept control by a minority, they disrupted the system and contributed to its eventual destruction.

George Phillips holds the Ph.D. from UCLA where he received training in both social anthropology and history. His appreciation of other viewpoints has grown out of experience in Africa and formal study in African history. Phillips was a school teacher in Tanzania and taught African History at the University of the West Indies in Jamaica for two years. He has also taught American Indian History at UCLA and is presently assistant professor of Indian and Southwestern History at the University of Colorado. His book, *Chiefs and Challengers: Indian Resistance and Cooperation in Southern California* (Berkeley: 1975) has won critical acclaim.

NOTE

1. Phillips is not alone in this effort. Sherburne F. Cook launched the first serious assault on the one-sided mission literature in *The Conflict Between the California Indian and White Civilization*, published serially in the 1940s and reprinted in a single volume in 1976 by the University of California Press. Two examinations of aspects of this question appeared recently in the *Journal of San Diego History:* Robert Heizer, "Impact of Colonization on the Native California Societies," 24 (1978): 121–39, and Robert Archibald's more temperate "Indian Labor at the California Missions: Slavery or Salvation?" 24 (1978): 172–82.

Indians and the Breakdown of the Spanish Mission System in California

Writing in 1769, a Franciscan missionary asserted that the California Indians were "without religion, or government, [having] nothing more than diverse superstitions and a type of democracy similar to that of ants." Similarly, in 1851 an Anglo-American visitor to California claimed that "the extreme indolence of their nature, the squalid condition in which they live, the pusillanimity of their sports, and the general imbecility of their intellects, render them rather objects of contempt than admiration."[1]

Because statements such as these abound in the primary documentation, it is not difficult to understand why historians (often the prisoners of their source materials) have considered the Indians of California backward and inferior. Thus in 1930 Fr. Zephrin Engelhardt, the author of a dozen or so books on the California missions, could write that "all accounts agree in representing the natives of California as among the most stupid, brutish, filthy, lazy and improvident of all the aborigines of America."[2] In the 1953 edition of his textbook, *California*, John Caughey wrote:

> The Californians lacked the military cunning and ferocity that inspired respect for the Indians of the Plains and Eastern Woodlands. They were not such expert craftsmen in woodworking as their neighbors on the Northwest Coast, nor had they so interesting an art form or so highly developed a social system. They were obviously inferior to the Pueblo Indians in the Southwest, who had developed multi-storied buildings, agriculture and irrigation, excellent textiles and pottery, and a complex social organization.[3]

And as recently as 1966 Florian F. Guest stated that California Indian existence was "haphazard, irresponsible, brutish, benighted, and barbaric."[4]

When Indians are viewed as either stupid and brutish or just culturally inferior, their historical importance is not appreciated. Even those historians genuinely sympathetic to the Indians seldom consider them anything more than passive observers of their own demise, doing little to alter the conditions imposed by succeeding waves of Whites and thereby playing an insignificant role in the historical process.

This picture of Indian passivity (and thereby historical unimportance) is no more clearly drawn than in the events known as the secularization of the California missions. During the late 1820s and 1830s, the Mexican government passed a number of laws that, while not intending to destroy the mission system, were designed to reduce the powers of the Spanish missionaries, to break up the mission estates, and to distribute lands and goods to the neophytes (as the Indian converts were called) and to deserving Mexicans. By the 1840s the mission system in California was in ruins.

Historians have attributed the collapse solely to the activities of land-hungry Mexican officials and aristocrats who cheated the neophytes out of their promised lands. They give no recognition to the possibility that the neophytes themselves might have played an active role in the process of breakdown. For example, according to Andrew F. Rolle, during secularization "the mission Indians stood apathetically by as deeply confused, helpless witnesses."[5] Furthermore, most historians claim that secularization forced the neophytes to leave the missions. To Hubert Howe Bancroft, "the mission, broken up and despoiled, no longer afforded shelter to its children, save a few of more solid character. . . . The rest had been dispersed to seek refuge among the settlers or in the wilderness."[6] Similarly, Robert Glass Cleland has stated that secularization "scattered the partly civilized neophytes like sheep without a shepherd."[7]

This paper challenges these views. It will be shown that most of the neophytes were not forced to leave the missions during secularization but withdrew willingly and thereby played an important and active role in the breakdown of the mission system. To support this assertion, it will be necessary to discuss neophyte behavioral patterns and mission social structure by drawing upon both historical documentation and sociological theory. Following the concepts of the social anthropologist M. G. Smith and the sociologist Erving Goffman, the mission will be analyzed as a plural institution.

The Plural Society and the Total Institution

To M. G. Smith, population groups found within societies sometimes form distinct cultural sections. According to the distribution and function of its cultural sections, a society will exhibit either heterogeneous or plural features. A heterogeneous society contains distinct cultural sections and manifests varying degrees of social, political, and economic differentiation. But the majority of the population forms a cultural section that shares a common belief in the society's traditions and institutions.[8] Those sections represented by minorities usually present no serious threat to the social order. In the plural society, however, a cultural section representing only a minority of the population regulates the affairs of the inclusive unit. Perpetually occupied in preserving its economic, social, and political supremacy, the dominant cultural minority often maintains its position through serfdom, peonage, slavery, colonialism, or through a restricted political franchise.[9] Thus, in a plural society the majority of the population are not citizens but subjects.[10]

Since individual mobility and collective assimilation are minimized, it is virtually impossible to transfer from one cultural section to another.[11] There is, of course, interaction between members of the distinct cultural sections and assimilation sometimes takes place. Some acculturated members of the dominated section even align themselves with their rulers as trusted but expendable aides and assistants. But most subjects are reduced to frustration and dissidence, since social identity is ascriptive and sectional in base.[12]

If the plural society is to remain stable, sectional identities and boundaries should be preserved by maintaining religious, familial, educational, occupational, economic, and political inequalities. And the cohesion and superior organization to which the rulers owe their initial dominance should be continued through collective action that preserves their exclusiveness.[13] Because of its sectional inequalities, however, the plural society is subjected to severe structural strains. Any change in intersectional relations produces changes in the inclusive unit.[14] And if the position of the dominant minority is weakened, control over the total unit becomes uncertain. As a result, the dominated majority will often blatantly challenge the authority of their rulers.[15]

Similar to the plural society is the total institution as defined by Erving Goffman. Fundamentally, it is an organization in which the majority of members, the inmates, are controlled by a small supervisory staff. The responsibility of the staff is not the guidance or periodic inspection of the inmates, as in many employer-employee relations, but surveillance. Because of the sharp divisions within the institution, staff and inmates may stereotype one another. The staff may view the inmates as untrustworthy, bitter, and secretive, while the inmates may see the staff as condescending, high-handed, and mean.[16]

Before incorporation into a total institution, the inmates had a conception of themselves that was a result of the social arrangements they found in their home environment. Upon entrance, however, this conception begins to change, and in some institutions the process is intensified when the inmates are forced into a series of abasements, degradation, humiliations, and profanations of self.[17] Because most members of the staff have the right to inflict punishment, the inmates may live with chronic anxiety about breaking the rules.[18] Thus, for many, the full meaning of being inside a total institution does not exist apart from the desire to get out.[19]

It is evident that Smith and Goffman are discussing very similar types of social structures. However, while Smith is dealing at the most inclusive level of political and social organization, Goffman is concerned with the social structure of subordinate units. The Republic of South Africa and many present-day ex-colonial countries constitute plural societies.[20] The total institution is represented by penitentiaries, slave plantations, mental hospitals, and monasteries to mention only a few.[21] As will become apparent, the mission clearly fits the model of Goffman's total institution and possesses most of the characteristics of Smith's plural society. Because it lacked societal inclusiveness, Smith would probably identify the mission as a community. But since the concepts of both scholars are being utilized, perhaps the compromise term "plural institution" might best be applied to the Spanish mission.

The Mission as a Plural Institution

The mission was the principal vehicle of the Spanish colonization of Alta California, not because it was thought to be the most suitable institution for the undertaking but because the Spanish lacked the men and motivation to engage in a large scale colonization effort. Actually, the acculturated Indians were to preserve California for the Spanish crown. By congregating them into the missions, by converting them to Christianity, and by teaching them the arts and sciences of Europe, missionaries would make the Indians the region's main colonizing force. Once an area had been effectively transformed, the missionaries would move on to new frontiers.

Because the Spanish provincial government issued few land grants to private individuals, the missionaries could claim as much territory as they thought they could administer. The general area controlled by each mission was arranged between church and government officials; fixed boundaries were not deemed necessary. Since the missions were regarded as only temporary establishments, eventually to be turned into pueblos, titles were held by the Spanish crown.[22] Only the mission itself, comprising the buildings, cemetery, orchards, and vineyards, belonged exclusively to the Catholic Church.[23] The missions were, however, semi-independent of the provincial government, for only in cases of serious crime did the state assert its authority.[24]

Many of the so-called Spaniards who arrived in Alta California, beginning in 1769, were of mixed ethnic and racial backgrounds. But as *gente de razón*, or people of reason, they considered themselves distinct from and superior to both the unconverted and Christian Indians. Their group identity was shaped not so much by their common interests as by their insignificant numbers, for they formed only a tiny minority at any one mission. In 1816, for example, the *gente de razón* at Mission San Buenaventura totalled only thirty souls.[25]

At most missions, however, the neophyte population averaged between 500 and 600 persons and sometimes ranged between 1,000 and 2,000.[26] Large numbers of Indians were needed to keep the missions operating. Neophytes planted, tended, and harvested wheat, barley, corn, peas, beans, and various other crops. Mission equipment was produced in the shops where the neophytes made bricks, tiles, pottery, shoes, saddles, hats, clothes, candles, and soap. Indians also tended the herds of cattle, sheep, and horses that grazed on the numerous ranchos possessed by each mission. Carpentry, tanning, shearing, spinning, and blacksmithing were other tasks undertaken by the neophytes.[27] They were, indeed, the economic backbone of the mission system.

Some neophytes, moreover, occupied positions of authority. In 1779 the governor of California issued a decree stating that the resident Indians at each mission should elect from their own ranks two *alcaldes*, or magistrates, and two *regidores*, or councilmen.[28] However, the "Spaniards" made sure that only the most acculturated and the most favored became mission officers. This point is emphasized by a neophyte, Pablo Tac, who noted that the padres "appointed alcaldes from the people themselves that knew how to speak Spanish more than the others and were better than the others in their customs."[29]

Apparently the alcaldes took their work very seriously. A visitor to Mission San Luis Rey remarked that they "are very rigid in exacting the performances of the allotted tasks, applying the rod to those who fell short of the portion of labor assigned them."[30] Another visitor to the same mission reported that while the majority of the neophytes attended mass on their own, "it was not unusual to see numbers of them driven along by alcaldes, and under the whip's lash forced to the very doors of the sanctuary."[31] According to an early Anglo-American resident, the alcaldes were chosen from the most lazy, the padres being of the opinion that they took great pleasure in making the others work. "They carried a wand to denote their authority, and what was more terrible, an immense scourage of raw hide, about ten feet in length, plaited to the thickness of an ordinary man's wrist! They did a great deal of chastisement, both by and without orders."[32]

Those neophytes who disobeyed the alcaldes or the padres were subjected to varying degrees and different kinds of punishment. Writes one Franciscan:

> The punishments resorted to at Santa Barbara are the shackles, the lash, and the stocks, but only when we find that corrections and

> reproofs are unavailing. Seldom are the women punished with any of the above instruments but the stocks. . . . A man, a boy, or a woman, runs away or does not return from the excursion, so that other neophytes must be sent after them. When such a one is brought back to the mission, he is reproached for not having heard holy Mass on a day of obligation. He is made to see that he has of his own free will taken upon himself this and other Christian duties, and he is warned that he will be chastized if he repeats the transgression. He runs away again, and again he is brought back. This time he is chastized with the lash or with the stocks. If this is not sufficient, as is the case with some who disregard a warning, he is made to feel the shackles, which he must wear three days while at work. This same punishment is meted out to such as are caught in concubinage.[33]

The documentation clearly demonstrates that Indian discontent with mission life was prevalent from the very inception of the system and was often manifested in fugitivism. In 1779 a padre admitted that even those Indians who were on the sick list, thereby receiving the best care the mission could provide, ran away. "The majority of our neophytes have not yet acquired much love for our way of life; and they see and meet their pagan relatives in the forest, fat and robust and enjoying complete liberty.[34] In 1819 a missionary lamented that "the spirit of insubordination, which is rampant in the world at large, has reached the Christian Indians. A considerable number have withdrawn from the mild rule of the friars."[35] An Englishman who visited California in the mid-1820s mentioned that "after they became acquainted with the nature of the institution, and felt themselves under restraint, many absconded. Even now, notwithstanding the difficulty of escaping, desertions are of frequent occurrence."[36]

Because the Indians were continually withdrawing from the missions, sometimes to return on their own, other times to be brought back by force, the neophyte population was never static, and so valid information on desertion rates is most difficult to come by. But according to Sherburne Cook, of the over 81,000 Indians who had been baptized by 1831, nearly 3,500, or one out of twenty-four, had successfully escaped. And from 1831 to 1834 some 2,000 more neophytes "illegally" withdrew from the missions.[37] Ironically, however, the life of the mission system, or at least the lives of individual missions, may have been prolonged because of the high rate of desertion. The missions witnessed few serious uprisings, presumably because those who were the most discontented and thereby potentially the most dangerous had an alternative to violence.

It should be apparent that the Spanish mission in California possessed all the characteristics of the plural institution. The "Spaniards," represented by two priests, a few soldiers and laymen, comprised the institution's staff whose primary occupation, given the problem of fugitivism, was surveillance. As the dominant cultural section that formed only a tiny minority of a mission's population, the "Spaniards" saw themselves as superior in all ways to the Indians and often viewed them as untrustworthy and secretive.

In contrast, as the inmates of the mission, the neophytes formed a cultural section that constituted a population majority with distinct burdens and disabilities. Since social identity was ascriptive, there was no way in which the neophytes could change their sectional status. Even those who adopted much of Spanish culture and became alcaldes were prevented from transferring into the dominant cultural section. The cruelty they exhibited toward their fellow neophytes is probably a reflection of the frustrations they felt at being rejected by the very group they sought to emulate and please. Subjected to various kinds and degrees of punishment, many neophytes were degraded and humiliated and certainly must have regarded the "Spaniards" and their trusted Indian assistants as mean and high-handed. Large numbers probably lived with chronic anxiety about breaking the rules. And for many, full meaning of being inside the mission probably did not exist apart from the desire to get out.

The Breakdown of the Mission System

By the 1820s, fugitivism, disease, and a declining mission birth rate were drastically reducing the neophyte population. For example, Mission San Juan Capistrano claimed a total of 1,361 neophytes in 1812, but by 1820 the number was down to 1,064, and by 1830 it had dropped to 925.[38] Unless the padres had been able to tap new population centers, it seems likely that the mission system would have come to a gradual and unspectacular conclusion. As it was, political developments in Mexico hastened its demise in a most sudden and dramatic way.

When the Mexican war for independence broke out in 1810, the annual stipend of 400 pesos issued to each missionary by the Viceroy of New Spain was terminated, and the missions were subjected to taxation and forced requisitions by the provincial government. Thrown back on their own resources, many of the missions subsisted by selling hides and tallow to American and English sea merchants. The end of the war in 1821 failed to improve the situation, for the new Mexican government, facing grave financial problems, was unable to send more than token assistance.[39]

The Mexican government, however, was not unconcerned as to the condition of the Indian. Infused with the egalitarian and humanitarian beliefs of the day, it sought to improve the lot of all the Indians within its vast territory. Government officials realized that only when released from their servile position in society would the Indians become useful citizens of Mexico.[40] Consequently, the first Mexican governor of California issued a Proclamation of Emancipation on July 25, 1826, which stated that certain neophytes within the military districts of San Diego, Santa Barbara, and Monterey would be released from missionary supervision. To be set free, however, were only those whom the Franciscans thought capable of supporting themselves.[41]

Neophyte response to the proclamation varied from mission to mission, but many Indians took immediate advantage of their new freedom. "In my former visit to this country," wrote an English sea captain in 1828,

> I remarked that the padres were much mortified at being desired to liberate from the missions all the Indians who bore good characters, and who were acquainted with the art of tilling the ground. In consequence of their remonstrances the government modified the order, and consented to make the experiment upon a few only at first, and desired that a certain number might be settled in the proposed manner. After a few months' trial much to his surprise, he found that these people who had been always accustomed to the care and discipline of schoolboys, finding themselves their own masters, indulged freely in all those excesses which it had been the endeavor of their tutors to repress, and that many having gambled away their clothes, implements, and even their lands, were compelled to beg or plunder in order to support life. They at length became so obnoxious to the peaceable inhabitants, that the padres were requested to take some of them back to the missions, while others who had been guilty of misdemeanor were loaded with shackles and put to work.[42]

Cutting through the paternalism and ethnocentrism of this statement, one realizes that the neophytes were not exhibiting the behavioral patterns of disobedient school boys but were manifesting the kind of psychological disorientation that often accompanies decolonization.

In August 1833, the Mexican government passed a law that secularized all the missions of Alta and Baja California. The governor of Alta California delayed implementing the law until a year later when he issued his own secularization decree. It stated that the missionaries were to relinquish all secular control over the neophytes and were to perform only religious duties until replaced by parish priests. The missions were to be converted into pueblos and their lands distributed among the neophytes. Each head of a family or adult male over twenty years of age was to receive thirty three acres of land. Half the missions' livestock, tools, and seeds were also to be distributed among the neophytes, but all surplus lands, cattle, and other property would become the responsibility of the missions' civil administrators who would be appointed by the governor. Furthermore, according to the decree, the government possessed the right to force the neophytes to work in the vineyards, orchards, and fields that remained undistributed. Indians could not sell or otherwise dispose of their newly acquired property. If an owner died without an heir, his lands would revert to the state.[43]

At many of the missions, the majority of the neophytes exhibited no interest in acquiring mission lands or in having anything more to do with the system. For example, in 1834 the newly appointed civil administrator of Mission San Luis Rey complained of neophyte disobedience.

> These Indians will do absolutely no work nor obey my orders. In consequence, though the season for sowing the wheat is at hand, and the necessary plows have been prepared, I must suffer the pain of being obliged to suspend work for want of hands. The men have mistaken the voice of reason and even of the authority which orders the work, for they declare they are a free nation. In order to enjoy their obstinancy better, they have fled from their houses and abandoned their aged parents, who alone are now at this ex-Mission.
>
> I have sent various alcaldes to the sierra in order to see if, with sweetness and gentleness, we might succeed in having them return to their homes; but the result was the opposite of my desires. Nothing would suit them, nothing would change their ideas, neither the well-being which must result for their good behavior, nor the privations which they suffer in their wanderings. All with one voice would shout. "We are free! We do not want to obey! We do not want to work!"[44]

In 1835 an English visitor to California predicted a quick end for the missions. The neophytes "have been compelled to live under a restraint they could not bear. . . . I believe a great deal both of force and fraud were used in congregating them together in the missions; and the moment that force shall be altogether withdrawn, I have no doubt that the majority of them will return to the woods."[45] Indeed, once force was withdrawn, the termination of the mission system came rapidly. Most of the neophytes either sought work on the great Mexican ranchos then being carved out of mission territory or wandered into the towns, such as Los Angeles, to work intermittently and to drink and gamble. Others trekked inland to join independent Indian societies. Between 1834 and

1843, it is estimated that the neophyte population declined from over 30,000 to under 5,000.[46]

Conclusion

Eurocentric in their attitudes and often prisoners of a biased documentation, historians generally view the Indian as having played only an insignificant role in California history and no role at all in the collapse of the Spanish mission system. Their commonly held position states that the mission system was brought to an end by the activities of land-hungry Mexican officials and aristocrats who forced the neophytes to leave the missions by cheating them out of their promised lands. This view, however, overlooks the documentation that discloses neophyte behavioral patterns and it fails to acknowledge the importance of mission social structure in determing neophyte activity.

It will be recalled that the plural institution is characterized by sectional divisions in which a dominant cultural minority, the staff, regulates the affairs of the entire unit. If the structure is to remain stable, sectional identities and boundaries should be preserved and the cohesion and superior organization of the rulers maintained. Changes in intersectional relations, however, produce changes in the entire unit, and once the position of the staff is weakened, control over the institution becomes uncertain. The dominated cultural majority, the inmates, will then often blatantly challenge the ruling section.

Exhibiting social and political inequalities in which "Spaniards" and Indians formed distinct cultural sections, the mission, from its inception, was subjected to perpetual structural strains. This is most clearly seen in the continuous process of withdrawal. But significant changes in intersectional relations did not occur until the secularization laws stripped the staff of each mission of its temporal powers and thus gave the inmates new alternatives of action.

Some of the neophytes attempted to salvage whatever they could from their years of labor and were often cheated out of their promised lands and driven from the missions. But contrary to established opinion, most were not forced to leave, but withdrew willingly. This was in keeping with much of their past activity, for the withdrawal taking place after secularization represents an intensification of a process that had been going on throughout the entire mission period. Prior to secularization, however, escape was usually a matter of individual initiative. Afterwards, the neophytes could blatantly challenge the authority of their now politically emasculated rulers by withdrawing *en masse* with little fear of capture and punishment.

Their action was a near unanimous rejection of an oppressive social system, the final and most dramatic manifestation of a long-standing and very profound discontent. Furthermore, it demonstrates that the neophytes played an important role in the breakdown of the Spanish mission system in California. Far from being passive observers of their own destruction, doing little if anything to alter their colonized status, the neophytes were active agents in the historical process and deserve to be recognized as such.

NOTES

1. Quoted in Jack Forbes, ed., *The American Indian in America's Past* (Englewood Cliffs, N.J.: 1964), pp. 15–16.

2. Fr. Zephyrin Engelhardt, *The Missions and Missionaries of California*, 2d. ed., vol. 2, *Upper California*, pt. I (Santa Barbara, California: 1930), p. 245.

3. John Caughey, *California*, 2nd ed. (Englewood Cliffs, 1953), p. 19. To Professor Caughey's credit, this passage was eliminated in later editions of his textbook.

4. Florian F. Guest, "The Indian Policy Under Fermín Francisco de Lasuén, California's Second Father President," *California Historical Society Quarterly*, 45 (1963): 206–7.

5. Andrew F. Rolle, *California: A History* (New York: 1963), pp. 157–58.

6. Hubert Howe Bancroft, *California Pastoral 1769–1848* (San Francisco: 1888), pp. 241–42.

7. Robert Glass Cleland, *The Cattle on a Thousand Hills: Southern California, 1850–1870*, 2d ed. (San Marino, Calif.: 1951), pp. 22–23.

8. M. G. Smith, "Institutional and Political Conditions of Pluralism," in *Pluralism in Africa*, ed. M. G. Smith and Leo Kuper (Berkeley: 1969), p. 36.

9. Ibid., p. 38.

10. Ibid., p. 33.

11. M. G. Smith, "Pluralism in Precolonial African Societies," in *Pluralism in Africa*, ed. M. G. Smith and Leo Kuper (Berkeley: 1969), p. 96.

12. Smith, "Conditions of Pluralism," pp. 57–58.

13. Ibid., pp. 54–55.

14. M. G. Smith, *The Plural Society in the British West Indies* (Berkeley: 1965), pp. 14–15.

15. Smith, "Conditions of Pluralism," p. 58.

16. Irving Goffman, *Asylums: Essays on the Social Situation of Mental Patients and Other Inmates* (New York: 1962), pp. 6–7.

17. Ibid., p. 14.

18. Ibid., p. 42.

19. Ibid., p. 14.

20. Smith, "Some Developments," p. 429.

21. Goffman, Asylums, pp. 4–5.

22. George W. Beattie, "Mission Ranchos and Mexican Grants," *San Bernardino County Historical Society*, 2 (1942): 2–4.

23. Manuel P. Servín, "The Secularization of the California Missions: A Reappraisal," *Southern California Quarterly*, 47 (1965): 136.

24. Guest, "Indian Policy," p. 206.

25. Fr. Zephyrin Engelhardt, *San Buenaventura: The Mission by the Sea* (Santa Barbara, Calif.: 1930), p. 42.

26. Sherburne F. Cook, *The Conflict between the California Indian and White Civilization: I, The Indian Versus the Spanish Mission*, Ibero-Americana, no. 21 (Berkeley: 1943), pp. 86.

27. Hugo Reid, *The Indians of Los Angeles County: Hugo Reid's Letters of 1852*, ed. Robert F. Heizer (Los Angeles: 1968), pp. 82–83; Benjamin Wilson, *The Indians of Southern California in 1852: The B. D. Wilson Report and a Selection of Contemporary Comment*, ed. John Caughey (San Marino, Calif.: 1952), p. 22.

28. Fr. Zephyrin Engelhardt, *San Gabriel Mission and the Beginnings of Los Angeles* (San Gabriel, Calif.: 1927), pp. 43–44.

29. Pablo Tac, *Indian Life and Customs at Mission San Luis Rey*, ed. and trans. Minna and Gordon Hewes (San Luis Rey, Calif.: 1958), p. 19.

30. James O. Pattie, *The Personal Narrative of James O. Pattie of Kentucky*, ed. Timothy Flint (Chicago: 1930), pp. 347–48.

31. Alfred Robinson, *Life in California during a Residence of Several Years in that Territory* (New York: 1846) pp. 25–26.

32. Reid, *The Indians of Los Angeles County*, p. 85.

33. Quoted in Fr. Zephyrin Engelhardt, *San Barbara Mission* (San Francisco: 1923), pp. 80–81.

34. Guest, p. 209. Quoted in Guest, "Indian Policy," p. 209.

35. Quoted in Fr. Zephrin Engelhardt, *The Missions and Missionaries*, vol. 2, *Upper California*, pt. 2 (San Francisco: 1913), pp. 33–39.

36. F. W. Beechey, *Narrative of a Voyage to the Pacific and Beering's Strait in the Years 1825–1828*, pt. I (London: 1831), p. 360.

37. Cook, *The Indian Versus the Spanish Mission*, pp. 58–61.

38. Fr. Zephyrin Engelhardt, *San Juan Capistrano Mission* (Los Angeles: 1922), p. 175.

39. C. Alan Hutchinson, "The Mexican Government and the Mission Indians of Upper California, 1825–1835," *The Americas*, 21, (1965): 335–36.

40. Ibid., p. 340.

41. Engelhardt, *San Juan Capistrano Mission*, pp. 81–82.

42. Beechey, *Narrative*, pp. 582–83.

43. C. Alan Hutchinson, *Frontier Settlement in Mexican California: The Híjar-Padrés Colony and Its Origins, 1769–1835* (New Haven: 1969), pp. 255–260.

44. Quoted in Fr. Zephyrin Engelhardt, *San Luis Rey Mission* (San Francisco: 1921), pp. 96–97.

45. Thomas Coulter, "Notes on Upper California," reprinted from *The Journal of the Royal Geographical Society*, 1835 (Chicago: 1835), p. 67.

46. William Carey Jones, *Report on the Subject of Land Titles in California, Senate Executive Documents*, no. 18, 31st Cong., 1st sess., 1850 (Washington: 1850); p. 27*n*.

Reprinted with permission of the International Folk Art Foundation from *New Mexico Santos: How To Name Them*, illustrated by Frances Breese. Santa Fe, Museum of New Mexico and International Folk Art Foundation, 1966.

16

The Flowering and Decline of the New Mexican *Santero:* 1780–1900*

William Wroth

Editor's Introduction

In political terms, Spanish hegemony over what would become the American Southwest ended in 1821, when the region fell under the control of newly independent Mexico. Culturally, however, Spanish influence remained strong and manifested itself in many ways. In the present essay, William Wroth traces the rise of an art form, the making of wooden images of saints or *santos*, which developed in late eighteenth-century New Mexico and continued under both the Mexican and American governments. *Santeros*—the makers of saints—never became important in Texas or California, but peculiar local circumstances, which Wroth outlines, caused the art to flourish in isolated New Mexico. There, as Wroth explains, *santeros* developed a style that

*This article originally appeared in *The Cross and the Sword* (San Diego: 1976), a catalogue to an exhibition at the Fine Arts Gallery of San Diego, April 3 to May 16, 1976. The essay is reprinted here in revised form with permission of the Director of the Fine Arts Gallery and the author.

did not conform to the ornate, realistic patterns of the day, but that hearkened back to more abstract and simple lines which characterized European *santos* of the twelfth to the fourteenth centuries.

Santos of the style made in New Mexico appeared elsewhere on the frontiers of colonial Spanish America. They are not, then, unique, but they remain of compelling interest. One specialist, Carl Dentzel, has termed them "one of the few indigenous artistic developments in what is now called the United States."[1] Today, *santos* have become fashionable collectors' items, and a twentieth-century revival of the art of the *santero* has reversed the nineteenth-century decline described by Wroth.[2]

A graduate of Yale who holds the Ph.D. in Political Science from the University of Oregon, William Wroth is curator of the Taylor Museum of the Colorado Springs Fine Arts Center and visiting professor at Colorado College's Southwestern Studies Institute. Specializing in the material culture of the Hispanic Southwest, Wroth has most recently edited and contributed to *Hispanic Crafts of the Southwest* (Colorado Springs: 1977), an ambitious exhibition catalogue published by the Taylor Museum. He has in press *The Chapel of Our Lady of Talpa: A Study in Spanish New Mexican Art and Culture* (Colorado Springs).

NOTES

1. "Regional Variations in *Santero* Art," in *The Cross and the Sword*, p. 28.

2. For a general discussion of this revival see Wroth's "Hispanic Southwestern Craft Traditions in the 20th Century," in *Hispanic Crafts of the Southwest*, ed. William Wroth (Colorado Springs: 1977), 1–7.

The Flowering and the Decline of the Art of the New Mexican Santero: *1780–1900*

The late eighteenth century witnessed the development of an indigenous Hispanic folk art in the isolated mountain villages of northern New Mexico. Local artisans began carving and painting images of saints, known as *santos*, to fill a void left by the weakening influence and gradual withdrawal of Spanish Franciscan ecclesiastical authorities.

After 1780 the colony of New Mexico was virtually forgotten in the worldwide turmoil of the Spanish empire. The main link with Spain, and thus with current European thought, was the Franciscan friars, who, because of conflicts with authorities in New Spain, were gradually losing their once great influence in the colony. The Franciscan friars were being replaced by secular Mexican priests under the jurisdiction of the Bishop of Durango, some 1,500 miles south of Santa Fe. The late 1700s and early 1800s saw a dramatic increase in Hispanic population in New Mexico and at the same time a decrease in the number of priests. The Franciscans were greatly reduced by the mid-1820s (nine in 1826 compared to thirty in 1788) and in spite of efforts from Durango there were not enough secular priests in the colony to meet the needs of the expanding population. Also, due to political chaos, a weakened secular authority extended from Spain over this distant colony. It was a moment in history when the usual restraints and influences of political and religious order and authority were at a low point, official institutions were in neglect, and the folk of Spanish New Mexico were obliged to take care of their own lives as best they could.

New Mexico had always been isolated from the main currents of thought and activity in Spain, just as Spain herself was somewhat removed from the humanistic trends in Italy and France and the Protestantism of the Low Countries. The extreme isolation of New Mexico allowed an essentially medieval world-view and cultural pattern to persist unchanged from early colonial days in the simple, hard life of remote villages scattered along the watersheds of the Sangre de Cristo range north of Santa Fe. Medieval forms survived in social and political arrangements, in material culture, and especially in religious organizations and observances. In particular, the lay Brotherhood of Our Father Jesus Nazarene (known as the Penitente Brotherhood and based to large degree upon the Third Order of the Franciscans) perpetuated these forms in their penitential practices, their hymns, and their spirit of communalism. In the first half of the nineteenth century the Penitente

Brotherhood provided, in the absence of church authorities, Holy Week observances and services of prayers and blessings for their remote communities and constituted a lay religious order to take care of both spiritual and material needs.

The diminishing of religious influence in late eighteenth-century New Mexico left a need not only for lay groups such as the Penitentes, but also for *santeros*—makers of *santos*—to provide religious images that formerly had been brought from Spain and Mexico or made by Franciscan friars while stationed in the colony. Nurtured in the medieval atmosphere of remote New Mexican villages, the indigenous *santeros* ignored the provincial baroque style of their Franciscan predecessors and produced, quite naturally, a simpler art form surprisingly close in style and intention to the religious images of Romanesque Spain. These untrained artists were part of a folk culture that still maintained the spiritually-unified medieval world-view in which all aspects of daily life were founded upon devotion and obedience to God. Thus, their art was the natural expression of this spiritual wholeness. Its purpose, like that of art of the Middle Ages, was purely religious: to aid concentration upon the one thing necessary—a virtuous life devoted to observing God's will.

The European humanism of intervening centuries had been completely bypassed. The glorification of human form and achievement which reached its height in the Baroque art and thought of the seventeenth and eighteenth centuries was totally alien to the simple medieval world-view and the hard, spare life of colonial New Mexico. Left on their own, the native *santeros* produced a linear, impersonal art of idealized form reflecting at the folk level the deductive intention of traditional Christian art and the absolutism and unity of the medieval world-view, before the rise of Renaissance humanism and the consequent schisms that afflicted every aspect of Western life and thought. A dramatic illustration of this medieval direction in nineteenth-century New Mexican folk art is seen in the representation of the Holy Trinity as *one being* (Plate 2). This Byzantine representation was banned by the Church in 1745 but persisted in New Mexico past 1850. It is perhaps symbolic of the unity still residing in the Hispanic New Mexican folk culture.

The art of the indigenous *santero* flourished from about 1780 to 1850, reaching its finest expression after 1820. Already by 1820, however, events were in motion that would lead to its demise soon after mid-century.

In 1821 Mexico won its independence from Spain and became a republic with a constitution modeled on that of the United States. This revolutionary change spelled the end of many traditional religious, political, and economic practices of the Spanish monarchy (as they affected New Spain) and opened the way for cultural change and the introduction of modernism in all aspects of life and culture.

PLATE 1. Retablo of Santiago (St. James Major) by the "Calligraphic Artist" (attributed to Pedro Fresquiz, working dates ca. 1780–1830). This artist was the first known to have worked in the distinctive folk art style of New Mexico, producing both sculpture and paintings in the villages of Santa Cruz de la Cañada and Las Truchas. His earliest pieces are estimated by tree-ring dating to be from the 1780s. Collection of the Taylor Museum of the Colorado Springs Fine Arts Center.

PLATE 2. La Santísima Trinidad (the Holy Trinity), artist unknown, first quarter of the nineteenth century. This ancient iconographic type of the Trinity as one being was banned by the Catholic church on several occasions but persisted in isolated areas such as New Mexico well into the nineteenth century. It symbolizes better than the "approved" rendering the Christian notion of unity residing in the triune Godhead. Collection of the Taylor Museum of the Colorado Springs Fine Arts Center.

PLATE 3. Nuestra Señora de los Dolores (Our Lady of Sorrows) by the "Santo Niño" *santero*, ca. 1825–50). The sorrowful Virgin Mary is particularly important to the Penitentes, who focussed in their rituals upon the suffering and crucifixion of Christ. This skillful rendering is representative of the finest New Mexican folk sculpture during the period of flowering of the art. Collection of the Taylor Museum of the Colorado Springs Fine Arts Center.

In 1849 the American Catholic hierarchy successfully petitioned for the appointment of a bishop for the new territory, the first in its history. Jean Baptiste Lamy, a French priest serving in Ohio, arrived in Santa Fe in 1851 and immediately embarked on a program to reform and modernize the practice of Catholicism in New Mexico. His program of reforms proved to be (whether consciously intended or not) influential in diluting many traditional aspects of indigenous Spanish-American culture.

In this program he had the full support of the new Anglo-American merchants, and in turn he aided them by successfully neutralizing the efforts of popular native priests such as Padre Antonio José Martínez to protect Hispanic cultural forms and to keep the territory independent from outside Anglo influence. Before 1850, Bishop José Antonio Laureano de Zubiría of Durango had begun—slowly, limited by lack of resources—to train native New Mexican secular clergy to replace the Spanish Franciscans. Native priests such as Martínez strongly opposed the American occupation and the arrival of the French Bishop Lamy. Martínez was accused of playing a major role in the Taos rebellion of 1847, an attempt to expel the Americans and establish the independence of Hispanic (and Indian) New Mexico. In a final confrontation with Martínez in 1857, when the native padre was excommunicated, Lamy had vocal (and physical if necessary) support of the "American party" in Taos, which included Kit Carson and other prominent nonnative merchants of that community.

Bishop Lamy was, in turn, eager to please the Americans at the expense of Hispanic traditions, for which he seemed to have little respect. In considering the preservation of traditional adobe churches Lamy revealed his insensitivity to this invaluable and central aspect of New Mexican culture, and proclaimed his full sympathy to the Americans, stating in 1851 that he "would rather see every church building in New Mexico destroyed than that one finger should be raised against the civil authorities." He went on to authorize the "improvement" of many native churches through alterations and repairs totally out of keeping with New Mexican architectural style and technique, and he supervised the building of several new churches in the eclectic revivalist Romanesque and Gothic styles then so popular in Europe and America.

With regard to religious art, Lamy brought the sophisticated aesthetic tastes of mid-century Europe to still medieval New Mexico, and his insensitivity to the native *santos* again neatly coincided with the opinions of the American observers of the time who spoke of the "miserable," "crude," and "barbarous" paintings and sculpture they saw in New Mexican churches.

In many churches native *santos* were replaced with bland, mass-produced plaster saints and cheap Currier and Ives prints. With trade routes firmly established, these commercial products flooded the New Mexican market and provided a lucrative business for local merchants. Rather quickly the art of the native *santero* was superseded and began to decline. The major *santeros* of the first half of the nineteenth century were gone before 1865. The prolific "Calligraphic Artist" (whose work has been attributed to Pedro Fresquíz) ceased working by the 1830s. Molleno worked perhaps no later than 1845. José Aragón of Chamisal migrated to Senesú near El Paso sometime after 1835, it is said, to avoid the American occupation. J. Rafael Aragón died in the early 1860s. With a few notable exceptions, there was no one to follow these *santeros* and the tradition died out by 1900.

In the period of decline major changes can be noted in the work of surviving *santeros*. First, native skill was soon lost and the images became much cruder. This is especially apparent in the later *retablos* (paintings on pine boards). Second, native technical knowledge for preparation and use of gesso and colors rapidly declined, and pieces of this period tend to disintegrate more rapidly than the earlier work or were painted with house paints. Finally, the major demand for native *santos* now came from the Penitente *moradas* (meeting houses), often in the more remote areas, north and west of Taos. Consequently, many images from this period are figures of the sorrowful Virgin Mary and the suffering Christ.

The Penitente brotherhoods survived as the bastion of New Mexican folk culture, withstanding an onslaught that began with Bishop Zubiría's condemnation in 1833 and was intensified after 1851 by Bishop Lamy and later Bishop J. B. Salpointe, and by the scandalized Protestant Americans. The pressures of the modern world against the Penitentes forced them to become more secretive. After 1833 they no longer used the churches for their observances and the *moradas* were established. After the American occupation (1846) Penitentes from Taos and farther south migrated northward settling in the San Luis Valley, motivated in part by the desire to avoid persecution.

The Penitentes became, as it were, the final preservers of the medieval folk culture of Spanish New Mexico. They stoically withstood criticisms and attempts at suppression and in fact became an important political force in the late nineteenth century. Against all attacks they maintained, into the twentieth century and in some communities to the present day, many of their traditional practices and observances, and they continued their important communal activities, which still serve to unify remote Spanish-American settlements.

Unfortunately, the art of the *santero* could not also be preserved. It was a spontaneous creative outpouring made possible by an unusual set of circumstances for a brief historical moment of perhaps less than a hundred years. During this period a unique and powerful religious folk art flowered in New Mexico. Such a strong visual expression must reflect a similar strength in the culture that produces it. At a time when "official" political and religious conditions were at their worst, the Hispanic folk culture of New Mexico reached its highest point. This is indeed an irony of history worth pondering!

SOURCES

Boyd, E. *Popular Arts of Spanish New Mexico.* Santa Fe: 1974.

Espinosa, José E. *Saints in the Valleys.* Albuquerque: 1967.

Horgan, Paul. *Lamy of Santa Fe.* New York: 1975.

Kubler, George. *The Religious Architecture of New Mexico.* Colorado Springs: 1940.

———. "An Essay" in *Santos, An Exhibition of the Religious Folk Art of New Mexico.* Fort Worth: 1964.

Lamar, Howard R. *The Far Southwest 1846–1912: A Territorial History.* New Haven: 1966.

Mills, George. *The People of the Saints.* Colorado Springs: [1967].

Shalkop, Robert L. *Wooden Saints; the Santos of New Mexico.* Colorado Springs: 1967.

Weigle, Marta. *Brothers of Light, Brothers of Blood: The Penitentes of the Southwest.* Albuquerque: 1976.

17

Spaniards, Environment, and the Pepsi Generation*

John L. Kessell

Editor's Introduction

In the first essay in this anthology, Donald Worcester explained the significance of the Spanish Borderlands. In this essay, historian John Kessell warns of the pitfalls of the search for "relevance"—a popular word on college campuses in the late 1960s. Those who rummage through the past in an effort to illuminate the present can contribute mightily to our understanding. At the same time, however, they run the danger of imposing the present on the past and so distorting it. Such was the case in the late 1960s and early 1970s when some conservationists, anthropologists, and historians began to extol American Indians as America's first environmentalists. Because of their reverence for nature, it was argued, Indians lived in perfect harmony with their environment, practicing true conservation long before the European intrusion.[1]

*This article appeared originally in *The Historian*, 36 (1973): 87–91, and is here reprinted with minor modifications with permission of the author and the publisher.

As the "noble savage" grew ever more noble under the pens of these writers, Europeans came to be depicted as the true "savages" who despoiled the environment. Kessell offers a useful corrective and balance to this overdrawn view in his brief and entertaining assessment of the relevance of Spaniards and Indians to the environmentalists of the Pepsi generation.

John Kessell, a well-known authority on the Spanish missionary experience in northern New Spain, has won plaudits for his unusual ability to combine meticulous research and painstaking care for historical accuracy with a vivid, imaginative style that makes his writing compare with good fiction. He is the author of three books: *Mission of Sorrows: Jesuit Guevavi and the Pimas, 1691–1767* (Tucson: 1970) and *Friars, Soldiers, and Reformers: Hispanic Arizona and the Sonora Mission Frontier, 1767–1856* (Tucson: 1976), and *Kiva, Cross and Crown: The Pecos Indians and New Mexico, 1540–1840* (Washington, D.C.: 1979). Formerly a historian for the National Park Service and currently an independent research historian, Kessell earned the M.A. at Berkeley and the Ph.D. at New Mexico.

NOTE

1. An excellent summary of the pros and cons of this argument is Douglas Hillman Strong's "The Indian and the Environment," *The Journal of Environmental Education*, 5 (1973): 49–51.

Spaniards, Environment, and the Pepsi Generation

How does the historian relate the epic explorations of Coronado in 1540–1542 to the polluted air hanging over the Southwest in 1973? Should he even try? Is it enough merely to observe that Coronado's Captain López de Cárdenas, as he beheld the incredible panorama of the Grand Canyon, must have felt much as Neil Armstrong did when he took his one giant leap?

Certainly the pressure on scholars of every stripe is to be relevant. At a recent meeting of the Western History Association, held in Santa Fe, New Mexico, one panel labored under the title "Environmental Historiography: Its Role in Crisis and Reform."

No honest historian, whatever his specialty, whatever his period, consciously sets out to influence current or future events in a preconceived manner. Not even for the sake of comfortable "relevance." Unchanging and inexorable, the first great commandment of his profession is, Thou shalt have no other goals but the Truth. The second is like unto it, Tell it like it was. When he perverts these cardinal precepts and manipulates the facts of history to support a cause he believes is socially desirable, when he imposes on the past his own concern for what things ought to have been and ought to be, the historian is no longer a historian but a propagandist.

Take the "Indian land ethic" or the Spanish-Americans' unique love for the land in the poor counties of northern New Mexico—history or propaganda? The historian who embraces the first will feel like suppressing the 1830 report of a major forest fire in the White Mountains of Arizona caused by Apaches driving game with fire.

The very word "ethic" implies that early man enjoyed a right relationship with the creation by choice rather than of necessity. Did he appease nature because he believed it was morally right or because he stood small and naked in a formidable landscape? Which came first, man's ability or his desire to lord it over nature? (Philosopher-ecologist Aldo Leopold, author of *A Sand County Almanac,* believed that a true land ethic could come about only through future social evolution, based not on economics but on an informed yet humble appreciation of man's place in the ecological order.)

Certainly when he did marshal population and technology, as in the Valley of Mexico, the Indian devastated the land. Spanish cows, plows, and deforestation merely put the finishing touches on what the Indian had all but accomplished by himself.[1]

Perhaps pre-Coronadan man in the Southwest was more capable of altering his environment than we give him credit for—through burning, hunting, gathering, irrigation, or human crowding. Underrating his ecological impact squares neatly with our romantic desire to see him as a true child of nature, part of the primeval wilderness, noble before the heroes of James Fenimore Cooper or savage before the civilizers of Frederick Jackson Turner. There is no need to indict early man for changes he may have caused, as some proponents of the "Pleistocene overkill" theory are wont to do, only to recognize him as a being possessed of human nature and all that that implies.

As for a love of the land being any more a part of the Hispano's *alma* [soul] in New Mexico than the Anglo's in New England, nonsense. The Spanish colonist who emerges from the historical documents was no less materialistic, no less prone to fight with his neighbor over boundaries, no less eager to encroach on Indian lands or to move on to a better spread if the opportunity presented itself.

A historian must not succumb to a longing for the imagined calm and sanity of a pre-industrial age, or to a desire to enhance the dignity of certain ethnic groups, or, for that matter, to his revulsion at the wholesale ravage of an ecosystem, lest he find himself seeking not the truth but what Aldous Huxley termed "retrospective utopism." A false window on the past too often proves nothing but a mirror of our own illusions.

What of the current cry that the anthropocentric orientation is outmoded? Personally I find encouraging the view of man as a part of the creation rather than above it, but I question how our study of history can be anything but man-oriented. Perhaps the animals who talked to Hugh Lofting's Dr. Doolittle have something to say to historians.

It would be blasphemy, I suppose, to reiterate that environmental awareness is nothing new, that the ecological determinist of today is the warmed-over geographical determinist of yesterday. Nearly a hundred years ago William James, writing in *The Atlantic Monthly*, protested "This shrieking about the law of universal causation being undone, the moment we refuse to invest in the kind of causation which is being peddled round by a particular school. . . . These writers have no imagination of alternatives. With them there is no *tertium quid* between outward environment and miracle."[2]

Surely a historian can help document past use and abuse of the environment without becoming an ecomaniac. Ecologist Sherburne F. Cook sounded the challenge: "Man adapts himself to an environment, but in the very process of such adaptation the environment is altered and thus reacts on man. Since the entire concept is dynamic, it must operate within the framework of time as well as of space. Thus the historical approach is not only logical; it is unavoidable."[3]

The Southwest invites such historical inquiry. One might begin—fully aware that partial answers, both scholarly and romantic, are already available—by asking how the Spaniards looked upon this fragile environment, how their occidental Christian view differed from that of the native American inhabitants, and what adjustments coexistence in an "ecological tension zone" required of them.

Lynn White, Jr., in his famous paper "The Historical Roots of Our Ecological Crisis" would in one breath lay the rape of the biosphere to Christianity and in the next install St. Francis as patron of ecology, new queen of the sciences. Driven by an injunction from God to "have dominion over the fish of the sea and over the fowl of the air, and over every living thing that moveth upon the earth" (Gen.1.28), the early Christian went about stamping out all the little guardian spirits who lived in trees. As a consequence, says White, "To a Christian a tree can be no more than a physical fact."[4] In other words, a Christian—and the Spaniard was very Christian—unlike the pagan or Indian, could whack down trees with impunity.

White's case seems too pat. He chooses to disregard the Christian tradition of stewardship—man's accountability to God for the state of the creation—and the doctrine of the blessed earth—that for the Christian, "hope remains loyal to this earth" rather than flying off into extraterrestrial realms of the spirit. How many Christians or "post Christians" would accept the fatalism of the traditional Navajo who opposed erosion control and stock reduction simply on the grounds that "nature is more powerful than man"?

Frankly, I doubt that the spirits dwelling in nature were all that effective. The pueblo builders of Chaco Canyon in northwestern New Mexico, during the eleventh century alone, cut down an estimated 75,000 to 100,000 young trees in an area of marginal forest.

When the man who killed the deer and apologized to its spirit was joined by many other apologetic killers, many deer died. When man in Chaco Canyon, or countless men in the Valley of Mexico, cleared the land and with all due propitiation scratched Mother Earth to plant their maize, too much water too fast cut into her exposed surface deep arroyos and barrancas.

Whatever the difference in their outlook, Indian *and* Christian Spaniard sought to placate nature in the arid Southwest. Spain found no compelling reason to bring population or techno-power to bear on the region, so sky continued to determine. The records of the Inquisition in New Mexico provide fascinating, perhaps indicative, glimpses of Christians accused of borrowing animistic "superstitions" from the Indians.

The region's overriding aridity may have kept the clash of cultures, the discontinuity in human and environmental history, to a minimum. One authority argues convincingly that continuing adjustment to environment and hostility between tribes, rather than pressures from the Spaniards, kept the Indians of the Southwest moving about until the United States finally put them on reservations.[5]

Assessing the ecological impact of what the Spaniards brought with them to the Southwest, aside from their world view, is an enormously complex process. Historians can help. Every reference to livestock, for example, is useful to the ecologist at the University of Arizona's Office of Arid Lands Research. Relating Spaniard and changing environment need not give rise to an ecological black legend. It serves no good purpose to brand Father Eusebio Francisco Kino, Arizona's pioneer cattleman, an environmental rapist, to damn him for mesquite invasion of grasslands every time an agronomist counts 1,670 mesquite seeds in one dry cowpie. Awareness of the link is quite enough.

The idea of conserving natural resources and native peoples in the New World seems to have struck the Spaniards first. The grievous devastation they themselves wrought in the first half century had a sobering effect. After that, they introduced the land, irrigation, and stock raising practices reflected today in the laws of our western states. By the 1570s strict fire regulations were on the books. Doubtless the 100-peso fine for Spaniards and 100 lashes for half-breeds deterred the careless smoker more effectively than a poster of Humoso el Oso [Smokey the Bear].

Spaniards, too, thought the buffalo herds inexhaustible. And surely not even the Provo Chamber of Commerce could match the high hopes of the Spaniard who in 1777 envisioned on the banks of Utah Lake a development as large as Mexico City! Father Serra was in the minority—as was John Muir a century later—sitting in a field of California wildflowers praising God not for the medicinal value of the poppy, not for its marketability as perfume, but for the sheer joy of the creation.

One small voice, I would urge historians to take note but be wary. We must not leave the environment to the propagandists, but neither should we jump in so eager to be relevant, so eager to play a role in crisis and reform, that we ourselves become propagandists. Our first concern is the past: if we adulterate it, we fail those who would build their future or their hopes upon it.

We in the Southwest can do no better than to pursue faithfully the goal geographer Carl O. Sauer set for himself: "to learn what the Spaniards found of nature and culture at their coming and what they did in accepting, adapting, and replacing prior conditions."[6]

If our findings have ecological implications for the Pepsi generation, so much the better.

NOTES

1. Sherburne F. Cook, *Soil Erosion and Population in Central Mexico*, *Ibero-Americana*, 34 (Berkeley, 1949), 86.

2. "Great Men, Great Thoughts, and the Environment," *The Atlantic Monthly*, 46 (Oct. 1880), 451.

3. *The Historical Demography and Ecology of the Teotlalpan*, *Ibero-Americana*, 33 (Berkeley, 1949), 1.

4. *The Subversive Science: Essays toward an Ecology of Man*, ed. by Paul Shepard and Daniel McKinley (Boston, 1969), 349.

5. Albert H. Schroeder, "Shifting for Survival in the Spanish Southwest," *New Mexico Historical Review*, 43 (1968), 291–310.

6. *The Early Spanish Main* (Berkeley and Los Angeles, 1966), v.

18

"Scarce more than apes." Historical Roots of Anglo-American Stereotypes of Mexicans*

David J. Weber

Editor's Introduction

Try as we might to see the past accurately, our vision is clouded by stereotypes and prejudices that abound in American popular culture. One common stereotype depicts Spanish-Mexicans before the American conquest of the Southwest enjoying a life of ease and comfort in a pastoral setting. Handsomely clothed *caballeros* and bejeweled *señoritas* dance the night away at colorful *fandangos* while contented mission Indians sleep peacefully, anticipating the welcome sound of the Church bells to summon them to morning Mass and another day of work. This highly

---

*An abbreviated version of this paper appeared under the title "Stereotyping Mexico's Far Northern Frontier," in *An Awakened Minority: The Mexican-Americans*, ed. Manuel P. Servín (Beverly Hills: 1974), pp. 18–26. This expanded essay appears here with permission of the publisher and was prepared for a bilingual symposium at the University of Texas at El Paso, September 1975.

romanticized view of the past, which is especially strong in California, has a negative counterpart that depicts Spanish-Mexicans as a lazy, dirty, depraved, superstitious, and inept people who lived sordid lives until The American Way of Life came to rescue them from themselves. The following essay explores the causes of Anglo Americans' negative stereotypes of Mexicans and suggests some of the pernicious results of those stereotypes.

David J. Weber, editor of this volume, is Professor of History at Southern Methodist University. He has written or edited nine books relating to the history of the Southwest, one of which explores questions raised by this essay: *Foreigners in Their Native Land: Historical Roots of the Mexican Americans* (Albuquerque: 1973).

NOTE

1. Students interested in pursuing this question further might be guided by my notes, but should also consult two articles by Raymund A. Paredes that have appeared since this article was revised: "The Mexican Image in American Travel Literature, 1831–1869," *New Mexico Historical Review*, 52 (1977): 5–29, and "The Origins of Anti-Mexican Sentiment in the United States," *The New Scholar*, 6 (1977): 139–65. Doris L. Meyer adds another dimension to the question in her article, "Early Mexican-American Responses to Negative Stereotyping," *New Mexico Historical Review*, 53 (1978): 75–91.

"Scarce more than apes." Historical Roots of Anglo American Stereotypes of Mexicans in the Border Region.

Many nineteenth-century, Anglo-American visitors to what is today the Southwestern United States (defined for present purposes as the four border states of Alta California, Arizona, New Mexico, and Texas), depicted the Mexican residents of that area in the most unflattering terms. Mexicans were described as lazy, ignorant, bigoted, superstitious, cheating, thieving, gambling, cruel, sinister, cowardly half-breeds. As a consequence of their supposed innate depravity, Mexicans were seen as incapable of developing republican institutions or achieving material progress.[1] These opinions of Mexicans, some of which endure to the present, are familiar to most Southwesterners and can be found in the writings of many early Anglo-American writers. One example will suffice. Thomas Jefferson Farnham, a New England attorney who toured Alta California in the early 1840s, described the *californios* thus:

> There never was a doubt among Californians that they were at the head of the human race. In cowardice, ignorance, pretension, and dastardly tyranny, the reader has learned that this pretension is well founded.
>
> Thus much for the Spanish population of the Californias; in every way a poor apology of European extraction; as a general thing, incapable of reading or writing, and knowing nothing of science or literature, nothing of government but its brutal force, nothing of virtue but the sanction of the Church, nothing of religion but ceremonies of the national ritual. Destitute of industry themselves, they compel the poor Indian to labor for them, affording him a bare savage existence for his toil, upon their plantations and the fields of the Missions. In a word, the Californians are an imbecile, pusillanimous, race of men, and unfit to control the destinies of that beautiful country. . . .
>
> No one acquainted with the indolent, mixed race of California, will ever believe that they will populate, much less, for any length of time, govern the country. The law of Nature which curses the mulatto here with a constitution less robust than that of either race from which he sprang, lays a similar penalty upon the mingling of the Indian and white races in California and Mexico. They must fade away. . . .[2]

Not all Americans who came to the Mexican frontier shared Farnham's passionate contempt for Mexicans, but many did and they expressed their feelings in no uncertain terms. Charles Bent, a merchant who became prominent in New Mexico in the 1830s and 1840s and took a Mexican woman as his common-law wife, wrote that "the Mexican character is made up of stupidity, obstinacy, ignorance, duplicity, and vanity."[3] Noah Smithwick, who settled in Texas in 1827, later recalled that "I looked on the Mexicans as scarce more than apes."[4] This image of Mexicans as subhuman creatures was shared by a Santa Fe trader who preferred not to consider Mexicans as part of "humanity," but to classify them separately as "Mexicanity."[5]

If Anglo Americans had portrayed individual Mexicans in a negative fashion, we might think little of it, for surely there were Mexicans, just as there were Anglo Americans, who fit the description. When such characterizations are applied to an entire people, however, they clearly are no longer based on empirical evidence and cannot be regarded as valid generalizations. Sweeping generalizations, which either have no basis in fact, or which are based on "overgeneralizations of facts," are known as stereotypes.[6] Negative stereotypes are, of course, an obstacle to communication and understanding for they are usually expressions of prejudice which, as Walter Lippman once put it, "precedes the use of reason."[7]

Stereotypes need not always be negative, of course. In describing Mexicans as a peculiarly depraved people, for example, early Anglo-American writers, who were almost always males, frequently took pains to exempt Mexican women from their disparaging remarks. Hence, the negative stereotype applies to the male half of the Mexican population; the feminine half has enjoyed a positive image. "The men of northern Mexico," wrote one early American settler in Arizona, "are far inferior to the women in every respect." Similarly, an English visitor to Alta California in 1842 concluded that women were "by far the more industrious half of the population."[8]

Male visitors to the Mexican frontier, who usually had not seen a woman for several months, were frequently impressed with the beauty, kindness, and flirtatiousness of Mexican women. In forming this positive stereotype, American males allowed their hormones to overcome their ethnocentrism. Indeed, one visitor to New Mexico put aside his characteristic chauvinism to pronounce Mexican women "more beautiful" than their counterparts in the United States.[9] Another young American traveler in New Mexico carried a stereotype to its extremes by asserting that "women is women the whole world over, no matter where she is found."[10]

Americans found some things to dislike about Mexican women, to be sure, but in general their high regard for Mexican women stands in sharp contrast to their contempt for Mexican men. Francis Parkman, traveling in the far West in 1846, revealed this dichotomy in American thinking clearly if unconsciously when he termed Mexican women "Spanish" and Mexican men "Mexicans."[11]

How did a negative stereotype of Mexican males develop? There are many approaches to that question which cannot be explored in a brief paper. As a historian, I would like to suggest that the answer has larger dimensions than usually suggested by Southwestern writers. One popular explanation, implied more often than it is stated, is that a negative stereotype of Mexicans developed as a result of the contacts made between Mexicans and Anglo Americans in the border region in the two and a half decades before the so-called Mexican War.

There is no doubt that Anglo Americans' first significant contact with Mexicans occurred in the border region. Anglo-American trappers, traders, and settlers first entered Texas, New Mexico, and Alta California in the 1820s, after Mexico achieved independence from Spain and relaxed restrictions against foreigners. The Anglo Americans who entered northernmost Mexico in the 1820s, 1830s, and 1840s, it is said, came to know an area of Mexico that was backward politically, economically, and culturally. Thus, it has been suggested, Anglo Americans formed a mistaken notion of what *all* Mexicans were like on the basis of contact with relatively *few* Mexicans in the border region.[12]

Writers who have taken this position have found support from a contemporary Mexican visitor to the frontier, General Manuel Mier y Terán, who, after inspecting Texas in 1828, reported to President Guadalupe Victoria:

> It would cause you the same chagrin that it has caused me to see the opinion that is held of our nation by these foreign colonists [i.e., Anglo Americans], since, with the exception of some few who have journeyed to our capital, they know no other Mexicans than the inhabitants about here, and excepting the authorities . . . the said inhabitants are the most ignorant of negroes and Indians.[13]

As literary historian Cecil Robinson summed up the situation, "Early American writers and chroniclers in dealing with Mexico generally mistook a part for the whole thing."[14]

I would like to suggest that no such mistake occurred. On the contrary, many Anglo-American writers held a contemptuous view of Mexican males wherever they encountered them. General Mier y Terán, for example, would have been even more chagrined had he known the private views that Stephen Austin expressed about Mexicans during a visit to Mexico City in 1822–23. Austin wrote that: "the people are bigoted and superstitious to an extreem [*sic*], and indolence appears to be the general order of the day." "To be candid the majority of the people of the whole nation as far as I have seen them want nothing but tails to be more brutes than the apes."[15]

It could be said that Austin's previous experience in Texas had predisposed him to dislike Mexicans wherever he found them. This was not the case with Joel Roberts Poinsett, who never set foot in what is today the Southwest.[16] In 1822 Poinsett visited Mexico for the first time, traveling to Mexico City by way of Vera Cruz. In his well-known *Notes on Mexico*, Poinsett pronounced Mexicans in general to be lazy.[17] The Indians and mixed-bloods were "indolent," he said, and the "lazy" creoles "are not remarkable for their attainments, or for the strictness of their morals." He described the upper class as a complacent, self-satisfied group. The clergy, Poinsett said, had too great an influence in society, and the people were superstitious.[18] Just as visitors to the frontier would note. Mexicans practiced terrible vices of gambling and smoking, and gave little thought to the future. Poinsett found the people to be generally ugly, and one can only wonder if this was because he had also discovered them to be "swarthy."[19] Compared to most of his contemporaries, Poinsett's observations tended to be sophisticated. The well-traveled Poinsett showed some awareness of his prejudices and tried, but often failed, to avoid overgeneralizing.[20]

More typical was another visitor to Mexico in 1822 whose notes, describing a journey from Tampico to Mexico City, appeared in the appendix to Poinsett's work. This anonymous traveler dismissed all Mexicans with the characteristic stereotype:

> Their occupation seems to consist, principally, in removing fleas and lice from each other, drinking pulque, smoking cigars, when they can, and sleeping.[21]

On a return visit to Mexico in 1825, Joel Poinsett brought with him a young secretary, Edward Thornton Tayloe, another person who had had no previous contact with Mexicans. Tayloe quickly judged the residents of Mexico City, including the upper class, to be superstitious and lazy. Not as gallant as some of his contemporaries, Tayloe singled out upper-class women, especially, as "idle and useless." "They can do naught but eat, sleep, smoke or talk, or visit the theatre." The Mexicans, Tayloe wrote, were ignorant, vicious, thieving, and incapable of governing themselves as republicans. In fact, Mexicans had no virtues whatsoever. "Should I attempt to find them out," Tayloe wrote, "I fear I shall fail."[22]

These remarks by a necessarily small sample[23] of Anglo-American visitors to Mexico City in the early 1820s, seem to indicate that Anglo Americans did not, as Cecil Robinson said, mistake "a part" of Mexico "for the whole thing." A negative stereotype of Mexicans was articulated very early, almost as soon as foreigners began to get a good look at Mexico City after 1821.[24] The relative uniformity of the stereotype suggests the possibility that the observers were making valid generalizations—that Mexicans were lazy, ignorant, bigoted, superstitious, cheating, thieving, gambling, cruel, sinister, cowardly half-breeds, incapable of self-government or material progress. Yet, a closer look at American thought suggests that the stereotype was based not so much on direct observation or experience with Mexicans, but was in large part an extension of negative attitudes toward Catholic Spaniards which Anglo Americans had inherited from their Protestant English forebears.

During the colonial period, English colonists on the Atlantic Coast had almost no contact with Mexicans or other Latin Americans. Nonetheless, seventeenth-century Protestant New Englanders, such as Samuel Sewall and Cotton Mather, took a jaundiced view of Catholic Latin America, based largely on what they had read in literature from England. Sewall believed that Mexican culture was doomed to fall before a triumphant Protestantism and hoped that Mexico would hasten the process by revolting against Spain. Mather took the trouble to learn Spanish in order to write a missionary tract for Spaniards in the New World, designed "to open their eyes and be converted . . . away from Satan to God."[25]

Anti-Spanish views inherited from England were far more complex than simple anti-Catholicism, however. The English colonists also believed that Spanish government was authoritarian, corrupt, and decadent, and that Spaniards were bigoted, cruel, greedy, tyrannical, fanatical, treacherous, and lazy. In attempting to respond to these charges, Spanish historians have found it convenient to give them a pejorative label: the Black Legend. Not surprisingly, in defending themselves from the "blackening" effect of this "Legend," Spaniards have often gone to the other extreme of whitewashing Spain of all faults, giving rise to what Spain's detractors called a White Legend.

The origins of the Black Legend are complex. Some of its roots lie in the New World where Spanish conquistadors have been viewed as the apotheosis of evil. Interestingly, Spain's enemies drew much of their inspiration from the self-critical writings of Spaniards themselves, most notably Bartolomé de las Casas, who was widely read in England and in her American colonies. In this literature, Spaniards were depicted as grasping adventurers who came to the New World, not to seek liberty or better homes for their families as did the English, but to search for treasure and to live in idleness on the sweat of enslaved aborigines. This image remained alive. In 1821, the same year that Mexico won independence from Spain, Henry Clay told Congress that if Anglo Americans moved into Texas "it will be peopled by freemen and sons of freemen, carrying with them our language, our laws, and our liberties." Should Texas remain part of Mexico, however, Clay warned that "it may become the habitation of despotism and slaves, subject to the vile domination of the Inquisition and of superstition."[26]

For our purposes, suffice it to say that Mexicans, the descendents of the Spanish conquistadors, inherited the reputation of their forefathers. As Phillip Wayne Powell recently put it: "We [Anglo Americans] transferred some of our ingrained antipathy toward Catholic Spain to her American heirs."[27]

Powell is one of the few historians to take note of this connection between the Black Legend and anti-Mexicanism,[28] but one does not need to read too carefully in the writings of Anglo-American visitors to the Mexican frontier to find evidences of the Black Legend. One of the most explicit statements comes from young Lewis Garrard, who visited New Mexico during the Mexican War. After briefly characterizing the New Mexican males as alternatively "servile," and "villainous," he explained the reason for their depravity in terms which show clearly the influence of the Black Legend. "The extreme degradation into which they are fallen," Garrard observed, "seems a fearful retribution on the destroyers of [the] Aztec Empire."[29]

In addition to the Black Legend, Anglo Americans found one other element to despise in Mexicans—racial mixture. Color-conscious Anglo Americans were nearly unanimous in commenting upon the dark skin of the "swarthy" Mexican *mestizos* who, it was generally agreed, had inherited the worst qualities of Spaniards and Indians, resulting in a "race" still more despicable than that of either parent group.[30] In suggesting that Anglo Americans were racists, I am not trying to ignore the racist nature of Mexican society. We do not have time to elaborate on this matter and for present purposes I simply want to suggest that a belief in the Black Legend, combined with a belief in the inferiority of mixed-bloods, enabled Anglo Americans to predict erroneously what Mexicans would be like (that is, to construct a stereotype) even before coming into significant contact with them. Not surprisingly, the Anglo Americans' expectations were fulfilled.

Anglo-American stereotypes of Mexicans, then, did not originate in the border region. Indeed, as early as 1822 the Mexican minister in Washington recognized that Anglo Americans viewed Mexicans as "inferiors."[31] There can be little doubt, however, that the growing number of travelers, merchants, trappers, and settlers who entered northernmost Mexico after 1821 nourished the stereotype and through writing and conversation, encouraged its growth throughout the United States.

To understand better the nature of Anglo American stereotypes of

Mexicans, let us examine how one of its components functioned—that is, the frequent charge that Mexicans were lazy.

Disparaging remarks regarding Mexicans' lack of initiative were widespread, and were especially abundant in literature describing the border region. Typical was a visitor to San Antonio who observed in 1837 that "The life of the Mexican here is one of unconcerned indolence and ease. As long as he is satisfied with a bare living for the present, there is no reason that he should give himself much trouble about the future."[32] Many writers expressed their disdain for Mexicans' work habits in more colorful terms. Albert Pike, visiting New Mexico in 1831, found the *nuevo mexicanos* "a lazy gossipping people, always lounging on their blankets and smoking the cigarrillos—living on nothing and without labor."[33] How Mexicans lived on nothing, Pike does not trouble himself to explain. An American resident of California told his readers that "you might as well expect a sloth to leave a tree, that has one inch of bark left upon its trunk, as to expect a Californian to labor, whilst a *real* glistens in his pocket."[34] Richard Henry Dana likened laziness in California to an endemic disease, terming it "California Fever," which, he said, might spare the first generation but which, "always attacks the second."[35] As an enduring monument to the laziness of Mexicans, there is said to be a gravestone somewhere in California which bears the inscription: "Aquí reposa Juan Espinosa. Nunca en su vida hizo otra cosa."[36] ("Here rests Juan Espinosa. Never did he do anything else.")

Contemporary accounts of the laziness of Mexican frontiersmen are abundant, then, and even include accusations made by officials from Mexico City and Mexican or Spanish-born clergy who had their own reasons for labeling the frontiersmen lazy.[37] Some historians have taken these contemporary accounts at face value and perpetuated the stereotype of Mexican indolence.[38] Yet, it is not only possible to refute the charge that Mexican frontiersmen were lazy, but there is reason to suppose that Mexicans on the frontier were energetic pioneers who worked as hard, if not harder, than their compatriots in the more "civilized" areas of central Mexico. With the exception of Alta California, it was more difficult to exploit Indian labor on the frontier than in central Mexico; frontiersmen had to work with their own hands. For example, the *encomienda* (a system of distributing Indian labor), was unsuccessful and short-lived in the Borderlands, operating only in seventeenth-century New Mexico.[39] Hard work by colonists from Mexico was necessary in some areas of the frontier to provide defense against hostile Indians. Moreover, hard work was probably rewarded on the frontier, where there seems to have been greater social mobility than in central Mexico.

The idea that Mexican frontiersmen were industrious has been suggested by historians such as Silvio Zavala and France Scholes, and anthropologist Miguel León-Portilla.[40] It was also mentioned by contemporaries such as Miguel Ramos Arizpe in Texas, Pedro Bautista Pino in New Mexico, Alexander von Humboldt, the German savant and traveler, and Zebulon Montgomery Pike, the "lost pathfinder."[41] Pike, for example, termed the inhabitants of New Mexico "the bravest and most hardy subjects in New Spain," because of "their continual wars with the savage nations who surround them," because of their isolation from the rest of New Spain, and because they lacked gold and silver, a source of easy wealth.[42]

It is possible, then, that Mexicans on the frontier were not lazy and were perhaps even harder working than their countrymen to the south.[43] Nevertheless, Anglo-American visitors generally described frontier Mexicans as lazy. How can this be explained? The Black Legend, which identifies Spaniards as lazy, offers part of the explanation. An understanding of Anglo American attitudes toward racial mixture also adds to the explanation, for Anglo Americans generally regarded persons of mixed blood as lazy. In 1844, for example, Thomas Jefferson Farnham, described the complexion of upper class Californians as "a light clear bronze; not white . . . not remarkably pure in any way; a lazy color."[44] Still a third explanation needs to be considered. Psychologists tell us that we stereotype ethnic groups in part because "in them we may perceive our own shortcomings."[45] According to Maurice Janowitz and Bruno Bettelheim, "ethnic hostility is a projection of unacceptable inner strivings onto a minority group."[46] The ethnic group, in other words, becomes our alter ego. Examined in this context, the Anglo-American observation that Mexicans were lazy may tell us more about the rigorous work ethic of nineteenth-century Americans than it does about Mexican culture.

The fact that many Anglo Americans blamed the economic and cultural under-development of Mexico's far northern frontier on the "indolent" character of the Mexican settlers not only reveals a bias, but is simplistic. Better explanations for underdevelopment could have been found by looking into historical, geographical, and economic circumstances that contributed to the relative backwardness of the region. Indeed, had they looked more closely, Anglo Americans might have found that under-development was not as much a result of the supposed laziness of Mexican frontiersmen, but instead, the frontiersmen's lack of initiative was a result of underdevelopment and of peculiar frontier conditions. As one astute Franciscan, José Señán, summed up the situation of the *californios;* "I have good reason to accuse the settlers of laziness, but there is equally good reason to excuse them in large part. Their lack of enthusiasm for their work is not surprising, inasmuch as they regard most of it as fruitless." In a province dominated by the military, Señán explained, a settler was prohibited from selling grain or other surplus crops to anyone except the quartermaster at "absurdly low prices" fixed by law, "while being charged exorbitantly for whatever goods he can procure." Clothing, farm implements, and household goods were in short supply and soldiers had first preference at purchasing them. Even if the settlers had cash, then, "there would be no place to spend it."[47] The situation in Texas was similar, according to Fray Mariano Sosa, who saw the lack of a market for agricultural goods as destroying "incentive to raise larger or better crops."[48]

Whereas some padres blamed the military system for economic stagnation and lack of incentive among the frontier settlers, some settlers, especially in California, criticized the padres for monopolizing Indian labor and the best lands.[49]

Those who truly understood the rugged conditions of life on the frontier and the legal restrictions on trade and commerce, then, were not so quick to label frontiersmen lazy. Indeed, some knowledgable officials expressed admiration for the frontiersmen's tenaciousness and initiative. As Governor Manuel Salcedo wrote of the *tejanos* in 1809: "one . . . marvels at how the most of them cultivate their lands without the necessary farming tools, . . . how some have built houses without artisans . . . how in this poverty they have been able to dress themselves and their families."[50]

For most Anglo-American observers, however, there was no need to look too closely for explanations of lack of economic progress on the Mexican frontier. The stereotype of Mexican laziness constituted a sufficient explanation. Historians of the border region need to be reminded, then, that Anglo Americans did not necessarily see what they said they saw. This contention may be unprovable, but it is not unreasonable. A stereotype, psychologist Gordon Allport tells us, "may interfere with even the simplest rational judgments."[51]

This discussion of the historical roots of Anglo-American stereotypes is not solely of academic interest, for stereotypes have had a profound impact on Mexican–United States relations and on the treatment of Mexicans and Mexican Americans in the United States. The stereotype of the inferior Mexican lay behind the arrogant sense of cultural and political superiority, known in United States history as Manifest Destiny, that led to the United States seizure of half the Mexican Republic in 1846–47. The stereotype of the inferior Mexican has been used to the present to justify efforts to "Americanize" Mexicans in the Southwestern United States, substituting their "folkways," with "superior" Anglo-American culture. Stereotypes have also helped Anglo Americans rationalize their exploitation and mistreatment of Mexican and Mexican-American workers in the fields and factories of the border region. Those who seek to improve the economic conditions of Mexicans in United States, or to make relations between Mexicans and Anglo Americans more harmonious, need to be reminded that deeply rooted stereotypes stand as a formidable obstacle to progress. We have come a long way since Noah Smithwick thought that Mexicans were "scarce more than apes," but we have not come nearly far enough.[52]

NOTES

1. This is the picture that emerges from such studies as Cecil Robinson, *With the Ears of Strangers: The Mexican in American Literature* (Tucson: 1963), and David T. Leary, "The Attitudes of Certain United States Citizens toward Mexico, 1821–1846" University of Southern California, 1970).

2. Thomas Jefferson Farnham, *Travels in California* (1st ed., 1844; Oakland, California: 1947), pp. 147–48, 161.

.3 In an article sent to Manuel Alvarez (a Spaniard), Taos, March 30, 1845, quoted in Ward Alan Minge, "Frontier Problems in New Mexico Preceding the Mexican War, 1840–1846" (Ph.D. diss., University of New Mexico, 1965), p. 309. Harold H. Dunham, "Charles Bent," in *The Mountain Men and The Fur Trade of the Far West*, ed. LeRoy R. Hafen, 10 vols. (Glendale, Calif. 1965), 2:44.

4. Noah Smithwick, *The evolution of a State: or, Recollections of Old Texas Days* (1st ed., 1900; reprint, Austin: 1935), p. 45.

5. Richard L. Wilson, *Short Ravelings from a Long Yarn, or Camp Sketches of the Santa Fe Trail*, ed. Benjamin F. Taylor (1st ed., 1847; reprint, Santa Ana, Calif., 1936), p. 120.

6. In this article I am following Gordon Allport's widely accepted distinction between a stereotype and a valid generalization. *The Nature of Prejudice* (Cambridge, Mass., 1954), pp. 190–91.

7. Quoted in Rosemary Gordon, *Stereotype of Imagery and Belief as an Ego Defence* (Cambridge: 1962), p. 5. Psychologists give Lippman considerable credit for popularizing the term *stereotype*.

8. Charles D. Poston, *Building A State in Apache Land* (Tempe: 1963), p. 75. Sir George Simpson, *Narrative of a Journey Round the World*, 2 vols. (London: 1847), 1:381.

9. Lansing Bloom, ed., "Santa Fe and the Far West in 1841," *New Mexico Historical Review*, 5 (1930): 300.

10. Lewis H. Garrard, *Wah-To-Yah and the Taos Trail* (Palo Alto, Calif. 1968), p. 194.

11. Quoted in James H. Lacy, "New Mexico Women in Early American Writings," *New Mexico Historical Review*, 34 (1959): 41.

12. This argument was put forth by Cecil Robinson, *With the Ears of Strangers*, pp. 29–30 and Samuel H. Lowrie, *Culture Conflict in Texas, 1821-35* (New York: 1935), pp. 82, 88. Herbert E. Bolton, in a more generalized essay, advanced a similar thesis. See "Defensive Spanish Exploration and the Significance of the Borderlands," in *Bolton and the Spanish Borderlands*, ed. John Francis Bannon (Norman: 1964), pp. 33–34.

13. Mier y Terán to Guadalupe Victoria, Nacogdoches, June 30, 1828, in Allaine Howren, "Causes and Origin of the Decree of April 6, 1830," *Southwestern Historical Quarterly*, 16 (1913):395.

14. Robinson, *With the Ears of Strangers*, p. 29.

15. To James Brown Austin, July 8, 1822, and June 13, 1823, quoted respectively in

Lowrie, *Culture Conflict*, p. 89, and William S. Red, *Texas Colonists and Religion, 1821–36* (Austin: 1924), p. 43.

16. See J. Fred Rippy, *Joel R. Poinsett, Versatile American* (Durham, N.C.: 1935).

17. J. R. Poinsett, *Notes on Mexico, Made in the Autumn of 1822 . . .* (London: 1825), p. 37. At one point Poinsett departs from his generalization to indicate that the "labouring class" in cities, towns, and countryside is "industrious" (p. 163).

18. Ibid., pp. 161, 162, 112.

19. Ibid., pp. 160, 100, 174, 51.

20. See, Ibid., p. 88.

21. Ibid., Appendix, p. 7.

22. C. Harvey Gardiner, ed., *Mexico, 1825-1828. The Journal and Correspondence of Edward Thornton Tayloe* (Chapel Hill, N.C.: 1959), pp. 54, 69, 116, 55.

23. The writings of Poinsett and Tayloe are the only book-length descriptions of Mexico by Anglo Americans to be published in the 1820s. See C. Harvey Gardiner, "Foreign Travelers' Accounts of Mexico, 1810–1910," *The Americas*, 8 (1952): 321–51.

24. Such views continued to be articulated by visitors to Mexico City in the 1830s and 1840s, as David Leary's dissertation suggests. By that time, of course, these views could have been influenced by reports about Mexicans on the frontier.

25. Harry Bernstein, *Making an Inter-American Mind* (Gainesville: 1961), pp. 6–10. See also Stanley T. Williams, *The Spanish Background of American Literature*, 2 vols. (New Haven, Conn.: 1955), 1:9, 18.

26. Quoted in Joseph Carl McElhannon, "Imperial Mexico and Texas, 1821–1823," *Southwestern Historical Quarterly*, 53 (1949): 137.

27. Philip Wayne Powell, *Tree of Hate: Propaganda and Prejudices Affecting United States Relations with the Hispanic World* (New York: 1971), p. 118. Mr. Powell's work is the best history of the Black Legend in English. *The Black Legend: Anti-Spanish Attitudes in the Old World and the New*, ed. Charles Gibson (New York: 1971), contains well-chosen selections of anti-Spanish writing.

28. The only other writers who have made this connection are Cecil Robinson, in discussing the notion that Mexicans are unusually cruel *(Ears of Strangers*, p. 190), and Harry Bernstein, who says that the Black Legend "became Americanized under the name of Manifest Destiny" *(Making an Inter-American Mind*, p. 4). Powell and Bernstein were both trained in Latin American history. Historians of Manifest Destiny, such as Federick Merk and Albert K. Weinberg, who were trained in United States history, seem to be unaware of the depth of anti-Latin feeling in the United States, or else believe it unimportant.

29. Garrard, *Wah-To-Yah and the Taos Trail*, p. 194.

30. For a discussion of this theme see Robinson, *With the Ears of Strangers*, pp. 67–74. In addition to those writers cited by Robinson, explicit statements about the evils of miscegination are found in the writings of men such as Rufus B. Sage, Thomas James, and Thomas J. Farnham.

31. Manuel Zozaya, quoted in McElhannon, "Imperial Mexico and Texas," p. 137.

32. Andrew Forest Muir, ed., *Texas in 1837: An Anonymous Contemporary Narrative* (Austin: 1958), p. 104.

33. Albert Pike, *Prose Sketches and Poems Written in the Western Country (With Additional Stories)*, ed. David J. Weber (Albuquerque, 1967), p. 247.

34. Alfred Robinson, *Life in California* (1st ed., 1846; Santa Barbara, Calif., 1970)), p. 99.

35. Richard Henry Dana, Jr., *Two Years Before the Mast*, ed. John Haskell Kemble (1st ed., 1840; 2 vols.; Los Angeles: 1964), 1: 172.

36. Quoted in Thomas Workman Temple, II, "Our Heritage from the Days of the Dons," *Southern California Quarterly*, 40 (1958); 70.

37. See, for example, José María Sánchez, "Trip to Texas in 1828," trans. Carlos E. Castañeda, *Southwestern Historical Quarterly*, 29 (1926): 250–51, 258; and Governor Juan

Bautista Elguézabal, A Description of Texas in 1803," ed. and trans. Odie B. Faulk, *Southwestern Historical Quarterly* 66 (1963): 513–15. For California, see C. Alan Hutchinson, *Frontier Settlement in Mexican California. The Híjar-Padrés Colony and Its Origins, 1769–1835* (New Haven: 1969), pp. 81, 138, 346–47. It is not my purpose here to analyze the reasons why some Franciscans and upper class Mexicans viewed frontiersmen as lazy. Manuel P. Servín has provided a good explanation of the case of the Franciscans in "California's Hispanic Heritage: A View into the Spanish Myth," *The Journal of San Diego History*, 19 (1973): 1–9.

It is interesting to note that *peninsulares* frequently regarded Mexicans as lazy (see, for example, Christon Archer, "The Key to the Kingdom: The Defense of Veracruz, 1780–1810," *The Americas*, 27 [1971]: 427, 430) while Mexicans regarded *peninsulares* as generally "disdainful of applying themselves to work which they look on as too servile." Benito María de Moxó, quoted in Hugh Hamill, *The Hidalgo Revolt, Prelude to Mexican Independence* (Gainesville: 1966), p. 30.

38. See, for example, Odie B. Faulk, *Land of Many Frontiers. A History of the American Southwest* (New York: 1968), p. 79; and Charles E. Chapman, *A History of California: The Spanish Period* (New York: 1921), pp. 391–92.

39. Charles Gibson, *Spain in America* (New York: 1966), p. 190.

40. Zavala, "The Frontiers of Hispanic America," in *The Frontier in Perspective*, ed. Walker D. Wyman and Clifton B. Kroeber (Madison: 1965), pp. 36–58. Scholes, "Civil Government and Society in New Mexico in the Seventeenth Century," *New Mexico Historical Review*, 10 (1935): 98. León-Portilla, "The Norteño Variety of Mexican Culture: An Ethnohistorical Approach," in *Plural Society in the Southwest*, ed. Edward H. Spicer and Raymond H. Thompson (New York: 1972), pp. 110–11. Not all historians, of course, would agree. Two recent works that suggest opposite conclusions are Hutchinson, *Frontier Settlement in Mexican California*, p. 399; Lynn I. Perrigo, *The American Southwest: Its Peoples and Cultures* (New York: 1971), pp. 416–17.

41. For Ramos Arizpe and Von Humboldt, see Zavala, "The Frontiers of Hispanic America," pp. 48–49. For Pino, see his comments about paupers in Mexico in H. Bailey Carroll and J. Villasana Haggard, eds., *Three New Mexico Chronicles* (Albuquerque: 1942), pp. 27–28.

42. "Pike's Observations on New Spain," in Donald Jackson, ed., *The Journals of Zebulon Montgomery Pike with Letters and Related Documents*, 2 vols. (Norman: 1966), 2: 58. Among the few Americans who agreed with Pike's analysis in later years was John Fox Hammond, who thought the New Mexicans indolent, but nonetheless more industrious than "the inhabitants of lower Mexico." See *A Surgeon's Report on Socorro, New Mexico, 1852* (Santa Fe: 1966), pp. 26–27.

43. Poinsett and Tayloe suggest this possibility in their observations on Mexico. Poinsett found rural Mexicans generally more virtuous than city dwellers *(Notes on Mexico*, pp. 266–67, 163, 175). Both men offered something of a "reverse frontier thesis." As Poinsett put it, "where nature has done much, man is indolent," and he added: "To no part of the world has nature been more bountiful, and in no part of it is there so little of comfort among people" (p. 181; see also Tayloe, *Mexico*, p. 69). This environmental explanation for indolence was popular through much of the nineteenth century in describing Anglo-American residents of Texas, too. See Marilyn McAdams Sibley, *Travelers in Texas, 1761–1860* (Austin: 1967), p. 100. A more detailed analysis of the question of indolence on Mexico's far northern frontier would need to distinguish between regions of the frontier. See, for example, how Pike's description of Texas differed from his description of New Mexico *(The Journals*, 2: 58, 80).

44. Farnham, *Travels*, p. 142.

45. Allport, *Nature of Prejudice*, p. 200.

46. Quoted in Ibid., p. 199. See, too, the fine discussion of this question by Joan W. Moore and Alfredo Cuéllar, *Mexican Americans* (Engelwood Cliffs, N.J.: 1970), p. 5.

47. Señán to the Viceroy, the Marqués de Branciforte, May 14, 1796, in *The Letters of José Señán, O.F.M. Mission San Buenaventura, 1796–1823*, trans. Paul D. Nathan, ed. Lesley Byrd Simpson (San Francisco: 1962), pp. 3–4.

48. Sosa to Governor Manuel de Salcedo, May 26, 1810, quoted in Carlos E. Castañeda, *Our Catholic Heritage in Texas, 1519–1936*, 7 vols. (Austin: 1936–1958), 5: 429.

49. See, for example, José Bandini, *A Description of California in 1828*, trans. and ed. Doris M. Wright (Berkeley: 1951), pp. 6–7. See, too, Robinson, *Life in California*, p. 152.

50. Nettie Lee Benson, ed. and trans., "A Governor's Report on Texas in 1809," *Southwestern Historical Quarterly*, 76 (1968); 611.

51. Allport, *Nature of Prejudice*, p. 190. For a different view of this question, see David J. Langum, "Californios and the Image of Indolence," *Western Historical Quarterly*, 9 (1978): 181–96; and my commentary and his reply, *Western Historical Quarterly*, 10 (1979): 61–69.

52. For a discussion of stereotypes in the late nineteenth and early twentieth centuries, as well as a good guide to sources on this question, see the recent article by José E. Limón, "Stereotyping and Chicano Resistance: An Historical Dimension," *Aztlán*, 4 (1973): 257–70).

Examples of the ways in which stereotypes have been used to justify imperialism and to exploit Mexicans are abundant. For historical treatments see the overview by Carey McWilliams, *North From Mexico: The Spanish-Speaking People of the United States* (New York: 1948), and my own *Foreigners in Their Native Land: Historical Roots of the Mexican Americans* (Albuquerque: 1973).

Suggestions for Further Reading and Research

The specialized articles in this anthology may inspire some readers to look at broader studies so that they do not lose the proverbial forest for the trees. The briefest and best surveys of the Spanish Borderlands are: *Land of Many Frontiers: A History of the American Southwest*, by Odie B. Faulk (New York: 1968), chapter 2; *The American Southwest: Its Peoples and Cultures*, by Lynn I. Perrigo (New York: 1971), chapters 1–5; and *Spain in America*, by Charles Gibson (New York: 1966), chapter 9. Gibson surveys the entire Borderlands, while Faulk and Perrigo, as their titles suggest, look at the region from California to Texas.

Herbert Bolton's slender and vividly written synthesis, *The Spanish Borderlands: A Chronicle of Old Florida and the Southwest* (New Haven: 1921) still makes rewarding reading. The most up-to-date and scholarly single-volume summary of the region's history is now John Francis Bannon, *The Spanish Borderlands Frontier, 1513–1821* (Albuquerque: 1974) which updates Bolton's half-century-old study. Due in part to the growth of modern scholarship, however, Bannon's volume is much heftier than Bolton's. A balanced picture, which gives Indians their due as historical figures, appears in anthropologist Edward H. Spicer's extraordinary synthesis, *Cycles of Conquest: The Impact of Spain, Mexico, and the United States on the Indians of the Southwest, 1533–1960* (Tucson: 1962). Spicer focuses on New Mexico and Arizona and the present-day Mexican northwest.

Emphasizing well-chosen words and phrases over accuracy, Paul I. Wellman has written *Glory, God and Gold: A Narrative History of the Southwest* (New York: 1954), and Paul Horgan has composed the lyrical and sweeping *Great River: The Rio Grande in History* (New York: 1954). Both Wellman and Horgan focus on New Mexico and Texas. In a still more popular vein, the editors of Time-Life have produced *The Spanish West* (New York: 1976), a book of handsome illustrations with a minimum of text.

Historiographical works often provide valuable guidance to readers and researchers, but no writer has yet produced a satisfying essay on the Spanish Borderlands from California to Texas. Félix Almaraz looks broadly at the region in "The Status of Borderlands Studies: History," in *The Social Science Journal*, 12 (1975): 9–18. Perhaps because he attempts to cover literature regarding the Spanish, Mexican, and American periods in ten pages, his essay is long on lists. Interesting essays by France Scholes, "Historiography of the Spanish Southwest: Retrospect and Prospect," in *Probing the American West*, ed. K. Ross Toole et al. (Santa Fe: 1962), pp. 17–25 and Eleanor B. Adams, "History of the Spanish Southwest: Personalities and Discoveries," in *Voices from the Southwest,* ed. Donald C. Dickinson et al. (Flagstaff: 1976), pp. 3–12, are both concerned primarily with New Mexico. A brief, but provocative essay by Antonio José Ríos-Bustamante criticizes earlier interpretations of Borderlands history and urges the use of an approach that the author calls "Dialectical socio-economic change." "A Contribution to the Historiography of the Greater Mexican North in the Eighteenth Century," *Aztlán*, 7 (Fall 1976): 347–56.

Jack D. L. Holmes has written a fine piece on the historiography of the eastern Borderlands, "Interpretations and Trends in the Study of the Spanish Borderlands: The Old Southwest," *Southwestern Historical Quarterly,* 74 (1971): 461–77. This, together with a series of essays on Louisiana, Mississippi, Alabama, and the Floridas, by Holmes, William S. Coker, Samuel Proctor, and J. Leitch Wright, Jr., published in the *Latin American Research Review*, 7 (1962): 3–94, suggest that the historiography of the Borderlands east of Texas has been explored in greater detail than that of the western Borderlands.

Those interested in a closer examination of some of the themes introduced in this anthology will find plentiful leads in the notes accompanying each article. To proceed systematically beyond that, bibliographies are especially useful. The best starting place is the well-organized and thorough bibliography in John Francis Bannon's *The Spanish Borderlands Frontier, 1513–1821* (Albuquerque: 1974). More concise lists of basic works are: "The Spanish Borderlands: A Selected Reading List," by Oakah L. Jones, Jr., in *The Journal of the West,* 8 (1969): 137–42, and "The Spanish Speaking Peoples in the West," in *The Frontier and the American West,* ed. Rodman W. Paul and Richard W. Etulain (Arlington Heights, Ill.: 1977), pp. 42–44. Henry R. Wagner, *The Spanish Southwest, 1542–1794: An Annotated Bibliography* (Albuquerque: 1937) remains useful. For periodical literature, an indispensable reference with excellent organization and indexing is Oscar O. Winther's *A Classified Bibliography of the Periodical Literature of the Trans-Mississippi West, 1811–1957* (Bloomington: 1961), and its *Supplement, 1957–1967* (Bloomington: 1970), coed. Winther and Richard A. Van Orman. New books and articles, however, appear more rapidly than bibliographies. The *Handbook of Latin American Studies,* an annual volume published by the University of Florida, Gainesville, is useful for keeping abreast of recent research. So too is the remarkable *Newsletter* of the Southwestern Mission Research Center, published at the Arizona State Museum, Tucson.

Among the books published in English in the last decade, which do not appear in Bannon's 1974 bibliography, general readers will find the following most rewarding: Carl Ortwin Sauer, *Sixteenth Century North America: The Land and the Peoples as Seen by the Europeans* (Berkeley: 1971); Robert S. Weddle, *Wilderness Manhunt: The Spanish Search for La Salle* (Austin: 1973); John L. Kessell, *Mission of Sorrows: Jesuit Guevavi and the Pimas, 1691–1767* (Tucson: 1970), and *Friars, Soldiers, and Reformers: Hispanic Arizona and the Sonora Mission Frontier, 1767–1856* (Tucson: 1976); Francis F. Guest, *Fermín Francisco de Lasuén (1736–1803): A Biography* [a Franciscan in California] (Washington, D.C.: 1973); Max L. Moorhead, *The Presidio: Bastion of the Spanish Borderlands* (Norman: 1975); Elizabeth A. H. John, *Storms Brewed in Other Men's Worlds: The Confrontation of Indians, Spanish, and French in the Southwest, 1540–1795* (College Station, Texas: 1975); Edwin A. Beilharz, *Felipe de Neve, First Governor of California* (San Francisco: 1971); Walter Briggs, *Without Noise of Arms: The 1776 Domínguez-Escalante Search for a Route from Santa Fe to Monterey* (Flagstaff: 1976); Félix D. Almaraz, Jr., *Tragic Cavalier: Governor Manuel Salcedo of Texas, 1808–1813* (Austin: 1971); Henry F. Dobyns, *Spanish Colonial Tucson: A Demographic History* (Tucson: 1976); Janet Fireman, *The Spanish Royal Corps of Engineers in the Western Borderlands: Instruments of Bourbon Reform, 1764–1815* (1977); Abraham P. Nasatir, *Borderland in Retreat: From Spanish Louisiana to the Far Southwest* (Albuquerque: 1976); and Warren L. Cook, *Flood Tide of Empire: Spain and the Pacific Northwest, 1543–1819* (New Haven: 1973). As this anthology goes to press, the University of Oklahoma Press has announced for publication: *Los Paisanos: Spanish Settlers on the Northern Frontier of New Spain*, by Oakah L. Jones, Jr.

The preceding list is meant to be suggestive, not exhaustive. It does not, for example, include articles or primary sources. For those who enjoy reading first-hand accounts, translators, editors, and publishers continue to bring fascinating documents into print. Recent years have seen the publication of *As the Padres Saw Them: California Indian Life and Customs As Reported by the Franciscan Missionaries, 1813–1815*, Maynard Geiger, ed. and trans. (Santa Barbara: 1976); José Mariano Moziño, *Noticias de Nutka: An Account of Nootka Sound in 1792*, ed. and trans. Iris Higbie Wilson [Engstrand] (Seattle: 1972); *Friar Bringas Reports to the King: Methods of Indoctrination on the Frontier of New Spain, 1796–97*, ed. and trans. Daniel S. Matson and Bernard L. Fontana (Tucson: 1977); *Desert Documentary: The Spanish Years, 1767–1821*, ed. and trans. Kieran McCarty (Tucson: 1976); *Fray Juan Agustín de Morfi's Account of Disorders in New Mexico, 1778*, ed. and trans. Marc Simmons (Isleta, N.M.: 1977); *The Domínguez-Escalante Journal: Their Expedition Through Colorado, Utah, Arizona, and New Mexico in 1776*, ed. Ted J. Warner and trans. Fray Angelico Chavez (Provo: 1976); *Guidelines for a Texas Mission. Instructions for the Missionary of Mission Concepción in San Antonio*, Benedict Leutenegger, ed. and trans. (San Antonio: 1976).

Readers and researchers, then, will find a rich, varied, and ever-growing historical literature on the activities of Spain's subjects and their interaction with Indians in what has become the American West. Notwithstanding the abundance of historical writing, old questions remain and new questions appear as we continuously seek to illuminate the present with light from the past. The Borderlands will continue to challenge and fascinate historians, would-be historians, and aficionados of history.

Index

DAVID J. WEBER is Robert and Nancy Dedman Professor of History at Southern Methodist University, where he has taught since 1976. He is the author or editor of twenty books, including the prize-winning *Spanish Frontier in North America* (Yale 1992), and is a past president of the Western History Association. Weber currently directs the William P. Clements Center for Southwest Studies at SMU.